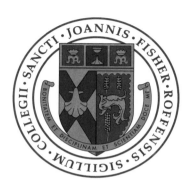

Lavery Library

St. John Fisher College

Rochester, New York

American Alliance Policy
in the Middle East, 1945–1992

American Alliance Policy
in the Middle East, 1945–1992

Iran, Israel, and Saudi Arabia

John P. Miglietta

LEXINGTON BOOKS
Lanham • Boulder • New York • Oxford

LEXINGTON BOOKS

Published in the United States of America
by Lexington Books
4720 Boston Way, Lanham, Maryland 20706

12 Hid's Copse Road
Cumnor Hill, Oxford OX2 9JJ, England

British Library Cataloguing in Publication Information Available

Library of Congress Cataloging-in-Publication Data

Miglietta, John P., 1962–
    American alliance policy in the Middle East, 1945–1992 : Iran, Israel, and Saudi Arabia / John P. Miglietta.
        p. cm.
    Includes bibliographical references and index.
    ISBN 0-7391-0304-0 (alk. paper)
        1. United States—Foreign relations—Saudi Arabia. 2. Saudi Arabia—Foreign relations—United States. 3. United States—Foreign relations—Israel. 4. Israel—Foreign relations—United States. 5. United States—Foreign relations—Iran. 6. Iran—Foreign relations—United States. 7. United States—Foreign relations—1945–1989. 8. United States—Foreign relations—1989–1993. 9. Iran—Foreign relations—1941–1979. 10. Iran—Foreign relations—1979–1997. I. Title.

E183.8.S25 M54 2001
327.73056'09'045—dc21

                                                                2001048267

Printed in the United States of America

♾™ The paper used in this publication meets the minimum requirements of American National Standard for Information Sciences—Permanence of Paper for Printed Library Materials, ANSI/NISO Z39.48–1992.

To my wife Beth and my grandmother Caroline Valentini

and to the memories of my parents and my brother,

Tullia, Mario, and James Miglietta

Contents

Tables

Graphs

Acknowledgments

This project originated as a dissertation written for the Department of Politics at New York University. I would like to thank my dissertation advisor Farhad Kazemi for his support and encouragement. He exhibited exceptional patience and understanding in guiding me through that process. The other members of the committee who provided me with detailed comments on the dissertation which I found useful in completing this book were Timothy Mitchell, David Denoon, Leah Haus, and John Entelis. I would especially like to thank John Entelis for introducing me to the complexities of Middle East politics while I was an undergraduate at Fordham University.

Other members, or former members, of the New York University Politics Department who assisted me in clarifying my research on this topic were Nasrin Abdolali, Donna Bahry, Zeev Maoz, Ben Moore, Miroslav Nincic, and Kenneth Rodman. Marilyn LaPorte and Sara Steinmetz remain constant sources of encouragement. The New York University Politics Department provided financial support which assisted me during the initial phase of research for this book as a graduate student.

I would like to thank the faculty, staff, and administration at Lock Haven University, Caldwell College, and Tennessee State University for their encouragement and patience while I was finishing this project. I am grateful to the editors at Rowman & Littlefield/Lexington Books for their patience and understanding in helping me see this project to its completion.

I cannot thank my family enough for their many years of support and assistance in my educational and research endeavors. My late parents Tullia and Mario Miglietta, and my late brother James Miglietta were constant sources of encouragement during graduate school, and in my early academic career. My grandmother Caroline Valentini remains a source of encouragement and understanding.

Finally, this book could not have been written without the love, patience, and understanding of my wife Elizabeth Dachowski. In addition to her moral support she also greatly assisted me in the proofreading and final preparation of this manuscript. She spent many hours utilizing her skills with computers in correcting my many errors in formatting and helping me organize the final printing of this manuscript.

Any errors or omissions in this book are, of course, mine alone.

Chapter 1

Alliances, American Foreign Policy, and International Relations Theory

Historical Interpretations of Alliances

Traditional definitions of alliances have focused on several factors. These are (1) a cooperative relationship that encompasses at least two nations; (2) the combining or complementing of the military forces of the member states; (3) a mutually perceived threat that encourages common national security interests; and (4) the value of collective action in defending or propagating foreign policy interests.[1] Alliances have been defined as "a limited set of states acting in concert at X time regarding the mutual enhancement of the military security of the members."[2] In the classical sense of the definition, alliances have been military in nature revolving around a formal agreement.

Contemporary definitions of alliances are more informal. Stephen Walt asserts that alliances are, "a formal or informal relationship between two or more sovereign states."[3] Robert Osgood's definition is more precise. He states that "an alliance is defined as a formal agreement that pledges states to cooperate in using their military resources against a specific state or states and usually obligates one or more of the signatories to use force, or to consider the use of force, in specified circumstances."[4]

Synder in his definition of alliance emphasizes explicit mutual declarations of future intent. He distinguishes this type of declaration from simply a vague promise of aid in the future. He also emphasizes the military components of alliances as opposed to groupings that deal with economic or political goals such as the Organization of Petroleum Exporting Countries (OPEC) or the British Commonwealth.[5]

In discussing contemporary views of alliances it is necessary to expand the scope of the definition to include other interests besides military.[6] The definition of an alliance must also include those nations that share a high level of common interests and seek to form working relationships to enhance these interests despite not having a formal treaty. This concept was reflected by Osgood when he reported that declarations of support for a particular state made in conjunction with that nation serves the same purpose as an alliance.[7]

Other scholars have argued that the definition of alliances in the modern period has become more informal by necessity. Some third world states are reluctant to enter into formalized alliances as a result of the possibility of charges from external as well as internal opponents that they are compromising their sovereignty. Many of the more significant alliances in the international system in the postwar period have lacked a comprehensive mutual security arrangement, yet the commitment of the parties has not been doubted.[8] In addition to national security arrangements established in formalized mutual security pacts, the study of alliances in international relations has also focused on less formalized arrangements such as nonaggression pacts, neutrality agreements, and ententes. These categories, which range from no framework for national security to a traditional formalized defensive alliance, have influenced the theoretical discussion on alliances. These classifications and their definitions are articulated by the data collection of the Correlates of War project. These categories are (1) alliances that have no arrangements pertaining to national security; (2) neutrality pacts that emphasize nonintervention against members; (3) ententes that provide for consultations among members during conflict; and (4) mutual defense pacts that provide for nations to assist each other if attacked.[9]

Other terms related to alliances include alignment and coalition. Alignment is the broadest of these terms and is defined as a grouping of either individuals or states for or against a specific cause. A coalition is defined as a temporary coming together to advance a specific goal or goals. Many historians have used this term to label combinations of states prosecuting a war on the same side. An entente is a more specific term that signifies an understanding between states formed as a result of conventions or declarations. It is more formal than either alignments or coalitions. However, it is less binding than an alliance as it gives the parties more freedom of choice than in a formalized alliance framework.[10]

Another question within the framework of alliances is decision making within the relationship. While in theory an alliance respects sovereignty, the relationship frequently is between unequals in power. It should be recognized that bargaining is always taking place in alliances. Also present within the alliance framework is a fair amount of coercion and tension, which can be present in times of conflict as well as stability.[11]

Historically, alliances have been focused on military relations and national security. Eighteenth-century alliances were established with specific stipulations. These included obligations to provide specific numbers of soldiers, as well as funds for the military. However, due to limitations in technology and communications, there were usually no provisions for establishing a joint command structure or consultations once hostilities began. The emphasis of the alliance was on assistance in military operations. This characteristic of military alliances was carried through the nineteenth century leading up to World War I. The Austro-German Alliance of 1879, which was known as the Dual Alliance and evolved into the Triple Alliance when Italy joined, provided for very limited military coordination. This was primarily carried out by the military attachés in the respective capitals. When hostilities started in 1914, German leaders were largely ignorant of their allies' mobilization plans.[12]

Alliances in the modern international system have changed their focus to deterrence. For the most part, they emphasize crisis prevention and diplomatic influence. Alliances for most of the postwar international system have been based largely on the formation of blocs and the presence of fairly permanent complementary foreign policy objectives and interests.[13] However, with the collapse of the Soviet Union as a superpower this may change. Now that the major external threat to the Western bloc has been removed, individual nations may view different threats as taking priority.

Alliances in the International System

The Functions of Alliances in International Politics

An important consideration in the study of alliances is their function in the international system, as well as why states align. The functions of alliances are identified by Liska and Osgood as the aggregation of power, as a means of controlling another state, and promotion of stability and the status quo in the international system. Robert Osgood discusses a fourth function of alliances, which is as a means of establishing internal security. He claims that this is especially pertinent for small states. This later point is discussed by Rothstein, who cites the bargaining advantages and the political-psychological effects of being associated with a powerful state.[14]

A further reason why nations align is articulated by Charles Kegley and Gregory Raymond. They assert that an alliance is produced when their tacit agreement to cooperate is made explicit through a written treaty. Alliances, in other words, are formal agreements between sovereign states "for the putative purpose of coordinating their behavior in the event of certain specified contingencies of a military nature." The degree of coordination may range from a detailed list of military forces that will be furnished by each party under certain conditions, to a guarantee of neutrality in the event that an alliance member is attacked, to the broader requirement of consultation should a military conflict erupt.[15]

Jack Levy, in rejecting the correlations of alliances as an independent predictor of war, states that nations form alliances when international and domestic conditions make the occurrence of war likely. He argues that when this occurs, states form alliances to meet the following criteria: in order to deter war; fight the war successfully in the event it occurs; or perhaps even to initiate war under more favorable circumstances.[16]

Historically, alliances have been formed for a variety of reasons. Paul Schroeder, in a discussion of alliances in the international system between 1815-1945, illustrates several reasons and implications of alliance formulation. First, a significant factor in alliance formulation during this period, and one that other scholars discussing contemporary American alliance policies have cited, is that while forming alliances illustrates a desire to increase a state's power against an outside threat, in some cases the formation of alliances has weakened a nation's military power. Second, alliances formed to face one threat had secondary functions that were not specified. Third, alliances by definition serve to restrain the freedom of action of the partners. This was frequently the goal of forming the alliance in the first place. Fourth, traditionally, alliances were used as a carrot-and-stick approach towards opponents, punishing them by isolating them within the international system, depriving them of allies, and thus limiting their power aggregation capabilities. Alliances were also used to mollify an opponent and attempt to bring it back into the international system as a full-fledged member. Finally, an alliance can either be used to balance a potential opponent or to join with that state in an attempt to dilute the threat.[17]

Ideology and Alliances

An important question in the literature is the significance of ideology on alliance formation and maintenance. In their discussions on alliances, Kegley and Raymond discuss the significance of necessity as opposed to ideology in explaining international alignments.[18]

Stephen Walt advances several hypothesis on ideology and alliances: (1) states with similar domestic ideologies are more likely to ally; (2) centralized and hierarchical movements will have greater difficulty in forming alliances, and those they do form will be more fragile; (3) ideological alignments are more prevalent in a bipolar international system; (4) states that lack domestic legitimacy will be more likely to align ideologically in order to facilitate external support as well as internal support for the regime; and (5) the impact of ideology on alliances is frequently exaggerated by statesmen and they will overestimate the degree of ideological agreement among their allies and adversaries.[19]

George Liska argues that the primary function of ideology in alliances is to provide a rationalization of a state's alliance choices. This has the effect of translating the alliance from simply being one of necessity into a social institution.[20]

While ideology is frequently the justification for alliances and the extension of aid, in reality this has not been the case. Many of America's allies in the third world have been authoritarian military, or quasi-military, governments with only limited popular support. Ideology has been used more as justification than a primary reason for alliances. This can be observed when looking at American alliances in the Middle East. The United States has allied itself with conservative monarchies, Saudi Arabia and Iran, modernizing authoritarian governments, Egypt, as well as parliamentary democracies such as Israel.[21]

Alliances As Components of Realist Theory

The realist perspective makes several assumptions concerning the nature of states and how they function in the international system. First, all states are unitary actors whose minimum objective is to survive. Second, the international system is one of anarchy, with no central authority to check behavior. As a result, individual states are left to their own devices. In order for states to maximize their power they increase their strength internally by building up their military capabilities and economic resources. In addition, states can enhance their power by forming external alliances.[22]

Realism is divided into two major components, classical and structural. There are four major assumptions of classical realist theory. First, nation-states are the key actors of the international system. Second, domestic politics are separate from foreign policy. Third, international politics is a struggle for power in an international system of anarchy. Fourth, there are measurable differences in power between greater and lesser powers.[23]

This theory also assumes that individuals are evil and lust for power; there is no utopian ideal and life is a struggle against all for control. The national interest of a state is identified as maximizing power. The nature of the international system and the assumptions discussed above require nations to build up their military strength. Part of the development of a nation's military power is forging military alliances based on necessity and not ideology. This is qualified by having a fluid system of alliances because they are temporary and serve limited purposes. Realist theory assumes self-help in international affairs, and therefore nations should not subordinate themselves to their allies.[24]

Alliances are a key component in maintaining the balance of power in the realist view. Morgenthau argues that nations form alliances to add the capabilities of other states to their own, as well as to withhold these from an adversary. Nations form alliances out of self-interest and will not align if the advantages outweigh the costs. He asserts that for an alliance to be effective there must not only be coordination of the general policies and objectives by the aligned nations, but there must also be agreement on specific policies and measures to be adopted as well. However, Morgenthau argues that nations that have weak power capabilities can be of great value to a larger power if they have strategic resources or occupy a geostrategic geographical position.[25]

Neorealist or structural realism agrees with much of the assumptions of realism described above. An important distinction, however, is the recognition that the structure of the international system is significant in this theoretical framework. The number of actors and their respective capabilities shapes the patterns of interactions that will take place. Changes in the structure influences behavior and the distribution capabilities among the units within the international system. Neorealists attempt to give greater clarity to terms in an effort to test this approach. The categories of inquiry are (1) system and decision (leadership); (2) interest and power; (3) perception and reality; (4) cooperation and conflict (behavioral strategy); and (5) norm or advantage.[26] Among the international relations theorists that articulate this approach is Kenneth Waltz. Waltz argues that the structure of the international system is significant in how states interact. "The concept of structure is based on the fact that units differently juxtaposed and combined behave differently and in interacting produce different outcomes."[27]

Neorealists attempt to explain the behavior of states as well as the outcomes of this behavior based on systemic factors. Two factors of the international system remain constant. First, the international system is characterized by anarchy as opposed to hierarchy. Second, the structure of the international system typically involves interaction of actors with similar functions. The third important element of structure is the distribution of power capabilities across the international system. This is not a constant but varies from system to system. The power capabilities of the greater nations are most important because they shape the structure of the international system.[28] Neorealism expands on classical realism by emphasizing the political preferences of the regime in the formulation of foreign policy. Stephen Walt discusses the importance of examining how elites seek to keep their political power. Walt argues that maximization of power at the international level is subordinate to keeping power at the domestic level.[29] Arms transfers are one way that states attempt to maximize their power both domestically and internationally. They are strategically and politically significant as they can illustrate the support of a larger power and imply a certain degree of political and military commitment. In addition, they can assist in deterring an attack or forcing an adversary to back down even though there is doubt about just how militarily significant these transfers were. An example of this was Iraq's agreeing to settle its territorial dispute with Iran in 1975, which occurred in part because of the perceived enhancement of Iranian military power.

In looking at the functions of alliances it is necessary to examine them in light of both international and domestic levels of analysis. The perception of most policy makers is that alliances enhance the power capabilities of the state as well as its national interests as defined by its leaders. However, in creating these alliances the leadership of a nation also hopes to enhance its domestic political credibility. By at least creating the popular perception that the state's power is increasing, this can translate into greater legitimacy for the regime, while the converse is also true. An example of this took place during the Carter administration. Several regimes with which the United States was allied were overthrown, notably the Shah of Iran and Somoza in Nicaragua. While setbacks to American foreign policy, these events did not threaten the basic security of the United States nor did they jeopardize the American position in the international system. However, the public perception both domestically and internationally was that American power was declining and this helped to contribute to the defeat of President Carter in 1980. Thus, the importance of alliances is the domestic and international credibility that is attached to them, rather than on the enhancement of the concrete power of the state.

Balancing, Bandwagoning, and Alliances

There are several implications of the process of bandwagoning as they relate to international relations literature. Bandwagoning occurs when a vulnerable state makes concessions to a dominant power as a form of appeasement. This involves tolerating hostile and illegitimate actions because of the disparity in power between the states. Detente is defined as more or less equal concessions from both states to attain mutual benefits. If one state in this arrangement attempts actions that the other finds threatening or contrary to the spirit or agreements of the detente, in all likelihood it would collapse.[30]

It has been suggested by those who favor the realist approach to international relations that states tend to bandwagon in an attempt to either appease a dominant power, as a means of deterring a possible attack, or to gain territory. Weak states are more likely to bandwagon than states that have moderate power capabilities. These states can only offer limited resources to a dominant power and cannot change the balance of power in the international system. Often weak states are able to free ride in an alliance relationship if they have a great deal of support from the major power.[31]

Stephen David discusses bandwagoning and the third world. He argues that bandwagoning could make the nation susceptible to takeover by the dominant power. However, he points out that bandwagoning has been apparent in the bipolar system by citing two examples. First, Finland bandwagoned with the Soviet Union after World War II. This was the reason it maintained its independence, despite having fought on the side of the Axis. Second, Egypt bandwagoned with the United States after the 1973 war. Egypt's credible military showing convinced the United States of its potential contributions to the American alliance system.[32]

David relates the importance of balance of power, bandwagoning, and ideology in alliance formation in the third world by focusing on the internal as well as the external factors in looking how third world nations align. For this he develops what he refers to as "omnibalancing." This adopts a realist approach to understanding third world alliance formation, combined with studying the internal politics and policy preferences of the leadership of the state, as separate from the nation. He argues that threatened states will bandwagon with secondary opponents in order to balance against the primary adversary.[33]

In order to better understand how third world nations align, factors of internal politics are studied. Elites will base their alliance policy on neutralizing key domestic contingency groups, or dealing with internal threats to the regime. David cites as examples the cases of Egypt under Sadat and Ethiopia under Mengistu. On his ascendancy to the presidency, Sadat was forced to align with the Soviet Union in order to maintain the support of the pro-Soviet elements of his regime until his power was consolidated. He shifted his alliance to America after 1973 in response to pressures from key groups in society, such as the military, who felt he was proceeding too slowly in taking steps to gain back the Sinai. In addition, the Soviet Union, because it wished to avoid potential direct conflict with the United States, was unwilling to supply Egypt with the equipment Sadat deemed necessary to take back the territories. The Ethiopian case revolved around similar dynamics. After the overthrow of the monarchy the Dergue, headed by Mengistu, was confronted by the rivalry with Soviet-supported Somalia. Despite Mengistu's personal preference for the Soviet Union, he could not weaken his dependence on the United States. However, the United States was unwilling to extend the support that the regime needed to confront internal threats such as the separatist movement in Eritrea. It was argued that Mengistu adopted a Marxist philosophy in order to gain Soviet aid and to lessen Soviet support of his internal and external rivals, Somalia, and the Eritrean rebels.[34]

Bandwagoning is significant in analyzing American policy in the third world for several reasons. Walt argues that states tend to balance as opposed to bandwagoning. The implication for the United States is that American pressure against Soviet allies would be counterproductive as these states would, in all likelihood, strengthen their ties with the Soviet Union. This also leads to the conclusion that the United States should not have worried about allies defecting or maintaining neutrality during the Cold War, as they would have needed to balance the Soviet threat. Therefore, Walt argues, it is more incumbent for the United States to be concerned with the wasting of its resources and the needless provocations sometimes caused by attempting to maintain credibility with its allies.[35]

Walt cites as examples of balancing in alliances the examples of Iran and Turkey. At the beginning of the Cold War, both states viewed the Soviet Union as a threatening power. Therefore, an alliance with the United States was viewed as being essential to balance the Soviet threat. In addition, the United States was a desirable ally as it could be counted on to provide protection without compromising the independence of these states. However, as relations between the United States and the Soviet Union eased, these states viewed the emergence of nationalistic states in the region as potentially more threatening. As a result, relations between Turkey, Iran, and the Soviet Union improved because the Soviets appeared less threatening and more as a status quo power desiring stability.[36]

Balancing verses bandwagoning has been a debate in American foreign policy. Many scholars have advanced the idea that the United States must remain committed to its global alliances. They argue that a failure to do so would result in states tilting toward the Soviet Union, a process known as bandwagoning. The opposite viewpoint, however, has been advanced that if the United States did less in terms of military commitments and aid, its allies would be forced to contribute more to balance against the Soviet threat.[37]

The validity of the bandwagoning hypothesis has been perpetuated in the history of American foreign policy in order to justify American commitments abroad, as well as to a particular policy toward a country or region. President John F. Kennedy stated, "if the United States were to falter, the whole world . . . would inevitably begin to move toward the Communist bloc." Henry Kissinger, although he frequently argued that the United States should adopt more of a balancing philosophy in maintaining its alliance commitment, also considered the element of bandwagoning in defending American interests. "If leaders around the world . . . assume that the U.S. lacked either the forces or the will . . . they will accommodate themselves to what they will regard as the dominant trend." This was further supported by Ronald Reagan. "If we cannot defend ourselves . . . then we cannot expect to prevail elsewhere. . . . Our credibility will collapse and our alliances will crumble."[38]

The balancing argument states that first, an American defeat in the periphery would not reflect a lessening of American resolve, but rather would result in the United States redoubling its efforts to counter the Soviets in other areas. Second, a Soviet victory in the international system would galvanize American allies to do more for their own defense and reduce the effectiveness of any Soviet pressure on them. Third, the same can be said for Soviet allies, as they would have to calculate a greater resolve by the United States in standing up to any attempt to increase their own power. In summary, the central tenet of the balancing hypothesis is that the traditional concept of falling dominoes in response to an American foreign policy setback must not be taken as an absolute given.[39]

The Benefits and Costs of Alliances

It is argued that alliances add precision and reduce the risk of uncertainty in the international system. Knowledge of the size of the coalition confronting the potential aggressor can reduce the likelihood of conflict withing the international system by serving as a deterrent to war.[40]

Singer argues that alliances can reduce the chance of conflict due to miscalculation. Osgood has also advanced the idea that firm alliance commitments can minimize the occurrence of potentially destabilizing shifts in the international system. Similar to this argument is one made by Gulick and Holsti, who claim that alliances prevent one nation or group of nations from exercising a preponderance of power. Therefore, alliances serve to reinforce the balance within the international system. This balancing argument is also made by Walt with reference to regional powers in the Middle East. It is also argued that alliances can reinforce the status quo by restraining a potentially belligerent actor. Morgenthau asserts that because this adds to precision within the international system, it imposes limitations on policies and how they can be implemented by individual states.[41] Liska claims that an alliance can enhance the prestige of a state, the collapse of which might destablize the international system.

Glenn Snyder argues that historically, states have gained greater security from alliances. First, the probability of their being attacked is decreased. Second, in the event that a country is attacked, they can call on their ally and thus have greater resources to repel the attacker. Third, an alliance precludes its ally from joining with its potential adversary.[42]

States form alliances in an effort to achieve the expectation of private benefits, which lead participants to support the formal alliance institutions. These institutions in theory are supposed to give the optimal benefit and share the costs. The benefits of alliances are divided into collective and private goods. Collective goods are defined as those that when supplied to one member of a group must be made available equally to the entire group. Francis Beer contends that collective goods possess either one or both of the properties of nonexclusivity and nonrivalness, maintaining that if the common goal is achieved, everyone who shares this goal will automatically benefit. This brings up the idea of the free rider who can gain benefits without contributing to the attaining of the good. A second point Beer makes is that if a good is available to one party, it is made available to other members at little or no cost.[43]

The arguments against alliances focus on the idea that they frequently lead to polarization within the international system.[44] Balance of power theorists identify two situations where permanent alliances can destabilize the international system. First, fixed alliance commitments reduce the number of possible coalitions that could form against a potential aggressor. This could embolden a revisionist state to initiate an aggressive war.[45] Second, the formation of permanent alliances eliminates potential balancers within the international system. Balancers are important as they bolster weaker coalitions, resulting in the greater likelihood of conflict within the system.[46] In addition, there is a body of international relations literature that considers alliances costly, as they limit cross-cutting pressures among states, leading to a rigid, polarized international system.[47]

Alliances can inflict costs in several ways. First, there are political costs in which initial promises are followed by the liabilities of acquiring the opponent of one's ally as an enemy as well. The enemy of my friend is also my enemy. Another political cost involved in postwar alliances occurs as a result of anticolonialism-nationalism within the third world where they are perceived as being an extension of Western colonial control.[48]

In addition, alliances cannot guarantee the peace, as a large number of allies may not be enough to deter a country intent on changing the status quo of the international system. This is especially true when the coalition consists of minor powers with only limited power capabilities, or if the coalition's credibility is questionable. In addition, a leader may view the initiation of a conflict as preferential to a protracted conflict, or be willing to take the risk of engaging in a quick strike before resistance can be brought to bear. In summarizing this view, one can take a quote from Virgil, "It never troubles a wolf how many the sheep be."[49]

Even if a state has been able to accrue allies of considerable strength it can still prove to be destablizing, and not deter war, for several reasons. First, alliances can be viewed as menacing, since what for one country is a defensive alliance can be viewed by a rival as an offensive coalition. This can lead to the formation of counteralliances, thereby creating and reinforcing existing cleavages within the international system. Second, alliances are entangling and require states in some cases to subordinate their own interests to that of their coalition partners. As a result, states can be drawn into conflicts when their vital interests are not threatened. Finally, alliances can lengthen the severity of a conflict, as states who are losing may continue to fight in hopes that their allies will rescue them.[50]

Obligations of alliances can cost more than other types of military commitments because it limits the political options available to a state. Thus, states have to be reassured periodically about their partners' commitment since there is no enforcement within an alliance framework except for mutual cooperation among the partners, common interests, and good faith. Alliances require members to clarify their liabilities and contribute further assets in order to satisfy their partners. A possible consequence of an alliance is it may lead to states becoming involved in each other's internal and external affairs. This occurs because changes in the regime or the state's power capabilities can have ramifications on the alliance.[51]

An important consideration for states in an alliance is their fear of entrapment or abandonment. The significance of entrapment is that states may find themselves in a conflict that they only have a limited interest in in order to facilitate the interests of its ally. Abandonment is the fear that in the event of a conflict an ally will simply stand aside and do nothing. This factor played a role in the origins of World War I. France feared that in the event of a Franco-German war, Russia would be tempted to stay out of the conflict. Therefore it was more desirable for France to have a Russo-Austrian dispute in the Balkans flare up into a general European war, as this would ensure Russian and perhaps even British participation.[52]

Alliances and Domestic Politics

Alliances are affected, and in many cases are predicated, on domestic politics. States that share common economic interests will form coalitions based on trade and other general economic issues.[53] An alliance can affect the internal politics of a nation by the pooling of resources, as well as the granting of subsidies, allowing the regime to maintain itself without mobilizing disaffected groups or interests. Alliances also can confer prestige on a regime and assist it in perpetuating itself in power, sometimes undercutting domestic opposition groups within the country. In this way, a state may be compelled to support an allied regime, since changes in the political elite could jeopardize the alliance, resulting in a loss of prestige, as well as power, for the major ally.[54]

When an alliance is determined by domestic factors, those groups and individuals who gain politically or economically are its strongest defenders. Oftentimes individuals and groups develop a personal stake in an alliance and invoke the concept of national interest as justification. It seems that when an alliance is based more on the personal preferences of the ruling groups, and the regime's interest becomes predominant, these relationships tend to be fleeting. Liska cites as an example the Iraqi monarchy's affinity for the Baghdad Pact, which ended once the regime was overthrown. The example of Iran is similar, as many scholars viewed the Shah's alliance with the United States as weakening his legitimacy with many Iranians, and the U.S. link was severed after the revolution. Liska discusses how alliances based on external interests are able to endure and have more legitimacy within a society. He cites the example of West Germany in which German membership in NATO has been supported by the major political parties and German public opinion, as well as by such diverse groups as constitutional democrats and neo-Nazis.[55]

In examining alliances, the domestic politics of third world states are often not given enough consideration in the study of international relations. Steven David discusses the importance of third world states more specifically, observing that during the bipolar system the superpowers tended to ignore third world leaders. It is important to recognize that these leaders have their own agendas and interests that they attempt to advance within the respective alliance frameworks established by the superpowers.[56]

Alliances between Great and Small Powers

Another body of literature on the theory of alliances revolves around relationships between large and small powers. Liska identifies three reasons why states align: (1) to deter and coerce; (2) to enhance the domestic stability of the nation; and (3) to convey status on a particular nation.[57] There is a fundamental difference between great powers and smaller powers as to why they form alliances. Great powers tend to form alliances for traditional geostrategic reasons such as bases and access to raw materials. Smaller powers have sought to use alliances for internal reasons, as well as a dynamic of their regional goals.

Historically, the international relations literature on alliances reflects the view that larger states gain more benefits in allying with smaller powers. Morgenthau asserted that alliance benefits tend to reflect the distribution of power in the relationship, with larger powers gaining greater benefits and influence over policy. He cites the United States-South Korean alliance as a example of this factor.[58] This argument was also illustrated in classical literature, as the political philosopher Machiavelli warned small states to ally with greater nations only when absolutely necessary.[59]

A more recent motivation for greater powers to align with lesser powers that is related to alliance management, deals with great power concerns over nuclear proliferation. Larger states may feel that they can forestall a state's nuclear development by aligning and increasing its leverage over it.[60] A component of these great-small power alliances is that the larger powers offer an abundance of conventional weaponry in order to influence its smaller ally away from developing nuclear weaponry. This was cited as a reason for the supplying of offensive weapons to Israel during the Johnson administration, as well as the decision by the United States to furnish Pakistan with weaponry.

Historically, the great powers have looked to ally with smaller states as a way of building up their own military status. An example of this occurred with the breakup of the Concert of Europe after 1890. Many decision makers felt if a major conflict should occur, minor military gains in strength could tip the balance for a coalition. This lead to states like Romania gaining in importance, as it was viewed that their resources could be the margin of victory to whatever coalition it allied with.[61]

This view of the significance of small powers lasted into the interwar period and was reinforced by the French alliance system in Eastern Europe. As a result of their alliance with France, these states gained military aid and the prestige of being allied with the most powerful nation in Europe. More significantly, they hoped this alliance would guarantee their independence gained as a result of the peace settlement after World War I. However, as war approached by the end of the 1930s, the influence of these powers, and small powers in general, became negligible in great power calculations. By this time, advances in technology had made warfighting more sophisticated and lessened the importance of minor powers.[62]

In the modern period, alliances may have other costs for a small power besides being dominated by the larger state. In the postwar period, alliances have been viewed as vestiges of colonialism by which developed states attempt to maintain control over less-developed states. Therefore, while scholars such as George Liska propose that alliances have a function of conferring status on nations, he also suggests that in the postwar international system an alliance can cost a third world state or regime legitimacy, both externally and internally.[63]

The prospect of great and small power alliances can lead to misconception and differences in policy. Due to the different levels of analysis of the alliance partners, the larger power must concern itself with issues at the systemic level, while the orientation of the smaller power is on the regional situation, and even the survival of the individual regime. In addition, the greater power frequently is in the middle, sitting between its allies that are directly impacted by a particular threat, and those states that are more remote from it. This latter group only has a limited interest and understanding of these threats, and is less likely to contribute to the alliance.[64]

Benefits for Small Powers

Rothstein argues that alliances with great powers increased the status of the small powers, since they were viewed as strategic assets capable of tipping the balance against the rival coalition. Rothstein also discusses the different interests of the respective allies that can lead to tensions in the relationship. The great powers tend to identify with problems on the systemic level, while small powers are more concerned with their respective regions and regime goals.[65]

Small powers can also achieve leverage in an alliance by reinforcing the view of the larger power that they are important strategically. This is achieved through emphasizing the importance of a strategic commodity or the geographical location of these nations. Therefore, smaller states are able to gain strength from the alliance that transcends the actual power capabilities they possess. Smaller powers have several opportunities to exert influence in their relationships with larger states: (1) the smaller state is able to focus more on a single foreign policy issue, while the larger state must pay attention to many different issues; (2) the smaller state may be willing to take more chances to maximize its power, while the greater power is afraid of having its power eroded; (3) a smaller power may sometimes be willing to sacrifice more than a larger power in a conflict because it is fighting for a more concrete interest than a larger power. An example of this was North Vietnam during its conflict with the United States; (4) the decision making institutions of the smaller power are frequently more centralized than the more fragmented institutions of a larger power; (5) the smaller state may possess an important commodity or a strategic location which the larger power values; and (6) the smaller state could threaten to align with an adversary of the greater power and, depending on the presence of the conditions cited above, the larger power may feel it is in its interest to placate it.[66]

Arms Transfers in International Relations Theory

Arms transfers can impact on alliances in several ways. First, they have become a central element of foreign policy for major as well as regional powers trying to expand their political influence and heavy industrial base. Second, arms transfers have increased in importance as other traditional instruments of foreign policy have decreased. In the contemporary international system, alliances have become more informal than they were in previous eras. Part of the reason for this is due to the growth of nationalism in the postwar international system. In many cases today, it is not considered politically feasible for smaller states to allow the basing of foreign troops. Finally, the credibility of intervention has lessened as a result of the political, economic, and military costs that could occur. For the United States, this became a problem after Vietnam, as decision makers are now aware of the political costs of an intervention lasting too long. In addition, with the growth of nuclear weapons, the great powers viewed attempting to enhance their interests through the arming of regional proxies as being more stable than direct confrontations. A third reason for the greater acquisition of arms in the international system is the proliferation of states in the world. These states and regimes have their own interests and desire to possess weapons and some of them, due to oil wealth, now have the ability to purchase large numbers of technologically advanced systems.

Arms transfers have increased in sophistication as a result of several factors, including the more advanced quality of armaments, particularly aircraft, being provided by the major powers to their respective allies in the third world. Technology has also spread around the international system with the growth of coproduction agreements. In addition, there has been a greater emphasis on the establishment of indigenous arms industries in the Third World.[67]

The literature dealing with arms transfers discusses both the causes and repercussions of arms sales at the systemic level, as well as the domestic level. At the systemic level is the traditional argument of arms sales enhancing the power of the nation by being used as a tool of foreign policy.[68] Much of the arms transfer literature deals with the pros and cons of selling arms. This is from the perspective of the selling country as well as the recipient.

There are several geostrategic reasons justifying arms sales: (1) to illustrate support for allies; (2) to provide a means for military burden sharing; (3) to enhance political influence and leverage over other, predominantly third world countries; (4) as a component in superpower competition; (5) to provide access to military bases; (6) to enhance access to political and military elites; and (7) to assist in the enhancement of international security in third world nations deemed critical to the interests of the great powers. In addition to strategic military rationales, economic justifications for selling arms are prominent in the literature. These economic considerations include the reduction of trade deficits; the absorption of surplus output; and the establishment of cost sharing in the research and development of major weapons systems. Proponents of arms transfers argue that they enable the United States to satisfy domestic economic problems and aid key high tech industries, in particular, the aerospace field. They also provide employment, particularly in states that are electorally significant, as well as aid the Pentagon in American domestic military production and research costs.[69]

Critics call into question the traditional views that arms transfers equal leverage, claiming states frequently enact policies that are counter to the interests of the supplier. Within the literature on arms transfers, the potential costs of supplying arms that have been discussed include the weakening of the national security interests of the supplier. Of primary concern is the possibility that weapons could fall into the hands of an opponent, either a state or terrorist group. Even if the original supplier retains control, the arms still could be used against the interests of the supplier. Supplying arms could also constrain the foreign policy options of the supplier nation, as frequently there is a quid pro quo of furnishing military bases or political considerations. The supplier not wanting to risk losing these gains would be likely to continue the arms relationship despite having misgivings. Additionally, excessive arms sales can deplete the stockpile of the supplier nation, weaken the readiness of its own forces, as well as impede nuclear nonproliferation policies. Finally, arms transfers could hurt the interests of the supplier by encouraging regional arms races and jeopardizing regional stability.[70]

Critics also charge that the economic value of arms transfers are also overstated. Arms sales constitute only a small percentage of total American exports and have not contributed significantly to remedying the American balance of payments deficits. The employment gains established by arms sales are relatively minor and most defense contractors do not depend on overseas sales. Also the costs of research/development as well as the price of a system are not lowered substantially as a result of arms transfers, nor do nations denied American arms necessarily purchase comparable arms from other suppliers.[71]

The Concept of Commitments

Alliances are predicated on an understanding of commitment, which is defined as the joint action during a contingency in which the alliance partners will complement each other's capabilities and secure a mutual advantage.[72] A problem with commitment in international alliances is that they are frequently misunderstood or misused. Misunderstandings can occur as coalition partners frequently misinterpret the goals and priorities of an alliance. In addition, nations may misinterpret what they each mean by an act of commitment.[73] There are many examples of these misunderstandings in international politics, such as the strains within the Atlantic alliance in the early 1980s. The United States sought to restrain the Soviet Union in all spheres of international interaction, strategic, political, as well as economic. Although many of the NATO countries agreed with the basic premise of containing the Soviets politically and militarily, as indicated by membership in NATO, they felt it was appropriate to enter into economic relations with Moscow.

An example of a misplaced commitment were the events leading up to the outbreak of World War I. The Triple Alliance, comprised of Germany, Austria, and Italy, was designed to be a defensive pact. However, there was a faction of the Austrian leadership that desired to punish Serbia for its complicity in the assassination of Archduke Francis Ferdinand and crush the Pan-Slavic threat to the Austro-Hungarian empire. Austria sought to provoke a war and they were supported in this by Germany, which still viewed its obligation to Austria as binding. Thus, Germany essentially allowed itself to be used to advance the internal politics of Austria-Hungary in order to promote Austria's security at the expense of her own.[74]

The commitments that the respective allies gave to Austria and Russia seem to be irrational as Britain, France, and Germany had virtually little or no interest in the situation in the Balkans. However, for various reasons, all of the major European powers valued their alliances, which reflects Schelling and Kahn's argument that despite the seemingly irrationality of specific commitments, the importance of commitment in general is one of national credibility. In reality, commitments are interdependent and if one is broken it leads to a loss of credibility that could imperil more fundamental national interests.[75] Therefore the notion of credibility has been and continues to be a significant factor in determining state action, particularly by the great powers. Robert Kann points out that states, and in particular great powers, fear the loss of credibility. This would weaken their ability to make future alliances and as a result, nations, "may in effect become a political prisoner of the credibility factor."[76]

The Significance of Global Commitments Theory

In discussing American alliances with other actors, there have been various interpretations of the utility of alliance commitments that the United States has made in the postwar period. One is that it was necessary and desirable to construct a worldwide alliance system in order to defend American interests. This was done for two reasons: to stabilize the local ally as well as to demonstrate American resolve to its friends and deter threats to other American allies.[77] This view is seconded by more contemporary authors, who argue that the United States should do more to help out its allies.[78]

Realist theory as articulated in the writings of Thucydides and Morgenthau places a great deal of emphasis on acquiring allies. However, the scholarly support for a policy of global commitments differs from the traditional realist approach in four respects. First, there is the assumption that commitments (alliances) have to be made on a global scale because threats are interdependent. Second, because of this interdependence, once a commitment is made it has to be maintained. Third, commitments must be backed up by political uses of military force and fourth, a domestic coalition must be kept in place in order to reinforce this policy.[79] Global commitment theories, unlike realists theories, did not make any distinctions among interests; all interests are essentially vital interests.[80] The cost of the commitment is not taken into consideration because of the credibility issue and it is significant for both allies and adversaries to understand that, regardless of costs, the United States would maintain its commitments.[81] The use of military force as a political instrument, as articulated by Robert Osgood, is "not just a problem of military strategy, but is, more broadly, the problem of combining military power with diplomacy and with the economic and psychological instruments of power within a coherent national strategy that is capable of supporting the United States' political objectives abroad."[82]

Ideological rivalry has often been emphasized in an effort to maintain support within nations for these worldwide commitments. Theodore Lowi has referred to this as a process of overselling the threat in reference to the Truman administration getting Congressional and public opinion to support the furnishing of aid to Greece and Turkey.[83] Historically, ideology has been a significant rationale in justifying American actions and U.S. presidents have sought to portray America as on a mission to enforce democracy in the world.[84] As a result, U.S. policy makers have overstated the impact of perceived threats to American global strategy, causing the United States to establish or reinforce commitments prematurely. This policy of global commitments has resulted in an inflexibility in American decision making concerning alliances.[85]

During the Cold War, global commitments were justified as a result of the domino theory in which commitments were considered interdependent. If one were allowed to fall this would initiate a process in which others could go down. This was a very simplistic notion and really did not happen, as regional and internal dynamics within these countries have to be taken into account.[86] The significance of political credibility is also a manifestation of the growing importance of American presidents in foreign affairs. Therefore, a situation that starts out as involving a national commitment can quickly take on the form of a personal commitment for an American president.[87]

American Interests in the Middle East

The goals commonly cited of American foreign policy in the region are in the literature on U.S. foreign policy in the Middle East and at times there has been debate over how best to achieve those goals. However, this general framework of American policy has, by and large, not been the subject of debate in American politics.

The first goal is defined as security in order to deny the area to the Soviets and fits generally into the postwar containment policy of the United States. The second goal involves a maintenance of oil supplies from the region to the West, and the third emphasizes stability, which is support of the status quo in order to fulfill the first two goals.[88] A fourth goal is American support for Israel which likewise can be stated as a U.S. goal in the region. Historically, the United States has been committed to aiding Israel, evidenced by the strategic importance that American policy makers, academics, and journalists have given to the value of Israel militarily. America has also psychologically committed itself to support for Israel and the ideological and religious links that the two nations share are frequently cited.[89] A fifth American goal in the Middle East involves the general economic importance of the region to the West. This includes placing value on the necessity of maintaining a stable and productive balance of trade by ensuring that the petrodollars from the Gulf are invested in ways that stabilize the economic structure of the West.[90]

The enhancement of these goals are usually done by emphasizing ideology in discussing U.S. foreign policy in the region. American support for its Middle East allies is usually justified by democratic principles, as with Israel, or profess anticommunist and or pro-Western values such as Iran and Saudi Arabia.[91]

However, in examining these interests there has been a contradiction between the stated interests of the United States and their implementation. The obvious contradiction involves the position of Israel in American foreign policy as, due to the Arab-Israeli conflict, this would seem to contradict the other security and economic goals previously mentioned. However, other inconsistencies exist as well. In order to maintain the other American interests in the region the United States has traditionally sought to bolster regional powers that share similar interests. In the 1970s these positions were taken by Iran and Saudi Arabia and in the last twenty years it has been Saudi Arabia and Egypt. The method of safeguarding American interests was in building up the military power of these states to serve primarily as a check on anti-Western political movements and states in the region. The vast transfers of sophisticated armaments in the region, however, threatened to upset the status quo and made the disruption of oil traffic and economic activity more likely. The development of Iranian military capabilities led to the exacerbation of territorial conflicts with Iraq in the early 1970s, which also included encouraging the Kurds to rebel in Iraq. Proponents will argue that a benefit of the Iranian arms purchases was that they contributed to the settling of the territorial boundary between the two countries on terms favorable to Iran. However, it is important to note that Iranian arms purchases escalated in the latter portion of the decade despite its favorable relationship with Iraq. In addition, while Saudi Arabia is often presented as a status quo power in the region, they have frequently sought to destabilize both North and South Yemen and have traditionally been opposed to Yemeni unity. Therefore, a primary motivation of increasing the power projection capabilities of these states both militarily and politically has been to exacerbate internal conflict within many states of the region.

Iran

Iran was considered an essential ally for several reasons. The United States came to value Iran very highly for providing it access to listening posts from which America could monitor Soviet nuclear missile and testing facilities in Central Asia. American policy makers viewed these installations as essential in any potential arms control agreement with the Soviet Union for verification purposes. The significance of these facilities influenced American policy towards the Iranian regime to a large degree.[92]

Tehran was also important for the United States as a regional surrogate to serve as a check to radical forces within the Persian Gulf and to a certain extent the third world as a whole. The Shah provided covert assistance to groups seeking to destabilize the governments of Soviet allies in the region such as Iraq and Afghanistan, as well as providing assistance to pro-Western governments such as Oman and South Vietnam. In an effort to further advance these goals, the Shah associated Iran with a group of conservative Middle Eastern and African states in an informal organization known as the Safari Club. This group was dedicated to blocking the spread of Soviet influence the third world.[93]

Other scholars argue that the relationship with Iran was important strategically for the United States as a way of signaling to the Soviet Union that in spite of the policy of detente, Washington would not abandon its interests in the world.[94] However, in pursuing these strategic goals some scholars have argued that the United States became too interlocked and dependent on the Iranian regime. This was a result of the emphasis American policy makers placed on the strategic importance of Iran regionally and internationally.[95]

Iran was also important because of its oil resources, which were strategically and economically essential to the West. In addition, Iran was considered important economically as a trading partner for the United States. The oil boom of the 1970s allowed the Iranian government to adopt grandiose development plans that ended up benefitting many American companies.

Israel

For the United States, Israel can also be viewed as a strategic asset in the political-military sphere. Steven Spiegel has outlined five perspectives that make Israel strategically significant for the United States: intelligence, battlefield experience, technological innovation, the factoring of Israeli military capabilities in Soviet strategic planning, and the enhancement of the reputation of American armaments versus Soviet arms.[96]

This premise has been challenged by other scholars who argue that the American relationship with Israel has jeopardized other, more important, goals in the region. It has been argued that Washington's support for Israel has weakened American relations with the Arab countries as a result of three factors. First, it had influenced some Arabs states to align with the Soviets. Second, the Arab-Israeli conflict has been the primary catalyst of regional instability. Third, the relationship with Israel has impeded American economic objectives in the Middle East.[97]

This view has been stated by George Ball, who challenged the utility of the American alliance with Israel and maintained that the two countries really have different perspectives on foreign policy. The United States has a global emphasis, where Israel is concerned with its own definition of security.[98]

In addition, Israel was significant strategically as a result of providing assistance to various pro-American movements and states that American administrations would find politically difficult. American administrations also generally find that it is a domestic political advantage to support Israel. While there are few tangible economic benefits for the United States in the American-Israeli alliance, the foreign aid extended to Israel subsidizes certain sectors of the American economy. This translates into some economic advantages as well as domestic political advantages for American policy makers.

Saudi Arabia

Politically, Saudi Arabia is important as a result of its capability to influence other regional actors. Militarily, the American relationship with Saudi Arabia is significant as a way of providing security for the region as a whole through arms sales, and the development of Saudi military infrastructure. Saudi Arabia is important for the United States, and the West in general, as a source of oil. In addition, the amount of commercial transactions between American corporations and Saudi Arabia is significant.[99] Saudi Arabia is also valued by the U.S. as Riyadh has assumed a leadership position in the Gulf Cooperation Council.[100]

While the United States looks to Saudi Arabia to provide stability in the region, the Saudis look to the United States as guaranteeing regional security. However, the Saudis are wary of having the perception of adopting too close of a relationship with the United States in order to preserve their internal and regional legitimacy.[101]

American Domestic Groups and Alliances

In all of these cases, domestic politics and interest groups have figured prominently in encouraging and reinforcing these alliances. In fully understanding these relationships, it is necessary to study the interaction of these private interests groups, along with sectors of the bureaucracy, Congress, the media, as well as the preferences of the executive branch in formulating American foreign policy toward these states.[102]

American alliances with Iran and Saudi Arabia were formed predominantly out of perceived national security interests. These interests included maintaining access by the West to Middle Eastern oil, the containment of the Soviet Union, as well as checking or preventing regional states from coming under Moscow's influence. With the Saudi case, the influence of oil company officials was significant in getting the U.S.

government to extend aid and support to Ibn Saud. It was these geostrategic and national economic interests that established the environment in which the early formation and implementation of these alliances took place. The military buildup of Iran and Saudi Arabia was a tool to accomplish these goals. However, once these arms sales were initiated, they served to contribute to the development of constituency groups in the United States that argued for the expansion of these relationships. As a result, the military links between the two states became predicated on Washington's continually supplying sophisticated armaments to these nations and these arms transfers fueled American trade in general with these states. Major American defense contractors, as well as companies selling civilian goods, lobbied in favor of extending this alliance and speculated about the dire consequences should a particular arms sale be rejected by Congress. Sectors of the bureaucracy also developed a stake in maintaining the relationship with these nations for their own bureaucratic interests. The conservative, status quo-oriented philosophies of these regimes also drew support from American decision makers, who continually testified in favor of expanding the military links between the United States and these countries while speculating about the negative repercussions should America attempt to scale back on these strategic commitments. These would include repercussions on bilateral relations as well as on Washington's position in the region and the international system in general. Therefore, American arms transfers to these states grew to be the key component of the alliance and became at least as important as the interests they were designed to protect. Furthermore, the pro-Western "modernizing" aspects of these regimes were continually emphasized in the American media with comparatively few dissenting views expressed. This was particularly true with regard to Iran. Saudi Arabia was criticized more in the media because expanded military links to Riyadh were viewed as threatening to Israel.

Israel represents a different case, as the dynamics of American domestic politics were mainly responsible for forging this alliance. Once this alliance was established, Israel became significant in serving as an important component of U.S. strategy in the region, and the third world as a whole and has remained the case even after the Cold War. Israel has traditionally enjoyed broad support in American society and the media as a whole, and because of the structure and processes of the American political system, it is looked on very favorably by most members of Congress. In addition, the national security bureaucracy overall has been in favor of maintaining the American-Israeli alliance despite the tensions this relationship has from time to time caused with various Arab states.

Thus these U.S. alliances were formed and reinforced out of a combination of national security considerations as well as domestic political implications. With Iran and Saudi Arabia, national security interests were predominant in forging and implementing the alliance. Domestic politics served as a reinforcement of the over-militarization of these alliances, and ultimately was a factor in American decision making. In the Israeli case domestic politics was responsible for the establishment and over-militarization of the alliance between the years 1960-1968, with strategic factors providing the justification and reinforcement for military links. This began in a major way during the 1967 war, and culminated with the privileged position and reputation that Israel enjoyed in American national security circles during the Reagan administration.

Notes

1. Michael Don Ward, *Research Gaps in Alliance Dynamics* (Denver, Colo.: Monograph Series in World Affairs, 1982), 5.
2. Edwin Fedder, "The Concept of Alliance," *International Studies Quarterly* 12, no. 1 (March 1968): 68-69.
3. Stephen M. Walt, *The Origins of Alliances* (Ithaca, N.Y.: Cornell University Press, 1987), 12.
4. Robert Osgood, *Alliances and American Foreign Policy* (Baltimore, Md.: Johns Hopkins University Press, 1968), 17. Other commentators have argued that Osgood's definition is narrowly restricted to military affairs. See George Modelski, "The Study of Alliances: A Review," *Journal of Conflict Resolution* 7, no . 4 (December 1963): 774.
5. Glenn H. Snyder, "Alliances, Balance, and Stability," *International Organization* 45, no.1 (Winter 1991): 123.
6. Charles Burton Marshall, "Alliances and Fledgling States," in *Alliance Policy in the Cold War*, Arnold Wolfers ed. (Baltimore, Md.: Johns Hopkins Press, 1959), 216. Francis Beer argues that alliances traditionally have been accepted by national decision makers as an appropriate strategy to pool national resources of several states to increase the power of their coalition, or to join the grouping that they felt was the strongest. See his *Alliances: Latent War Communities in the Contemporary World* (New York: Holt, Rinehart, and Winston, 1970), 4-5.
7. Osgood, *Alliances and American*, 19.
8. Walt, *The Origins of Alliances*, 12. He cites the American-Israeli relationship as an example of an extremely close alliance relationship that lacks a formalized mutual security treaty. Conversely, he pointed out that the presence of a formalized agreement can signal a weakness in an alliance. He cites as an example the Soviet-Egyptian Treaty of Friendship and Cooperation in 1971. This treaty was concluded a year prior to the expulsion of Soviet advisors from Egypt by President Sadat.
   This view is also reflected by Steven R. David who has written extensively on third world states and alliances. He argues that, "a state has aligned when it brings its policies into close cooperation with those of another state. 'Close cooperation' can take many forms, from a formal written treaty to working together for mutually beneficial goals." Steven R. David, *Choosing Sides: Alignment and Realignment in the Third World* (Baltimore, Md.: Johns Hopkins University Press, 1991), 29. Patrick McGowan and Robert M. Rood argue that alliances differ from alignments. Alliances are geared toward an actual or anticipated enemy. They plan for military engagement at a risk of war and are based on either reinforcing or revising the status quo of the international system. See their "Alliance Behavior in Balance of Power Systems: Applying a Poisson Model to Nineteenth-Century Europe," *The American Political Science Review* 69, no. 3 (1975): 859.

24 Chapter 1

9. Ward, *Research Gaps*, 5. See also the various writings by J. D. Singer and M. Small, notably, "Formal Alliances, 1815-1939: A Quantitative Description," *Journal of Peace Research* 3, (January 1966): 1-31. Also, "Alliance Aggregation and the Onset of War, 1815-1945," in *Quantitative International Politics: Insights and Evidence*, J. David Singer ed. (New York: The Free Press, 1968), 247-86. For a further discussion of the definitions of defense pacts, nonaggression agreements, and ententes see also Charles Kegley and Gregory Raymond, *When Trust Breaks Down: Alliance Norms and World Politics* (Columbia, S.C.: University of South Carolina Press, 1990), 53.

A good discussion of the differences between Alliances and Ententes was discussed by Robert Kann, "Alliances Versus Ententes," *World Politics* 28, no. 4 (July 1976): 611-21. In assessing the differences between the two he points out that in a formal alliance, states frequently attempt to minimize their commitments by finding loopholes in the wording of the agreement. Ententes, on the other hand, are based on common interests that produce similar policies. As an example of this he cites the pre-World War I entente between Britain, France, and Russia, the Triple Entente of 1907.

10. Roger V. Dingman, "Theories of, and Approaches to, Alliance Politics," in *Diplomacy: New Approaches in History, Theory, and Policy*, Paul Gordon Lauren ed. (New York: Free Press, 1979), 249. Michael Ward also discusses the differences between alignments and alliances. He agrees that alignments are more informal than alliances as they are derived from behavioral actions as opposed to formal agreements. Ward states that alignments do not focus solely on the military sphere but also on political, economic, and cultural issues. See Ward, *Research Gaps*, 7-8; George Modelski further elaborates on the differences between alliances and alignments. He asserts that alliances are essentially military in nature, while alignments cover all forms of international cooperation. See Modelski, "The Study of Alliances," 774-75.

For a discussion of how alignments are derived and measured see Henry Teune and Sig Synnestvedt, "Measuring International Alignment," *Orbis* 9, no. 1 (Spring 1965): 176. Among the indicators of measuring alignment with a respective superpower are: military alliances, visits by heads of state or government as well as other important officials, recognition of controversial noncommunist countries, recognition of East Germany, agreements, advisors, and military aid from either superpower, among other factors.

11. Julian Friedman, "Alliance in International Politics," in *Alliance in International Politics*, Julian Friedman et al ed. (Boston: Allyn and Bacon, 1970), 10.

12. K. J. Holsti, "Diplomatic Coalitions and Military Alliances," in *Alliances in International Politics*, Julian Friedman et al eds. (Boston: Allyn and Bacon, 1970), 97. Some of the specific stipulations of eighteenth century alliances included subsidies to support another state's troops, a guarantee to provide military forces under specific circumstances, pledge of nonintervention in a conflict, and division of territory or other acquisitions of war. In the eighteenth century, alliances were the means by which nations aggregated their military power due to the limitations on increasing one's own armed forces internally. See Osgood, *Alliances and American*, 25-26.

13. Holsti, "Diplomatic Coalitions," 97-98.

14. Robert Keohane, "Lilliputians Dilemmas: Small States in International Politics," *International Organization* 23, no. 2 (Spring 1969): 301. Liska also stresses prestige in his discussion of why states align, George Liska, *Nations in Alliance: The Limits of Interdependence* (Baltimore, Md.: Johns Hopkins

University Press, 1962), 30. See also Robert Rothstein, *Alliances and Small Powers* (New York: Columbia University Press, 1968), 227-28.

The importance of leverage in alliance formation is also brought out by Kegley and Raymond. As an example of a greater power restraining a lesser power(s), they cite the Suez War and the United States forcing the British, French, and Israelis to cease attacking Egypt. However, they also point out the advantages that smaller states have over the larger state in influencing policy. They cite the examples of Saudi Arabia in getting the United States to agree to the sale of AWACS in 1981, as well as the case of Castro's Cuba in which alliance with the Soviet Union had given the state and regime protection from the United States, economic assistance, and ideological legitimacy. See Kegley and Raymond, 58. Also see Andrew Pierre, *The Global Politics of Arms Sales* (Princeton, N.J.: Princeton University Press, 1982).

15. Kegley and Raymond, *When Trust Breaks Down*, 52.

16. Jack S. Levy, "Alliance Formation and War Behavior," *Journal of Conflict Resolution* 25, no. 4 (December 1981): 611. He argues that states form alliances to maximize their power. This theme is also reported by Glenn Synder as he cites alliances as being one way states attempt to aggregate their power. He also mentions armaments and territorial expansion as other means by which states gain power. See "The Security Dilemma in Alliance Politics," *World Politics* 36, no. 4 (July 1984): 461.

17. Paul W. Schroeder, "Alliances, 1815-1945: Weapons of Power and Tools of Management," in *Historical Dimensions of National Security Problems*, Klaus Knorr ed. (Lawrence, Kans.: University Press of Kansas, 1976), 230-31. An illustration of commitments formed to manage allies to gain advantage was illustrated with the Prussian-Austrian alliance in 1863 against Denmark over Schleswig-Holstein. This led to a joint administration of these territories with Austria that provoked a conflict that culminated in the Seven Weeks War. The reason Bismarck drew Vienna into an alliance against Denmark was to isolate Austria by alienating her from Britain, the German nationalists, as well as the smaller states of the Confederation. The Austrians also sought to control this alliance by pinning down the Prussians in these provinces and reviving the previous Holy Alliance. See Schroeder, "Alliances, 1815-1945," 240-41.

Examples of the fourth reason for alliances can be seen in international relations history. Knorr himself discusses Bismarck's alliance system after the Franco-Prussian War in which France was isolated by a system of German alliances that limited French diplomacy while at the same time kept German commitments to a minimum. See Schroeder, "Alliances, 1815-1945," 228-29. It can be argued that an example of the use of alliance to conciliate a defeated power was the general treatment of France by the other essential powers in the aftermath of the Napoleonic wars. This stands in marked contrast to the treatment of Germany after World War I. A more significant example of this was the Dual Alliance between Germany and Austria in 1879, which was done to insure Austrian friendship with Germany despite Berlin having displaced Vienna as the leader of the German Confederation and ultimately unifying Germany. As a result of the subsequent German alliance with Russia, the Dual Alliance linked Austria and Russia despite their rivalry in the Balkans. This forced the Austrians to recognize Russian interests in the region. See Schroeder, 243. Another example of alliance control, done in more brutal fashion, was Hitler's alliances during World War II in which Germany de facto controlled most of its allies domestic and foreign policies, and actively intervened to perpetuate German influence in these nations. Schroeder, "Alliances, 1815-1945," 252.

18. Kegley and Raymond, *When Trust Breaks Down*, 58.

19. Walt, *The Origins of Alliances*, 40.

20. George Liska, *Nations in Alliance*, 62.

21. Walt, *The Origins of Alliances*, 199.

22. James M. Goldgeier and Michael McFaul, "A Tale of Two Worlds: Core and Periphery in the Post-Cold War Era," *International Organization* 46, no. 2 (Spring 1992): 470.

23. James E. Dougherty and Robert L. Pfaltzgraff Jr., *Contending Theories of International Relations: A Comprehensive Survey* (New York: Harper and Row Publishers, 1990), 81.

24. Hans J. Morgenthau, *Politics among Nations: The Struggle for Power and Peace* (New York: Alfred A. Knopf, 1978), 3-4, and 188-93. Morgenthau defines traditional measurements of power that help to define a nation's status in the international system, including geography and natural resources. The latter consists of agricultural production, raw materials, industrial capacity, technological innovation, leadership, quantity and quality of armed forces, population, the quality of diplomacy, and legitimacy 117-55.

25. Morgenthau, *Politics among Nations*, 192-93.

26. Dougherty and Pfaltzgraff, *Contending Theories*, 119.

27. Kenneth Waltz, *Theory of International Politics* (London: Addison-Wesley, 1983), 81.

28. Robert O. Keohane, "Theory of World Politics: Structural Realism and Beyond," in *Neorealism and Its Critics*, Robert O. Keohane ed. (New York: Columbia University Press, 1986), 166. Also Waltz, *Theory of International Politics*, 93.

29. Stephen Walt, *The Origins of Alliances*, 46-48. See also Robert O. Keohane, "Alliances, Threats, and the Uses of Neorealism," *International Security* 13, no. 1 (Summer 1988): 173.

30. Stephen M. Walt, "Alliance Formation in Southwest Asia: Balancing and Bandwagoning in Cold War Competition," in *Dominoes and Bandwagons: Strategic Beliefs and Great Power Competition in the Eurasian Rimland,* Robert Jervis and Jack Synder eds. (New York: Oxford University Press, 1991), 55.

31. Walt, *The Origins of Alliances*, 30-31. Walt cites as examples of states bandwagoning to gain territory the cases of Italy and Romania in World War I. Both these nations switched alliance partners after hostilities broke out. Italy in World War II also could fall in this category. Although already aligned with Germany at the outbreak of hostilities, Mussolini had held off from committing Italy to entering the war. However, in seeing the rapid German advance across Western Europe and especially the successes against France, the Italians entered the war on Germany's side in order to gain the spoils of victory. A similar example was the Soviet Union's breaking of its nonaggression pact with Japan in the last month of World War II in an effort to gain territory and influence in Asia, (21).

32. Steven David, *Choosing Sides*, 4-5.

33. Steven David, *Choosing Sides*, 6-10.

34. Steven David, *Choosing Sides*, 185-88.

35. Stephen M. Walt, "Testing Theories of Alliance Formation: The Case of Southwest Asia," *International Organization* 42, no. 2 (Spring 1988): 313-15. However, he argues that the United States should not disengage from its allies. He asserts that weak, vulnerable states do have a tendency to bandwagon, and that the United States cannot count on its major allies devoting additional resources for defense in the absence of U.S. support. In addition, he argues that the Soviet Union could have been more emboldened if it felt the United States would not respond to

a challenge. Finally, he says that American alliances have served the purpose of protecting U.S. allies from each other (316).

36. Walt, "Alliance Formation in Southwest Asia," 71.

37. This view of bandwagoning was advanced by the former supreme allied commander in Europe General Bernard Rogers. See Edgar Ulsamer, "The Potential Checkmate in Europe," *Air Force Magazine* 69 (November 1986): 55-56. The opinion that the United States should do less in its alliances is particularly advanced by those writers who discuss NATO. See Christopher Layne, "Atlanticism without NATO," *Foreign Policy*, no. 67 (Summer 1987): 22-45; Earl Ravenal, "Europe without America: The Erosion of NATO," *Foreign Affairs* 63, no. 5 (Summer 1985): 1020-35; Irving Kristol, "What's Wrong with NATO?" *New York Times Magazine* (September 25, 1983): 64-71; and David P. Calleo, *Beyond American Hegemony: The Future of the Western Alliance*, (New York: Basic Books, 1987). These arguments are summarized in Walt, "Testing Theories of Alliance Formation," 275. This view is also reflected in Josef Joffe, *The Limited Partnership: Europe, the United States, and the Burdens of Alliance* (Cambridge, Mass.: Ballinger, 1987), 14. He cites a quote from Henry Kissinger who viewed the Europeans as having "a monopoly on detente and America a monopoly on defense."

38. The statement by Kennedy was cited in Seyom Brown, *The Faces of Power: Constancy and Change in United States Foreign Policy from Truman to Johnson* (New York, 1968), 217; For Kissinger's comments see U.S. House of Representatives, Committee on Foreign Affairs, *The Soviet Union and the Third World: Watershed in Great Power Policy?* 97th Congress, 1st sess. 1977, 157-58; The statement by Reagan was in a speech quoted by *New York Times*, 28 April 1983, 12(A). These were cited in Walt, *The Origins of Alliances*, 20.

39. Ted Hopf, "Soviet Inferences from Their Victories in the Periphery: Visions of Resistance or Cumulating Gains?" in *Dominoes and Bandwagons: Strategic Beliefs and Great Power Competition in the Eurasian Rimland*, Robert Jervis, and Jack Snyder eds. (New York: Oxford University Press, 1991), 148.

40. Jack Levy, "Alliance Formation and War Behavior," *Journal of Conflict Resolution* 25, no. 4 (December 1981): 582. Singer, Bremer, and Stuckey have argued that alliances give a clear structure of the power relationships present within the international system. See "Capability Distribution, Uncertainty, and Major Power War, 1820-1965," in *Peace, War, and Numbers*, Bruce Russett ed. (Beverly Hills, Calif.: Sage, 1972), 19-48.

41. Hans J. Morgenthau, "Alliances in Theory and Practice," in *Alliance Policy in the Cold War*, Arnold Wolfers ed. (Baltimore, Md.: Johns Hopkins University Press, 1959), 186.

42. Glenn H. Snyder, "Alliance Theory: A Neorealist First Cut," *Journal of International Affairs* 44, no. 1 (Spring 1990): 110.

43. Francis A. Beer, *The Political Economy of Alliances: Benefits, Costs, and Institutions in NATO* (Beverly Hills, Calif.: Sage, 1972), 7-8. Beer's study of NATO concluded that larger powers incur more burdens in some aspects of alliances, while smaller nations take on a disproportionate share in other areas of the alliance. Morgenthau argues that the distribution of benefits in an alliance is related to the power distribution of the members. Therefore, a great power will be more likely to incur benefits than a smaller ally. See Hans Morgenthau, "Alliances," *Alliance in International Politics*, Julian Friedman, et al. eds. (Boston: Allyn and Bacon, 1970), 84.

For a definition of collective goods see Mancur Olson Jr., *The Logic of Collective Action* (Cambridge, Mass.: Harvard University Press, 1965). Also Mancur Olson Jr. and Richard Zeckhauser, "An Economic Theory of Alliances,"

The Review of Economics and Statistics 48, no. 3 (1966): 266-79. For a comprehensive assessment of the theory of collective goods see Joe Oppenheimer, "Collective Goods and Alliances," *Journal of Conflict Resolution* 23, no. 3 (September 1979): 387-407.

44. Ole R. Holsti, Terrence P. Hopmann, and John D. Sullivan, *Unity and Disintegration in International Alliances Comparative Studies* (New York: Wiley, 1973); Morton H. Kaplan, *System and Process in International Politics* (New York: John Wiley and Sons, 1957); Quincy Wright, *A Study of War* (New York: W. W. Norton, 1955).

45. See Morgenthau, *Politics among Nations*. Reflects the realist view of nonpermanent, nonideological alliances. See 3-15 and 188-93 for a general discussion.

46. This is discussed in the works of Inis Claude, *Power and International Relations* (New York: Random House, 1962); and Edward Gulick, *Europe's Classical Balance of Power* (New York: W. W. Norton, 1955).

47. J. D. Singer and M. Small, *The Wages of War 1816-1965* (New York: John Wiley, 1972); Robert E. Osgood and R.W. Tucker, *Force, Order, and Justice* (Baltimore, Md.: Johns Hopkins University Press, 1967); E. Gulick, *Europe's Classical Balance of Power*; Holsti, Hopmann, and Sullivan, *Unity and Disintegration,* 1973; Walt, *The Origins of Alliances*; George Liska, *Alliances and the Third World* (Baltimore, Md.: Johns Hopkins University Press, 1968); Morgenthau, *Politics among Nations*; Bruce Bueno de Mesquita, "Measuring System Polarity," *Journal of Conflict Resolution* 19, no. 2 (June 1975): 187-216; Bruce Bueno de Mesquita "Systemic Polarization and the Occurrence and Duration of War," *Journal of Conflict Resolution* 22, no. 2 (June 1978): 241-67; K. W. Deutsch and J. D. Singer, "Multipolar Power Systems and International Stability," *World Politics* 16, no. 3 (April, 1964), 390-406; Michael Wallace, "Alliance Polarization, Cross-Cutting, and International War, 1815-1964," *Journal of Conflict Resolution* 17, no. 4 (December 1973): 575-604.

48. Liska, *Nations in Alliance*, 207-9.

49. Kegley and Raymond, *When Trust Breaks Down*, 220.

50. Kegley and Raymond, *When Trust Breaks Down*, 220-21. For a further discussion of these issues using the historical example of World War I see George Kennan, *The Fateful Alliance: France, Russia, and the Coming of the First World War* (New York: Pantheon Books, 1984) and Paul Kennedy, "The First World War and the International Power System," *International Security* 9, no. 1 (Summer 1984): 7-40. Stephen Van Evera also looks at these issues by comparing the Bismarckian alliance system of the 1880s, with the alliance blocs that solidified prior to World War I. He argues that the Bismarckian alliances increased the security of the status quo powers by providing them with sufficient allies. At the same time conflicts could be averted as potential aggressor states may not be able to count on their allies to assist them in a war that they provoked. See "The Cult of the Offensive and the Origins of the First World War," *International Security* 9, no. 1 (Summer 1984): 58-107.

The opposing view that alliances generate counter alliances is discussed in Brian Healy and Arthur Stein, "The Balance of Power in International History," *Journal of Conflict Resolution* 17, no. 1, (March 1973): 33-61; and H. Brooke McDonald and Richard Rosecrance, "Alliance and Structural Balance in the International System," *Journal of Conflict Resolution* 29, no. 1, (March 1985): 57-82.

51. Osgood, *Alliances and American Foreign Policy*, 20-21. Christensen and Snyder argue that another drawback of alliances is that not only can they lock nations into a course of action, they can also foster a free rider situation in which

nations don't contribute their share. See Thomas J. Christensen and Jack Snyder, "Chain Gangs and Passed Bucks: Predicting Alliance Patterns in Multipolarity," *International Organization* 44, no. 2 (Spring 1990): 140-41.

52. Glenn Synder, "The Security Dilemma in Alliance Politics," 474. Discusses the concepts of abandonment and entrapment in different international systems.

53. K. J. Holsti, "Diplomatic Coalitions and Military Alliances," 93-94.

54. Liska, *Nations in Alliance*, 37-38. He cites as an example of the conveying of prestige on an ally the Triple Alliance in which Germany and Austria essentially conferred great power status on Italy. This enhanced the legitimacy of the Italian government and allowed it to better cope with domestic opposition.

55. Liska, *Nations in Alliance*, 23.

56. David, *Choosing Sides,* 16-21. This view is shared by Barnett and Levy. They argue that in the international relations literature pertaining to alliances, "There is also a tendency to focus on relatively well endowed and politically stable great powers, and this gives inadequate attention to domestic resource constraints and the political fragility of many regimes, either of which might provide a powerful reason for seeking an alliance." See Michael Barnett and Jack Levy, "Domestic Sources of Alliances and Alignments: The Case of Egypt, 1962-1973," *International Organization* 45, no. 1 (Summer 1991): 370-72. They challenge the assumption that looks at alliances as a consequence of external policies and systemic conditions. Among the conditions that Barnett and Levy analyze are budgetary constraints, domestic political interests of the regime, resource constraints, and threats to domestic political stability (378).

57. Liska, *Nations in Alliance*, 26.

58. Hans J. Morgenthau, "Alliances in Theory and Practice," 190. Also see the previous discussion of Bismarck's alliance policies with respect to Austria, where Germany was able to manipulate the weaker Austria in an effort to control it and stabilize relations with Russia over the Balkans.

59. Niccolo Machiavelli, *The Prince*, translated by George Bull (New York: Penguin Books, 1961), 119-23.

60. Liska, *Alliances and the Third World*, 34. The term leverage is used in this case to mean ways the larger power tries to gain influence over the smaller power in an effort to prevent that state from engaging in policies that the greater power views as detrimental to its own interests.

61. Rothstein, *Alliances and Small Powers*, 14. Rothstein discusses this issue in some detail. He cites the work of the historian A. J. P. Taylor, who argued that the great powers were locked into the mindset of traditional views of power. This meant adding up the number of troops and supplies that could be put into the field. World War I was a struggle between the great powers, where smaller states were more of a liability than a gain. He maintained that statesmen, "still thought in terms of a casual accumulation of man-power and failed to recognize that war had become a struggle solely between Great Powers. Every alliance with a small state meant an additional liability, not a gain."

This point was brought home to German leaders in both World Wars as their alliance policies tied Germany to relatively weak states. Austria-Hungary, Bulgaria, and the Ottoman Empire in World War I and in World War II Germany's allies included Italy, Bulgaria, Hungary, Romania, and Finland, none of which could aid it significantly. One can also include Japan in this set. Although not a drain on Germany, both states were too remote to be able to offer any meaningful assistance to each other. The German-Japanese alliance did increase Germany's liabilities, as the German declaration of war on the United States after the Japanese attack on Pearl Harbor did not require Japan to issue a reciprocal declaration of war on the

Soviet Union. Thus, President Roosevelt was able to mobilize American resources against Germany with no domestic political resistance. Conversely, the Japanese nonaggression pact with the Soviet Union enabled Stalin to shift Red Army troops from the Soviet Far East to the eastern front, which proved significant in stopping the Germans just outside Moscow in December of 1941.

62. Rothstein, *Alliances and Small Powers*, 227. Rothstein discusses the reasons why the French aligned with smaller powers such as Belgium, Rumania, Yugoslavia, and Czechoslovakia. This was done in order to compensate for the inability of France to ally with its traditional partner Russia, as well as to counterbalance the U.S.-Great Britain relationship. He argues however, that on balance the small powers lost out in this relationship (see 228). Rothstein discusses the inconsequential military assistance of small powers by the late 1930s (267). In his discussion of why small states align with major powers, George Liska also discusses this argument and cites the French alliances listed above to illustrate the point that smaller states ally for reasons of security, stability, and status. See Liska, *Alliances and the Third World*, 227.

63. Liska, *Nations in Alliance*, 39.

64. Arnold Wolfers, "Stresses and Strains in Going it with Others," in *Alliance Policy in the Cold War*, Arnold Wolfers ed. (Baltimore, Md.: Johns Hopkins University Press, 1959), 7.

65. Robert Rothstein, *Alliances and Small Powers*, 14-15.

66. Maria Papadakis and Harvey Starr, "Opportunity, Willingness, and Small States: The Relationship between Environment and Foreign Policy," in *New Directions in the Study of Foreign Policy*, Charles F. Hermann, Charles F. Kegley, and James N. Rosenau eds. (Boston: Allen and Unwin, 1987), 426-27. Papadakis and Starr point out that in general, smaller powers are able to gain leverage over a larger power because the larger power frequently places more value in the alliance than the smaller state. This results in the larger power finding it difficult to reduce its contribution to the smaller power. Larger states have less to gain by hard bargaining and are more willing to acquiesce to the demands of the smaller state. Finally, the larger power, because of the value placed on the alliance, would find it difficult to accept the strategic, economic, and political losses associated with a defeat of its smaller ally. This view is also articulated by Glenn Synder as he argues that those allies that are less dependent on an alliance will have greater control of the relationship, as they can afford to incur the breakup of the alliance. See Glenn H. Synder, "Alliance Theory: A Neorealist First Cut," in *The Evolution of Theory in International Relations*, Robert Rothstein ed. (Columbia, S.C.: University of South Carolina Press, 1991), 94.

67. Pierre, *The Global Politics of Arms Sales*, 275-76; See also Andrew J. Pierre, "Arms Sales: The New Diplomacy," *Foreign Affairs* 60, no. 2 (Winter 1981/82): 266-68. In the neorealist international relations literature, arming and alliances are viewed as attempts at balancing. The building up of a country's military is viewed as internal balancing, bringing political benefits of acquiring additional power capabilities coupled with the political-economic costs of allocating resources for the military. Alliances, external balancing, provide more immediate increases in power, although with less reliability. See James D. Morrow, "Arms versus Allies: Trade-offs in the Search for Security," *International Organization* 47, no. 2 (Spring 1993): 208.

68. Among the writers who discuss this are Barry M. Blechman et al. "Pushing Arms," *Foreign Policy*, no. 46 (Spring 1982): 138-54; Alexander George, *Managing the U.S.-Soviet Rivalry: Problems of Crisis Prevention* (Boulder, Colo.: Westview Press, 1983); Bruce W. Jentleson, "American Commitments in the Third

World: Theory vs. Practice," *International Organization* 41, no. 4 (Autumn 1987): 667-704; Geoffrey Kemp and Steven Miller, "The Arms Transfer Phenomenon," in *Arms Transfers and American Foreign Policy,* Andrew J. Pierre ed. (New York: New York University Press, 1979); Michael T. Klare, *American Arms Supermarket* (Austin, Tex.: University of Texas Press, 184); Robert S. Litwak, *Detente and the Nixon Doctrine: American Foreign Policy and the Pursuit of Stability, 1969-1976* (New York: Cambridge University Press, 1984); Andrew J. Pierre, *The Global Politics of Arms Sales*; and Stephen Walt, *The Origins of Alliances.*

69. See Klare, *American Arms Supermarket,* 29-34, which provides a concise comprehensive discussion of these factors. Also see Kemp and Miller, "The Arms Transfer Phenomenon," as well as Roger P. Labrie et al, *U.S. Arms Sales Policy: Background and Issues* (Washington, D.C.: American Enterprise Institute, 1982); Pierre, *The Global Politics of Arms Sales*; and John Stanley and Maurice Pearton, *The International Trade in Arms* (New York: Praeger Publishers, 1972). In addition to these broad reasons, other scholars have discussed the question of actually integrating recipients into military production. It is argued that by allowing American allies to reproduce military components, a process known as offsets, builds up their military capabilities and also leads to their economic development. This, it is argued, serves to benefit the United States. In addition, the production of American spare parts further encourages the process of standardization between the United States and its allies in specific military systems. For a good discussion of this issue and its ramifications see Stephanie G. Neuman, "Coproduction, Barter, and Countertrade: Offsets in the International Arms Market," *Orbis* 29, no. 1 (Spring 1985): 210.

70. Labrie et al, *U.S. Arms Sales Policy,* 58-60.

71. Labrie et al, *U.S. Arms Sales Policy,* 59-60. See also Paul Y. Hammond, David J. Louscher, Michael D. Salomone, and Norman A. Graham, *The Reluctant Supplier: U.S. Decisionmaking for Arms Sales* (Cambridge, Mass.: Oelgeschlager, Gunn & Hain, 1983).

72. Franklin B. Weinstein, "The Concept of a Commitment in International Relations," *Journal of Conflict Resolution* 13, no. 1 (March 1969): 41.

73. Weinstein, "The Concept of a Commitment," 39.

74. Weinstein, "The Concept of a Commitment," 44-45.

75. Weinstein, "The Concept of a Commitment," 46, which discusses the work of Schelling and Kahn regarding the importance of maintaining commitments.

76. Robert A. Kann, "Alliances vs. Ententes," *World Politics* 28, no. 4 (July 1976): 618-19.

77. Authors who make this argument include Thomas C. Schelling, *The Strategy of Conflict* (Cambridge, Mass.: Harvard University Press, 1960) and *Arms and Influence* (New Haven, Conn.: Yale University Press, 1966); John H. Herz, *International Politics in the Atomic Age* (New York: Columbia University Press, 1959); Glenn H. Synder, *Deterrence and Defense: Toward a Theory of National Security* (Princeton, N.J.: Princeton University Press, 1961); Robert E. Osgood, *Limited War: The Challenge to American Strategy* (Chicago: University of Chicago Press, 1957).This argument is summarized very well in Jentleson, "American Commitments," 667-704. He has labeled this idea of universal alliance commitments as "Global Commitments Theory."

78. Jeanne Kirkpatrick, "Dictatorships and Double Standards," *Commentary* 68, (November 1979): 34-45; and Michael Ledeen and William Lewis, *Debacle: The American Failure in Iran* (New York: Knopf, 1981).

79. Jentleson, "American Commitments," 670-71.

80. John Herz argues that the American-Soviet security interests, "touch each other everywhere, with few ways out into neutral or unoccupied ground." Therefore, "any unit anywhere would concern every other unit in the world." *International Politics in the Atomic Age,* 240-41. Schelling emphasized the importance of credibility, see *The Strategy of Conflict,* 55. These were cited in Jentleson, "American Commitments," 671.

For a discussion of a comparison between the Classical Realist Model and the Cold War Model in which interests come first in the former and last in the latter see Alexander George and Richard Smoke, *Deterrence in American Foreign Policy* (New York : Columbia University Press, 1974), 559, cited in Jentleson, "American Commitments," 703. See also Richard Feinberg, *The Intemperate Zone: The Third World Challenge to U.S. Foreign Policy* (New York: W. W. Norton, 1983), 184-86; Robert H. Johnson, "Exaggerating America's Stakes in Third World Conflicts," *International Security* 10, no. 3 (Winter 1985/86): 42.

81. George and Smoke, *Deterrence in American Foreign Policy,* 41. See also David Baldwin, *Economic Statecraft* (Princeton, N.J.: Princeton University Press, 1985), 108. Baldwin argues that in cases of economic sanctions, the more costly it is for the power enacting the sanctions the greater their credibility in the state where sanctions are being applied. An example of this during the Reagan administration was the strategic importance attached to Central America, specifically, the ability of the U.S.-sponsored government in El Salvador to quell a rebellion. The success of the United States in dealing with this insurrection would reflect on American alliance commitments worldwide, such as in Europe and Asia. See Johnson, "Exaggerating America's Stakes," 64. He cites *New York Times,* 28 April 1983, 12(A); as well as the conclusions of the Kissinger Commission. See *Report of the National Bipartisan Commission on Central America* (Kissinger Commission) (Washington, D.C.: U.S. Government Printing Office, January 1984), 92. For a further discussion of the significance of Central America see also Jerome Slater, "Dominos in Central America," *International Security* 12, no. 2 (Fall 1987): 105-34.

82. Robert E. Osgood, *Limited War: The Challenge to American Strategy* (Chicago: University of Chicago Press, 1957), 7. Cited in Jentleson, "American Commitments," 674.

83. Theodore Lowi, "Making Democracy Safe for the World," *Domestic Sources of Foreign Policy,* James N. Rosenau ed. (New York: Free Press, 1964), 295-331. Cited in Jentleson, 675. For a comprehensive discussion on the ramifications of overselling a threat, or threat inflation, see Johnson, "Exaggerating America's Stakes," 67-68.

84. Jentleson, "American Commitments," 675 discusses quotes made by various Presidents, Woodrow Wilson, John F. Kennedy, and Ronald Reagan to illustrate this point. See also Frank L. Klingsberg, "The Historical Alternation of Moods in American Foreign Policy," *World Politics* 4 (January 1952): 248 for the quote by Wilson "the stage is set, the destiny disclosed. It has come about by no plan of our conceiving, but by the hand of God who led us in this way." Jentleson cites quotes from Kennedy at his inauguration speech, "pay any price, bear any burden." Also this theme was present in Ronald Reagan's inaugural speech, "the city on the hill." This idea of the significance in ideology establishes a universality of American commitments. Occurring as a result of the establishment of universal values, it establishes an American definition of a world order and carries with it an embracing political symbol. Johnson, "Exaggerating America's Stakes," 44.

85. Jentleson, "American Commitments," 684. See also Johnson, "Exaggerating America's Stakes," 43. He argues that in a crisis the case was not important but the emphasis was on maintaining credibility in regard to the Soviet Union.

86. Robert H. Johnson, "Exaggerating America's Stakes," 40. He cites the example of the Middle East, where rivalries among the Arab countries have limited American-Soviet attempts to manipulate politics in the region.

87. Jonathan Schell, *The Time of Illusion* (New York: Alfred A. Knopf, 1976), 376-87. He cites as examples Kennedy and Berlin, Nixon and Indochina, and Carter and Afghanistan.

88. John C. Campbell, "The Middle East: A House of Containment Built on Shifting Sands," *Foreign Affairs* 60, no. 3 (1981-82): 593-628.

89. See the work of Wolf Blitzer, *Between Washington and Jerusalem* (New York: Oxford University Press, 1985); Stephen Green, *Taking Sides: America's Relations with a Militant Israel* (New York: William Morrow and Company, 1984); William J. Olson, *U.S. Strategic Interests in the Gulf Region* (Boulder, Colo: Westview Press, 1987); and Seth Tillman, *The U.S. and the Middle East* (Bloomington, Ind.: Indiana University Press, 1982), among others.

90. Anthony Cordesman, *The Gulf and the West: Strategic Relations and Military Realities* (Boulder, Colo.: Westview Press, 1988), 27-29.

91. See Tillman, *The U.S. and the Middle East*, 50-62. For a further discussion of American interests in the Middle East, see Richard Cottam, "U.S. Policy in the Middle East," in *The United States and the Middle East: A Search for New Perspectives.* ed. Hooshang Amirahmadi (Albany, N.Y.: State University of New York Press, 1993), 35-64; and Phebe Marr, "Strategies for an Era of Uncertainity: The U.S. Policy Agenda," in *Riding the Tiger: The Middle East Challenge after the Cold War.* eds. Phebe Marr and William Lewis (Boulder, Colo.: Westview Press, 1993), 211-35.

92. Barry Rubin, *Paved with Good Intentions* (New York: Penguin Books, 1980), 187; see also Gary Sick, *All Fall Down*, 25.

93. Leeden and Lewis, *Debacle*, 56-57.

94. Alexander George, *Managing the U.S.-Soviet Rivalry: Problems of Crisis Prevention* (Boulder, Colo.: Westview Press, 1983), 107-18; Jentleson, "American Commitments, 678-79; Robert Litwak, *Detente and the Nixon Doctrine*, 141-43.

95. James Bill, *The Eagle and Lion: The Tragedy of American-Iranian Relations* (New Haven, Conn.: Yale University Press, 1988), 183-215; Jentleson, "American Commitments," 667-704; and Sick, *All Fall Down*, 3-21.

96. Steven Spiegel, "U.S. Relations with Israel: The Military Benefits," Orbis 30, no. 3 (Fall 1986): 475-97. Also see Blitzer, *Between Washington and Jerusalem*, 66-82.

97. Cheryl Reubenberg, *Israel and the American National Interest* (Urbana, Ill.: University of Illinois Press, 1986), 1-22.

98. George Ball, "What is an Ally?" *American-Arab Affairs* 6, no. 6, (Fall 1983): 5-14.

99. David E. Long, *The United States and Saudi Arabia: Ambivalent Allies* (Boulder, Colo: Westview Press, 1985), 134-41.

100. Cordesman, *The Gulf and the West*, 1-44.

101. Long, *The United States and Saudi Arabia,* 142.

102. See the work of Mitchell Geoffrey Bard, *The Water's Edge and Beyond: Defining the Limits to Domestic Influence on United States Foreign Policy* (New Brunswick, N.J.: Transaction Publishers, 1991); Peter Grose, *Israel in the Mind of America* (New York: Alfred A. Knopf, 1983); Bernard Reich, *The United States and Israel: Influence in the Special Relationship* (New York: Praeger, 1984); and

Rubenberg, *Israel and the American National Interest*, 1986, among others. With regard to Iran, the best work is Bill, *The Eagle and Lion*, 1988. In discussing the Arab lobby, and particularly Saudi Arabia, see Bard, *The Water's Edge and Beyond*,1988. He discusses both the Israeli and Arab lobbies while comparing and contrasting them. Also, or a critical analysis o Saudi in luence in the United States see Steven Emerson, *The American House of Saud: The Secret PetroDollar Connection* (New York: Franklin Watts, 1985).

Chapter 2

The United States and Iran: The Forging of an Alliance

World War II and the Growing American Influence in Iran

In an effort to ensure the supply of lend-lease materials to the Soviet Union and to strengthen the central government of Iran, the United States began in 1942 to establish a strong military, diplomatic, and eventually an economic presence in the country. By 1943, six major military, diplomatic, and economic missions were operating in Iran. The diplomatic mission was in the embassy headed by Ambassador Louis Dreyfus Jr. and it coordinated the entire American presence in the country. A second diplomatic source of ties, although more informal, was the role played by General Patrick J. Hurley. He visited Iran in 1943 and 1944 as a personal representative of President Roosevelt. Military interactions between the two countries, which would become a formidable component of relations later on, were initiated during this period. General Clarence Ridley headed the American mission to the Iranian army (ARMISH) from 1942 to 1947, which sought to strengthen and develop Iranian forces. The second mission, and by far the largest and broadest in scope, was the Persian Gulf Service Command (PGSC) headed by General Donald Connolly. This force included 30,000 troops whose primary function was to maintain the supply line transversing Iran to the Soviet Union. The third mission, GENMISH, headed by General H. Norman Schwarzkopf, was to build up and aid the Iranian Gendarmerie, the rural police force. Both the ARMISH and GENMISH military missions became permanent and continued in various forms until the revolution. The final mission, to reorganize Iranian finances, was led by Dr. Arthur Millspaugh.[1]

Other lower-level missions and individuals also performed important functions and enhanced contacts between the two countries. A mission advising the urban police was headed by L. Stephen Timmerman, as well as a group advising the Iranians on food and supply led by Joseph Sheridan. The Organization of Strategic Services (OSS) was also active in Iran gathering intelligence as well as a military intelligence group led by the military attaché. This latter group was especially active, having representatives in such crucial areas of the country as Kurdistan, Azerbaijan, as well as in the Qashqai tribal area between Isfahan and Shiraz.[2]

These missions offered American policy makers an opportunity to mold Iranian opinion and enabled the country to become a partner in the anti-Axis coalition. These factors were reflected in a report by Undersecretary of State Sumner Welles to President Roosevelt:

> I believe that the work of these various missions will be of great benefit since the officers and experts we have sent to Iran will not only be able to exert considerable personal influence upon Iranian opinion in a sense favorable to the general cause of the UN, but they will also be able to assist in the rehabilitation of the country which would seem to be a fundamental requisite for the ultimate conversion of Iran into an active and willing partner on our side. I feel now more than ever that the United States Army mission to work with the Iranian Army could in fact play an extremely important role in this work.[3]

The necessity of building up Iran to secure Allied war aims offered America a unique advantage that could work to its benefit after the war. This was reflected by Roosevelt's special representative to Iran, Patrick Hurley:

> American advisers indoctrinated in U.S. policy would have an important role in rendering American assistance, but closer commercial ties, a treaty covering the PGSC, American control over Lend-Lease distribution and the strengthening of loyal American security forces were other necessary steps toward the realization of American objectives.[4]

While initially these contacts were established in the general context of meeting immediate American needs in fighting World War II, they quickly began to take on an intrinsic importance of their own. The United States began to broaden its aims in the country and the region as a whole. These centered around acquiring control of Iranian oil, as well as maintaining Iran as a strategic bulwark against the Soviet Union during the Cold War. Oil was one of the primary reasons why Iran became important to America and this resource had become more significant during the war. In 1938 Iran accounted for 4.4 percent of the noncommunist world's oil supply. By the late 1940s this total increased to 6.8 percent.[5] America had been expanding its quest for oil in the Middle East during the 1920s and as a result frequently clashed with Britain. The State Department actively assisted American companies in 1928 in gaining a concession from Britain and France for American interests to acquire 24 percent of the output from the former Ottoman territories and was known as the Red Line Agreement. This process continued during World War II, with reference to Iran, as in January of 1942 the United States insisted that British and Soviet pipelines constructed with lend-lease aid be available to American oil interests after the war.[6]

Iran prior to the war had been interested in attracting American companies as part of their policy of playing off the British and Soviets with a third power. In 1937 a concession was awarded to Seaboard Oil, which was later canceled in 1938. In 1940 a concession was almost given to Standard Oil of New Jersey but had to be put off due to Soviet objections.[7]

It became apparent to American decision makers that because of oil, Iran would be significant after the end of World War II. It was evident that the United States, as a result of war time needs and the depletion of American reserves, would have to become an oil importer instead of an oil exporter. This position was stated by Harold Ickes who wrote, "There is no denying the possibility in fact, the probability– that in future years the United States may have to yield its position as the number one oil producer in the world."[8] Besides Ickes, other prominent converts to this view included Secretary Hull as well as many officials within the State Department who had been previously affiliated with oil companies.[9]

In addition to oil, economic relations in general, and specifically trade, were considered significant. Decision makers were anticipating America's future political, strategic, as well as economic position in the international system. Wallace Murray in particular stressed economic implications, maintaining that the wartime occupation of Iran could enable either Britain or the Soviet Union to gain a more favorable economic position in the country at the expense of American interests. United States bilateral trade was not very significant from Washington's point of view, although American wartime involvement in the country did create contacts for broader economic contacts later on. This point was emphasized as the State Department negotiated a trade agreement with Iran in 1943.[10]

Iran, the United States, and the Cold War, 1946-1953

The beginnings of the Cold War had a severe impact on Iran and Iranian-American relations. This was particularly true with regard to three events that illustrate the development of Iranian importance, as well as the Middle East in general, to American decision makers: the crisis over Soviet withdrawal from Azerbaijan, the Truman Doctrine, and the royalist coup against Prime Minister Musadiq.

The Crisis over Azerbaijan, 1946

A major crisis in Iranian-Soviet relations occurred as a result of the failure of the Soviets to withdraw from the provinces of Azerbaijan and Kurdistan, in northwestern Iran. This became the first real crisis of the Cold War. In 1942 the Tripartite Treaty of Alliance was concluded between Iran, Britain, and the Soviet Union. Among the stipulations of this agreement was that foreign military forces would be withdrawn from Iran six months after the end of hostilities. The Soviets, however, delayed for several reasons. First, there was concern on the part of the Soviets concerning the security of their oil fields in Baku. Second, the Soviets wanted to use their military forces to assist communist groups and separatist movements within the country. Third, the Soviets wanted a similar oil concession in the north to what the British received in the south. Finally, the Soviets hoped to use the leverage of the occupation in order to gain more general political and economic concessions from Iran.[11]

American policy makers attributed Soviet policy toward Iran to two possible objectives. First, the Soviets wanted a communist regime in Iran that would in effect be a Soviet satellite. Second, the Soviets wanted a pliant regime in Tehran tolerating an autonomous communist regime in Azerbaijan and willing to grant the Soviets favorable oil concessions in the north. Either of these policies were considered aggressive by the United States and this served to shape American policy makers view of an expansionist Soviet Union.[12]

The United States supported Iran in its effort to force Moscow to withdraw by giving Iran political support in diplomatic notes to the Soviets as well as in the U.N. Security Council. The Soviets eventually did withdraw in May of 1946 after obtaining an oil concession from the Iranian government. Under Ahmad Qavam the Iranian government started to crackdown on pro-Soviet forces in the country and October of 1946 the government, using tribal unrest in the south as an excuse, cracked down on the pro-Soviet Tudeh party. In November the Iranian army was sent in to attack the pro-Soviet separatist republics of Azerbaijan and Kurdistan. These separatist republics quickly collapsed and Soviet influence in the country was neutralized. The Iranian Parliament eventually rejected the Soviet oil concession that had been negotiated in May.[13]

The Truman Doctrine, 1947

The United States involvement in Iran deepened as a result of the Truman Doctrine, which was an attempt to institutionalize in American politics a strong policy against the Soviet Union in the aftermath of World War II. At this time the administration was confronted with political pressures from public opinion and Congress for demobilization, as well as ending wartime taxes and price controls. In addition, many Americans were not in favor of Churchill's belligerent tone towards the Soviets or the large loan that the United States was extending to Britain. It was especially significant for the administration to gather support from public opinion and Congress in this endeavor. The Truman Doctrine, which was proclaimed in March 1947, was an attempt by the Truman administration to cast the ensuing Cold War in ideological terms to gain public support and shock Congress into supporting the President's foreign policy.[14]

The Truman Doctrine, while immediately concerning itself with events in Greece and Turkey, had importance for American policy toward the third world as a whole, and consisted of two goals. First, to contain potential revolutionary movements in the third world. Second, to maintain order and stability in the third world in order to maintain the political, economic, and strategic orientation of these areas toward the West. This had the implication of viewing as subversive those movements that sought to challenge established authorities. The implication of the Truman Doctrine was that it viewed any threat to the Shah as hostile to American interests.[15]

The Royalist Coup in Iran: The Creation of the American-Iranian Alliance

The third major event involving the United States in Iran was the oil nationalization crisis, which lasted from 1951-1953. This situation pitted the nationalist Prime Minister Muhammad Musadiq against both the Shah and the British. British interests in Iran were represented by the Anglo-Iranian Oil Company (AIOC), which was the dominant economic force in the country and the largest employer. The AIOC had complete control over accounting procedures and profit reporting, which dictated how much the company was to pay Iran in any given year. In addition, there was dissatisfaction with the company in terms of its payment and treatment of Iranian workers in comparison to British technicians. For the British the AIOC was an economic and strategic asset. Iranian oil was essential for powering the domestic economy, supplying the British armed forces, and an important source of revenue for the British treasury at a time when London's financial leadership was declining. These factors account for the refusal of the British to surrender control of the AIOC.[16]

The emphasis on nationalization gained ground as a result of favorable agreements oil companies concluded with other nations. In the late 1940s Venezuela negotiated an agreement giving it half of the revenues derived from oil. Saudi Arabia during this period also entered into a similar arrangement. In 1948 the Iranian government sought to initiate the process of negotiations by identifying six major areas of dissatisfaction in a document to the British government.[17] It was in this period that Iran was trying to draw closer to the United States to gain security guarantees against the Soviet Union. In a 1949 visit to Washington the Shah asked for increased military and economic assistance. He was told by Secretary of State Dean Acheson that rather than relying on military assistance from the United States, he should initiate economic and social reforms and attempt to get a better deal from the Anglo-Iranian oil company to finance these initiatives.[18]

In 1951 the Iranian Majlis, under the leadership of Muhammad Musadiq, voted for nationalization. This caused a clash within Iranian politics between the prime minister and the Shah. Internationally it caused a rift between Iran and Britain, and later on the United States. The initial reaction of the Truman administration was to try to reconcile Iran and Britain in order to preserve the stability of the region. The Truman administration felt that American interests would be better served by having Iran develop politically into a constitutional, Western-type democracy. The oil nationalization issue caused some tensions in the Anglo-American relationship. The revenues that Britain derived from Iranian oil were necessary to aid the country's balance of payments, maintain oil supplies, and to gain tax revenues. The United States, however, felt it was more important to support a stable, secure Iran and to maintain the supply of Iranian oil without disruption. Although the Truman administration advocated compromise between the Iranians and British, American oil companies were siding with the AIOC, as they felt that Iran's nationalization attempt would have repercussions elsewhere.[19]

The goals of the Truman administration were to prevent Iran from defecting from the Western camp and to maintain the stability of world oil markets in an effort to promote both economic and strategic security.[20] Despite the fact that Iran was a traditional British sphere of influence, the United States had been using Iran as a key component in the emerging Cold War. The CIA had become active within Iran in the late 1940s in order to both gain intelligence and destablize the Soviet Union, as well as attempt to subvert and discredit the Iranian left. The covert activities that the CIA carried out in Iran consisted of five components. First, Washington organized stay-behind networks to carry out acts of sabotage in case of a Soviet invasion and occupation of the country. Second, escape and evasion routes were set up within the country in case of a major conflict with the Soviet Union. Third, the CIA carried out infiltration and subversive operations along the Iran-Soviet border using personnel from ethnic groups such as Armenians and Azerbaijanis that saddled the border areas. Fourth, America monitored Soviet activities within Iran. Fifth was the establishment of an operation code named BEDAMN in 1948, the purpose of which was to limit Soviet influence in Iran by discrediting the Tudeh Party and other groups considered to be on the Iranian left. This would also eventually come to include the National Front.[21]

The Eisenhower administration viewed Musadiq and the nationalist movement very differently and shifted American policy from mediation to confrontation with Iran. James Bill identifies four factors for this change in American policy. First was the fear of communism. The Eisenhower administration viewed Iran as sliding towards anarchy and instability under Musadiq. In their view this invited communist subversion, and they justified this position by focusing on the growth in influence of the Tudeh Party in the government, and society in general. Second, American decision makers were concerned about access to oil. The United States was afraid that instability in Iran and the potential growth of Soviet influence would imperil American oil interests in Saudi Arabia that had been established during the 1930s. Third, America accepted the British view of the situation and fourth, there seemed to be personal animosity toward Musadiq from

U.S. decision makers.[22]

At the same time, within Iran, Musadiq's power base was eroding. Important leaders within the National Front started to conspire against him in the summer of 1952. A series of events in early 1953 illustrated that Musadiq was losing his grip on power. Ayatollah Kashani, who was speaker of the Majlis, attempted to oust the prime minister in January. Riots occurred in February as there were rumors of coup plots fomented by General Zahedi. In April the chief of the National Police, General Afshartous, was kidnapped and murdered. Musadiq's rivals within the National Front were implicated along with General Zahedi. Prior to the August coup, the American effort to destablilize Musadiq went into high gear and the BEDAMN network continued its anti-Musadiq activities. In addition, American officials such as Ambassador Loy Henderson held meetings with the Shah in an effort to persuade him to support General Zahedi, the American favorite.[23]

In August of 1953 the United States and Britain in cooperation with the Shah, the majority of the military, as well as other conservative groups in society, in particular the leadership, cooperated in overthrowing the National Front government. Initially the coup seemed like it would not succeed. The firmans signed by the Shah dismissing Musadiq and appointing General Zahedi in his place were delivered to the prime minister by Colonel Nassiri, the commander of the Imperial Guard, who was promptly arrested. Troops who were loyal to Musadiq were called out to the streets. A warrant was issued for Zahedi's arrest, and troops loyal to him who were supposed to arrive in Tehran in conjunction with the delivery of the firmans failed to appear. The Shah then fled the country. The CIA team coordinating the coup, led by Kermit Roosevelt, undertook a number of activities in order to complete the operation. They circulated copies of the firman removing Musadiq, encouraged support for Zahedi within the Iranian military, and also coordinated with the American military mission in the country to distribute weapons to pro-Shah groups. The CIA team also sought to gain support for the monarchy by appealing to the garrison commanders of other cities. Finally, through coordination with Iranian contacts they encouraged a spark to set off a provocation that would lead to an uprising against the government. Ayatollahs Kashani and Behbehani led a demonstration that was eventually joined by elements of the police and army. This demonstration came at the same time that pro-Zahedi troops captured the radio station and marched on Musadiq's residence. The prime minister escaped the battle that took place at his home and surrendered to General Zahedi the following day.[24]

The United States benefitted from this coup in two ways. As a recognition of American cooperation in this coup, as well as geostrategic realities in general, Britain agreed to allow American companies to control 40 percent of Iran's oil market. This was something that the Eisenhower administration encouraged over the objections of the oil companies. Washington viewed oil as a strategic commodity and wanted American companies to establish a direct presence in such an important area. In addition, American decision makers concluded that in order to stabilize Iran, oil production had to be restored quickly. This necessitated the presence of major American oil companies in the Iranian market to stimulate rapid production. Both the Truman and Eisenhower administrations encouraged this by changing an antitrust suit against the oil companies from a criminal to a civil case.[25]

The United States also benefitted by installing a pro-American government which became America's most important ally in the third world economically, politically, and strategically. The United States moved to solidify this regime by dramatic increases in foreign aid. General Zahedi's government was furnished with military and economic credits. In 1953, $60 million was given to Iran, double the amount of aid in the previous decade. This amount was doubled the following year.[26]

The most dynamic repercussion of the royalist coup of 1953 was that in supporting the monarchy, America initiated a policy that would culminate in the eventual locking in of U.S. interests with the fate of the Shah. The coup also alienated many Iranians and prevented a liberal nationalist movement from emerging, led to the establishment of the Iranian-American alliance, and initiated the process where Iran would eventually become the most important ally of the United States in the third world. Critics of American policy also make the argument that this coup served as a precedent for the overthrowing of other governments, notably Arbenz in Guatemala and Allende in Chile. It also tied American interests to the fortunes of the monarchy and as a result, the United States along with the Shah was an object of condemnation by the Iranian people during the revolution of 1978-1979.[27]

American Aid to Iran and the Establishment of the Alliance

The interest of American policy makers after World War II was to strengthen Iran in order to enable the regime to maintain its territorial integrity and internal security, as opposed to trying to build it up militarily as a counterweight to the Soviet Union. This view was illustrated in correspondence between the State Department and the American Embassy in Tehran:

> Power relations Iran and USSR cannot be altered appreciably by provision U.S. military supplies. Iranian arms program intended (1) replace lost or obsolete equipment Iranian Army to permit effective display central Government power, patrol border areas and insure quick repression of foreign inspired uprisings, and (2) increase effectiveness Gendarmerie in maintaining law and order throughout country. We inclinded think provision of arms for first-line defense would be fruitless and provocative to USSR.[28]

The emphasis this time was to try to strengthen Iran economically. "As you know, in the European arms program we are emphasizing that economic recovery is the first objective and all military programs must be subordinated to that. In our view this applies equally to Iran."[29]

The Growth of Military and Economic Assistance

After the restoration of the Shah, America began to provide large amounts of economic and military aid. Economically, American assistance came in the form of both grants and loans. From 1953-1957 the United States provided Iran with a total of $250.6 million in grants, and $116.2 million in loans. These figures increased in the early 1960s. It was also during this period that a significant amount of two-way trade between Washington and Tehran began to develop. In 1963 Iranian imports from the United States totaled 103.7 million while American imports of Iranian goods reached $40.4 million.[30]

In addition to direct economic assistance and funds from the purchase of Iranian oil, the International Bank for Reconstruction and Development, as well as private American banks such as Chase Manhattan, assisted in the development of the Iranian banking system. An important institution to further Iranian economic development was the Industrial and Mining Development Bank of Iran (IMDBI), created by the Second Development Plan of October 1959. Its goal was to facilitate foreign exchange to import industrial machinery and raw materials.[31]

In the military sphere an extensive relationship also began to develop after the coup. A militarily strong Iran came to be viewed as a complement to American interests in the region.[32] The military assistance given by the United States included grants in aid for the purpose of purchasing arms, as well as for the extensive training of Iranian personnel both within Iran and the United States. Between 1953-1963, $535.4 million was provided in grants to the Iranian military. In addition, through the presence of American advisors, the Shah was able to build the army to a total of 190,000 men as well as establishing a modern navy and air force. American advisory teams expanded their roles in the country by participating in direct planning with the military authorities. ARMISH, the team of American officers that assisted the Iranian army, aided the general staff in organization and planning. The reasons for creating ARMISH as articulated by the State Department were: (1) the extension of the Truman Doctrine to the Middle East; (2) the furnishing of military aid to Iran for internal security; and (3) the growing importance of Iran strategically from its border with the Soviet Union, coupled with its position as a valuable exporter of oil.[33] The Military Assistance Advisory Group (MAAG) assisted in military procurement for the Iranian armed forces. The American Military Mission with the Imperial Iranian Gendarmerie (GENMISH) was to advise the Interior Ministry. In addition, the American CIA assisted in the formation of the Iranian State Intelligence and Security Organization (SAVAK) in 1957.[34]

The growth of military relations between the two countries was also reflected in the growing sophistication of the Iranian Armed Forces. By the mid to late 1950s the Iranians acquired from the United States 24 Lockheed T-33 training and reconnaissance planes in 1956, between 1956 and 1958, 75 F-84G Thunderjet fighter bombers were delivered. In 1959, 70 Sabre jets built under license in Canada were delivered to the Iranians. The Iranian army received 200 Patton tanks in 1958, and the Iranian navy also began receiving front line equipment. Aid to the navy went from $166 million from 1949 to 1953, to $387 million from 1953 to 1960.[35]

The Development of the American-Iranian Alliance: CENTO and the Bilateral Defense Agreement

Iran was formally integrated into the American alliance system with the creation of the Baghdad Pact in 1955. This alliance was composed of Britain, Iran, Iraq, Pakistan, and Turkey, with the United States as an associate member. It was renamed the Central Treaty Organization (CENTO) in 1958 after the revolution in Iraq resulted in that country's withdrawal from the alliance.

For the United States this alliance was a component of the American worldwide alliance system that was being constructed at this time to blunt perceived Soviet expansionism. CENTO linked Iran with other American allies in NATO and SEATO due to overlapping memberships.

Because of its geographical location vis-à-vis the Soviet Union, Iran was especially important in this alliance. This was articulated in a memorandum of the Joint Chiefs of Staff Joint Intelligence Committee written on April 13, 1955:

> From the viewpoint of attaining U.S. military objectives in the Middle East, the natural defensive barrier provided by the Zagros Mountains must be retained under Allied control indefinitely. Because Western Iran includes the Zagros Mountain barrier, geographically, Iran is the most important country in the Middle East, excluding Turkey. Iranian participation in a regional defense organization would permit the member countries to take full advantage collectively of the natural defensive barrier in Western Iran and would permit utilization of logistical facilities of the area. The relative importance of Iran in relation to other countries of the Middle East would be significantly increased if she became a partner in a regional defense organization which included Turkey, Iraq, and Pakistan.[36]

The alliance was much more significant from the point of view of Iran. It is argued that Iran joined CENTO for four major reasons. First, to establish a military commitment in order to gain American support. Second, to increase the capabilities, status, and prestige of the armed forces. This latter point was a special interest of the Shah.[37] From 1953-1961 Iran, according to official sources, received a total of $1.31 billion in military and economic assistance. The economic portion of this figure was $548.1 million, $197 million as loan and $351.1 million as grants. The military portion of this figure was $482 million, $436.1 million as a Military

Assistance Program (MAP) grant and $45.9 million as trans-excess stock.[38]

The last two reasons for Iran joining CENTO deal more with issues of psychology and domestic politics. Membership in the Baghdad Pact/CENTO gave Iran a psychological boost by placing it on a equal footing with Turkey in the region. Lastly, but just as important membership in the alliance would provide American support for the Shah's regime.[39]

Membership within CENTO gave Iran several benefits: it served as a deterrent to possible Soviet advances; it allowed Iran to claim extra benefits such as military and economic aid; it served as a vehicle for upgrading the capability of its military forces through joint military exercises with the United States and other nations; it provided a link between the Iranian military and other regional military forces; and it served a crucial support role for the Iranian elite, in particular the monarchy.[40]

However, while overall the CENTO alliance was beneficial to Iran from the Shah's perspective it was limited. While CENTO provided some guarantees on paper against a Soviet threat, it was during the 1960s that the Shah became more concerned with local threats. The Shah's faith in CENTO was weakened as a result of the clash between India and Pakistan in 1965, in which the United States did not come to the assistance of Pakistan, a CENTO member. Therefore, the Shah was conscious of maintaining diplomatic freedom and seeking to ease tensions with the Soviet Union.[41]

In 1959, a Bilateral Defense Treaty was concluded between the two nations, influenced by the revolution in Iraq and that country's subsequent withdrawal from the Baghdad Pact. The Iraqi revolution resulted in a greater emphasis on Iran by American policy makers. The aid program was increased and Iran received high level visits from the secretaries of the treasury and defense.[42] The Bilateral Defense Treaty was concluded on March 5, 1959 and specified:

> In the case of aggression against Iran, the Government of the United States of America, in accordance with the Constitution of the United States of America, will take such appropriate action, including the use of armed forces, as may be mutually agreed upon and as is envisaged in the Joint Resolution to Promote Peace and Stability in the Middle East, in order to assist the Government of Iran at its request.[43]

The Evolution of the American-Iranian Alliance in the1960s:
The Development of Iranian Security Interests in the Region

Relations with the Kennedy Administration

The importance of Iran in American foreign policy calculations did not change when the Democratic administration of John Kennedy succeeded the Republican Dwight Eisenhower. The new administration was presented with a crisis in Iran almost immediately upon taking office. State Department analyst John W. Bowling, in a departmental report, recognized the disenchantment with the Shah in particular from the middle classes. The report, after considering the alternative of a nationalist, more broadly based government akin to that of Muhammad Musadiq ten years earlier, viewed the possibility of an American shift in policy as being too costly in the short term strategically, economically, and politically. Specifically he discussed the possibilities of: (1) the breakup of the CENTO alliance; (2) withdrawal of American military advisers from Iran; (3) abandonment of attempts at economic stabilization; (4) attempts to get more money from the oil consortium; (5) a blow to U.S. global prestige; (6) an opportunity for communist influence in the regime; (7) the loss of Iranian support in the United Nations; (8) viewing neutralism as a positive alternative to other third world states; and (9) the potential growth of Soviet influence through the acceptance of Soviet aid. However, the report did acknowledge the possible long-term advantage of a more stable, broad-based regime in Iran.[44]

The Kennedy administration sought to press the Shah to adopt internal reforms and establish a more broad-based regime. The administration favored the establishment of the government of Ali Amini as an effort to provide economic reforms as well as promote anticorruption policies. The Amini government lasted 15 months, and while it introduced some reforms with American encouragement, it was forced to resign as a result of conflicts with the Shah and the inadequacy of American aid to bring about substantial reforms.[45]

The White Revolution initiated by the Shah in early 1963 was an attempt to appease the Kennedy administration and had six major features: (1) land reform; (2) sale of government-owned factories that would go to finance land reform; (3) woman suffrage; (4) forest conservation; (5) national literacy corps that would target rural areas; and (6) profit sharing for industrial workers.[46] These reforms, however, have been criticized for not being very comprehensive and simply designed to appease the Shah's American critics while giving the appearance of reform.[47] In addition some scholars have argued that land reform actually enhanced the Shah's authority by weakening the power of conservative landlords as well as the ulema.

During the Kennedy administration military aid to Iran was scaled back. Between 1959-1962 the total amount of military assistance furnished by the United States dropped from $91 to $44 million, and during this period Iran received few arms or major weapons systems.[48] The Kennedy administration sought to substitute economic aid for military aid.[49]

Relations with the Johnson Administration

While there was some friction with the Kennedy administration over the issue of reform, relations with the Johnson administration were much more amicable. It can be characterized that President Johnson had a very warm, cordial relationship with the Shah. President Johnson had limited experience in foreign policy and was more inclined to support existing regimes without pressing for reforms. In addition, because of the conflict in Southeast Asia the Johnson administration was not likely to distance itself from traditional American allies. High-level contacts between the Shah and President Johnson became a regular occurrence as W. Averell Harriman embarked on four presidential missions to Iran between May 1965 and November 1967. Also, Johnson's National Security Advisor W. W. Rostow was a strong backer of the Iranian monarchy.[50]

The Shah likewise sought to exploit the more favorable political climate in the United States by emphasizing his importance to American concerns in meetings with administration officials and prominent Americans. In a meeting with Kermit Roosevelt, the Shah listed the factors that made Iran important to American foreign policy: (1) geostrategic, as a result of Iran's 1,250-mile border with the Soviet Union that checked Soviet expansionism; (2) the Shah supported the American intervention in Vietnam; (3) Iran was willing to assume the role of regional leader in the Persian Gulf after the British withdrawal; (4) Iran served as a counterweight in the region to Nasser's Arab Socialism; and (5) the Shah provided assistance and supported Israel.[51]

The Shah sought to press the Johnson administration to increase the volume and sophistication of American arms aid to Iran, as well as to increase oil production from the consortium, in order to implement his modernization program. The Shah was especially interested in acquiring sophisticated aircraft, in particular the F-4 Phantom. The Shah also wanted to revise the entire American arms sales program to Iran. He felt that the Defense Department was overcharging Iran and cited as evidence the fact that the F-4 cost over three million dollars, while a Soviet fighter jet costs between $600,000-$700,000. The Shah also resented the limitations placed by the United States on arms sales to Iran that were based on Iranian economic conditions in general. In an effort to gain more favorable terms, the Shah threatened to distance Iran from the United States and to turn toward the Soviet Union.[52] It seems that he was holding open the possibility of purchasing arms from Moscow in an effort to force Washington to sell him the F-4. While there was some disagreement among American officials on the policy of selling the F-4 to Iran, it was also felt by some within the administration that the failure to do so would cause the Shah to establish an arms relationship with the Soviet Union.[53]

The argument was also made by policy makers that the sale of two squadrons of F-4 fighters would heighten the probability that the Shah would not purchase similar arms from the Soviet Union. There was a strategic justification for this sale with the growth of Egyptian and Iraqi air power. This arms sale was also justified in part to appeal to the Shah psychologically that the United States still supported him even though the American grant program was ending.[54] This illustrated a patten that would repeat itself until the revolution of 1978-1979.

There was some initial hostility to the Shah's demands from certain quarters of the American government, notably from the embassy in Tehran, the International Security Agency in the Defense Department, as well as from Senator William Fulbright, chairman of the Senate Foreign Relations Committee. The Johnson administration, however, was pressured to support the Shah's position by both international and domestic considerations. Internationally, the conflict in Southeast Asia was requiring an ever greater commitment of American financial and military resources. In addition, the Soviets were also active in the Middle East, supplying arms such as MiG fighters to their regional allies. This served as a justification for the sale of the F-4 to Iran. In addition, the sale would assist in maintaining a more favorable American balance of payments deficits.[55]

These policies were reinforced and approved by various high-ranking members of the Johnson administration. The economic importance of these sales was illustrated by Secretary of Defense Robert McNamara, who stated that "Our sales have created about 1.4 million man-years of employment in the U.S. and over $1 billion in profits to American industry over the last five years."[56] President Johnson sought to encourage major defense contractors, in particular Boeing and McDonnell Douglas, to sell more abroad in an effort to reduce American balance of payments deficits.[57]

Under the Johnson administration military aid to Iran increased. A significant factor in this military assistance that would become apparent during the 1970s was the increasing sophistication of this assistance as well as its economic implication for the United States. In 1967-1968 America sold on credit to Iran just under $96 million in military goods. In 1969-1970 this figure rose to $289 million. The sophistication of these transfers included the F-4 Phantom, 768 Sidewinder and Sparrow air-to-air missiles, and 40 AB205 Iroquois, among other items.[58]

The Changing Strategic Environment during the 1960s

During the 1960s Iran was becoming America's major ally in the Middle East, particularly in light of the British disengagement from the region. It therefore became American policy to attempt to fill this strategic gap by building up the militaries of Iran and Saudi Arabia and fostering their close cooperation.[59]

The strategic component of the alliance began to change in the 1960s. While CENTO and the Bilateral Defense Treaty provided a good defense for Iran against possible Soviet threats, during the 1960s regional threats tended to become more of a source of concern. Several circumstances during the 1960s led to the Shah downgrading his reliance on CENTO somewhat. The Shah's faith in CENTO weakened during the early to mid 1960s, one of the primary reasons being CENTO's failure to come to the assistance of Pakistan in 1965 during their conflict with India. In addition, the Shah was growing suspicious of Egyptian activity in the Gulf and he feared the growth of Arab nationalism in the region. The Shah was also disappointed with the United States as President Kennedy recognized the republican regime in Yemen. These regional factors, coupled with the possibility of Britain's military withdrawal from the region, lead the Shah to take a more active foreign policy.[60] The Shah had three main objectives in the Persian Gulf. The first was to safeguard the regime against internal threats emanating either directly or indirectly from hostile Arab states, and/or pro-Soviet groups. The second objective was to ensure unimpeded passage through the major regional waterways, the Straits of Hormuz, the Persian Gulf itself, as well as the Shatt al-Arab. Third, to protect Iranian oil resources and oil facilities from attack. Most of these were located in the south of the country, bordering on the Persian Gulf. These resources would include not only the oil fields themselves, but port facilities and refineries as well.[61]

Beginning in the mid 1960s the Shah became more attentive to military planning toward the Persian Gulf. This led to the vast upgrading of the Iranian navy, which included the construction of new naval facilities, notably at Bandar Abbas, as well as new weapons systems. Iran was the first country in the world to procure a squadron of hovercraft. In addition to procuring new military equipment, and the construction and expansion of infrastructure, Iranian forces were repositioned toward the Gulf. In 1967 the Government announced the formation of a new Third Army Corps to be based in the southern city of Shiraz. At the same time it was also announced that the headquarters of the Second Army Corps was to be moved from Tubat-i Haydari, which is in northeastern Iran near the Soviet border, to Tehran. The major strategic concern of the Iranian government was the threat from Iraq, which stemmed from the potential growth of Iraqi political influence. The Iranians were especially concerned about the politically fragile nature of the monarchies of the Arabian peninsula, and the opportunities this could provide for the spread of Iraqi influence, especially with regard to the smaller states of the area such as the United Arab Emirates, Oman, Qatar, and Bahrain. An important component of the Shah's foreign policy during this period, which also served American interests, was the potential of Iranian intervention in the region to support conservative regimes. This possibility was put forth by the Shah himself when in response to a question of whether he was seeking to absorb more territory as a result of Iran's military buildup he stated, "What do I need more territory for? All I am concerned about is the security of my country, and Iran's security is intimately related to the security and stability of the Persian Gulf region."[62]

Although Iraq was emerging as Iran's main rival, during the early 1960s the Shah viewed Nasser as his main regional rival. The Shah was concerned about the impact of Arab nationalism, particularly on Iran's oil rich Khuzistan province. In many respects he viewed Baghdad, especially after the 1963 coup, as being surrogates of Nasser's Egypt. The basing of Egyptian troops in Iraq and the anti-Shah propaganda broadcasts emanating from Cairo encouraged this view.[63]

The Shah's activist foreign policy was illustrated with Iran's intervention in Oman in the mid-1970s. In addition to sending ground troops to assist the

Sultan, the Shah also committed air and naval forces. Critics argued that these forces were not militarily useful, but reflected the Shah's goal of seeking to provide combat training to as much of the military as possible.[64]

In response to Britain's withdrawal from the region, Iran placed a greater emphasis on improving relations with its neighbors in the Persian Gulf. Among the policies adopted by the Shah was Iran's dropping of the claim on Bahrain, the acceptance of the formation of the United Arab Emirates, as well as a better understanding with Saudi Arabia. This rapproachment was symbolished by the Shah's acting as spokesman in the oil negotiations that followed the December 1970 OPEC conference in Caracas.[65]

Notes

1. James Bill, *The Eagle and the Lion: The Tragedy of American-Iranian Relations* (New Haven, Conn.: Yale University Press, 1988), 19-20. For a more detailed discussion concerning the military missions see Thomas M. Ricks, "U.S. Military Missions to Iran, 1943-1978: The Political Economy of Military Assistance," *Iranian Studies* 12, no. 3-4 (Fall 1979): 163-93.

2. Bill, *The Eagle and Lion*, 20.

3. Under Secretary of State (Welles) to President Roosevelt, Washington D.C., October 20, 1942. Quoted in Yonah Alexander and Allan Nanes eds., *The United States and Iran: A Documentary History* (Frederick, Md.: University Publications of America, 1980), 110-11.

4. *Foreign Relations of the United States* (1943) 4: 423-24. Hurley to Roosevelt, December 21, 1943. Quoted in Lytle, 103.

5. William Roger Louis, *The British Empire in the Middle East: 1945-1951* (Oxford: Clarendon Press, 1984), 55.

6. Justus D. Doenecke, "Revisionists, Oil, and Cold War Diplomacy," *Iranian Studies* 3, no. 1 (Winter 1970): 24.

7. Stephen L. McFarlane, "A Peripheral View of the Origins of the Cold War: The Crises in Iran, 1941-1947," *Diplomatic History* 4, no. 4 (Fall 1980): 340-41.

8. Harold Ickes, *Fighting Oil* (New York: A. A. Knopf, 1943), 125 Quoted in Mark Hamilton Lytle, "American-Iranian Relations 1941-1947 and the Redefinition of National Security," (Unpublished Ph.D. dissertation, Yale University, 1973), 112. For a further discussion of the importance of oil to the United States during World War II see also Mark Hamilton Lytle, *The Origins of the Iranian-American Alliance: 1941-1953* (New York: Holmes and Meier, 1987), 71-78.

9. For a complete discussion of this see Lytle, "American-Iranian Relations," 116-20.

10. Lytle, "American-Iranian Relations," 32.

11. Bill, *The Eagle and Lion*, 32.

12. Richard W. Cottam, "The United States, Iran and the Cold War," *Iranian Studies* 2, no. 1 (Winter 1970): 4.

13. Cottam, "The United States and Iran," 36.

14. John Lewis Gaddis, *The United States and the Origins of the Cold War: 1941-1947* (New York: Columbia University Press, 1972), 317.

15. William Dorman and Mansour Farhang, *The U.S. Press and Iran* (Berkeley, Calif.: University of California Press, 1987), 32.

16. Mary Ann Heiss, *Empire and Nationhood: The United States, Great Britain, and Iranian Oil, 1950-1954* (New York: Columbia University Press, 1997), 3.

17. Bill, *The Eagle and Lion*, 61. Discusses the major points of redress that the Iranians sought from Britain.

18. Mustafa Elm, *Oil, Power, and Principle* (Syracuse, N.Y.: Syracuse University Press, 1992), 60.

19. For a comprehensive discussion of the events leading up to and during the oil nationalization crisis see Heiss, *Empire and Nationhood*, as well as Mostafa Elm, *Oil, Power, and Principal*, 105-23. The United States attempted to mediate this dispute by sending an envoy, Averell Harriman, to facilitate negotiations between Britain and Iran, but this mission ended in failure. Occurring at the same time was a last ditch attempt by the British to negotiate with what has been called the Stokes mission. This attempt also did not succeed and Great Britain prepared to use force against Iran to end the oil nationalization issue. However, as a result of American pressure they were forced to temporarily abandon this, and the dispute was placed before the United Nations. For a discussion of this see Mark J. Gasiorowski, "The 1953 Coup D'Etat in Iran," *International Journal of Middle East Studies* 19, no. 3 (August 1987): 264.

20. Gasiorowski, "The 1953 Coup D'Etat in Iran," 267.

21. Gasiorowski, "The 1953 Coup D'Etat in Iran," 268-69.

22. James A. Bill, "America, Iran, and the Politics of Intervention, 1951-1953," in *Musaddiq, Iranian Nationalism, and Oil*, James A. Bill and William Roger Louis eds. (Austin, Tex.: University of Texas Press, 1988), 274-76.

23. Gasiorowski, "The 1953 Coup D'Etat in Iran," 270-75.

24. Mark J. Gasiorowski, *U.S. Foreign Policy and the Shah: Building a Client State in Iran* (Ithaca, New York: Cornell University Press, 1991), 76-79. He provides a detailed account of the events leading up to Musadiq's downfall.

25. Stephen D. Krasner, *Defending the National Interest: Raw Materials Investments and U.S. Foreign Policy* (Princeton, N.J.: Princeton University Press, 1978), 124-26.

26. Mark J. Gasiorowski, *U.S. Foreign Policy and the Shah: Building a Client State in Iran* (Ithaca, N.Y.: Cornell University Press, 1991), 109.

27. Gasiorowski, "The 1953 Coup D'Etat in Iran," 261.

28. State Department and United States Embassy in Iran Exchanges on Strategic Importance of Iran and Proposed United States Aid. "The Acting Secretary of State (Lovett) to the Embassy in Iran," Cable, Washington D.C., January 3, 1948. Quoted in Alexander and Nanes, *The United States and Iran*, 190.

29. Secretary of State (Acheson) to the Ambassador in Iran (Wiley). Washington May 16, 1949. Quoted in Alexander and Nanes, *The United States and Iran*, 194-95.

30. Amin Saikal, *The Rise and Fall of the Shah* (Princeton, N.J.: Princeton University Press, 1980), 51-53.

31. Jane Perry Clark and Andrew G. Carey, "Industrial Growth and Development Planning in Iran," *Middle East Journal* 29, no. 1 (Winter 1975): 5.

32. See various American government documents. "United States Policy toward Iran: A Report to the National Security Council by NSC Planning Board," (December 21, 1953) and "Memorandum by the Joint Chiefs of Staff for the Secretary of Defense on the MDA Program for Iran," (October 12, 1954) Quoted in Alexander and Nanes, *The United States and Iran*, 265-71.

33. Thomas M. Ricks, "U.S. Military Missions to Iran, 1943-1978: The Political Economy of Military Assistance," *Iranian Studies* 12, no. 3-4 (Fall 1979): 174.

34. Ricks, "U.S. Military Missions," 54-55.

35. Ulrich Albrecht, "Militarized Sub-imperialism: The Case of Iran," in *The World Military Order*, Mary Kaldor and Asborn Eide eds. (New York: Praeger, 1979), 164.

36. "Joint Chiefs of Staff Joint Intelligence Committee Memorandum for the Joint Strategic Plans Committee and the Joint Logistic Plans Committee," (April 13, 1955). Quoted in Alexander and Nanes, *The United States and Iran*, 273.

37. John Marlowe, *Iran* (New York: Praeger, 1963), 110-11.

38. Office of Program and Information Analysis Services, Bureau for Program Policy and Coordination Agency for International Development, "U.S. Overseas Loans and Grants and Assistance from International Obligations and Loan Authorizations, July 1945-September 1977," (Washington, D.C.: U.S. Government Printing Office, 1977), 17. Quoted in K. R. Singh, *Iran: Quest for Security* (New Delhi, India: Vikas Publishing House, 1980), 62.

39. Singh, *Iran: Quest for Security*, 62.

40. Singh, *Iran: A Quest for Security*, 75-76.

41. Alvin Cottrell, "Iran, the Arabs and the Persian Gulf," *Orbis* 27, no. 3 (Fall 1973): 979. Central Intelligence Agency Directorate of Intelligence, "The Shah of Iran and His Policies," June 5, 1967.

42. Bill, *The Eagle and Lion*, 119.

43. "Agreement on Defense and Cooperation between the Government of United States of America and the Imperial Government of Iran," (March 5, 1959). Quoted in Alexander and Nanes, *The United States and Iran*, 306-7.

44. John W. Bowling, *The Current Internal Political Situation in Iran: A Report by the Deputy Director of the Office of Greek, Turkish, and Iranian Affairs*, Department of State Report to the President (February 11, 1961). Quoted in Alexander, and Nanes, *The United States and Iran*, 320-21. Also cited in Bill, *The Eagle and Lion*, 133.

45. Nikki Keddie, *Roots of Revolution: An Interpretive History of Modern Iran* (New Haven, Conn.: Yale University Press, 1981), 155. The Shah was against reducing the military budget, which provoked Prime Minister Amini's resignation. It should be noted this was the last prime minister to exercise any kind of authority independent of the monarchy. Ali Amini was replaced as prime minister by the Shah's close friend Asadollah Alam. A similar argument is reflected in the National Security Archive, "Survey of U.S.-Iranian Relations 1941-1979: The Evolution of the U.S.-Iranian Relationship," in *The Making of U.S. Policy, Iran: 1977-1980* January 29, 1980, Document no. 03556 (Washington, D.C.: National Security Archive, 1989), 34. James Bill also points out the significance of the Amini premiership and the leverage that the United States used to induce the Shah to appoint him. Statement by former American Ambassador Armin Meyer, in Abbas Amirie and Hamilton A. Twitchell eds., *Iran in the 1980s* (Tehran: Institute for International Political and Economic Studies, 1978), 382. Quoted in Bill, *The Eagle and Lion*, 143.

46. Keddie, *Roots of Revolution*, 156.

47. Bill, *The Eagle and Lion*, 149-53. Discusses the Kennedy administration's policy towards Iran, as well as aid to the third world in general. While he argues that Washington's emphasis on reform had some benefits, such as the Peace Corps, Bill argues that its aim was to preserve the status quo. In addition it should be noted that it was during this period that the Shah sought to normalize and establish broader links with the Soviet Union as a warning to the United States should it seek to push its leverage too hard.

48. Safqat Shah, "The Political and Strategic Foundations of International Arms Transfers: A Case Study of American Arms Supplies to and Purchases by Iran and Saudi Arabia, 1968-1976" (Unpublished Ph.D. Dissertation, University of Virginia, August 1977), 15.

49. Nicole Ball and Milton Leitenberg, "The Iranian Domestic Crisis: Foreign Policy Making and Foreign Policy Goals of the U.S.," *Journal of South Asian and Middle East Studies* 2, no. 3 (Spring 1979): 44.

50. Bill, *The Eagle and Lion*, 169-70. Although Walt Rostow supported the monarchy he did criticize the Shah's squandering of Iran's resources on large arms purchases. He argued that Iran's economy would not be able to support it. However, he further stated in the same memo that the United States should sell arms to Iran if the Shah was determined to purchase them so the United States would not lose market share and Washington could retain some influence over the process. See W. W. Rostow, Memorandum for the President, May 21, 1966, LBJ Documents, NSF Country File: Middle East/India, Box no. 136, Document no. 266B.

51. Bill, *The Eagle and Lion*, 170-71. Iran's strategic importance to the United States was illustrated with the Shah's foreign policy of supporting conservative states and seeking to check pro Soviet states. See Director of Intelligence. *National Intelligence Estimates, Iran*, March 24, 1966, LBJ Documents, (4). Among the Iranian policies cited as benefitting the United States were Tehran's attempt to weaken Iraq by supporting Kurdish nationalism and his support for Saudi Arabia in its conflict with Egypt over Yemen.

52. Bill, *The Eagle and Lion*, 171-72.

53. Harold Wiggins, Memorandum for Mr. Rostow, Call to Secretary McNamara re F-4s to Shah, LBJ Documents, NSF Country File: Middle East/India Box no. 136, Document no. 265, 1.

54. Wiggins, Memorandum for Mr. Rostow.

55. Walt W. Rostow, Memorandum to President Johnson, November 8, 1966, LBJ Library, Confidential File, FO3-2(January-March 1966), Box 48. Quoted in Bill, *The Eagle and Lion*, 172. This argument was made in response to Senator Fulbright's opposition to the sale due to the sophistication of the equipment.

56. Memorandum Robert S. McNamara to President Johnson, February 9, 1967. Quoted in Bill, *The Eagle and Lion*, 173.

57. John D. Stempel, *Inside the Iranian Revolution* (Bloomington, Ind.: Indiana University Press, 1981), 68. Also Bill, *The Eagle and Lion*, 173.

58. Bill, *The Eagle and Lion*, 173.

59. Zbigniew Brzezinski, *Power and Principle* (New York: Farrar, Strauss, Giroux, 1983), 356-57.

60. Alvin J. Cottrell, "Iran, the Arabs, and the Persian Gulf," *Orbis* 27, no. 3 (Fall 1973): 979-80.

61. Rouhollah K. Ramazani, "Emerging Patterns of Regional Relations in Iranian Foreign Policy," *Orbis* 28, no. 4 (Winter 1975): 1052.

62. Cottrell, "Iran, the Arabs and the Persian Gulf," 980-88. Offers a discussion of the development of Iranian military resources, as well as the tensions between Iran and Iraq.

63. U.S. Directorate of Intelligence. *Intelligence Memorandum: The Arab Threat to Iran*, May 21, 1966, LBJ Documents, NSF Country File: Middle East/India , Box no. 136, Document no. 270, 2.

64. Eric Pace, "Shah of Iran Uses Oman to Train Armed Forces," *New York Times*, 25 January 1976, 22(A).

65. Hossein Amirsadeghi, *Twentieth-Century Iran* (London: Heinemann, 1977), 120.

Chapter 3

The United States and Iran: The Establishment and Implications of the New Persian Empire

The Importance and Ramifications of the American Alliance with Iran

The American-Iranian alliance achieved its importance in American foreign policy calculations from 1969 to 1978 for geostrategic, political, and economic reasons. This chapter will seek to explore these reasons and illustrate their importance, which increased over time and was reflected over several American administrations encompassing both political parties.

Geostrategically, Iran was important for three reasons. The first was that a pro-Western Iran was considered vital in American-Soviet relations pertaining to arms control. Listening posts located on the Iranian-Soviet border were considered necessary by American decision makers to monitor Soviet compliance with potential arms control agreements. This became particularly important after the first Strategic Arms Limitation Talks (SALT) and Anti-Ballistic Missile (ABM) treaties of 1972. Second, it was considered essential by American policy makers that the United States illustrate to the Soviet Union that despite detente, America would not abandon important allies in the third world. Third, Iran was considered important to the United States as a regional surrogate to serve as a check to radical forces within the Persian Gulf and in the third world as a whole. This was illustrated by the cooperation Iran established with other status quo powers in the region such as Israel and Saudi Arabia. In addition, Iran assisted in providing aid to pro-Western states such as Ethiopia, Oman, Somalia, South Vietnam, and Zaire.

Politically, the United States viewed Iran as one of its most important allies in the third world. In addition to attempting to establish Iranian military power, the United States also appreciated Iran's growing political clout in the third world, and the support Iran provided to other pro-Western states.

Economically, Iran was important because of its role as a major oil exporter to the West, as well as Israel. The broadening strategic and military relationship was envisioned by policy makers as opening the door for more expanded economic contacts, both civilian and military, and heightened speculation that these would increase in the future.

Changing Regional Conditions: The British Withdrawal and the Formation of the Nixon Doctrine

In 1968, the British government decided to withdraw its military forces from the Gulf by the end of 1971 and grant all of their protectorates full independence. American policy makers viewed this as a disruption of the status quo, which could lead to the destabilization of the pro-Western regimes in the region. In order to compensate for this, as well as to extricate the United States militarily from Southeast Asia, the Nixon Doctrine was announced on Guam in November of 1969.

This doctrine asserted that the United States would honor its treaty obligations and provide economic and military assistance to friendly nations. These states would provide the armed forces necessary to preserve the status quo in the region from Soviet threats, from internal revolution, and from anti-Western states within the region. The preservation of the status quo would serve American interests regarding containment, the control of oil, and access to the markets of these countries for Western business interests in general.

The Nixon Doctrine was a "twin pillar policy," as America counted on Iran and Saudi Arabia to provide regional security. It was initiated as a result of America's strategic overcommitment, illustrated by the stalemate in Vietnam. The conflict in Southeast Asia illustrated the loss of strategic hegemony by the United States. Iran was looked upon as the main military pillar, as it possessed the armed forces and population to enable itself to be a credible military power in the region. In addition, the Shah was only too eager to assume this role. Saudi Arabia, although it too received substantial amounts of military equipment, was looked upon as more of a stabilizing influence due to its financial resources and the influence it held in the Arab and Muslim worlds.[1] American policy makers viewed the United States as having strategic interests in both countries and to support one exclusively would isolate and alienate the other. It was argued that for regional stability to be achieved, both states had to work together in partnership, which was reinforced by the Nixon Doctrine.[2]

The doctrine was further refined in the early 1970s in order to incorporate two important political factors. The first was the American defeat in Vietnam. The second was the dramatic increase in the price of oil during the early 1970s, which gave OPEC nations tremendous political and economic clout. The American defeat in Vietnam was significant, as it radically changed the domestic political environment of the United States. The negative consequences of the Vietnam experience led to the growth of quasi-isolationist sentiments within America. The U.S. Congress responded to this by restricting the resources allocated the Military Assistance Program, as it was felt this program increased the chances of American involvement in local conflicts. In order to compensate for this the Nixon administration sought to encourage direct arms sales between the United States and certain regional powers like Iran, who were counted on to preserve the status quo in the Third World. The rise in oil prices gave Iran and Saudi Arabia the opportunity to purchase a large quantity of sophisticated armaments.[3]

These conditions allowed Tehran to be the ideal regional partner for Washington, serving a strategic purpose as the strongest military power in the region. Related to this were the economic implications. As a result of its oil wealth, Iran was able to pay hard currency for weapons that served to assist in maintaining American balance of payments, and providing employment and filling orders in key defense industries, lowering the cost of weapons systems for the American military by subsidizing research and development costs. Iran also was a reliable supplier of oil to the West, which became even more important after the 1973 Arab oil embargo. Iran was the fourth largest oil producer in the world and an alternative supplier should the Arab states attempt another oil embargo.

A related point to the rise in oil prices in the early 1970s is the role of the United States in these increases. During this period the Saudis seemed generally interested in establishing a stable price of oil, whereas the Shah advocated higher prices in order to create the necessary capital to further Iran's developmental needs and especially to embark on his military buildup. The United States did not put pressure on the Shah to moderate his price, despite the political leverage it had on Iran. Rather, it seemed that the Nixon administration viewed this positively, as a wealthy Iran coupled with its large population would serve as an ideal market for major American corporations. Given the Shah's desire for sophisticated weapons systems, this list would also include most of the largest American defense contractors.[4]

Iran and the Nixon Doctrine

The Shah saw the Nixon Doctrine as an opportunity to enhance Iranian policy in the region as well as in international politics in general. For Iran, this required major arms expenditures to upgrade and enhance its military capabilities. The path for this was cleared in May 1972 when President

Nixon promised the Shah that Iran could purchase any weapons, short of nuclear weapons, it felt necessary for its defense. These requests would be granted automatically by the executive branch and would only be reviewed superficially by the Defense Department. This arrangement continued up until the Shah's fall in 1979.

This policy was justified as, with the British withdrawal from Southwest Asia, American policy makers viewed the potential for Soviet expansionism as a threat. Iran, they argued, was particularly vulnerable, as it shared a 1,250-mile border with the Soviet Union and also controlled the Straits of Hormuz, the narrow waterway through which a good portion of the oil headed to Western markets passed. In addition, Iran itself was viewed as having a strategic location, a large population, and a large military to serve American objectives in the region. At the same time Iran would serve as a barrier to the Soviet's goal of reaching the Gulf and increasing their influence in the Middle East in general.[5] Iran came to be seen as a prime example of the Nixon Doctrine in action. American allies would be helped by the United States, but ultimately would have to defend themselves.[6]

The Importance of Oil

Oil was a key component of why the United States became involved with Iran during World War II and the postwar period. The significance of Iranian oil would only increase throughout the 1970s. American imports of Middle East oil virtually doubled from 1975 to 1976 from 6.6 percent to 12.4 percent respectively. In total, imported oil accounted for 45 percent of American oil consumption in 1976 as compared to 23 percent in 1970. The Middle East supplied 44 percent of total American oil imports.[7] While arguments were made concerning the dependence of the West on oil, it must also be remembered that oil was significant for the Iranian economy as well. In 1973 Iranian oil revenues were $4.8 billion, in 1974, after the oil shocks, it was $18.7 billion. The proportion of oil to total exports was about 95 percent.[8] Therefore, both countries had an incentive to ensure that the sea-lanes would be kept open.

Reasons for American Arms Sales

The Shah took advantage of this pledge by President Nixon, purchasing an enormous amount of military equipment and greatly expanding his armed forces. The Iranian armed forces grew from 161,000 in 1970 to 413,000 by 1978. Much of the equipment that was purchased consisted of sophisticated weapons systems for the navy and air force in particular. Iran possessed the largest hovercraft fleet in the world and it also ordered Spraunce class destroyers and Tang-class submarines. With regard to its air force, the Iranians had purchased F-4s, F-14s, and had ordered F-16s and Airborne Warning and Control System (AWACS) aircraft among others.[9]

In total, during the 1970s Iran spent about 27 percent of its budget on the military and more than one-third of these purchases came from the United States.[10] To illustrate the amount of petrodollars that circulated back to America in the form of arms purchases, it should be noted that arms sales to Iran increased from $35 million in the early 1970s to $3 billion by the mid-1970s.[11]

There were six reasons for this rapid increase in American arms sales to Iran: (1) it was in American interests to convert Iran into a "surrogate gendarme" in the Persian Gulf; (2) a strong Iran, it was felt, would block the spread of Soviet influence southward in the Persian Gulf and the Arabian Peninsula; (3) the arms relationship would enhance American influence over Iran; (4) the sale of armaments to Iran would help offset the U.S. balance of payments deficits that the rise in oil prices had caused; (5) the sale of sophisticated arms to Iran would offset the recession in the aerospace industry; and (6) the sale of armaments to Iran would lower the production costs of these weapons, making them cheaper to acquire for the Defense Department itself.[12]

The Political Implications of the Nixon Doctrine

The Nixon Doctrine was the turning point in the alliance, in particular for the United States, as it was here that America lost control of it. A major factor behind the making of this agreement was the broader strategic message it was designed to send to the Soviet Union. The 1972 agreement between President Nixon and the Shah came subsequent to the signing of the Basic Principles Agreement between the United States and the Soviet Union. In initiating this policy toward Iran, the United States was attempting to indicate to the Soviet Union that it would not allow the policy of detente to mean that America would not defend its interests in various parts of the world, or that it would hesitate to make commitments to defend those interests.[13]

In assessing American interests in the Middle East, United States strategic interests as defined by American policy makers were served by this alliance. Both the United States and Iran shared a number of common goals and Washington valued the alliance with Tehran. One reason was that Iran was the principal vehicle of America's containment strategy for the Persian Gulf and Southwest Asia. Iran was also valued for serving as a counterweight to Soviet allies in the region, especially Iraq, which was of special concern to the Iranians given Iraq's ties to the Soviet Union at that time. Iraq had developed a close military relationship with the Soviet Union shortly after the Iraqi revolution of 1958 as the Soviets began providing arms. This relationship accelerated during the late 1960s and 1970s. By mid-1971 Iraq had a formidable arsenal that included: 110 MiG-21 and SU-7 fighters; 20 helicopters and trainers; 100-150 tanks; 300 armored personnel carriers; and 500 field guns and artillery rockets.[14]

This relationship was formalized by the 1972 Soviet-Iraqi Treaty of Friendship and Cooperation as the quality of Soviet weapons to Iraq increased. Iraq then acquired: SA-3 surface-to-air missiles; Scud-surface-to surface missiles; TU-22 medium bombers, the first deployment outside of Eastern Europe; and the MiG-23 fighter, at that time the most sophisticated aircraft in the Soviet arsenal.[15] The USSR also illustrated its military and political support in other ways, such as the Soviet navy's visit to the ports of Basra and Umm Qasr. There was increased hostility along the border between Iran and Iraq as there were estimated to be 10 exchanges of fire. The Shah felt that Iran was at a disadvantage, claiming that the Iraqis outnumbered Iran in tanks and aircraft.[16]

Iran's economic role was another important factor in the alliance with the United States. It was the world's second largest oil exporter, as well as being the leading purchaser of American arms.[17]

This last point is the most significant, as the selling of arms to Iran ultimately led to the destabilization of the alliance. The vast arms sales program begun with the Nixon Doctrine and reinforced by the 1972 agreement served to weaken rather than enhance America's strategic interests. The main reason for this was the reverse leverage that developed in the relationship. As a result of these policies, American strategic interests became irrevocably linked with the monarchy. More significantly, it established an environment whereby American policy makers viewed Iran's security and the security of the monarchy as being inseparable.[18] Equally important, it served to tie American interests with the fate of the monarchy. The opposition groups that emerged against the monarchy after World War II, while varying in orientation between Islamic, left wing, and the more moderate National Front, took the view that military spending was to support the Shah politically, rather than Iranian national security interests.[19] This process began with the coup against Musadiq and was reinforced as a result of the enormous amount of economic and military aid, as well as political support furnished by subsequent administrations. This idea was articulated by T. Cuyler Young in 1962:

> During the last decade . . . the United States has furnished Iran more than a billion dollars in economic and military aid. Like it or not, justly or unjustly, this has served to identify the U.S. with the Shah's regime, together with responsibility for what that regime has done, or failed to do. . . . For this reason the United States is distrusted if not indeed throughly disliked by all those who have come to distrust the Shah and oppose his policies.[20]

As a result of these agreements American decision makers were unable to conceive of Iran without the Shah. The presence of the monarchy was viewed as being essential for the maintenance of America's position in the region. The 1972 agreement between President Nixon and the Shah effectively locked the United States into supporting the Iranian military buildup by severely limiting internal debate within the United States government over this issue.[21]

American Economic Imperatives for Expanded Military Cooperation

In addition to the United States providing Iran with the opportunity to purchase the most sophisticated armaments in the American arsenal, the arms sales served as a reinforcement of the existing relationship. As mentioned previously, the economic incentives for selling arms were: (1) to reduce the balance of payments deficits; (2) to absorb surplus output; (3) to establish cost-sharing in the research; and (4) to develop major weapons systems. A further incentive, which is stated in the international relations literature on arms transfers, was also functioning in the American-Iranian case, namely, the emphasis on maintaining market share. This would prove problematic, as other suppliers could conceivably move to fill the vacuum should the United States chose to abandon arms sales. This factor was stated by President Carter in a report discussing American arms sales policy in which he argued that it was difficult for the United States to limit arms transfers as other suppliers would move aggressively into the market, notably communist countries.[22]

American policy makers also viewed arms sales as satisfying domestic economic problems as well as aiding the Pentagon in domestic military production. It was during this period that the United States began to show trade deficits. The impending OPEC price increases would have the effect of worsening the American balance of payments deficits. As a result, arms sales were viewed as a way of recycling the petrodollars from the Middle East back to the United States. In addition, the increasing volume of arms sales would provide much needed revenues for American defense contractors at a time when the end of the Vietnam War meant decreasing defense budgets, keeping many of them in business. Finally, the sales of expensive weapons systems would stimulate production and thus decrease the unit cost per item. These savings could then be put into other programs for research and development.[23]

The United States found itself in the best of both worlds as its strategic interests in the region were safeguarded without any direct costs to itself; because of its oil revenues, Iran was able to pay for its armaments. It could be said that Iran, to a certain extent, was being used to subsidize American armament manufactures and the U.S. military itself.[24]

The Significance of the AWACS Sale

This subsidization concept is especially illustrated with regard to the AWACS sale of 1977-1978. It was argued in hearings before the United States Congress that not only would the sale be beneficial strategically, but would be economically significant. Strategically, it was argued that AWACS was essential to Iran for a variety of reasons. The administration position held that the development of an air defense system for Iran was essential to security. In testimony before Congress, Alfred Atherton, the assistant secretary of state for Near East and South Asia affairs, in his support of the AWACS sale, argued that Iran's use of AWACS was consistent with U.S. strategy and represented a defensive response by the government of Iran to upgrade its air defense capabilities.[25]

Another consideration that was discussed by proponents of the sale was the strategic position of Iran as a result of its long border with the Soviet Union. This was stressed in the testimony of Senator Barry Goldwater (R-Ariz.). He stated, "The sale of AWACs to Iran serves the best interest of the United States not only because Iran is one of our staunchest allies, and has been for 30 years, but also because she occupies such a strategic position in relation to the Soviet Union."[26]

In testimony before the House Subcommittee on International Security and Scientific Affairs, Eric Von Marbod, acting director of the Defense Security Assistance Agency, stated:

> Any sale of a weapon system that is in production does involve the recovery of certain costs by the U.S. government. In this case there would be a prorated recoupment of research and development costs and the buying of greater quantities does in fact reduce unit costs. However, that is not the justification for approving or considering the sale.[27]

He went on to indicate that it was estimated that the recovery of research and development costs on the system as a result of the sale to Iran would result in the saving of $20 million per aircraft.[28]

Similar themes were advanced in corresponding hearings in the Senate. Senator Thomas Eagleton (D-Mo.) in his criticism of the sale of AWACS to Iran, argued that the only utility of the sale was the corresponding reduction in the price of the system as a result.[29] In the same hearing, the State Department's Alfred Atherton argued that in addition to being necessary from a strategic viewpoint it was important economically to the United States. He maintained that the sale of aircraft by American companies, military as well as civilian, was necessary in order for the United States to meet its balance of payments deficits:

> This further refusal to continue in the engagement of the sale of aircraft whether it be military or airliners to other countries will in my opinion just continue to destroy this country's ability to meet its balance of payments. It is only thought the aircraft industry that we have met our balance of payments when we have met them, and they have been declining more rapidly lately than ever, mainly because we have not had the aircraft to sell.[30]

The importance of the sale of AWACS from a political as well as an economic perspective seemed to outweigh other costs. This was especially apparent as the development costs of the system became more prohibitive ($2.8 billion), which alarmed the NATO countries who were interested in buying it. Therefore, a sale to Iran became significant in order to recoup research and development savings.[31] Critics charged that the AWACS sale by the United States had potentially disastrous consequences and there were several arguments put forth by leading Democratic senators against the sale. These centered around the potentially offensive nature of the AWACS system, the existence of a cheaper, alternative ground-based system, and especially stressed was the repercussions to the strategic balance if one of these planes should fall into Soviet hands. It was argued that the U.S. technological air advantage over the Soviets would be compromised.[32] This was initially reflected in opposition to the sale by the director of the Central Intelligence Agency, Admiral Stansfield Turner. In a letter to the U.S. General Accounting Office he argued that the sale could jeopardize American military secrets.[33]

Later, however, Turner changed his stand and reportedly supported the sale in a closed door hearing of the Senate Foreign Relations Committee. This occurred as a result of pressure from Secretary of State Vance, and National Security Advisor Brzezinski, who were in favor of the sale. It was reported that these officials favored the transaction for political reasons, as they did not wish to jeopardize relations with Iran. In addition, they felt that there had been an understanding between the two countries, stemming from the 1972 arms transfer agreement made between President Nixon and the Shah, that the United States would provide Iran with an air defense system.[34]

While economic and foreign policy incentives were important in this sale, American domestic politics also played an important role. Politically, the AWACS sale was linked to American domestic politics, as some sources pegged the sale of the aircraft to the status of President Carter's energy legislation in Congress. This is because Senator Henry Jackson(D-Wash.) was chair of the Energy and Natural Resources Committee in the Senate, and also represented the state where the Boeing Corporation, the major contractor of the AWACS program, was located.[35]

In addition to these political considerations there was also the dynamic of interservice rivalry that also manifested itself in this transaction. A criticism of the AWACS sale was that the air force was attempting to push the plane, supported by the Defense Department, in order to recover some of the costs of research and development. Therefore, in order to maintain the air force program it was argued the Defense Department suppressed an attempt by the navy to sell Iran a cheaper radar control plane, the E-2C, in favor of the air force system.[36] The Iranians had asked for budgetary information on the purchase of 5 to 10 E-2Cs. However, it was charged that Secretary of Defense Schlesinger had ordered the American military mission in Iran not to provide the Iranians with the requested information. In addition, attempts to show off the Hawkeye to the Shah at Andrews Air Force Base in 1975 was not authorized by the secretary of defense.[37]

Iran's Military Expansion

Another significant aspect of this arms relationship was that it enabled Iran to expand its foreign policy goals in the region. Prior to the Nixon Doctrine and the 1972 agreement the emphasis on the regime was, for the most part, on internal security and, to a lesser extent, to defend itself against Soviet pressure. However, the Shah used these agreements, with American encouragement, to take a more active role in defending Iran from possible Soviet threats, and also to become the regional hegemon of Southwest Asia. In order to accomplish these goals it would be necessary to massively increase the size of the Iranian military, along with a corresponding increase in both the quantity and quality of the armaments at its disposal. In order to fulfill this goal the subsequent military buildup was designed to give the Iranian armed forces power projection capabilities not only in the Persian Gulf, but in the shipping lanes of the northwest quadrant of the Indian Ocean as well.[38] This desire to expand the power projection capabilities of the Iranian military as well as maintaining the oil shipping lanes was evident in the seizure of the three islands in the Persian Gulf, Abu Musa and Greater and Lesser Tumb. The Shah and the Iranian military felt that if a hostile power gained control of these islands, the Strait of Hormuz could be blockaded. In addition, they calculated that these islands could be used to attack Iran's southern ports, cities, and oil facilities. As justification, they cited the relative military weakness of the shiekdoms of Ras al-Khaimah and Sharjah in defending these islands.[39]

The Iranian military buildup during the 1970s has been called "the most rapid buildup of military power under peacetime conditions of any nation in the history of the world."[40] The scope of these sales can be characterized by several factors: volume, sophistication, technology transfer, and military technical assistance. Between 1970 and 1978 the United States agreed to sell Iran $20 billion worth of weapons; nine billion dollars worth of these weapons had been delivered before the regime fell in 1979. This is seen in tables 3.1 and graph 3.1 which illustrates U.S. Military Sales Agreements to Iran from 1969-1978, and table 3.2 and graph 3.2 which shows U.S. Military Sales Deliveries to Iran from 1969-1978. Another significant factor concerning these orders was that Iran represented 25 percent of all Foreign Military Sales (FMS) orders for this period.[41]

The number and variety of weapons involved in these orders was also significant. Among the Shah's purchases were 80 F-14 high performance aircraft costing about $2 billion. Mid-level systems purchased included 169 Northrop F-5E and F-5F fighter planes that cost $480 million; 209 McDonnell-Douglas F-4 Phantom fighter-bombers for $1 billion; 160 General Dynamics F-16 fighters costing $3.2 billion; and 202 Bell Ah-IJ Cobra helicopters gunships that cost $367 million. In addition, the Shah also ordered 326 Bell model 2I4 troop-carrying helicopters that cost $496 million, as well as 25,000 TOW and Dragon antitank missiles and 4 DD-

Table 3.1. U.S. Military Sales Agreements with Iran, 1969-1978 (in thousands of U.S. dollars)

Years	Worldwide	Near East and South Asia (NESA)	Iran
1969	1,183,723	355,886	235,821
1970	1,155,817	412,126	134,929
1971	1,388,955	725,365	363,884
1972	3,065,867	1,274,614	472,611
1973	4,480,390	3,095,380	2,171,355
1974	10,740,639	8,916,152	4,325,357
1975	13,938,200	7,684,967	2,447,140
1976	13,233,157	9,644,172	1,794,487
1977	11,341,906	8,487,684	5,713,769
1978	13,534,389	9,671,762	2,586,890
FY1950-1978	84,610,525	52,099,690	20,751,656

Sources: U.S. Department of State. *Security Assistance Programs, FY 1980* (Washington D.C.: U.S. Government Printing Office, 1978), 467; Also U.S. Department of Defense. *Foreign Military Sales. Foreign Military Construction Sales, and Military Assistance Facts* (Washington, D.C.: U.S. Government Printing Office, 1978), 1.

Graph 3.1. U.S. Military Sales
Agreements with Iran, 1969-1978

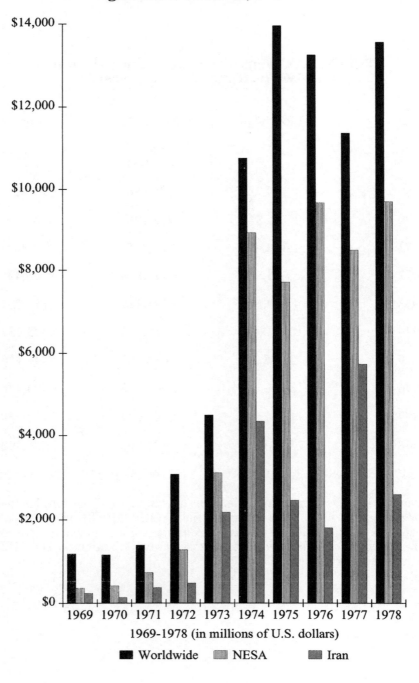

1969-1978 (in millions of U.S. dollars)

■ Worldwide ▥ NESA ▨ Iran

**Table 3.2. U.S. Military Sales Deliveries to Iran,
1969-1978 (in thousands of U.S. dollars)**

Years	Worldwide	Near East and South Asia (NESA)	Iran
1969	1,277,212	253,428	94,881
1970	1,342,257	469,259	127,717
1971	1,372,165	477,543	78,566
1972	1,460,473	584,197	214,087
1973	1,516,448	681,278	248,391
1974	3,177,735	1,992,717	648,641
1975	3,478,510	2,057,101	1,006,131
1976	5,932,594	3,886,348	1,927,860
1977	7,132,324	5,192,772	2,433,050
1978	7,699,233	5,593,441	1,792,892
FY 1950-1978	40,971,341	21,755,738	8,715,810

Source: U.S. Department of Defense. *Foreign Military Sales, Foreign Military Construction Sales, and Military Assistance Facts* (Washington, D.C.: U.S. Government Printing Office, 1978), 4.

Graph 3.2. U.S. Military Sales Deliveries to Iran, 1969-1978

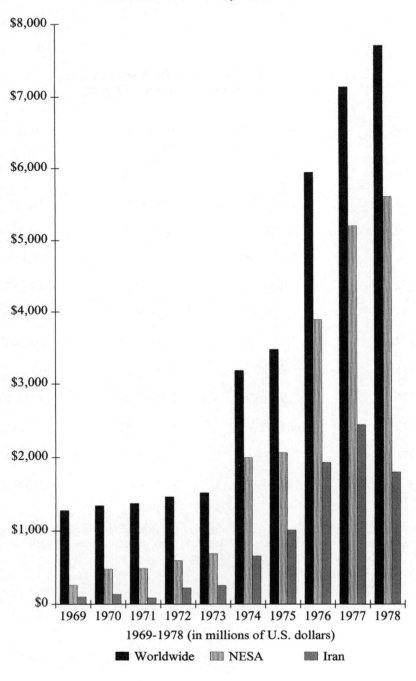

1969-1978 (in millions of U.S. dollars)

■ Worldwide   ▥ NESA   ▨ Iran

963 Spruance-class missile destroyers. These items cost $150 million and $ 1.5 billion respectively. In addition to these major systems, Iran also purchased or agreed to purchase submarines, transport planes, assault vehicles, and artillery pieces, as well as police equipment.[42]

Besides purchasing arms, the Shah sought to develop these industries domestically. Iran engaged in licensing and production agreements with such corporations as Northrop and Bell Helicopter and it was the government's hope that it could start an indigenous aerospace industry. The agreement with Northrop in 1969 established the Iran Aircraft Industries, which was owned jointly by Northrop and the Iranian government. This company's primary responsibility was maintaining the extensive amounts of equipment purchased from abroad while at the same time developing the capability to produce aircraft under license. In addition, it served as a training program to educate Iranian managers. A similar arrangement was made with Bell Helicopter, which agreed to construct a helicopter industry in Iran.[43]

The Shah used the arms sales program to enhance the industrial potential of the country through the development of domestic production lines. This was illustrated by General Katorijan (head of Iran's Armed Forces Control Bureau), when he stated that the development of an indigenous arms industry was viewed as a precondition for industrialization.[44] It was assumed that investment in the military would have a beneficial effect for the civilian economy, as it would promote education and technical innovation and training, development of infrastructure, the integration of isolated areas under the central government, and improvements in health care. The Shah felt that military development would be a useful tool in modernizing the nation.[45]

The Importance of Advisors

Another repercussion of the Nixon Doctrine and the escalation of military ties between the United States and Iran was the vast presence of American advisors, both military and corporate, which were needed to assist the Iranians in operating and maintaining their newly purchased weaponry. This presence required a long time frame, as the increasing volume of these purchases necessitated a continuation of the American maintenance link for the foreseeable future. It is estimated that in 1973 there were 3,600 American technicians, both military and corporate personnel, working on Iranian defense-related projects. As a by-product of the increased volume of arms sales, this number increased to 10,000 in 1978.[46]

For most foreign military sales, American advisors arrive in the nation between 18 to 30 months after the placement of the order. Given the volume and sophistication of Iranian orders in the mid-1970s this necessitated a heavy presence of American advisors. The American government estimated the community would number at least 50,000 by

1980.[47]

These advisors were especially significant in the air force and army aviation forces. By mid-1977 the army helicopter program was the largest employer of American personnel, with 2,600 civilian contractor personnel and 26 U.S. Army employees working with the Iranian military. These levels were projected to remain stable through 1981 before starting to taper off. The number of advisors involved in the helicopter coproduction effort between the Iranian government and Bell Helicopter was scheduled to peak at 500 by 1981-1982, and fall to 80 by 1985.[48] The number of Americans was also scheduled to increase as a result of air force programs. The American advisory efforts for the air force was scheduled to peak in the early 1980s as a result of the number of sophisticated arms program being conducted simultaneously, such as the F-16, AWACS, and I-HAWK, as well as the logistics program. The total number of contractor personnel involved in these programs, as well as the ongoing F-14 program, was estimated to be 2,800 by 1980.[49]

The expansion of the Iranian navy, both in volume and sophistication, also required an American presence. Central to Iran's naval expansion was the purchase of Spruance-class destroyers. It was argued that these ships were significant in that they would contribute to the Iranian navy possessing a blue-water capability and allow the Shah to project Iranian power well out into the Indian Ocean. However, this program required a great deal of technical sophistication, as these ships were even more advanced in terms of electronics than those procured by the U.S. Defense Department. It was estimated that about 3,000 Iranian personnel would have to be trained to adequately maintain and staff these ships. This would require about 50 American advisors to accompany the ships on their initial cruises. In addition to the ships themselves it was estimated that 167 contractor personnel, as well as the U.S. Navy Technical Advisory Field Team (TAFT), which consisted of 109 men, would be required for the maintenance of the Iranian port of Bandar Abbas through 1985.[50]

American advisors were also active in assisting the Iranians in intelligence gathering. While the links between the CIA and its Iranian counterpart SAVAK were strong, American companies were also involved in establishing an intelligence-gathering infrastructure in controversial project known as IBEX. This project had as its goal an elaborate electronic surveillance system in which Iran could intercept communications of other countries. This system would consist of specially configured EC-130 aircraft to pick up signals and relay them to a network of ground stations, where they would be decoded and analyzed. Iran retained the services of the Rockwell Corporation to set up this system and train Iranian personnel. Many analysts viewed this as a long-term program due to its complexity.[51] This program was controversial, as many Iranians felt that it would have a dual purpose of spying on the Shah's domestic opponents.

The Repercussions of Advisors

Due to the nature and size of the United States military commitment to Iran, the Iranian military needed a steady flow of spare parts and technical assistance in order to operate efficiently.[52] Thus, in the event of major hostilities involving Iran, the Iranians at the very least would have needed American support personnel in order to sustain a major conflict for any period of time. The scope of the arms sales program was one of the major problems in the relationship. In addition to the strategic ramifications that could be detrimental for the United States, there was also a political and economic cost.

Politically, the vast American presence in the country, the most visible being in the security sectors, reinforced the American association with the monarchy in the perception of the Iranian public. In addition, a significant congruence was that the American technical and military presence increased in Iran from the mid-1970s onward, which was the period that the public opinion of the Shah began to decline significantly. Also, since the advisors worked in military capacities, their presence in the country became linked to the survival of the monarchy rather than promoting Iran's national interest.[53]

Socially, the American advisors also promoted the Westernization of the country, which many traditional-religious Iranians viewed as cultural domination. Furthermore, the policies initiated by the government illustrated the view that the Shah not only condoned this Westernization but was encouraging it. Therefore it appeared to many Iranians that the monarchy was facilitating the foreign domination of the country.[54] Economically, the advisors not only placed strain on the Iranian economy by contributing to soaring inflation rates, they were also a large drain on the budget. An example of the economic effects of foreigners on Iranian society was in rents. Foreigners tended to displace upper and middle class Iranians for the better housing. This was particularly true in Tehran. Landlords had a preference for renting to Westerners, as they payed more and would only be there temporarily. As a result, rents increased in the more affluent areas of the city, which in turn pushed up rents in the poorer sections of Tehran, further breeding resentment of foreigners by average Iranians.[55]

The Development of Military Infrastructure

An important repercussion of these arms sales was the corresponding development of infrastructure that they required. This was particular true with regard to the air force and navy. In order to accommodate the procurement of these weapons, as well as adapt itself to the role of regional hegemon by projecting its forces throughout the Middle East and the Indian Ocean, Iran had to build up its military infrastructure. The Iranian air force had established 10 major bases within the country in strategic locations. In addition, they were planing 50 smaller airfields that would house Hawk antiaircraft missile batteries. By 1976 the Iranian navy had constructed six naval bases along the Gulf Coast. The Shah also planned to expand the already existing facility at Bandar Abbas by constructing a new naval base and headquarters, improving the facilities at Khorramshahr, as well as acquiring a hovercraft fleet based on Kharg Island. The centerpiece of Iranian naval development was the construction of the huge naval station at Chah Bahar on the Indian Ocean. This would give the Iranian fleet direct access to the open ocean. In conclusion, during this period the Iranians were making a conscious effort to increase their force posture on the Gulf and Indian Ocean. Most of the military construction was taking place in the south of the country, as there were plans to invest $30 billion in the provinces bordering the Gulf between 1975 and 1982.[56] The social effects of this development was seen with the construction at Bandar Abbas as the population of this city rose from 18,000 in 1960 to 200,000 in the early 1970s.[57]

The rapid pace and scale of the military acquisition process was justified by the regime in order for each service to undertake the military and political functions they were assigned. The air force was given the responsibility for defending the country's airspace which, as a result, gave it the opportunity to acquire high quality aircraft as well as a comprehensive air defense system. The navy, which had been given the mission of defending the Persian Gulf as well as projecting Iranian power into the sea-lanes of the Indian Ocean, needed both small maneuverable craft that could operate in shallow water as well as large ships for the open seas. The ground forces were given the assignment of defending the country's borders as well as contributing forces to intervene in the Gulf. Therefore, the ground forces were composed of three armored divisions, four infantry divisions, two infantry brigades, and one special forces brigade.[58]

American Business and Iranian Military Development

In looking at this vast armaments buildup it is important to analyze the role that American business played in implementing this policy. The results of the United States relationship with Iran was a windfall for Wall Street. For most of the 1970s, Iran was the largest recipient of American armaments in the third world. Between 1973-1978 Iranian military orders averaged $3.2 billion per year, representing on average 28 percent of all U.S. foreign military sales worldwide.[59]

In addition to just increasing sales, the Iranian arms program also accomplished the two-fold purpose of bailing out some major American defense contractors who were threatened with bankruptcy while subsidizing the Pentagon's own procurement policies. The most notable example of this was the Iranian government's relationship with the Grumman Corporation.

Grumman had been awarded a contract in 1969 to build a new, technically advanced fighter for the navy. The company had severe problems with cost overruns and it appeared that the plane's cost would be prohibitive for the navy, as the price was approaching $11 million per plane. Even before the plane was being mass produced, Grumman began looking for foreign buyers to help defray the research and development expense.[60]

As a result, it became the policy of Grumman to lobby the Shah into purchasing the F-14. The navy, seeking to defray the cost of the plane, also assisted in lobbying Iran and along with the Air Force, which was sponsoring the F-14's rival the McDonnell Douglas F-15, sent teams to Iran to insure this purchase.[61] The Shah ultimately agreed to purchase 80 F-14s along with Phoenix missiles.

However, even after an agreement was concluded to sell Iran the aircraft, Congress cut off a loan that the navy was extending to Grumman to finance the project. In order to insure the completion of this purchase the Iranian National Bank stepped in and loaned Grumman $75 million, followed by additional credits provided by other banks.[62] Thus Grumman was saved from possible bankruptcy and the navy was able to acquire the F-14 at a reasonable cost. The president of the Grumman Corporation, Joseph Gavin, stated in congressional testimony that the Iranian order reduced the cost of the aircraft. This made the company more competitive in other arms sales, as well as reduced the unit costs to the navy.[63]

This strategy of enticing the Iranians into purchasing weapons systems still in production was carried to new levels in the case of the F-18. The Pentagon had not made a decision on the F-18 and the contractors, Northrop and McDonnell Douglas, sought to get the Shah interested in purchasing the plane as a way of placing pressure on American policy makers to approve production. In addition to attempting to sell the F-18 to Iran, Northrop was successful in selling 140 of its Tiger fighters to the Shah. Iran was able to acquire a half-share of the Iran Aircraft Industries, as well as part of a telecommunications consortium.[64]

This practice was not without its critics, as it was argued that these aggressive marketing techniques were undermining the decision making process concerning weapons procurement in the United States. Among those articulating this viewpoint at congressional hearings regarding the sale of fighter aircraft to Iran was Senator Frank Church (D-Idaho) who stated:

> Investigations of my subcommittee have shown that the big arms corporations get out in that area of the world and start soliciting for the sale of their latest equipment long before the Federal government has decided to make that equipment available to the foreign government.[65]

While these two cases are significant, they represent just part of American businesses' stake in Iran. All the major aerospace companies, as well as other defense contractors, benefitted from the American relationship with Iran. The previously financially troubled Lockheed Corporation sold 64 Hercules transport planes as well as six Orion reconnaissance planes to

Iran. In addition, Lockheed also won a contract for an inventory system to keep track of Iran's military supplies. General Dynamics was able to sell Iran 160 F-16 fighters along with their accompanying missiles. The total cost of this package was $4 billion.[66]

When these sales are added to Iran's other purchases, one can observe that during the 1970s the Shah subsidized American defense contractors to the point of keeping major production lines, as well as many minor ones, working at full capacity. This presented a dilemma for some policy makers and military officials since the selling of first-rate American military equipment as well as the export of this technology could erode American advantages in weapons development. This placed American decision makers in a similar position to British military leaders in the Victorian era who, in allowing the British armament companies Armstrong and Vickers to export arms, were able to subsidize Britain's military buildup. At the same time this eroded Britain's technological lead in arms.[67]

However, in the opinion of most American decision makers this was more than compensated for by the revenue these sales generated and the jobs that they saved. American policy makers, particularly military officials, have always maintained that a vibrant aerospace industry is essential for national security.[68] Therefore, it is necessary to keep these production lines open and at full capacity in order to keep the potential for production in existence, as well as fostering technical innovation, which is the cornerstone of any armaments industry. In addition, these goals can also be extended in one form or another to other defense industries.

Nonmilitary Economic Incentives for the United States

In addition to the U.S. defense industry in general, other sectors of the American economy were hoping to benefit from the oil money that Iran was willing to spend on imported manufacturing goods and technology. In an effort to take advantage of this potentially lucrative market, many felt that the demand for American arms should be encouraged as this would act as a magnet for other industries to get involved. This concept was illustrated in a report to the Committee on Foreign Affairs in the U.S. House of Representatives:

> To abandon the military market in the Persian Gulf would lead to a reduction of U.S. participation in other markets as well. The finished benefits generated by arms sales cannot, therefore be added up in terms of arms sales alone, but extend to earnings gained from an entire range of nonmilitary sales and activities as well.[69]

In addition, the same report stated that for each $1 billion in military sales about 47,000 jobs are created.[70]

The American policy toward Iran as articulated by the Nixon and Ford administrations was supported by many prominent American corporations, in particular major defense contractors, electronic, and telecommunications companies. Among them were Bell Helicopter International, General Electric, Grumman Aerospace, International Telephone and Telegraph, Litton Industries, Lockheed, McDonnell Douglas, Northrop, Page Communications, Philco-Ford, Raytheon, Stanwick, Sylvania, and Westinghouse.[71]

At the time of the Nixon Doctrine, U.S. exports to Iran totaled $409.7 million in 1972 and it increased to $558.4 million in 1973. By 1975 total American investment in Iran was set at $1.2 billion with over 200 firms being represented in Iran. This economic activity was facilitated by the establishment of a trade development center in Tehran in 1973.[72]

With regard to specific sectors of the Iranian economy, the most important nonmilitary sector was oil. In the mid-1970s about 15 percent of total American oil imports came from Iran; the dollar value of this investment was estimated at being $900 million. Twenty-four American oil companies were in partnership with the National Iranian Oil Company in 11 concessions and 11 American oil companies held 40 percent of the international oil consortium. In addition, five American banks were associated with joint banking ventures in Iran. The American industrial presence in the country was also quite significant. There were 14 American firms engaged in mining, equipment sales, and mineral exploration and one of the most significant companies involved was the Anaconda Mining Company, which had a major project near Kerman. Anaconda had signed a 15-year agreement with Iran to provide technical assistance in the development of a copper smelter and refinery and it was expected that the number of Anaconda employees in Iran would eventually reach 100. Other major American corporations with interests in Iran included Union Carbide, ESB, General Motors, FMC, General Tire, B. F. Goodrich, Park Davis, Kimberly Clarke, and Westinghouse. In total 29 American telecommunications and electrical firms, and 31 engineering, architectural and planning organizations were involved in the Iranian market.[73]

The potential of the Iranian market was illustrated by the economic agreement signed in March 1975 that committed Iran to purchasing $15 billion in goods from the United States over a five-year period. This was to be distributed as $5 billion in normal trade that would rise 20 percent each year; $5 billion in armaments and related services and $7 billion on developmental projects that would include such items as nuclear power plants, water desalting installations, etc.[74]

This was viewed as an extremely significant economic agreement for the United States that could be built on in future years and would benefit both nations. The 1975 economic agreement was viewed as being a potential economic bonanza for the United States, while at the same time eventually allowing Iran to become a member of the club of industrialized nations.[75] Certain American officials were projecting that the dollar value of trade would go even higher, especially when factoring the total expenditures for military equipment. Indeed, it seemed to some, notably James Bill, that "this highly publicized agreement seemed to weld the two countries into one huge, commercial, binational conglomerate."[76]

These views of the importance of Iran, not only strategically, but from an economic perspective as well, were further illustrated by President Carter himself. In a letter to House Speaker Tip O'Neill he discusses the importance of Iran to the United States: "Our relationship with Iran is broad, it bolsters significant U.S. security interests and helps to assure the uninterrupted flow of oil to an energy short world. Our engagement in developing Iran's civilian economy is of daily importance to our own manufacturers and farmers."[77]

The pinnacle of American economic involvement in Iran occurred in 1978 for several reasons: American investments in Iran totaled more than $682 million; the number of Americans stationed in Iran was more than 50,000; the military purchases and commitments from American defense contractors totaled over $12 billion; and the United States nonmilitary imports to Iran totaled $12.7 billion. This made America the second largest supplier of nonmilitary goods to Iran.[78]

American banks were also heavily involved in Iran. It was estimated that by late 1978-1979, a dozen major American banks had made loans in Iran totaling $2.2 billion. This position was even more precarious when it is considered that most of these loans were either to the Iranian government directly, or to semigovernmental institutions, such as the Agriculture Development Bank of Iran and the Industrial Mining and Development Bank of Iran. It is maintained that most of these loans were very risky, as they either were not guaranteed or were backed only by the Iranian Central Bank. Some analysts argue that the decision by the Carter administration to freeze Iranian assets on November 14, 1979, in the aftermath of the embassy takeover, helped preserve the assets of American banks, as Iran could not default on loans.[79]

The interests in Iran were fueled by trends in the Iranian market that were touted by the American government. The U.S. Department of Commerce published a comprehensive survey of Iranian market conditions designed to assist American business. The major conclusions of this survey were: (1) it was estimated that the capital goods market was to grow around 17 percent per year with an estimated total of $13.4 billion by 1980; (2) Iran's domestic production of capital goods was expected to grow, reaching 30 percent of a total of around $4 billion by 1980; and (3) while the percentage of American capital goods was to decrease from 28 percent in 1975 to 18 percent in 1980, in absolute terms the American exports of capital goods to Iran was expected to increase to $1.66 billion. The highest increases were expected to come from the transportation and construction sectors, which combined were projected to be 60 percent of the total market.[80]

American Strategic Advantages

While these economic benefits were important, it should be noted that the United States did gain some geostrategic advantages from this relationship. The first of these was the building up of the Iranian military to preserve American interests in the region by being able to intervene in the Persian Gulf, as was illustrated in Oman. Second, this relationship had broader strategic implications for the United States, as America had access to listening posts within Iran in order to maintain surveillance on the Soviet Union. American policy makers viewed these installations as essential for verification purposes in any potential arms control agreement with the Soviet Union. The presence of these bases, in the view of American policy makers, was one of the primary reasons why the United States needed to defer to the Shah.[81] Therefore the Iranian relationship had broader implications for the United States. This was particularly a problem for the Carter administration, as anti-SALT treaty opponents charged that the Soviets were cheating on SALT I by encoding their missile technology. The administration was thus under pressure to redouble their verification efforts in order for SALT II to get Senate ratification.[82]

Iranian Foreign Relations

Iran served to safeguard American interests in the Middle East and the third world in general. The Shah provided covert assistance to groups seeking to destabilize the governments of Soviet allies in the region such as Iraq and Afghanistan, as well as providing military assistance to pro-Western governments, such as Oman and South Vietnam. Also, Iran was the principal oil supplier for like-minded states such as Israel, South Africa, and Rhodesia. He maintained good relations with Pakistan as well, in an effort to keep that country oriented towards the West. In addition, the Shah was associated with a group of conservative Middle Eastern and African states in their efforts to block the spread of Soviet influence. This association was known as the Safari Club and it included as it's principal members Iran, Saudi Arabia, Egypt (after Sadat's break with the Soviets), the Ivory Coast, and Senegal, with France also associated with this group.[83] In addition to providing oil to Israel, Iran was considered to be the Jewish state's only ally in the region.

An important component of American foreign policy in the Middle East and Indian Ocean region during the 1970s was the close relationship between the United States and Iran, Saudi Arabia, and Ethiopia. This relationship was known as the Red Sea Entente or the three kings principle. The common threads running through these relationships were: (1) support for these three states, which were pro-Western conservative monarchies; (2) security and other forms of assistance to enable these states to deal with internal and external threats; (3) cooperation in resisting the spread of Soviet influence in the region; and (4) coordination of policies of the states concerning security issues and other problems.[84]

The entente began to break down in 1975 with the collapse of the Ethiopian monarchy and the establishment of a military regime that espoused Marxist doctrines and became dependent upon the Soviet Union. As a result of these and other perceived Soviet gans in the area, the Saudis and the Iranians sought to take a much more interventionist stance in the region. They were especially active in assisting regional states who previously were aligned to the Soviets, to draw away from the USSR and move toward the Western bloc. Examples of this include Egypt, Sudan, and Somalia. The techniques used by both Iran and Saudi Arabia and facilitated by the United States included increased financial aid and American military assistance to these countries. With regard to Somalia, Iran and the Saudi Arabia supported Somali claims to the Ogaden region at Ethiopia's expense.[85]

The latter point caused some tension between these countries and the United States in the aftermath of the Somali invasion of Ogaden in 1977, resulting in the final break between Moscow and Mogadishu. The Soviets ended their military relationship with Somalia while they initiated a massive airlift to Ethiopia that included 17,000 Cuban troops. The United States, however, did not provide Somalia with any military goods and condemned the invasion. American military goods were provided by Egypt and Iran, which transferred excess arms from their inventories. It was said that American M-48 tanks sold to Iran were shipped to Somalia via Oman.[86] This led the Red Sea Entente countries of Saudi Arabia and Iran, as well as Somalia, to view Washington as having let them down and backing away from its commitments at the last moment. It has been argued that this affected the Shah's perception of the Carter administration and the potential impact this could have on his own position in Iran and the region.[87]

Another related point was the relationship that developed between Iran and Saudi Arabia. This became an important component in American foreign policy, as the Saudis were viewed as being important because of their anti-communism and their control of a good portion of the world's oil wealth. The close political relationship between these two countries and American support for each was known as the "twin pillar" policy, which was stated earlier.

While Iran and Saudi Arabia had good relations for most of the 1970s, American aid and support for Iran, as well as Iranian policy itself, caused problems with Saudi Arabia. The relationship between the two was somewhat strained in the early 1970s due to incidents like the Iranian takeover of three islands, Abu Musa, Greater Tumb and Lesser Tumb, at the mouth of the Persian Gulf. More importantly, the Arab states of the Persian Gulf were suspicious in general of Iran's growing military power, which they viewed as a potential threat to their sovereignty.[88] In addition, the two nations had disagreements over the price of oil, as the Saudis with their much smaller population and development needs, argued for a more stable price, while the Shah was a leading advocate of higher prices. The two countries had opposing interests within OPEC and were frequently on opposite sides of the price question. In 1975 Iran supported a price increase of 21 percent in the price of oil, while the Saudis were steadfast in maintaining a 10 percent price increase.[89]

However, from the mid-1970s onward, these fears subsided as Saudi Arabia and Iran came together on many diverse issues. They both cooperated in forming a united front against Baathist Iraq in the latter's attempt to gain port concessions from Kuwait. The Saudis also supported Iranian attempts to subvert the Iraqi government and force it to make concessions on the Shat-al Arab question. Both states opposed the radical forces present in the region such as the Popular Front for the Liberation of the Occupied Arab Gulf (PFLOAG), as well as the Marxist regime in South Yemen. In addition to combating left-wing states and movements, they also cooperated in providing support for the pro-Western Sultan Qabus of Oman in defeating the Dhofar rebels supported by South Yemen.[90] As indicated previously, the United States supported the creation of the Red Sea Entente to limit Soviet influence in the region by providing financial and military incentives to states to move closer to the pro-Western bloc.[91]

In the arena of political and military cooperation, both Iran and Saudi Arabia favored conservative, status quo, pro-Western governments and actively cooperated to promote their establishment, which complemented American interests very well. The Saudis, however, were less than enthusiastic with the Iranians becoming the hegemonic military power in the region. At the same time, Iran resented the Saudis being able to dominate the oil market.[92]

Iran and the Kurds

The Shah wanted to use the Kurds in an effort to destabilize the Iraqi regime and prevent Iraq from challenging Iran for regional hegemony, as well as redress certain disputed border areas. The Israelis also sought to keep the Iraqi regime off balance. Iraq was potentially the greatest adversary for Israel as it combined population, oil revenues, military strength, and a tightly controlled political and military apparatus. This had ramifications for the United States for many of the same reasons, as Iraq was one of the strongest Soviet allies in the region and the third world in general. In addition, the Baathist government in Iraq advocated socialism and principles of Arab nationalism that both directly and indirectly attacked American allies in the region such as Iran, Israel, and the conservative Arab monarchies.[93]

There were some reports that aid began as early as 1969 with an agreement between the United States and Kurdish leader Mustafa Barzani.[94] The relationship between the United States and the Kurds was concretely established by 1972. During the May 1972 visit by President Nixon to Tehran, Iran presented the possibility of joint cooperation in aiding the Kurds. The Shah viewed the Iraqi regime as a threat for various reasons.

First, numerous Iranian opposition groups were headquartered in Baghdad; after leaving Iran, the Ayatollah Khomeini had established himself in Iraq. Second, the government in Baghdad was also encouraging separatist movements among the Arab and Baluch populations of Iran.[95] Third, prior to the Tehran meeting between President Nixon and the Shah there had been severe tensions and military incidents along the Iranian-Iraqi frontier. After some period of study the United States agreed with the plan that would also involve the Israelis. The logistics of the military assistance provided was to purchase captured stocks of Soviet equipment from the Israelis and give these weapons to the Kurds. This was done in an effort to both hide the origins of these supplies as well as perhaps sow tensions within the Iraqi-Soviet relationship. This later point did not succeed, as it provided further evidence to the Iraqis that Iran and the United States were aligned against them.[96]

There are various reasons for the United States' justification of its support for the Kurdish rebellion: (1) to support Iran, which felt threatened by Iraq and as a quid pro quo for past cooperation; (2) to weaken the abilities of the Iraqi regime to spread its influence in the region and therefore, by association, limiting the spread of Soviet influence in the region; (3) to restrict the abilities of the Iraqis to aid revolutionary groups in the conservative Arab states of the Middle East; (4) to weaken Iraq so it could not challenge Iran in the Persian Gulf, while at the same time limiting its abilities to aid dissident Iranian groups; and (5) to impede Iraq militarily so it could not participate in the Arab-Israeli conflict, or oppose efforts by the United States to achieve a peace settlement.[97]

However, the primary motivation for Washington intervening in Iraq on the side of the Kurds was oil. The decision to aid the Kurds was made by the United States just two weeks after the Iraqi Petroleum Company was nationalized. In an effort to entice America into an aid relationship, in large part because he did not trust the Shah, Barzani promised to essentially turn over the oil fields to the Americans. He also indicated that an independent Kurdistan would be a friend to the United States in OPEC councils.[98]

While American intervention gave added impetus to the Kurdish independence movement, both Washington and Tehran had no intention of allowing the Kurds to emerge victorious. The Kurdish movement in Iraq represented a possible boomerang effect, because if it was successful in Iraq it could serve as a model for the Kurdish populations of Turkey and Iran. Rather than try to break up Iraq, the goal was to place pressure on Baghdad and encourage a coup to bring in a more amenable government.[99]

Iranian-Israeli Relations: Political, Economic, and Military

Iranian foreign policy complemented American interests with the tacit alliance that developed between Israel and Iran. This alliance was initiated in March of 1950 when the Iranian cabinet defacto recognized Israel, and was defended by Prime Minister Saed during the 18th session of the Iranian Senate.[100] The Iranian-Israeli relationship became significant for both countries and also to Washington for a variety of reasons. First was Iran's facilitation of the immigration of Iraqi Jews after the first Arab-Israeli war in 1948. Second, the two-way trade that was established once Israel became independent, which was mutually beneficial to both countries. The centerpiece of this trade was oil, although it involved other goods as well. Third, the strategic cooperation between the Israeli and Iranian militaries as well as the security services designed against anti-status quo Arab states such as Iraq and radical groups active in the Middle East. Fourth, a related point to both security and trade was the cooperation between the two countries in developing their respective military industries and infrastructure, as well as cooperation in training, and in particular Israeli economic assistance to Iran designed to help support the regime. Finally, the broader cooperation between the two countries that existed in supporting various conservative states and groups in the Middle East. This generally functioned as a complement to American policy in the region to one degree or another.

The Iranian-Israeli alliance, while being an open secret in Middle East politics, was carried out discreetly by both parties. The countries cooperated in security and economic relations and had a vested interest in assisting conservative, pro-Western forces in the Middle East. It can be pointed out that the Israeli-Iranian contacts go back to ancient times, as it was the Persian King Cyrus the Great that ended the Babylonian captivity of the Jews; since ancient times there has been a Jewish population in Iran. However, while Reza Shah in 1925 sought to ease discrimination of Iranian Jews unofficial discrimination persisted and became particularly acute during and in the immediate aftermath of World War II.[101]

In modern day politics, Iranian-Israeli links were established during the first Arab-Israeli War of 1948 when the Mossad established contacts to facilitate the evacuation of Iraqi Jews. Between October 1948 and mid-1949 the Israelis managed, through a number of means, to gain the tacit support of the Iranian prime minister and the imperial court to establish a network to allow Iraqi Jews to leave Iraq. During this period Iran came under pressure from Iraq to cease this assistance by, among other actions, sealing the border. The Iranians sought to resist these pressures for a time, but appeared to cave in during early 1949 as they sought to deport Iraqi Jews back to Iraq. The Israelis, however, persuaded the Iranians to change their minds on this issue.[102]

The second major impetus driving the Iranian-Israeli relationship was trade and specifically oil. By the late 1960s Iranian-Israeli trade amounted to $250 million annually and the most important component of this trade was oil. From Israeli independence until about 1957, Iran was not a major oil supplier for Israel. A credit agreement was concluded between Persian and Israeli banks to purchase Iranian oil in 1953, but because of Egypt's control over the Straits of Tiran, it could not be delivered. During this period Israel counted more on Venezuela, Romania, and the Soviet Union for its oil supplies. The Suez War caused these relationships to change. First, the Israelis were able to gain control of the Straits militarily, ending the Egyptian blockade. Second, the Soviets in the aftermath of the Suez War began to orient themselves more toward the Arabs and ceased supplying Israel with oil.[103] Therefore, Israel quickly became Iran's largest oil purchaser in the Middle East.

Iran's rationale for selling oil to Israel was twofold: the first reason was an economic incentive, as Iran needed markets for its oil and funds for its economic development; second, the Shah was aware of the special relationship that was developing between the United States and Israel. He felt providing oil to the Israelis would help his standing to receive economic and military aid from Washington.[104]

In addition, there was a strategic benefit not only for Iran and Israel but for the West in general. As a result of Israeli access to Iranian oil, Israel rapidly acquired a tanker fleet and also constructed a pipeline between Eilat via Beersheba to Haifa where oil was refined. This would allow an alternative route for oil to be transhipped to Europe without transiting the Suez Canal. This became significant with the closing of the Suez Canal as a result of the 1967 war. As a result of this conflict, Israel's Eilat to Ashkelon pipeline grabbed an increasing share of the oil shipping industry and by 1970 this pipeline carried 10 million tons of oil.[105] The Israelis came to rely very strongly on Iranian oil and this influenced the Israelis to be more accommodating toward the Egyptians in regards to returning the Sinai. In 1975 Israeli Prime Minister Rabin made a visit to Iran in order to receive the Shah's personal assurance that Iran would continue to supply oil to Israel.[106]

Another important bilateral component between Israel and Iran was in military cooperation. This assistance was very extensive and had several components. One aspect consisted of Mossad-CIA cooperation to create SAVAK, the Iranian secret police. In addition, the military and political leadership were very close at the highest levels, most senior Iranian officers had traveled to Israel for training, and every Israeli prime minister had traveled to Iran to meet with the Shah and other senior officials. These visits were kept very quiet and were done without fanfare. Diplomatic ties between the two countries were maintained, with the Iranian diplomatic delegation in Israel operating out of the Swiss embassy. In Tehran the Israeli delegation officially functioned as a trade mission having low-level diplomatic status. However, in reality, this trade mission functioned as an embassy in everything but name only. The Israeli representative enjoyed close access to high-level Iranian officials despite not having the title of ambassador.

In practical military matters Iran-Israeli relations were also close. Both countries were cooperating with each other to develop high technology industries with military applications and the Iranians sought to learn from Israeli expertise. An example of this was the copying by Iran of Israeli modifications on the F-4 Phantom, including the installation of machine guns to aid in dogfighting and the modification of the exhaust system to make the plane less susceptible to heat-seeking missiles.[107]

It was the Shah's hope that military procurement and modernization could be used to assist the country's industrialization in general. This strategy was illustrated by a comprehensive military cooperation agreement concluded between the Shah and Shimon Peres in 1977. This agreement was estimated as a $1-billion oil-for-arms agreement which, among other projects, covered the development of a nuclear-capable missile system. It was hoped by the Shah that these types of projects would allow a diversification of Iran's industrial base using Israeli technical expertise that would be easy to maintain and cost effective. It was also a goal of the Shah to develop an indigenous arms capability to decrease dependency on foreign sources and reduce Iran's dependency on the American supply link.[108]

The missile project required a vast amount of development. The missiles were to be shipped to Sirjan, in central Iran, where a runway capable of handling 747 jets was scheduled to be constructed. In addition, Iran was to be used as a testing site, as one was to be constructed near Rafsanjan. From this area the missile could be test-fired 300 miles either north into the Lut Desert or south into the Gulf of Oman. A side benefit of this project from the Iranian perspective was to increase development in central Iran. An example of this was the 3,000 new housing units that were constructed by 1979 to accommodate the Iranian military personnel working on the project. This was to be an arms-for-oil swap, with the first payment occurring in 1978 when Iran sent $260 million worth of oil to Israel.[109]

Another example of this close military cooperation was the cooperation in producing artillery guns. This was to involve a joint project in Iran where a factory would be set up to produce Israeli-designed artillery guns. A site was selected near Isfahan for the factory and the Iranians were in the process of making a deal with Pakistan to purchase the guns that would have gotten Iran involved in the export market in a significant way. However, the Iranian revolution ended this project.[110]

In addition to military-industrial projects, the Israelis provided assistance in rural and agricultural development. This was illustrated by enormous Israeli cooperation in the digging of wells and irrigation channels. The Israeli government corporation Tahal (Water Planning) received a contract from the Iranian government in 1962 to develop the Ghazvin Plain in the aftermath of an earthquake. Between 1966 and 1971 the amount of irrigated land in the Ghazvin Plain increased from 2,600 hectares to 23,000 hectares; the number of wells increased from 95 to 272; field crops increased from 5,500 hectares to 20,600 hectares and deciduous irrigated fruit trees from 910 hectares to 1,630 hectares. In addition, the yield in tons per hectare increased in wheat, sugar beets, and tomatoes. The average income per family by 1975 increased to about $620 for a family of six.[111]

Joint planning between the two countries' militaries were also significant. Another part of the 1977 agreement concluded by Shimon Peres and the Shah involved the installation of Israeli-manufactured electronic countermeasures (ECM) on Iranian aircraft to better protect them from antiaircraft missiles. In order to implement this program, Iranian Air Force General Gholam Reza Rab'ii visited Israel to consult with the Israeli Aircraft Industry Company. Similar planning was also being made between the navies of the two countries that would be comprehensive in scope. This involved discussions with Iranian Naval Commander Admiral K. M. Habibollahi. Both nations had strategic goals for naval cooperation. From Iran's perspective her interest in Israeli cooperation was to better protect the shipping lanes of the Persian Gulf, Gulf of Oman, as well as the Indian Ocean from Iraqi and Indian threats. From the Israeli perspective she was interested in obtaining Iranian financing for military projects, notably the purchasing of three British-made Vickers-class submarines that would potentially extend the range of the Flower missile.[112]

Iranian-Israeli Foreign Policy Cooperation

The foundations of the Israeli-Iranian strategic alliance was based on mutual needs and driven by an emphasis on the maintenance of a pro-Western status quo region. This included attempting to destabilize those states that were pro-Soviet and was accomplished with Iraq by cooperating in aiding the Kurds. It was thought that this would enhance the security of both Israel and Iran, as well as complement American foreign policy. Initially, at the establishment of Israeli-Iranian relations, a major consideration from the Iranian perspective was to counterbalance the Egyptian alliance with the Soviets in the region.[113] Both states found themselves in a similar position in the 1950s and 1960s as they feared the growth of Arab nationalism and isolation within the region. Iran felt caught between a potential hostile Soviet Union to the north and the uncertainty that Arab nationalism posed to the south and west. Israel thought itself in a similar position, which necessitated both states reaching out in an attempt to break this perceived encirclement.[114]

This alliance cooperated in assisting antiradical forces in the region as illustrated by two major episodes that occurred in Yemen and with the Kurds of Iraq. In Yemen, Iran assumed a prominent role cooperating with both the Saudis and Israelis in assisting the royalist forces. A close relationship was established between SAVAK and the Saudi intelligence services to coordinate aid to the royalists, while SAVAK agents were dispatched to northern Yemen to establish liaison with Imam al-Badr and to assure him of support in the form of military hardware and training. The Iranians flew in equipment on transports twice a week from Tehran to Taif where it was then transported on trucks into Yemen. The Israelis became involved later when additional equipment was needed. The Israelis flew captured Soviet equipment to Tehran where it was repaired and renumbered and then sent to Yemen. On at least two occasions Israeli aid was more direct, as Israeli planes, with Iranian markings, overflew Saudi Arabia in order to drop supplies to the royalists.[115] The purpose of such cooperation was to contain the spread of Arab nationalism and also, more concretely, tie down Egyptian forces in the Arabian Peninsula, which payed military dividends for Israel in the 1967 war. The aid to the Kurds was done for the same reasons. Israeli and Iranian aid to the Kurds, which was initiated as early as 1961, served to distract and keep the Iraqis tied down. This resulted in a drain in resources, as it was estimated that 80 percent of the Iraqi military was occupied in fighting the Kurds and suffering significant loses.[116]

In conclusion, from the Shah's point of view the benefits for the Iranian alliance with Israel outweighed the risks. A fundamental strategic gain of the alliance was to take pressure off Iran, which would be accomplished by Israel serving as a strategic decoy to the Arab states. The close political, military, and economic relationship, as well as the strategic cooperation between the two countries, would potentially give the impression that should an Arab state attack Iran, the Israelis might in turn attack them.[117]

Iran and Nuclear Power

Iran planned to achieve a generating capacity of 23,000 MWe by 1990 at a total cost of $27.6 billion. It was argued that this was an enormous amount of electric power: half of the American capacity as of 1974, over four times that of Great Britain, five times that of the Federal Republic of Germany, and almost eight times that of French capability as of 1974.[118] U.S. companies were significant in assisting the Shah in setting up a nuclear industry. The Shah was interested in involving American companies as the United States had the reputation of ensuring fuel enrichment and reprocessing arrangements. The two companies most involved in this Iranian effort were Westinghouse and General Electric, two major defense contractors.[119]

While the basic technology was to be obtained from the United States, Iran also had to consider the purchase of fuel for these reactors. Similar to other areas in which Iran sought to invest money in foreign-owned companies such as Krupp in Germany, the government of Iran concluded an agreement to lend the French Atomic Authority $1 billion for 15 years in order to purchase a 10 percent stake in a multinational enrichment plant being built at Tricastin. In was stated in the press that the Iranian share in the Tricastin plant would later rise to 15 percent. The Iranians also sought to procure nuclear fuel from America. Iran concluded two contracts with the United States to fuel two 1,200 MWe light water reactors as well as a provisional agreement to provide fuel for six more reactors totaling 8,000 MWe.[120]

The Iranian nuclear industry was projected to supply 52 percent of the country's energy needs by 1990, at a cost of $126 billion by 1994. By 1976 Iran began a program to build four nuclear reactors with a capacity of 4,200 megawatts.[121] Arguments for this emphasis on nuclear power were several. These nuclear plants had a long time frame and they would not be on-line until the 1980s. It was predicted that at this time, Iranian oil supplies and corresponding revenue would start to diminish. In addition, given other sectors of economic development at this time there would be a need for new sources of energy.[122]

A serious argument, however, can be raised concerning the question of nuclear proliferation. Critics charged that the investment in nuclear power was premature and wasteful as the electrical consumption of the nation in 1977 totaled only 14,000 megawatts. In addition, there was the problem of not having trained personnel to operate this equipment.[123]

There were fears that the Shah was actually seeking to develop nuclear weapons. In answering a question of whether or when Iran would acquire nuclear weapons, the Shah stated, "Without a doubt, and sooner than one would think." A statement was issued later denying the meaning of these comments and stating that Iran would not acquire nuclear weapons if other, smaller nations did not do so.[124] Further evidence of this is the scale of the nuclear program as well as the Iranian attempt to diversify nuclear fuel sources. To provide the hoped for goal of 34,000 megawatts by 1995, Iran would need about 25 nuclear reactors. The Iranians approached the French Atomic Authority to help locate indigenous sources of uranium, as well as expressed interest in purchasing uranium from Australia.[125]

This would complement the Shah's goals of increasing Iranian power in the international system. The arguments for turning Iran into a nuclear power from a military economic standpoint revolved around cost and opportunity. First, it would be cheaper to upgrade the military and increase power capabilities by focusing on nuclear forces and cutting conventional forces. Second, the development of a civilian nuclear power industry would provide the opportunity, at reduced costs, to develop nuclear weapons.[126]

The limitations for acquiring nuclear weapons, however, seemed to outweigh any possible benefits. First, in order for Iran to pursue its legitimate and more easily obtainable security considerations specifically, ensuring the control of oil shipping lanes as well as regional security, nuclear weapons would not be effective. Second, Iran was linked by treaty obligations with the United States that placed it under the American nuclear umbrella; if Iran acquired nuclear weapons of its own that arrangement could change. In addition, some maintained that the presence of an Iranian nuclear force could serve to invite a preemptive nuclear strike. At the very least Soviet-Iranian relations, which were improving since the mid 1960s, would suffer. Finally, the acquisition of nuclear weapons by Iran would give further impetus to other nations in the region to acquire them. This would not only extend to India and Iraq, but to less powerful states like Saudi Arabia. The acquisition of nuclear weapons might be more enticing to a nation like Saudi Arabia with its armed forces limitations, enabling it to compare more favorably with a nation like Iran militarily. Another ramification would be Iran losing its military hegemony within the region, both quantitatively and qualitatively. This would seriously downgrade Iranian strategic capabilities acquired until that point.[127]

Weaknesses of American Intelligence Gathering in Iran

A significant failure in the American-Iranian relationship was the lack of solid intelligence being provided on Iran to U.S. policy makers. In the aftermath of the Iranian revolution, a report of the intelligence procedures and interpretations on Iran was compiled by the House of Representatives Select Committee on Intelligence. The conclusion of this staff report was that there was a failure by both intelligence professionals and policy makers and that the methods of intelligence gathering were weak. The religious opposition was underestimated as well as the degree and scope of opposition to the regime. In addition, the report found that policy makers confidence in the Shah served to skew intelligence on Iran. As Iran became more important to the United States there was no incentive for analysts to challenge conventional wisdom. In addition, the Shah's suspicion of plots against him led the CIA and State Department to ignore opposition figures as well as scale back their intelligence reporting within Iran. The conclusion of the report was that within the intelligence community, the political environment established by the American-Iranian relationship lead to an acceptance of the Shah's position in Iran and of the importance of Iran in the region. This led to the lack of candid reporting and the inattention to alternative hypotheses concerning the monarchy.[128]

Repercussions on the Iranian Economy

In the late 1960s and early 1970s it seemed that Iran was experiencing a great deal of economic growth due in large part to the increase in the price of oil. The 10 year period prior to the revolution illustrated a period of sharp economic growth, as well as a period of economic downturn that contributed to the revolution.

In analyzing the economic performance of Iran from 1968-1978, analysts have divided this 10-year span into two distinct periods. The years between 1968-1972 saw the country's GDP grow 9.86 percent, which slightly exceeded the goals of the Fourth Development Plan. As a result of the oil price increases economic growth rates rose spectacularly. In 1973 real economic growth rose 24 percent and 56.73 percent in 1974. The growth level tailed off from 1975 to 1977 as a result of stabilizing oil prices and reduced production to 3.81 percent. On the surface, the economic growth rates just prior to the revolution were impressive; during the Fifth Development Plan it reached 18.6 percent. During the 10-year period from 1968-1978 Iran's GNP increased from $8.3 billion to exceed $30 billion in 1977. Per capita income increased in the country from $306 to $880, which resulted in a 186 percent increase in real purchasing power.[129]

During the Fourth Development Plan (1968-1972) both the industry and service sectors grew at the rates of 14 percent and 14.2 percent respectively. The agricultural sector, where the majority of the population was situated, grew at only 3.9 percent. The manufacturing sector, while growing, was oriented more toward the production of consumer goods and relied on imports in order to sustain production. In addition, the type of industries that were developed increased dependency on foreign technology, skilled manpower, and capital goods. The development of heavy industry, which was fueled by oil, happened rapidly and without consideration for efficiency. The implications of this was rapid industrialization and development of infrastructure coupled with food imports and government subsidized food prices that were at the expense of agriculture. This fueled the migration to the cities and turned the society into a consumption oriented, largely urban society with balance of payment deficits.[130]

Despite the growth of the Iranian economy during the 1970s, oil remained the most significant sector. Oil prices slumped in 1975, which coupled with the worldwide recession resulted in non-oil GDP growth averaging 5.8 percent during 1976-1977.[131] Prior to the 1973-1974 oil price increases, oil made up 55 percent of government revenues and 76 percent of foreign exchange receipts in 1972-1973. After the price increases, oil revenues provided 84 percent of government revenue and 80 percent of foreign exchange earnings. The value of oil to the Iranian economy increased from $4 billion in 1973 to $18 billion in 1974. The raising of oil revenues allowed the Iranian government to embark on various economic strategies. First, oil revenues financed the purchase of imports. Second, they provided a means of savings that made heavy taxation unnecessary. Third, Iran sought to use oil revenues to stimulate private investment as the government sought to encourage private industry through government spending and the extension of credits.[132]

A repercussion of the rise in oil revenues was inflation. The former Prime Minister Amuzegar has established six reasons why inflation occurred after 1973: (1) the burst of expenditures in both the public and private sectors; (2) increased credit by the banking system caused private liquidity to grow an average of 42 percent a year; (3) bottlenecks increased, which made barriers against further importation of goods and equipment; (4) domestic agricultural production could not keep up with rising demands; (5) the rapid development of technologically advanced industries added to the shortage of skilled manpower in the country; and (6) the sharp rise in the prices of raw materials caused inflation, which increased prices in general.[133]

A significant problem that Iran experienced prior to the revolution was unemployment. While the increase in oil revenues spurred a certain amount of economic development and, more important, created the expectation of economic development, the decline in oil revenues impacted negatively on employment. This decline forced the government to put off development projects that had drawn semi and unskilled workers into the cities from rural areas. In addition, there was a shortage of skilled workers and by 1978 it was estimated that 7 to 8 percent of the labor force was unemployed. Unofficial estimates placed this figure at between 15 percent and 20 percent.[134]

Another factor that impacted negatively on Iran's economic situation, specifically employment, during this period was defense expenditures. During the Shah's reign the defense budget never dropped below 23 percent of the budget. The military was also a big employer in the country. During the 10 years prior to the revolution, 1968-1978, the Iranian military employed 3.2 percent on average of the labor force. By 1978 the military employed more than 500,000 and represented 4.7 percent of the country's labor force. More significantly it employed 17.2 percent of those employed outside of the agricultural sector of the economy.[135]

The oil price rise in 1973 enabled the Shah to realize his goal of modernizing the economy and the style and implementation of this program in many cases was wasteful and inefficient. The Shah was motivated by two factors. First, oil exports were projected to peak by the early 1980s, therefore it was imperative for the country to develop an industrial base in order to generate both domestic growth and foreign exchange. Second, the Shah wanted to make certain that Iran was firmly on course to becoming a mid-level industrial power prior to his relinquishing power to his son.[135]

Despite the increasing oil revenues, the attempt to develop rapidly led to major structural problems, with the transportation and communications systems overburdened. While Iran was an exporter of oil during 1977, Tehran experienced blackouts for up to six hours a day. These factors had a negative impact on industrial production and Iran actually experienced an industrial decline in 1977-1978 from 1975-1976. Aluminum production was down 50 percent, textiles 60 percent, brick-making 50 percent, automobiles and tractors 30 percent. In addition, by late 1977 there was an acute housing shortage, particularly in Tehran, which helped to fuel unrest against the regime.[136] The years 1977-1978 saw Iran's GNP per capita fall after steady rises during the 1970s. This contributed to dissatisfaction within society against the monarchy.

Another economic problem was the effect of military modernization. This was a fundamental tenet of the Shah's development program, as he sought to use the military to spur economic development. The military was active in promoting the industrializing of the Iranian economy.[137]

The military was also part of the process of developing infrastructure. New communities, roads, water supplies, ports, and housing and utilities, while developed for military use, would also provide a benefit to the civilian economy. An example of this was the construction of the Khatami Air Base outside of Isfahan. The construction of the base involved the building of roads, water and electricity lines, development of transportation, an infusion of money into the local economy, which provided employment, and the training of local teachers at the base schools.[138]

Although the excessive spending on the military did not cause the revolution, it contributed to severe economic and social dislocation. At least one-fourth of the official Iranian budget, the actual figure was probably higher, went to the military. If this money had been channeled in ways to assist the population in social services and meaningful employment opportunities this could have alleviated some of the pent up tensions toward the regime. The heightened expectations that the oil revenues brought coupled with the lack of benefits spread out over the population, caused resentment and frustration from those segments of the population that the monarchy traditionally relied on for support, such as the peasantry, rural migrants, and the urban lower middle classes.[139]

The arms program was an example of the Shah's development program in general. The military development was in response to minimal threats. American intelligence estimates as early as 1970, before major arms sales were initiated, concluded that there was no sufficient external threat to Iran to justify the acquisition of sophisticated military equipment. There were two major economic reasons that also impacted on Iranian security. First, Iran did not have the capability to produce sophisticated weaponry. Second, it was estimated that the Iran could not finance both major weapons purchases and the level of economic development the Shah felt desirable.[140]

The military acquisitions involved the most sophisticated and expensive technology as well as foreign expertise. It appeared to average Iranians that the Shah was selling the country to foreigners and this heightened resentment against the regime and the United States, which was identified as the main supporter of the monarchy.

Furthermore, these military expenditures, it can be argued, were not necessary. This is particularly true when examining the possible threats that Iran could conceivably face in the region. Iran could not hope to match the Soviet Union in military capabilities. However, relations with the Soviet Union, as previously stated, had been improving steadily since the mid-1960s. Iran also had fairly good relations with the Arab states of the Arabian Peninsula. Despite some tensions with Saudi Arabia in the early 1970s, there was a good deal of strategic cooperation. Iran was linked by treaty obligations to Turkey and Pakistan through CENTO, and as previously noted, enjoyed a quiet but very close political, economic, and strategic relationship with Israel. Therefore, the only state that could pose a potential threat to Iran was Iraq. In the early 1970s this threat was apparent as the two states contested for regional power. They engaged in border skirmishes as well as aided each other's dissidents.

However, in measuring military strength and expenditures in this period Iran was able to maintain superiority throughout the 1970s. This is particularly true when looking at the figures concerning military expenditures as a whole, as well as total number of troops in the armed forces. In examining military expenditures as a percentage of GNP, as well as changes in military expenditures, the statistics can be divided into two periods. The period encompassing the years 1970-1974 illustrates Iraq as spending a greater percentage of its GNP on the military as well as greater changes in the percentages of military expenditures from year to year. This is reflected in table 3.3 and graph 3.3 which illustrate Iranian military expenditures as a percentage of GNP compared to the Middle East region and Iraq. A good portion of the expenditures during this period were being devoted to combating the Kurds who were being supported by Iran, Israel, and the United States.

The 1975 Algiers Agreement was a watershed period in Iranian-Iraqi relations. The border dispute was settled on Iranian terms and a normalization of relations was established in return for Iran ending its support for the Kurds. The second period illustrated by the statistics covers the years 1975-1978. This illustrates Iran spending a greater percentage of its GNP on military expenditures, as well as higher percentage changes in military expenditures during this period. This despite the fact that relations with Iraq were improving and there were no other discernable threats.

Table 3.3. Military Expenditures As a Percentage of GNP

Years	Middle East	Iraq	Iran
1970	10.3	12.9	7.8
1971	10.1	12.3	8.4
1972	10.1	11.5	8.5
1973	11.9	13.6	8.3
1974	11.9	15.7	11.8
1975	15.1	11.8	14.3
1976	14.5	11.0	13.5
1977	12.7	10.7	11.6
1978	13.5	8.8	14.6

Source: U.S. Arms Control and Disarmament Agency. *World Military Expenditures and Arms Transfers, 1970-1979* (Washington, D.C.: U.S. Government Printing Office,, 1982), 45, 62.

Graph 3.3. Military Expenditures
As a Percentage of GNP

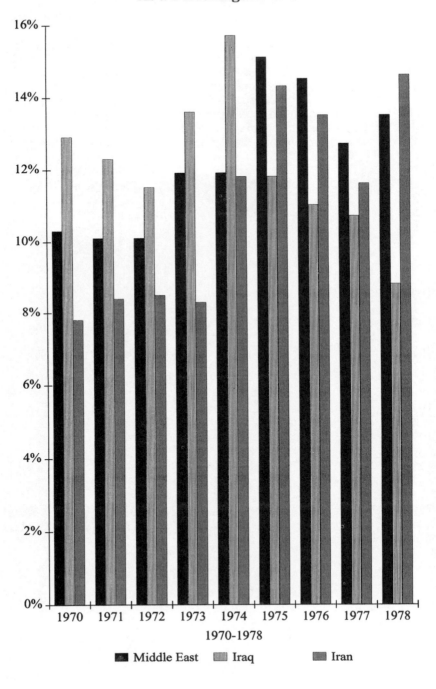

1970-1978

■ Middle East   ▥ Iraq   ▦ Iran

Conclusions

The United States and Iran

During the 1970s there were three conditions that shaped the alliance between the United States and Iran. These were: (1) American geostrategic interests; (2) reverse leverage; and (3) the economic benefits that the alliance brought for the United States.

The motivations for the United States to become involved in Iran resulted from largely geostrategic interests. During W.W.II the Americans sought to become involved in Iran in order to preserve the allied supply lines to the Soviet Union. In addition, the Americans wanted to use their presence in the region to protect their economic interests in Saudi Arabia, while at the same time gain access to Iranian oil.[141]

After the war the American interests became geared toward the elimination of Soviet influence in the country. The 1953 coup, which placed the monarchy back in power, began in earnest the relationship between the United States and the Shah, was done in order to forestall what American decision makers felt would have been a possible communist coup. Also, the United States, as a result of the intervention, was allowed by Britain to acquire a share of the Iranian oil market that policy makers felt was a significant geostrategic interests.[142]

Similarly, the main reason for the Nixon Doctrine and the subsequent agreement between President Nixon and the Shah was the result of a congruence of strategic interests between the two countries. It was at this time that the United States desired to limit its security commitments to the third world, while Iran was seeking to broaden its security responsibilities in the region.

Iran's new agenda was due to several factors. First, it had lost confidence in American support through treaty obligations as a direct result of the 1971 India-Pakistan War, which resulted in Pakistan's partition. This conflict also reinforced the Shah's desire to build up his own military forces to assert Iranian power. Second, as a result of the Vietnam War, a form of isolationism developed in America during the 1970s that made it politically difficult for American officials to expand as well as maintain existing military commitments. Therefore, the United States was unable to fulfill its strategic role in the Middle East at a time when Iran was willing to expand its military capabilities. Consequently, the primary motivation for the United States to cease restraining arms transfers and agree to sell Iran the arms it wanted was one of mutually shared interests.[143]

While the regional goals of the United States and Iran were similar, this relationship was also influenced by more broader strategic goals. It was the American intention not to allow detente with the Soviet Union to compromise United States interests and commitments in the third world. As a result, the American commitment to Iran was in part driven by the broader context of American-Soviet relations. This would seem to indicate why the United States concurred with the Shah in the perception that Iranian defense needs should be based on Soviet capabilities.[144]

Because of these regional, and more broadly, geostrategic considerations, the Shah was able to acquire a good deal of leverage in his relationship with the United States. This was institutionalized by the Nixon Doctrine, and especially by the 1972 agreement that served to permanently link American interests in the region with the Shah. Thus the relationship between the United States and Iran became a client-centric one in which the highly valued geostrategic client state was able to gain control of this particular alliance.[145]

The ability of Iran to purchase vast quantities of American military equipment at will helped to further this situation. American business interests were exposed to the potential for enormous profits that were to be made in the selling of armaments to Iran. In addition to private sector interests, various elements of the American bureaucracy also became involved in promoting, or at least not discouraging, arms sales to Iran. The worsening balance of trade that the United States was facing promoted the Treasury and Commerce Departments to look with favor on the recycling of petrodollars back to the United States in the form of arms sales. In addition, segments of the American foreign policy and military bureaucracies felt that it was important to maintain this relationship out of policy convictions, or personal, career-oriented goals. It was even felt by some within the military that Iran's military buildup could bring direct military benefits to the United States by enabling American military forces to have access to strategic bases that would be maintained by Iran.[146]

Therefore, it seems that although the original decision to give Iran wide access to American arms was done out of strategic rationale, it ultimately led to the United States losing control over the alliance. The Shah was able to use this to further reinforce the belief that his position was essential in order for the United States to maintain it's influence in the region. In this way the arms sales were able to serve the double purpose of establishing a constituency base of support within the United States, as well as reinforcing the already existing beliefs of American decision makers of the importance of Iran, and specifically the Shah himself, in their strategic calculations.

This was illustrated by observing the Carter administration's attitude toward arms sales to Iran. Although President Carter had campaigned on a platform to reduce arms transfers, by the time he entered office American security interests in the Middle East had become so associated with the Shah that this dependency could not be lessened.[147] In addition, it should be noted that arms sales actually increased during 1977, as almost $6 billion in agreements were concluded during that year.[148]

Furthermore, these agreements included the most sophisticated armaments in the American arsenal, such as AWACS aircraft and the F-16. Also, President Carter expressed his willingness to sell nuclear power plants to Iran. In agreeing to these sales the President reaffirmed the importance of Iran to the stability of the Persian Gulf and the preservation of American interests, as well as its value as a listening post enabling the United States to monitor the Soviet Union.[149]

In conclusion, the one major weakness of this relationship for Washington was that it allowed the focus of the alliance to shift from an emphasis on American strategic interests to the arms sales themselves. As a result, the arms sales ultimately compromised the strategic goals they were designed to maintain.

The Effect of the Alliance on Iran

Another repercussion of these arm sales were their effect on the internal situation in Iran, which included: the draining of a large share of the national budget; the volume and sophistication of the arms transfers were such that the Iranian military could not operate at peak efficiency; an extensive arms program was unnecessary given the regional situation; the vast military development detracted from the country's internal efforts to develop industry; and the arms sales served to reinforce the Shah's already large reliance on military support as opposed to attempting to broaden his base of support in society as a whole.

The first condition that these arms transfers exacerbated was the growth of military spending in Iran's national budget. It is estimated that prior to 1978 about one-fourth of the Iranian budget was devoted to military expenditures. There were also indications that additional resources that were spent on civilian projects really were military oriented. An example of this were funds for public housing. It is estimated that 70 percent of these funds actually went for military construction. The characteristics of Iran's procurement of arms reflected the goals of the regime, which were: the rapid creation of an industrial base to earn foreign exchange once oil exports peaked; and the development of industry to insure a more stable environment to facilitate the succession of the monarchy.[150]

A follow-up component to this was that while the vast spending on armaments weakened the country economically, it helped to create pockets of very capital-intensive industries in a nation that for the most part still possessed a basically traditional economy and infrastructure. Examples of this include enterprises such as Bell Helicopter's plant in Isfahan and Westinghouse's and Hughes Aircraft's partnership with the Iran Electronics Industry to construct a missile repair and assembly plant in Shiraz. While these ventures would introduce high technology and some skilled employment, critics charged that these projects were taking up too many resources at the expense of broadly based, labor-intensive enterprises. This resulted in many Iranians viewing these military industries as being foreign dominated and contributing little to the internal economic and social development of the country.[151]

The third glaring defect of this arms relationship for Iran was manifested in the Iranian military itself. As a result of the rapid rate of arms acquisition, along with their increasing technological sophistication, the

Iranian military experienced problems with absorbing these arms, causing severe problems in both training and maintenance. A prime example of this was the conditions that existed in the Iranian air force. The air force was the Shah's favorite service and he paid special attention to procuring the most technically advanced equipment for it. In rapid succession he purchased the F-4, F-5, and F-14 aircrafts. He also ordered the F-16 and was interested in purchasing the F-18, as well as AWACS aircraft. Because of this rapid procurement, the best pilots and ground crews were constantly shifted to higher series of aircraft and only few personnel were ever able to master the technology needed to operate one series of aircraft efficiently and effectively.[152]

Fourth, the American arms sales to Iran were unnecessary given the regional situation. One of the justifications used to support this program by both American officials and the Shah was that it was necessary to contain Soviet expansion in Southwest Asia and the Arabian Peninsula. Historically, Russian-Iranian relations were not good, the Russians having long sought to turn northern Iran into a protectorate. Relations were particularly bad from 1945 to 1961 as the Soviet Union had supported the separatist movements in Azerbaijan and Kurdistan after World War II. After 1962, however, relations began to improve as the Shah announced that he would not permit American bases on Iranian soil. By the late 1960s high-level visits were exchanged and substantial economic agreements were concluded. The Soviets participated in developing numerous large economic projects in Iran, such as the creation of an indigenous steel industry. In addition, the Shah sold large quantities of natural gas to the Soviet Union as well as purchased small amounts of military equipment.[153] It would seem that the Soviets viewed the Iranian monarchy favorably as providing stability on their southern border and as a result of the 1975 Algiers Accord relations with Soviet ally Iraq were also stable. Therefore, the large quantity of arms acquired by Iran during this period were unjustified.

The last major weakness of the arms sales program was that it contributed to the regime's strategy of isolating the military from the rest of society. Once officers left the service they usually received generous pensions and were given jobs in other parts of the government apparatus, such as seats on the board of state companies or quasi-military positions in SAVAK or the Imperial Inspectorate. Under the Shah the military in Iran was treated as a privileged class.[154]

The military enjoyed these benefits as long as they held favor in the court and military officers, with a few exceptions, were primarily loyal to the Shah rather than the nation.[155] This caused a dual dependence to develop; the military was dependent on the monarch and could not exist as a separate institution detached from the monarchy. Therefore, the military could not exert any influence during the revolution to restore the status quo and preserve some form of American interest in the country. This had been a goal of the United States as it was thought the military could serve as a pro-Western force despite a change of government.

The military was dependent on the Shah. The arms program was a primary component of this dependency as it gave them status, power, and resources that in turn were channeled in ways to support the regime. The emphasis on the military also enhanced the Shah's dependency on this institution, which contributed to his failure to build significant support among other groups in society likely to support his goals, such as the new middle class and state bureaucrats. Thus during the revolution his overemphasis on the military left him isolated and vulnerable.

There was a concern among certain analysts that American policy in Iran was contributing to the postponement of fundamental social changes in that country. This allowed power to be concentrated in the narrow circle of the Shah and his supporters.[156]

Critics charged that American support for Iran was a holdover from the Cold War era. This support also held the danger of becoming a self-fulfilling prophecy that could cause Iraq to further view Iran as a threat and develop their military capabilities accordingly. Therefore the building up of the Iranian military had the potential of leading to the destablization of the region by promoting regional arms races.[157]

American arms transfers to Iran also had the potential to increase the level of violence should hostilities occur as a result of the technological sophistication of the weaponry involved. The level of military involvement between the United States and Iran increased the chances of America being drawn into a conflict, thus widening it. While this was a potential threat, it can be argued that the arms sales program did contribute to a destabilization of oil prices as the Shah sought to pay for these arms, as well as leading to the crash of the Iranian modernization program in general.[158]

Notes

1. Charles G. MacDonald, "U.S. Policy and Gulf Security," in *Gulf Security into the 1980s*, Robert G. Darius et al eds. (Stanford, Calif.: Hoover Institution Press, 1984), 99.

2. National Security Archive, "Survey of U.S.-Iranian Relations 1941-1979: The Evolution of the U.S.-Iranian Relationship," in *The Making of U.S. Policy, Iran: 1977-1980*, January 29, 1980, Document no. 03556, (Washington, D.C.: National Security Archive, 1989), 47.

3. Michael T. Klare, *American Arms Supermarket* (Austin, Tex.: University of Texas Press, 1984), 40.

4. Mark Hulbert, *Interlock* (New York: Richardson and Snyder, 1982), 76-81. This factor is discussed later in the chapter in the section labeled "Nonmilitary Economic Incentives for the U.S."

5. Hulbert, *Interlock*, 73-74.

6. Bernard Gwertzman, "It Was Like Coming Home Again," *New York Times*, 29 July 1973, 5(IV).

7. Hossein Amirsadeghi, *Twentieth-Century Iran* (London: Heineman, 1977), 212.

8. Amirsadeghi, *Twenthieth-Century Iran*, 126.

9. Fred Halliday, *Iran: Dictatorship and Development* (New York: Penguin Books, 1979), 95-96.

10. Barry Rubin, *Paved with Good Intentions* (New York: Penguin Books, 1980), 158.

11. Klare, *American Arms Supemarket*, 35.

12. Klare, *American Arms Supermarket*, 35.

13. Alexander L. George, "The Basic Principles Agreement of 1972: Origins and Expectations," in *Managing the U.S.-Soviet Rivalry: Problems of Crisis Prevention*, Alexander L. George ed. (Boulder, Colo.: Westview Press, 1983), 107-18. Quoted in Bruce Jentleson, "American Commitments in the Third World: Theory vs. Practice," *International Organization* 41, no. 4 (Autumn 1987): 678-79.

14. Roger F. Pajak, "Soviet Military Aid to Iraq and Syria," *Strategic Review* 4, no. 1 (Winter 1976): 52.

15. Pajak, "Soviet Military Aid to Iraq and Syria," 53.

16. U.S. House of Representatives Committee on International Relations. *U.S. Arms Policies in the Persian Gulf and Red Sea Areas: Past, Present, and Future.* 95th Cong., 1st sess., December 1977, 130. Also U.S. House of Representatives, Committee on International Relations, Special Subcommittee on Investigations, *The Persian Gulf, 1975: The Continuing Debate on Arms Sales.* 95th Cong., 1st sess., 1975, 26. Testimony of Joseph Sisco, under secretary of state for political affairs, on security concerns of the Gulf States. In addition to Iraq, Sisco discussed Iran's concern about the Soviet Union, India, and the Indian Ocean in general with respect to oil access routes.

17. Jentleson, "American Commitments," 678. See also Robert Litwak, *Detente and the Nixon Doctrine: American Foreign Policy and the Pursuit of Stability, 1969-1976* (New York: Cambridge University Press, 1984), 143.

18. Litwak, *Detente and the Nixon Doctrine*, 143.

19. Ann Tibbitts Schulz, *Buying Security: Iran under the Monarchy* (Boulder, Colo.: Westview Press, 1989), 98.

20. T. Cuyler Young, "Iran in Continuing Crisis," Foreign Affairs 40, no. 2 (January 1962): 291-92. Also see Hossein Mahdavy, "The Coming Crisis in Iran," *Foreign Affairs* 44, no. 1 (October 1965): 145. Author's Note: The inability of the Shah to develop a strong political base of support is discussed later in this chapter in the section labeled "The Repercussions of the Alliance on Iran."

21. Rubin, *Paved with Good Intentions*, 135; See also Gary Sick, *All Fall Down* (New York: Random House, 1985), 18-19.

22. Bernard Weintraub, "Controversy Grows over Carter's Move to Sell Iran Planes," *New York Times*, 12 July 1977, 1(A).

23. Klare, *American Arms Supermarket*, 118; Halliday, *Iran: Dictatorship*, 101.

24. Halliday, *Iran: Dictatorship*, 101.

25. U.S. Senate Foreign Relations Committee, Subcommittee on Foreign Assistance, *Sale of AWACS to Iran.* 95th Cong., 1st sess., 1977, 29-45.

26. Senate Committee, *Sale of AWACS to Iran,* 79. Testimony of Senator Barry Goldwater (R-Ariz.).

27. U.S. House of Representatives Committee on International Relations, Subcommittee on International Security and Scientific Affairs, *Perspective Sale of Airborne Warning and Control System to Iran.* 95th Cong., 1st sess., 1977, 24.

28. House Committee, *Perspective Sale,* 24.

29. Senate Committee, *Sale of AWACS to Iran,* 5.

30. Senate, Committee *Sale of AWACS to Iran*, 86.

31. "Arms Business as Usual," *Washington Post*, 27 July 1977, 22(A).

32. Bernard Weintraub, "Congressional Agency Denounces Plan to Sell Radar System to Iran," *New York Times*, 16 July 1977, 34(A). Also see additional articles in bibliography. For reasons against sale of AWACS see House Committee, *Perspective Sale*, 104, which includes the GAO report, "Issues Concerning the Proposed Sale of the Airborne Warning and the Control System E-3 to Iran."

33. Harold Logan, "Turner Stands by Warning on Radar-Jet Sale to Iran," *Washington Post*, 22 July 1977, 2(A).

34. Laurence Stern, "CIA Expected to Alter Iran Radar Stand," *Washington Post*, 18 July 1977, 1(A).

35. Bernard Wientraub, "Carter Approves Pentagon's Offer to Sell Surveillance Planes to Iran," *New York Times*, 27 April 1977, 10(A).

36. Bernard Weintraub, "Controversy Grows over Carter's Move to Sell Iran Planes," *New York Times*, 12 July 1977, 1(A). Also Weintrab, "Congressional Agency Denounces," 34(A).

37. Weintraub, "Controversy Grows," 8(A).

38. Shahram Chubin, *Security in the Persian Gulf: The Role of Outside Powers* (London: Allanheld and Osmun, 1982), 59.

39. R. M. Burrell, "The Indian Ocean: An Iranian Evaluation," in *The Indian Ocean: Its Political, Economic, and Military Importance*, Alvin J. Cottrell and R. M. Burrell eds. (New York: Praeger, 1972), 94-95.

40. Klare, *American Arms Supermarket*, 108.

41. Klare, *American Arms Supermarket*, 108-9.

42. U.S. Department of State, *Iran*. February 28, 1978 (Washington, D.C.: National Security Archive, 1989), 116-17.

43. Shahram Chubin, *Security in the Persian Gulf*, 67.

44. Ulrich Albrecht, "Militarized Sub-imperialism: The Case of Iran," in *The World Military Order*, Mary Kaldor and Asborn Eide eds. 172.

45. Albrecht, "Militarized Sub-imperialism," 172.

46. Klare, *American Arms Supermarket*, 117-18. Also see James Noyes, *The Clouded Lens* (Stanford, Calif.: Hoover Institution Press, 1979), 65.

47. U.S. Department of Defense, *The Growing U.S. Involvement in Iran*. January 22, 1975 (Washington, D.C.: National Security Archive, 1989), 1.

48. U.S. Department of State, *Iran*. February 28, 1978 (Washington, D.C.: National Security Archive, 1989), 36-37.

49. U.S. Department of State, *Iran*. February 28, 1978, 9.

50. U.S. Department of State, *Iran*. February 28, 1978, 39.

51. Michael Klare, "America's White-Collar Mercenaries," *Inquiry* (October 16 1978): 17.

52. Halliday, *Iran: Dictatorship*, 98-99.

53. Joseph P. Englehardt, "American Military Advisors in Iran: A Critical Review," *Joint Perspectives* (Summer 1981), 29.

54. Englehardt, "American Military Advisors in Iran," 36.

55. Hossein Razavi and Firouz Vakil, *The Political Environment of Economic Planning in Iran, 1971-1983* (Boulder, Colo.: Westview Press, 1984), 86.

56. Halliday, *Iran: Dictatorship*, 96. See also Safqat A. Shah, "The Political and Strategic Foundations of International Arms Transfers: A Case Study of American Arms Supplies to and Purchases by Iran and Saudi Arabia, 1968-1976" (Unpublished Ph.D. Dissertation, University of Virginia, August 1977), 213.

57. Robert E. Looney, "The Role of Military Expenditure in Pre-Revolutionary Iran's Economic Decline," *Iranian Studies* 21, no. 3-4 (1988): 55.

58. Chubin, *Security in the Persian Gulf*, 59.

59. Klare, *American Arms Supermarket*, 127.

60. Anthony Sampson, *The Arms Bazaar* (New York: Viking Press, 1977), 249-55. Sampson provides a detailed account of this process.

61. Klare, *American Arms Supermarket*, 120-21.

62. Sampson, *The Arms Bazaar*, 254.

63. U.S. Senate Foreign Affairs Committee, Subcommittee on Multinational Corporations, *Multinationals and U.S. Foreign Policy, Part 17.* 94th Cong., 2nd. sess., 1976, 120. Testimony of Joseph Gavin, President Grumman Corporation.

64. Senate, Committee, *Multinationals and U.S. Foreign Policy, Part 17*, 257-58.

65. U.S. Senate Foreign Affairs Committee, Subcommittee on Foreign Assistance, *U.S. Arms Sales Policy.* 94th Cong., 2nd., sess., 1976, 109.

66. Senate Committee, *U.S. Arms Sales Policy,* 257-58.

67. Senate Committee *U.S. Arms Sales Policy*, 243.

68. James R. Kurth, "Why We Buy the Weapons We Do," *Foreign Policy*, no. 11, (1973), 64.

69. U.S. House of Representatives Committee on Foreign Affairs, *United States Arms Sales to the Persian Gulf, Report of a Study Mission to Iran, Kuwait, and Saudi Arabia.* 94th Cong., 1st., sess., 1975, 26.

70. House Committee, *United States Arms Sales*, 26.

71. Bill, *The Eagle and Lion*, 209.

72. U.S. Department of Defense, Special Regional Studies, *The Growing U.S. Involvement in Iran*, January 22, 1975 (Washington, D.C.: National Security Archive, 1989), 21.

73. U.S. Department of Defense, *The Growing U.S. Involvement in Iran,* 21-23.

74. New York Times, "Iran Will Spend $15 Billion in U.S. over Five Years," *New York Times*, 5 March 1975, 1A.

75. C. L. Sulzberger, "The Biggest Deal of All," *New York Times*, 15 March 1975, 27.

76. Bill, *The Eagle and Lion*, 204.

77. U.S. House of Representatives Committee on International Relations, *Letter from President Carter to Speaker O'Neill.* 95th Cong., 1st., sess., 1977, 1.

78. Khosrow Fatemi, "The Iranian Revolution: Its Impact on Economic Relations with the United States," *International Journal of Middle East Studies* 12, no. 3 (November 1980): 303.

79. Fatemi, "The Iranian Revolution," 310; Also Nikki Keddie, *Roots of Revolution: An Interpretive History of Modern Iran* (New Haven, Conn.: Yale University Press, 1981), 178. For a discussion of American corporate interests in Iran and influence on foreign policy see Mark Hulbert, *Interlock: The Untold Story of American Banks, Oil Interests, the Shah's Money, Debts, and the Astounding Connections between Them* (New York: Richardson and Snyder, 1982).

80. Fatemi, "The Iranian Revolution," 312.

81. Rubin, *Paved with Good Intentions*, 168, 187. In addition, in the event of a global conflict with the United States, the Soviets would have to allocate resources to guard against an American attack from Iran.

82. George C. Wilson, "U.S. Dismantling Intelligence Gear, Storing It in Iran: Selling of SALT II Could be Affected," *Washington Post*, 12 January 1979, 1.

83. Michael Ledeen and William Lewis, *Debacle: The American Failure in Iran* (New York: Vintage Books, 1982), 54-57. Discusses Iran's regional diplomacy.

84. Ledeen and Lewis, *Debacle: The American Failure*, 86.

85. Ledeen and Lewis, *Debacle: The American Failure*, 87-88.

86. Ledeen and Lewis, *Debacle the American Failure*, 92-93. Also see Jeffrey A. Lefebvre, *Arms For The Horn* (Pittsburgh, Pa.: University of Pittsburgh Press, 1991), 45, 188.

87. Ledeen and Lewis, *Debacle: The American Failure*, 94-96. Discusses comprehensively the ramifications of events in the Horn of Africa and the impact on American-Saudi-Iranian relations.

88. Anthony Cordesman, *The Gulf and the Search for Strategic Stability* (Boulder, Colo.: Westview Press, 1984), 158.

89. Robert Graham, *Iran: The Illusion of Power* (New York: St. Martin's Press, 1980), 100.

90. Cordesman, *The Gulf and the Search for Strategic Stability*, 155-57.

91. See Ledeen and Lewis, *Debacle: The American Failure*, 91. Discusses the ramifications and implications this had on the Soviet position in the Middle East.

92. Richard W. Cottam, *Iran and the United States* (Pittsburgh, Pa.: University of Pittsburgh Press, 1988), 147.

93. Edmund Ghareeb, *The Kurdish Question in Iraq* (Syracuse, N.Y.: Syracuse University Press, 1981), 138.

94. Ghareeb, *The Kurdish Question*, 138. Gives detailed information on the alleged agreement. Allegations of this secret agreement were made by *Al-Ahad* (Beirut), 10 August 1969.

95. Richard W. Cottam, "American Policy and the Iranian Crisis," *Journal of Iranian Studies* 13, no. 1-4, (1980): 290.

96. Cottam, *American Policy*, 290. Also see Ghareeb, *The Kurdish Question*, 140, *New York Times*, 2 November 1975.

97. Ghareeb, *The Kurdish Question*, 141-42. See also *The Village Voice*, 11 February 1976.

98. Ghareeb, *The Kurdish Question*, 140.

99. Ghareeb, *The Kurdish Question*, 140-41.

100. Sohrab Sobhani, *The Pragmatic Entente: Israeli-Iranian Relations, 1948-1988* (New York: Praeger, 1989), 10.

101. For a brief history of Jewish Persian contacts see M. G. Weinbaum, "Iran and Israel: The Discreet Entente," *Orbis* 28, no. 4 (Winter 1975): 1070-73.

102. Uri Bialer, "The Iranian Connection in Israel's Foreign Policy: 1948-1951," *The Middle East Journal* 39, no. 2 (Spring 1985): 299-300.

103. Weinbaum, "Iran and Israel," 1078. Also see Stephen H. Longrigg, *Oil in the Middle East* (London: Oxford University Press, 1968), 333.

104. Sobhani, *The Pragmatic Entente*, 53. See also Weinbaum, "Iran and Israel," 1078-79.

105. Weinbaum, "Iran and Israel," 1078-79. See also Robert Reppa, *Israel and Iran: Bilateral Relationships and Effect on the Indian Ocean Basin* (New York: Praeger, 1974), 84.

106. Sobhani, *The Pragmatic Entente*, 118. Quoted from a personal interview with Shmuel Segev in Israel, 1988.

107. Sobhani, *The Pragmatic Entente*, 116-17.

108. Sobhani., *The Pragmatic Entente*, 117. See also Aaron Klieman, *Israel's Global Reach: Arms Sales as Diplomacy* (New York: Pergamon-Brassey's, 1985), 128-29.

109. Sobhani, *The Pragmatic Entente*, 131.

110. Sobhani, *The Pragmatic Entente*, 117-18. Also see U.S. Department of State, *Documents of the United States Embassy in Tehran*, Volume 19, 1979, 13. Quoted in Sobhani.

111. Sobhani, *The Pragmatic Entente*, 55-57.

112. Sobhani, *The Pragmatic Entente*, 131-33. Discusses these processes in comprehensive details.

113. Sobhani, *The Pragmatic Entente*, 19.

114. Sobhani, *The Pragmatic Entente*, 33-35. Discusses Ben-Gurion's periphery strategy of Israel's attempt to break its isolation within the region by aligning with like-minded states on the edge of the Middle East, namely Turkey, Iran, and Ethiopia, and the reasons the Shah came to view this strategy favorably.

115. Sobhani, *The Pragmatic Entente*, 45.

116. Sobhani, *The Pragmatic Entente*, 47. Data taken from U.S. Government sources. See U.S. Department of State, *Documents*, Volume 31, 1979, 15. Although it should be noted this had the potential of causing problems with Turkey due to that country's own Kurdish population.

117. Sobhani, *The Pragmatic Entente*, 115. See also Avner Yaniv, *Deterrence without the Bomb: The Politics of Israeli Strategy* (Lexington, Mass.: Lexington Books, 1987), 159.

118. Alvin J. Cottrell and James E. Dougherty. *Iran's Quest for Security* (Cambridge, Mass.: Institute for Foreign Policy Analysis, 1977), 22.

119. Cottrell and Dougherty, *Iran's Quest*, 25.

120. Anne Hessing Cahn, "Determinants of the Nuclear Option: The Case of Iran," in *Nuclear Proliferation and the Near Nuclear Countries*, eds. Marwah Onkar and Ann Schulz (Cambridge, Mass.: Ballinger Publishing Company, 1975), 190.

121. Amirsadeghi, *Twentieth-Century Iran*, 245.

122. George Quester, "The Shah and the Bomb," *Policy Sciences*, Volume 8, no. 1, (March 1977), 23.

123. Quester, "The Shah and the Bomb," 21.

124. Quester, "The Shah and the Bomb," 22.

125. Heshing Cahn, "Determinants of the Nuclear Option," 190.

126. Cottrell and Dougherty, *Iran's Quest*, 37.

127. Hessing Cahn, "Determinants of the Nuclear Option,"195-97.

128. U.S. House of Representatives Select Committee on Intelligence, *Iran: Evaluation of U.S. Intelligence Performance Prior to November 1978*. 96th Cong., 1st., sess., 1979, 1-8.

129. Springfield, Va.: National Technical Information Service, 1980, Gregory Francis Gates, *An Analysis of the Impact of American Arms Transfers on Political State in Iran*, AD-A093255, 55.

130. Hossein Razavi and Firouz Vakil, *The Political Environment of Economic Planning in Iran, 1971-1983* (Boulder, Colo.: Westview Press, 1984), 61-62.

131. Gates, *An Analysis of the Impact*, 58.

132. U.S. Senate Committee on Energy and Natural Resources, *Access to Oil-The U.S. Relationship with Saudi Arabia and Iran*, Staff Report by Fern Racine and Melvin Conant, 95th Cong., 1st sess., 1977, 85-86.

133. Razavi and Vakil, *The Political Environment*, 81.

134. Gates, *An Analysis of the Impact*, 63.

135. Theodore H. Moran, "Iranian Defense Expenditures and the Social Crisis," *International Security* Vol. 3, no. 3 (1978-1979), 180.

136. Moran, "Iranian Defense Expenditures," 181-82.

137. Stephanie Neumann, "Security, Military Expenditures and Socioeconomic Development: Reflections on Iran," *Orbis* Vol. 22, no. 3 (Fall 1978): 591.

138. Neumann, "Security, Military Expenditures," 589-90.

139. Moran, "Iranian Defense Expenditures," 179. Gates, *An Analysis of the Impact*, 79-111. Makes argument that the American military program did not hinder Iran's economic and political development, but that the revolution would have occurred anyway.

140. U.S. Department of State, Bureau of Intelligence and Research, *Iran: The External Threat to Iran*. June 9, 1970, (Washington, D.C.: National Security Archive, 1989), 9.

141. Bill, *The Eagle and Lion*, 48.

142. Bill, *The Eagle and Lion*, 82-83.

143. Litwak, *Detente and the Nixon Doctrine*,140-43. Discusses the similar interests between Iran and the United States

144. Litwak, *Detente and the Nixon Doctrine*, 142-43.

145. Christopher C. Shoemaker and John Spanier, *Patron-Client State Relationships* (New York: Praeger, 1984), 47. Discusses this concept.

146. Ledeen and Lewis, *Debacle*, 58-59. Also see Rubin, *Paved with Good Intentions*, 183, Gary Sick, *All Fall Down* (New York: Random House, 1985), 21. Also Robert Keohane, "The Big Influence of Small Allies," in *Foreign Policy* Vol. 1, no. 2 (Spring 1971): 161-82. Discusses how foreign governments can manipulate the American political system and bureaucracy.

147. Sick, *All Fall Down*, 21.

148. U.S. Department of Defense, *Foreign Military Sales, Foreign Military Construction Sales, and Military Assistance Facts*. (Washington D.C.: U.S. Government Printing Office, 1978). Quoted in Klare, *American Arms Supermarket*, 109.

149. Sick, *All Fall Down*, 25.

150. Theodore H. Moran, "Iranian Defense Expenditures and the Social Crisis," in *International Security*, Vol 3, no. 3 (Winter 1978): 180. It should also be noted that conditions present in the country also exacerbated the economic situation. These included corruption among some government officials and members of the royal family, as well as the flight of capital from Iran to the West.

151. Klare, *American Arms Supermarket*, 122.

152. Moran, "Iranian Defense Expenditures," 188-89.

153. Alvin Rubinstein, "The Evolution of Soviet Strategy in the Middle East," *Orbis* Vol. 24, no. 2 (Summer 1980), 325. It would seem therefore that Soviet policy toward Iran was in trying to maintain the status quo in order to preserve stability on its southern borders.

154. Robert Graham, *Iran: The Illusion of Power* (London: Croom Helm Ltd., 1978), 181-82.

155. Graham, *Iran: The Illusion of Power*, 181.

156. U.S. House of Representatives Committee On International Relations, *New Perspectives on the Persian Gulf,* 93rd Cong., 1st sess., 65. Testimony of Marvin Zonis, Center for Middle East Studies, University of Chicago, July 23 1973.

157. House Committee, *New Perspectives on the Persian Gulf,* 41, 111. See testimony of Richard Cottam, Professor of Political Science, University of Pittsburgh, July 24, 1973, and Marvin Zonis, July 23, 1977. See also Richard P. Berman, *The Shah's Iranian Empire: Old Games, New Stakes* (Washington, D.C.: Center for Defense Information) cited in U.S. House of Representatives Committee on International Relations, Subcommittee on Near East and South Asian Affairs, *The Persian Gulf 1974: Money, Politics, Arms and Power*. 93rd Cong., 2nd. sess., 1974, 254. Also see U.S. House of Representatives, Committee on International Relations, *United States Arms Sales to the Persian Gulf.* 94th., Cong., 1st., sess., 1975, 13. The same observations could be made in regard to the Soviet Union. See

Leslie M. Pryor, "Arms and the Shah," *Foreign Policy*, no. 31 (Summer, 1978): 68.

158. Senate Committee, *U.S. Arms Sales Policy,* 1976, 102. Testimony of Theodore Moran, Visiting Associate Professor Johns Hopkins University School of Advanced International Studies, September 24, 1976. See also U.S. Department of Defense, David Ranfeldt, *U.S.-Iranian Arms Transfers Relationship: A Historical Analysis, The Rand Corporation.* (Washington, D.C.: National Security Archive, 1989), 10. A working note prepared for the Office of the Assistant Secretary of Defense International Security Affairs, October 1976.

Chapter 4

The Origins of the American-Israeli Alliance, 1948-1960

The American-Israeli relationship began during the Truman administration as the United States was the first country to officially recognize Israel on May 6, 1948. During Truman's presidency Washington extended small amounts of aid to the Jewish state. The rationale for these decisions have more to do with American domestic politics than foreign policy considerations. During the Eisenhower period this relationship deteriorated somewhat as the primary emphasis of the administration was focused on questions of international affairs, and the preservation and enhancement of American strategic interests in the region. While Eisenhower's relationship with Israel was tense at times, strategic cooperation between the two nations had its origins during this administration.

The Truman Administration and the Politics of the Recognition of Israel

The issue of whether to recognize Jewish aspirations for a state in Palestine posed a great problem for the United States. The issue of Palestine-Israel was one of the fundamental concerns of the Truman administration heading into the Presidential election of 1948. President Truman encountered pressures from a variety of different sources both inside and outside his administration. These pressures manifested themselves in the form of interest groups, personal friendships, domestic political advisers, Democratic party leaders and contributors, as well as National Security advisers. Another factor that had to be taken into account was the President's weakened political position going into the election of 1948. In addition, Truman and the Democrats were confronted by a strengthened Republican party. The Republicans had recaptured Congress in the midterm elections of 1946 and were determined to win the White House in 1948. This led to a great deal of politicalization of the Palestine issue by both parties, and gave Truman incentive to preempt the Republicans by supporting Israel in an attempt to sway Jewish voters.[1]

Another factor impacting Truman's decision making was his personal preferences, which were generally supportive of the Zionist position, although at times he disagreed with their tactics. As a senator, Truman opposed the British attempt to limit Jewish immigration to Palestine prior to World War II. During the war, then-Senator Truman, while still articulating support for Israel, withdrew from the American Christian Palestine Committee when he interpreted their newspaper advertisements as possibly detracting from the war effort. In addition, he refused to endorse a resolution, which many of his Senate colleagues supported, which called for the establishment of a Jewish Commonwealth. Truman did not support this as he felt it could detract from the war effort.[2] Therefore, Truman's preferences seem to indicate that he had an appreciation for the possible repercussions of the Palestine issue that led him to take a cautious attitude. This was reflected in his decision making regarding this issue as President.

The Pressure Groups Confronting Truman

The Anti-Zionist Faction

The issue of Palestine caused conflicts within the executive branch and the bureaucracy and this had been the case since Truman assumed the presidency in 1945. The opposition to aiding the Jewish claims was primarily in the State Department, the newly created Defense Department, and consultants on military affairs. They were primarily concerned about security, oil, and economic advantage.[3] The more important of these individuals were Secretary of State George Marshall, Secretary of Defense James Forrestal, Undersecretary of State Robert Lovett, Loy Henderson, the head of the Near East Bureau in the State Department, and others such as George Kennan and Dean Rusk.[4]

The primary concern of this group was access to Middle Eastern oil. It was during the late 1940s that Secretary of Defense James Forrestal warned that domestic production would not meet the needs of the United States and access to Middle East oil was essential.[5] It is significant to note that secure access to, then cheap, oil was also important for the reindustralization of Western Europe. Postwar Europe's main source of oil, between 70 and 80 percent, was from the Middle East. The economic development of Europe was essential for American containment strategy in order to ensure that it would remain a bulwark against Soviet expansionism.[6]

By early 1948 American companies had invested a substantial amount of economic resources in the region. There were 11,000 Americans employed in the Arab countries. A symbol of United States economic involvement in the region were the pipelines being constructed by American corporations that connected the oil fields of Arabia with the Mediterranean. Most importantly, the Middle East was seen by many in the national security and foreign policy bureaucracies as an important arena in the forming of America's containment strategy versus the Soviet Union. This last point was important for two reasons. First, the geographical situation of the Middle East could provide the West with a greater air and sea capability to threaten the Soviet Union. Second, it was thought that regional instability could open up the possibility of Soviet intervention and control of the region's vast oil resources. Many defense and foreign policy experts viewed this possibility as potentially tipping the balance of power in favor of the Soviets.[7]

In the private sector the major groups supporting the Arab viewpoint were the oil companies; the oil lobby was very active and enjoyed access to decision makers, particularly in the State and Defense Departments. Much of this contact was informal as many oil company executives were former State Department officials. The oil industry attempted to refute support for Israel by emphasizing the possibility of jeopardizing oil concessions in the Arab world, as well as increasing the potential for regional instability and the increase of Soviet influence. Oil officials frequently provided information to the State and Defense Departments in their attempt to influence the administration to oppose partition in November 1947, or to recognize the establishment of Israel the following May.[8]

The Zionist Lobby within the Administration

In opposition to this view were Truman's personal political advisors. Among the more prominent of these individuals was David Niles, an administrative assistant to the President. Niles had served in the Roosevelt administration and was one of the few Roosevelt advisers that Truman kept on. He served as an invaluable aid to Truman in advising him on Jewish and labor politics in the Northeast, and in particular New York.[9] Another important advisor was Clark Clifford who was a special counsel to the President and strongly pro-Zionist. The third major pro-Zionist advisor was Max Lowenthal who served as an assistant on Palestine to special counsel Clifford and it was he who drafted the memoranda on Palestine for consideration by the president. In accomplishing this he was in frequent contact with the Jewish Agency for Palestine's office in Washington. President Truman would later give him a good deal of credit for the recognition of Israel.[10] In addition, there was also pro-Zionist pressure from important sectors of the Democratic Party, such as members of Congress and state party officials in such electorally essential states as New York.

The Zionist Lobby

Other pressures were coming from pro-Zionist interest groups, many of these centered in key states, and parts of the media. The major vehicle for Zionist lobbying in the United States was the Emergency Committee for Zionist Affairs, established in 1939. This group coordinated the various Jewish organizations in the United States who had been lobbying independently. In 1941 this organization established a public relations department and in 1943 it opened a Washington office. The organization later changed its name to the American Zionist Emergency Council.[11] Finally, personal considerations and connections in Presidential decision making must be taken into account. Truman at various times spoke to Jewish leaders informally concerning Palestine such as Rabbi Stephen Wise and Chaim Weizman, and especially Truman's longtime friend and business associate Eddie Jacobson. In addition there were those wealthy Jewish supporters of Israel who helped finance his campaign for vice-president in 1944 and who were invaluable in helping to provide resources for his 1948 reelection bid.

Palestine and Politics in the United States: The 1946 Congressional Elections

The importance of Palestine in American Politics manifested itself almost from the beginning of the Truman presidency. Truman was under a great deal of political pressure leading up to the midterm Congressional elections of 1946. An important issue at this time involved immigration of European Jews to Palestine, which at this point the British were severely restricting. The United States Congress in December 1945 had approved a resolution calling upon the president to use "its good offices" to allow Jewish immigration to Palestine and to assist in establishing a Jewish homeland there.[12] The resolution was adopted by both houses of Congress in a one-sided voice vote.

The election of 1946 and the issue of Palestine galvanized many Democrats into placing additional pressure on Truman. This was particularly acute in New York State, where Zionist groups and appeals had great sympathy. Brooklyn Congressmen Emanuel Cellar sought to arrange a session between the New York State congressional delegation and the president to make him more fully aware of the Pro-Zionist sentiments of the state. Truman resisted this meeting initially. Representative Cellar pointed out that Truman's refusal to meet with the delegation would give political capital to upstate Republicans. Truman eventually did attend, although was not enthusiastic about it.[13]

In addition to Congress, Truman was also facing pressure from Democratic party leaders, as well as his own political advisers. David Hannegan, chair of the Democratic National Committee, and David Niles encouraged him to make a statement in support of the Zionist position.

Niles and other political advisors argued that failure to do so would hurt local Democratic candidates in New York, as well as the President in the 1948 general election. They were concerned that Thomas Dewey, the likely Republican nominee for president in 1948, would issue a statement of support first. This would have given the Republicans control of the issue.[14]

Members of the national security bureaucracy sought to prevent this by appealing to the president to delay any statements that could damage American interests in the region. Truman was reminded by Acting Secretary of State William Clayton in September of 1946 that among other things, the Joint Chiefs of Staff had urged "that we take no action with regard to Palestine which might orient the peoples of the entire area away from the Western powers."[15]

In October 1946, on Yom Kippur eve, President Truman announced that the administration supported increased Jewish immigration into Palestine and called for the setting up of a Jewish state. This for a time stole the political initiative from Dewey and the Republicans who were also using the Palestine issue for domestic political purposes. Two days later, Dewey echoed Truman's sentiments and even called for immigration of several hundred thousand Jews into Palestine.[16] The Republicans went even further in July 1948 when representatives of the campaign met in New York with prominent Zionists to seek their support in the upcoming election. They promised to recognize an independent Jewish state, provide a substantial loan, and lift the arms embargo.[17]

Ironically, the attempt to play the Palestine issue did not have much of an effect on Democratic electoral fortunes in 1946. The Democrats lost their majority over both houses of Congress, and outside of the then solid Democratic south, only held seven of thirty-two governorships. The Democratic party lost for several factors unrelated to the question of Israel, such as the rate of inflation and disenchantment by both New Deal supporters and conservatives over the direction of the Truman administration.[18] The 1946 congressional elections saw the Democrats confronted with a six-seat minority in the Senate, and a fifty-eight-seat minority in the House. These legislative loses led to a weakening of the president's ability to coordinate an independent foreign policy and did not bode well for Truman's own reelection fortunes in two years.[19] This issue reflected the fine balance between foreign and domestic policy in American politics although the ramifications of Truman's decision were not apparent in the congressional elections of 1946, it could be argued that the Democratic loses might have been bigger had Truman not conveyed his support for Israel.

Truman and the Partition Vote of 1947

Establishing the Borders of the States for Partition

Many Zionists groups were not entirely satisfied with Truman's support, viewing it as lukewarm. They pressed Truman for a more definitive policy on an independent Israel and were frustrated by his unwillingness to pressure Great Britain.[20]

In early 1947 Britain attempted to bring the Zionists and Arabs together to hammer out a compromise in order to maintain the mandate until a settlement could be reached. The failure of the Arab-Zionist conference held in London in January-February 1947 led the British to declare that they were ceding the Palestine issue to the United Nations. The United Nations General Assembly in May of that year created a special committee to study the issue. The committee report issued in September unanimously recommended that Britain end its mandate and Palestine be granted independence. The committee, however, differed in their recommendations of how this was to be achieved. The majority of the committee (Australia, Canada, Czechoslovakia, Guatemala, the Netherlands, Peru, Sweden, and Uruguay) favored the partition of Palestine into separate Jewish and Arab states to be granted independence after a two-year transition period. These states would be joined in an economic union. The city of Jerusalem would remain under an international trusteeship. The minority report of this committee (India, Iran, and Yugoslavia) favored a single federal state to become independent after a three-year U.N. trusteeship.[21]

Truman began to take a more active role during the debate over the boundaries and the actual partition vote in the U.N. General Assembly. A big issue prior to the vote concerned the borders of the future states. American representatives at the United Nations were arguing that the partition would be more equitable if a portion of the Negev desert were allocated to the Arab state. This would not assign so many Arabs under the authority of the future Jewish state and could make partition more palatable to the Arabs. This mobilized the Zionist's leadership, who valued the future potential of the Negev as well as the port of Aqaba, of which Israel would now be deprived. Chaim Weizmann in his meeting on November 19 with Truman argued the importance of Aqaba and its future potential as a port that could benefit the West. Truman agreed with Weizman and instructed the American delegation to cease in their objections. Eventually, Israel received the bulk of the Negev with access to the Gulf of Aqaba, although the actual port was given to Jordan.[22]

American Pressure in the General Assembly

Leading up to the final vote on partition, pressure was put on the Truman administration from various quarters to line up nations to support the majority report. Congressmen Cellar urged the president to pressure nations that were hostile to partition, in particular Greece. He argued that Greece, "is immeasurably and morally indebted to us . . . and other countries friendly with us that we expect their cooperation on the matter of Palestine."[23]

The Truman administration was initially slow in actively supporting the Zionist cause in the U.N. However, in the last days before the General Assembly vote the American delegation became more active in attempting to solicit support for partition among other members. It has been argued that this occurred as a result of pressure from Zionists supporters.[24] Two prominent congressmen who supported the Zionist position indicated that Truman changed the instructions in the final days to the delegation. Congressmen Cellar, in a letter to Truman several days after the partition vote, stated his "sincerest gratitude for the effective work you did in actively assisting the passage of partition." Another Congressmen who supported the Zionist cause Arthur Klein stated, "there can be no doubt that the successful fight of the American delegation was made at the personal direction of President Truman."[25]

It has been established that there was considerable pressure brought to bear on several American allies to change their vote by various prominent Americans who supported the Zionist position. Ultimately the Philippines, Liberia, and Haiti switched their votes to enable the partition plan to pass by the necessary margin. The Philippines changed its vote as a result of heavy lobbying. Among those active in this activity was Clark Clifford, who held discussions with the Philippines ambassador in Washington on November 28.[26] In addition, the government of the Philippines was also lobbied by two members of the U.S. Supreme Court and 10 senators warning of possible consequences if the Philippines did not go along.[27]

The pressure placed on Liberia was more overt. Former Secretary of State Stettinus used his business connections with Harvey Firestone to inform Liberian President Tubman that unless Liberia changed its vote the Firestone company would reconsider its plans to expand its rubber plantations in the country.[28] The American lobbying pressure was not limited to small third world nations, as France also was pressured into voting for partition. The French were concerned initially about voting for partition as they were afraid this would cause unrest in the North African colonies. David Niles enlisted the aid of Barnard Baruch to indicate to the French that they risked a cutoff of aid if they did not vote for partition. The French were also being lobbied by Chaim Weizman, who had discussions with Prime Minister Leon Blum. As a result of this two-front lobbying effort, the French ultimately cast a positive vote for partition.[29] In addition, other countries such as Haiti, Cuba, and Greece also came under enormous pressure. Of the 17 nations that had abstained on the original vote on November 25, seven of them switched their votes in favor of partition four days later, November 29, when the second vote was taken. These were Belgium, France, Haiti, Liberia, Luxembourg, the Netherlands, and New Zealand. This was in contrast to the lobbying efforts of the Arab states. They managed to get only Greece and Chile to change their votes. Greece had abstained on the first ballot and voted negative in the final vote. Chile had initially voted in favor of partition, and was persuaded to abstain on the second vote.[30]

Political Pressures on Truman Leading to Partition Vote

Truman's political advisers as well as Democratic party leaders were attempting to influence Truman to take a more positive stand toward the Zionist cause. The Democrats were receiving large amounts of contributions from Jewish donors as a result of the President's Yom Kippur statement. Postmaster General Robert Hannegan told the president in September of 1947 that further favorable statements could assist in fund-raising. He followed this up a month later by telling Truman that some of the party's contributors wanted assurances that the administration would support the Jewish claim to Palestine before making further contributions.[31]

Truman understood the importance of fund-raising in American campaigns and was aware firsthand of the potential resources that many Zionists could contribute. In 1944 Truman's vice-presidential election was financed largely by Dewey Stone, a wealthy Zionist. It has been argued that Truman was particularly dependent on Jewish financial support in his first term. Many of these individuals were pro-Zionist and sought to use their influence in lobbying for Israel.[32] This was particularly true for the Democratic party as a whole. A political commentator at the time noted that, "the Democrats are always poor, they're always scrounging around for dough, and this makes them much more vulnerable."[33]

The possibility of exploiting this issue for greater campaign funding from Jewish sources was especially apparent to leaders of the national Democratic Party. This was evident in October 1946 after President Truman's favorable statement of support for a Jewish state, as the Democratic National Committee received greater amounts of contributions from Jewish sources.[34] In addition, it was indicated by high Democratic Party officials that additional contributions would be needed to carry out the 1948 electoral campaign.[35]

During the 1948 election Truman was particularly dependent on contributions to finance his famous whistle-stop train tour that he credited with turning the election around. Among the individuals who helped raise money for this campaign was Abe Feinberg. President Truman himself expressed his gratitude by stating, "If not for my friend Abe, I couldn't have made the trip and I wouldn't have been elected."[36] The ramifications of this were that prominent Zionist supporters gained access to the White House. Abba Eban, Israel's first ambassador to the United States, noted that after the election Dewey Stone and Abe Feinberg, "enjoyed fairly free access to the White House in times of crisis."[37] In addition to Democratic Party contributors, prominent Democratic politicians urged the president to accept partition. J. Howard McGrath, chairman of the Democratic National Committee, told Secretary of Defense Forrestal that unless Truman supported the Zionist position, two or three pivotal states in the 1948 election would be lost.[38] The Jewish vote was considered important for the election of 1948. In November 1947 the President's special counsel Clark Clifford drew up a memorandum to Truman on the importance of the Jewish vote for the 1948 election. This memorandum especially emphasized the importance of the Jewish vote in New York State: "The Jewish vote, insofar as it can be thought of as a bloc, is important only in New York. But (except for Wilson in 1916) no candidate since 1876 has lost New York and won the Presidency, and its 47 votes are naturally the first prize in any election."[39]

The New York vote was the major prize in the election. The Jewish population of New York State was estimated at 14 percent, in New York City it was estimated at 20 percent. However, as a group they are active in politics, and in particular within the Democratic Party. Nationally, the Jewish population composed 3 percent of the total population, and cast an estimated 4 percent of the vote in national elections. This one-percent difference translated into about 750,000 votes, most of which were concentrated in states with large electoral votes that would be significant in a close election. The difference between winning and losing the New York vote by itself was a swing of 94 electoral votes out of the necessary 266 needed for election. In addition, while Clifford did not emphasize this, the Jewish vote was also significant in Pennsylvania (36 votes), Illinois (27 votes), and Ohio (23 votes).[40]

Opposing this view of partition was the national security bureaucracy. The major concern of this group was that American support for the Zionists would weaken its position in the Middle East. The presence of an independent Israel, they argued, would lead to conflict and destabilize the region. As a result this would jeopardize American access to oil, as well as other commercial interests. More importantly, this could result in an opening for the Soviets to expand their influence. Among the groups that by and large supported this position were the State Department, especially the Near Eastern and Policy Planning Sections, the Defense Department, in particular the navy, which was concerned about oil accessibility, and the Joint Chiefs of Staff.[41]

Attempts to Reverse Partition

Personal Pressure Kept Truman on Partition Course

Despite the vote in the United Nations, the matter of American support for partition and the formation of the Jewish state was not yet finalized, particularly from the Zionist perspective. In early 1948 American relations became increasing strained with the Soviet Union as a result of the February 1948 coup in Czechoslovakia. Also, there was concern that the Communists would come to power in the 1948 election in Italy. This led some within Washington to suggest that another showdown over Palestine at this juncture would be unwise.[42] Zionist leaders were thus interested in restating their case to President Truman so as to firm up his support. The president at first refused to see Chaim Weizman until the personal intervention of Truman's longtime friend and business associate Eddie Jacobson changed his mind. As a result, Truman met with Weizman and gave him assurances of his concern for the Jewish people.[43]

Election Year Pressures

If Truman was wavering in his support for the Zionist cause, the pressures of election year American politics quickly ended this. Truman was especially concerned about New York State. New York City Democratic leader Edward Flynn informed Truman of the political problem he would have if he did not back the Zionists.[44] New York had a very large Jewish population; 47 percent of the nation's Jewish population lived in New York, and made up 17 percent of the state's vote. This was made more significant by the fact that New York held 47 electoral votes and was the most important state in the election. Democratic hopes were also shaken by the emergence of a third party candidate, Henry Wallace, the vice-president who Truman replaced on the Democratic ticket in the 1944 election, who was running for president with the support of the American Labor Party. He was considered a political threat by the Democrats as he was advocating more liberal policies than Truman, as well as supporting the Zionist position wholeheartedly.

A potential harbinger of things to come occurred in early 1948 in a special election to fill a congressional vacancy in Bronx County. The Democratic party candidate, Karl Popper, was defeated by the ALP candidate, Leo Isacson, by the handy margin of 55 percent to 31 percent. The district had a Jewish majority and was sympathetic to the pro-Zionist rhetoric of Isacson and Henry Wallace, who campaigned for him. Commentaries at the time stated that Isacson's election occurred as a result of dissatisfaction with Truman's policy toward Palestine.[45] Subsequently many New York State Democrats, as well as the Liberal Party, which was backing Truman, urged him to be more supportive of Zionist concerns, such as a lifting of the arms embargo and enforcing the partition of Palestine.[46]

Recognition and Support

It became apparent to Truman's domestic advisers, in particular David Niles and Clark Clifford, that it was important for Truman to mend fences with the Jewish community. They encouraged him to recognize Israel as soon as its independence was announced and this position was made public in a White House conference on May 12, 1948. The State Department advised caution and argued that it was necessary for the new government to demonstrate administrative control over the territory. Undersecretary of State Robert Lovett warned that to do otherwise would undermine American relations with the Arab world. Secretary of State George Marshall felt that domestic politics should be kept out of foreign policy matters.[47]

Truman in the end gave in to his political advisers and recognized Israel shortly after it's independence was proclaimed. This was quickly followed up with more concrete assistance. Truman publicly welcomed President Weizmann at the White House on May 25, where a loan to Israel was discussed. Truman supported the loan proposal, which eventually grew to

$100 million, and officially endorsed it shortly before the election. It was authorized by the president on January 19, 1949 from the Export-Import Bank and marked the beginning of official American financial support for Israel.[48] Truman further demonstrated his support for Israel by naming James G. McDonald as ambassador to Israel. McDonald sympathized with the Zionist position while serving on the Anglo-American Committee of Inquiry.[49] Ambassador McDonald attempted to encourage the Truman administration to be more supportive of Israel by emphasizing the communist threat to the country and advocated American aid.[50] He proved to be a firm advocate for Israel's interest and had direct influence with the President.

These acts were accompanied by firm statements of support in the Democratic platform established at the convention in July of 1948. These included diplomatic and financial assistance, supporting Israeli membership in the United Nations, not to agree to modifications on Israel's boundaries, and a lifting of the arms embargo. The 1948 election cemented the interests of American Jews with the Democratic Party for the next 30 years.[51]

However, despite the Democratic platform there were still points of contention between Truman and the American Jewish community. Truman did not lift the arms embargo for several reasons. First, the State Department advised against it, arguing that it would initiate a virtual American-Israeli alliance and be seen as an act of war by the Arab countries. Second, Truman determined that public opinion was overwhelmingly against the lifting of the embargo.[52] The Truman administration also agreed to the Tripartite Declaration issued jointly by the United States, Britain, and France. This was an agreement by the major Western powers seeking to regulate arms shipments to the region and opposing attempts to change boundaries by force.[53] The United States followed this plan during the Truman and Eisenhower administrations, started to break away under Kennedy, and eventually abandoned it under Johnson. However, during the 1950s America allowed the French to assume a very close arms supply relationship with the Israelis.

In the economic sphere, however, a modest relationship developed. Economic aid started in 1949 with a $100-million Export-Import Bank loan, which later was supplemented by another loan of $35 million in 1951. These loans were used for agricultural, industrial, and infrastructure development. In 1952 the United States began a program of economic grants in an effort to help resettle refugees, finance commodity imports, as well as help pay the balance of payments deficits.[54]

Conclusions

The Truman administration's policy toward Israel was driven by domestic politics in the United States. Truman, faced with electoral pressures, sided with his domestic political advisors over his foreign policy councilors. American support for Israel was based on domestic politics as opposed to perceptions of American national interest.[55]

It is difficult to say what factor Truman's attempt to secure the Jewish vote played in his reelection. Truman won only 75 percent of the Jewish vote. While this initially seems compelling, it is a substantial decrease from Roosevelt's 90 percent. As a result of the heavy turnout for Wallace in New York, Truman lost the state, becoming the first president to win without carrying New York since Woodrow Wilson in 1916. In addition to New York, he also lost Michigan and Pennsylvania, two other states with a substantial Jewish population. However, Truman did win in California, Ohio, and Illinois and it is argued that Jewish voters provided the margin for victory in these states.[56]

Eisenhower and Israel

The Eisenhower administration viewed the importance of the Middle East the same way as the foreign policy bureaucracy did during the Truman years. The Middle East was important because of its oil and thus needed to remain squarely in the Western camp. The Eisenhower administration saw the Middle East and Europe as being interconnected. In order for NATO to remain strong the economies of Western Europe must be strong. Therefore, they depended on access to abundant, and cheap, oil. Eisenhower's strategy toward the Cold War, which was implemented by his Secretary of State John Foster Dulles, was to form pro-Western alliances around the world linked to the United States. However, any attempt to draw Arab states into an alliance would flounder due to American support for Israel. Therefore the Eisenhower administration saw Israel as an impediment to America's containment strategy in the region.[57] This view was articulated by Secretary of State John Foster Dulles in the 1950s, as he felt that continued identification with Israel and the perception that the United States was continuing the colonial legacy of Britain and France in the region would limit American policy options.[58] This view was expressed by Secretary Dulles during a meeting with Egyptian officials in Cairo on May 11, 1953:

> The new Administration's policies will be based on the Communist threat. The Communists already rule one-third of the world . . . nothing has happened to change the philosophy of the Communists. The death of Stalin did not change Communist philosophy which, like a religious creed, keeps on and on. Faced with the Communist threat, the U.S. naturally seeks the help of others. The U.S. considers the Middle East to be a danger area which heretofore has been somewhat neglected by the U.S. . . . . In the past the U.S. has perhaps centered too much on its interest on Israel as a result of pressure groups in the U.S. The new Administration is seeking a balanced view of the Middle East directed against neither the Arabs nor the Jews.[59]

Another significant factor that affected the conduct of the relationship between the two countries was domestic politics in the United States. The pro-Israeli lobby did not have the same amount of influence with Eisenhower as they did with Truman. This posed a problem for Israel's supporters for several reasons. First, they had felt comfortable in dealing with the Truman administration, as he was viewed as a supporter of Israel. In addition, as has already been documented, when Truman did waver in his support for Israel there were numerous pro-Zionist advisors present among his inner circle to give pro-Israeli groups access to the White House. There were also party considerations, as Jews formed a core constituency within the Democratic Party, particularly in key electoral states. Second, the support of the White House was able to neutralize the negative attitudes prevalent in the national security bureaucracy of the United States that viewed support for Israel as an impediment to American security and foreign policy. For supporters of Israel, the incoming Eisenhower administration represented uncertainty as to whether American support for Israel would continue.[60] As a result of this ambiguity, the Israelis clearly favored Adlai Stevenson in the 1952 election. It was perceived by the Israelis that as a Democrat, Stevenson would provide continuity and build on the U.S.-Israel relationship established by Truman. This was illustrated by comments made by Abba Eban:

> Stevenson is a man of vision, an intellectual, eloquent and articulate. His intellectual superiority over Eisenhower is self-evident . . . he is equally charismatic as the General. His fondness for Israel and Zionism runs deep, he understands and is familiar with our case in every detail both in its historical and moral dimensions.[61]

While it was acknowledged by Israeli embassy officials in Washington that there were supporters of Israel around Eisenhower, notably Senator Henry Cabot Lodge Jr., as well as prominent American Jews within the Republican Party, they felt that Eisenhower was the weaker candidate when it came to Israel. The first secretary of the Israeli embassy, Esther Herlitz, summed up the embassy view of Eisenhower when she stated: "Eisenhower as a military man would not view the problems of the Middle East on the basis of justice and moral merit as Truman had, but solely on the cold considerations of balance of power and national interest."[62] The United States and Israel came into conflict several times during the Eisenhower administration. The first occurred in 1953 when the Israelis sought to divert water from the Jordan River which would dramatically alter its flow and thus negatively affect the economic development of Syria and Jordan. There were also tensions as a result of the formation of the Baghdad Pact, the Suez War, and over the sale of arms.

Points of Contention between the U.S. and Israel

The Diversion of Water from the Jordan River

The Eisenhower administration opposed the Israeli initiatives to divert water from the Jordan River in 1953, led to political tension with the United States and eventually caused a cutoff of a $26-million dollar aid allocation. This led to a great deal of lobbying by various Jewish groups as well as criticisms by members of Congress who supported Israel, such as Emanuel Cellar and Jacob Javits.[63] Eisenhower, however, did attempt to diffuse the crisis, dispatching Eric Johnston, the former president of the United States Chamber of Commerce, to the region in an effort to get the parties to agree to share the resources of the Jordan River. The Johnston Plan was based on a study financed by the United Nations Relief and Works Agency for Palestine Refugees (UNRWA), and was conducted by the Tennessee Valley Authority (TVA), backed by the State Department. While this plan to a certain extent contradicted Israel's own plan, it also had some complementary points as well, and as a result was acceptable to Israel.[64] On October 29, President Eisenhower announced that aid would be restored, as Israel had agreed to abandon its diversion project and cooperate with the Security Council's attempt to put into place a plan for the development of the Jordan River.

The Baghdad Pact

Another political problem occurred as a result of the formation of the Baghdad Pact in 1955. The Eisenhower administration viewed the Middle East as a major area of superpower confrontation to block the expansion of Soviet influence. Both Eisenhower and Dulles felt that it was essential to get key Arab states such as Egypt and Iraq to join a regional alliance framework. The fact that the United States was the first country to recognize Israel and extended to Israel political support and aid during the Truman administration, in the view of the Eisenhower administration, was an impediment to the formation of a pro-Western regional security framework.[65] The philosophy of the Eisenhower administration, was illustrated in a position paper prepared by the State Department prior to Secretary Dulles' journey to the Middle East in May of 1953:

> The part played by the United States in the establishment and support of Israel contributes very substantially to (a) continued and increasing anti-American and anti-Western sentiment in the Arab world; (b) western instability to create an atmosphere of confidence; (c) lack of progress in strengthening the defense of the Near East; and (d) delay in improving the fundamental economic and social conditions in the area. The Arab states continue to believe that U.S. policy in the Near East is partial to Israel although they are hopeful that the change in Administration in the United States will bring a change in this. They believe that Israel harbor additional territorial ambitions and they fear continued immigration into Israel will stimulate the desire for more territory.[66]

The Baghdad Pact reflected the different aspirations of the principal nations involved. For the United States it represented an attempt to increase its influence in the Middle East. The British goal was to maintain the little influence it retained in the region as it was rapidly becoming displaced by the United States. The Iraqi justification for participation in this alliance was to gain protection against the Soviet Union as well as improve its stature within the Arab world.[67]

The Baghdad Pact not only caused tensions with Israel but with the Arab world as well. The pact consisted of Turkey, Iraq, Iran, and Pakistan, with the United States as an associate member. The alliance caused conflict in the Arab world because it destablized Jordan. King Hussein at first announced he would join the pact, but as a result of popular protest in the country, was forced to withdraw. Egyptian membership was initially solicited as well. Nasser distrusted the motivations behind the pact, since it served to arm his rivals the Hashemites of Iraq. He viewed this as an attempt to prop them up as a counterweight to Arab nationalism. Ultimately, it led to better relations between Egypt and the Soviet Union, allowing Moscow to gain a foothold in the Middle East. Ironically, Israel also viewed Baghdad Pact with some trepidation. It viewed the provisions of the pact that armed Iraq as threatening Israel's national security. From the Israeli perspective, Jerusalem and Baghdad were still at war, as Iraq had participated in the war of 1948 and had not signed an armistice agreement. In compensation for this pact, the Israelis demanded greater military assistance from the United States, as well as membership in NATO and a bilateral defense treaty.[68]

American-Israeli tensions eased as the Iraqi revolution of 1958 took Iraq out of the alliance. Israel began to cultivate close relations with two other pact members, Iran and Turkey. Israeli-Iranian relations would eventually develop into an extensive strategic, economic, and political relationship until the fall of the Shah.

The Suez War

Another major stress point in American-Israeli relations during the Eisenhower administration was the 1956 Suez War. The Eisenhower administration was opposed to the war as it threatened to destablize the Middle East. Eisenhower had previously warned the Israelis not to resort to violence and afterward sought to end the conflict through the United Nations. In the events leading up to the conflict, Eisenhower informed the Israeli leaders that he would not be swayed by domestic political considerations in the conduct of Middle East policy. However, scholars point out that his policy leading up to the Suez War was unclear, and that he only threatened Israel with the withdrawal of aid on October 27, after the general mobilization of Israeli forces had already occurred.[69]

Aid was an important component in resolving this conflict. The primary goal of the Eisenhower administration was a restoration of the status quo by Israel returning to the original border. However, Israel refused to do so unless its freedom of navigation in the Strait of Tiran was assured, and its hold on the Gaza Strip could be maintained. Gaza was important to serve as a buffer to better defend Israel proper from Palestinian border raids. The Israelis wanted the United States to guarantee this. The United States threatened from time to time to withdraw all aid, public as well as private, in an attempt to coerce Israel to withdraw.[70]

While the Eisenhower administration was seeking to place pressure on Israel there was domestic pressure in the United States sympathetic to Israeli claims. In early February 1957, 41 Republican Congressmen signed a statement calling on America to oppose Israeli withdrawal until the Egyptians negotiated. At the same time, 75 Democratic Congressmen in a letter to Eisenhower argued that the United States should insist on Israeli passage through the Suez Canal and access to the Strait of Tiran as a condition for the evacuation of Gaza and Sharm el-Sheikh. Other notable figures who were against sanctions were Republican Senate Leader William Knowland, as well as prominent Democratic Senators Paul Douglas and Senate Majority Leader Lyndon Johnson.[71]

Senator Johnson wrote a letter to Secretary Dulles indicating his opposition to sanctions against Israel:

> I feel that I should tell you, most frankly, how disturbed I have been by recent stories in the press . . . that serious consideration is being given in the General Assembly of the United Nations to imposing economic sanctions against the state of Israel. . . . This imposition of sanctions would, or so it appears to me, be a most unwise move. . . . To put it simply, the United States cannot apply one rule for the strong and another for the weak, it cannot organize its economic weight against the little states when it has not previously made even a pretense of doing so against the large states.[72]

In addition to politicians, some major organizations were advocates of the Israeli position. This included the AFL-CIO, which supported a demilitarized Sinai and Israeli control over Gaza. Support for Israel could also be found in segments of the American media, notably *the Washington Post*, which supported Israel's position of wanting guarantees against guerrilla attacks and passage through the strait. Rubenberg argues that this domestic pressure served to undercut the credibility of the Eisenhower administration in enforcing sanctions against Israel.[73]

Eventually, in March of 1957, the Israelis withdrew from Gaza and Sharm al-Sheikh. They did gain passage through the strait along with freedom of navigation. This lead to the development of the port of Eilat, and gave Israel an outlet to the Red Sea. They also received personal assurances from President Eisenhower for Israel's security.[74]

Disagreements over Arms Sales

A further point of disagreement between the two countries centered on the issue of arms sales, which would later serve to define the relationship between the two countries. After the Czech arms deal with Egypt, which initiated the growth of Soviet influence in Egypt, the Israelis argued that the military balance in the Middle East was being disrupted and as a result the United States should become active in arming Israel. Secretary Dulles argued this was not the case and Israel should look to European sources for arms.[75]

The specifics of this Czech arms purchase were announced on September 27, 1955, when the United States refused to honor Egypt's outstanding arms orders. The sale was worth about $200 million and included the transfer of MiG aircraft, tanks, artillery, small arms, as well as submarines.[76]

The Israelis were alarmed by the Czech arms sales because it meant that Egypt was in the process of building an alliance with the Soviet Union, and this would add a superpower dimension to the Arab-Israeli conflict that threatened the Israeli military position. The Israelis felt that the arms being supplied to Egypt would give them a qualitative edge in technology and they were especially concerned about the supplying of aircraft to Egypt. The Illyushin bomber could operate at high altitude and be invulnerable from Israeli Meteor fighters. In addition, the MiG-15 was a superior fighter to the Israeli Meteor.[77]

The Israelis sought to upgrade their armaments by turning to France, whose military relationship with Israel began in the early 1950s. The French-Israeli alliance was more firmly established as a result of Nasser's nationalization of the Suez Canal in 1956 and the situation in Algeria. The French sought to destablize the Egyptian regime in an effort to end its support for the Algerian nationalists. The by-product of this was a French-Israeli alliance which lasted until 1967.[78]

Support for Israel

Military Support

Critics have stated that while the United States was not supplying arms to Israel directly, it was facilitating sales from European countries such as France, Canada, and others while Washington provided the funds to pay for this equipment. It is argued that this contributed to Israel's military superiority and served as a disincentive for it to negotiate with its Arab neighbors. In addition to facilitating the acquisition of conventional weapons, it is also argued that the United States enabled Israel to begin to acquire nuclear technology.[79] This aid was further facilitated in 1956 when the United States allowed the French to ship military equipment to Israel, rather than insist that NATO hold priority.[80]

The Tacit Alliance: France and Israel

As indicated above, the United States did not want to become directly involved with Israel militarily and preferred to encourage other Western nations to supply the Jewish state with weapons. Up until the 1967 war, Israel's primary military ally was France during the war, almost the entire Israeli air force was equipped with French planes. It was during this conflict that the French embargoed arms to Israel and the United States officially took over as Israel's primary arms supplier.[81]

The French-Israeli alliance had its origins in 1949 and was initiated as a quid pro quo arrangement centered around scientific contacts. An Israeli physicist, Israel Dostrofsky, invented a process of producing heavy water which was shared with the French. This began a relationship by which the two countries cooperated in sharing nuclear technology.[82] The arms relationship began during the same year as the Israelis received 155 mm howitzers and light arms.[83] The arms transfers advanced from these simple beginnings to a more complex stage by the mid 1950s. In 1954 Israel's Chief of Staff Moshe Dayan made an official visit to Paris and concluded agreements with his counterpart, General Augustin Guillaume. These agreements called for Israel to purchase Ouragon and Mystere jet fighters, AMX tanks, radar equipment, 75 mm cannon, antitank missiles, and various other weapons. By the next year additional agreements were concluded in which additional Ouragon as well as the new Mystere fighters were sent to Israel. The Mystere fighter was significant as it was considered to be the equal of the Soviet MiG-17, then being supplied to Egypt.[84]

An important reason why this Israeli alliance came about was the result of ideology, both on the left and right of the political spectrum. The French Left had a long history of being pro-Jewish dating back to the 18th century and the Dreyfus affair. In addition, both governments were controlled by Socialist parties so the political elites had an ideological affinity. On the political right, French conservatives, and in particular those in the military, saw Israel as a natural ally against the rising tide of Arab nationalism. They admired the Israeli military effort against the Arab countries in 1948 and felt that Israel's victory postponed the Algerian uprising by 10 years.[85] Also, both states did not approve of the American-sponsored Baghdad Pact concluded in 1955 as the French argued that this alliance threatened to destabilize the region.[86]

In the late 1950s a strong pro-Israel parliamentary grouping had emerged in France. It numbered over 100 deputies, at least 50 senators, and five ministers of the Gaillard government. In addition, the French President, Jacques Soustelle, was also very pro-Israel. He argued that Israel blocked the Syrians from intervening in the Algerian civil war.[87]

Military contacts escalated in the late 1950s for strategic reasons. The French viewed Israel as occupying a strategic position in the Middle East. French military planners envisioned Israel as having a role in protecting French oil supplies from the Middle East, as well as being conveniently located to French bases in Djibouti, Reunion, and Madagascar. In addition, the French navy envisioned a common strategy for both countries in the Red Sea. In January 1958 the navies of the two countries participated in joint maneuvers where the French trained the Israelis in new submarine fighting techniques. This was especially significant as the Soviets were supplying submarines to the Egyptians.[88] The United States knew about the French-Israeli arms connection as a result of the monitoring mechanisms established under the Tripartite Declaration of 1950. This declaration between Britain, France, and the United States pledged they would take action against Middle East states that violated borders and armistice lines.

Under this declaration, the Near Eastern Arms Coordinating Committee was established, which allowed these states to monitor all arms transfers to the region. This alliance complemented American strategy in the region. The Eisenhower administration was put in the favorable political position of being able to turn down Israeli arms requests, which facilitated relations with Arab states without really endangering Israeli security.[89]

Cooperation in Intelligence and Arms

An important development that took place during the Eisenhower administration was the cooperation in the sharing of intelligence and American access to captured Soviet military equipment. This would eventually evolve into one of the centerpieces of strategic cooperation between the two nations. A few days after the 1956 war, American military attachés were allowed to travel into Sinai to examine and photograph captured Soviet military equipment.[90]

A significant policy of President Eisenhower was his emphasis on not getting the United States involved with becoming Israel's major arms supplier. The Eisenhower administration wished to avoid this in an effort to maintain some independence from Israel and attempt to serve as an "honest broker" for peace. He did, however, retreat slightly from this position when the administration sold 100 recoilless guns to Israel in 1958, as well as sophisticated radar and communication equipment in 1960. However, his Secretary of State Christine Herter specifically informed Ben-Gurion that the United States was not willing to provide HAWK air defense missiles.[91]

Conclusions

The Eisenhower Presidency was the low water mark for American-Israeli relations. Eisenhower was guided more by issues of international politics and containment strategy than he was domestic political considerations. Although Eisenhower was subject to domestic pressures even in his own party, he was not as politically vulnerable as Truman was. He told Zionist leaders that the policy of whether or not to arm Israel would not be predicated on domestic politics. This illustrated that Eisenhower was more politically secure and popular with the electorate than Truman had been. Rabbi Hillel Silver, leader of the Zionist Organization of America, stated, "you can be re-elected without a single Jewish vote."[92]

A consideration in Eisenhower's policy toward Israel was that Jewish voters were not a major constituency group for the Republican Party. Therefore, Eisenhower felt he would not be hurt politically by threatening Israel with sanctions. However, the Eisenhower administration also greatly facilitated the emergence of the French-Israeli alliance. It was also under Eisenhower that arms started to be sold to Israel and that battlefield intelligence-sharing was initiated. These would later become fixtures, and in large part define the future relationship between the two nations.

Notes

1. Mitchell Geoffrey Bard, *The Water's Edge and Beyond* (New Brunswick, N.J.: Transaction Publishers, 1991), 182.

2. Bard, *The Water's Edge*, 132.

3. John Snetsinger, *Truman, the Jewish Vote and the Creation of Israel* (Stanford, Calif.: Hoover Institution Press, 1974), 12.

4. Bard, *The Water's Edge*, 132.

5. Snetsinger, *Truman, the Jewish Vote*, 13. Also see Walter Millis, ed. *The Forrestal Diaries* (New York: Viking Press, 1951), 323.

6. Snetsinger, *Truman, the Jewish Vote*, 13. See also John C. Campbell, *Defense of the Middle East* (New York, 1960), 250-52. Kermit Roosevelt, "The Partition of Palestine: A Lesson in Pressure Politics," *Middle East Journal*, Vol. 2, (January 1948): 9. Roosevelt stated that oil from the Middle East would be cheaper in Western Europe than Western Hemisphere oil, as well as allow the United States and other producers in the Americas to conserve their own domestic supplies. Also *The New York Times*, 15 May 1947, 12; 13 February 1948, 16.

7. Snetsinger, *Truman, the Jewish Vote*, 13-14.

8. Michael J. Cohen, *Truman and Israel* (Berkeley, Calif.: University of California Press, 1990), 95-100. Good discussion summarizing activities of oil companies in concert with State and Defense Department officials.

9. Cohen, *Truman and Israel*, 35-36. He points out that Niles was a valuable contact as he worked closely with the Zionist leadership. Eliahu Epstein, a member of the Jewish Agency Executive, said that Niles was "our friend" in the White House. (Epstein to Nahum Goldman, October 9, 1946, Weizman Archives). Cited in Snetsinger, *Truman, the Jewish Vote*, 36.

10. Cohen, *Truman and Israel*, 77-78, 81.

11. Bard, *The Water's Edge*, 130.

12. *New York Times*, 13 December 1945, 10. Quoted in Snetsinger, *Truman, the Jewish Vote*, 24-25.

13. Snetsinger, *Truman, the Jewish Vote*, 40-41.

14. Snetsinger, *Truman, the Jewish Vote*, 41. Also see Millis, *The Forrestal Diaries*, 346-47.

15. Memorandum Clayton to Truman, 12 September 1946. Quoted in Snetsinger, *Truman, the Jewish Vote*, 41-42.

16. *New York Times*, 7 October 1946, 1. Quoted in Snetsinger, *Truman, the Jewish Vote*, 42.

17. Confidential, unsigned memorandum, July 28, 1948, Box 30, Niles Papers, Harry S. Truman Library. Cited in Cohen, *Truman and Israel*, 250.

18. Snetsinger, *Truman, the Jewish Vote*, 44. Discusses Truman's problems with organized labor and the disaffection of prominent New Dealers like Henry Wallace and Harold Ickes, as well as opposition by conservative Democrats dissatisfied by Truman's initiatives on civil rights and welfare.

19. Bard, *The Water's Edge*, 182.

20. Snetsinger, *Truman, the Jewish Vote*, 53. He quotes among others Eliahu Epstein, the Washington Representative of the Jewish Agency who in a letter dated October 9, 1946, stated that people "will not let President Truman make of it a pre-election statement even if he would like to do so." Epstein to Nahum Goldman, Weizman Archives. In addition, Snetsinger cites a telegram from a Zionist group

in Sussex County New Jersey stating that Truman's inaction on the Palestine issue has lead the group not to support Truman in the election of 1948.

21. Cohen, *Truman and Israel*, 149.

22. Snetsinger, *Truman, the Jewish Vote*, 60-61. He argues that Zionist territorial ambitions were satisfied largely due to Weizman's presidential access.

23. Telegram Cellar to Truman, November 26, 1947. of 204-Misc., Truman Papers. Quoted in Snetsinger, *Truman, the Jewish Vote*, 67.

24. Snetsinger, *Truman, the Jewish Vote*, 68.

25. Cellar to Connelly, December 3, 1947, of 204-Misc., Truman Papers, and *Congressional Record*, 80th Cong., 1st sess., 1947, 100. Quoted in Snetsinger, *Truman, the Jewish Vote*, 69.

26. Eben A. Ayers diary, November 29, 1947, Harry S. Truman Library. Ayers was a special assistant in the White House and also functioned as assistant press secretary. Cited in Cohen, *Truman and Israel*, 169.

27. Cohen, *Truman and Israel*, 169.

28. Cohen, *Truman and Israel*, 169.

29. D. B. Sachar, "David Niles and American Policy," (unpublished Harvard senior honors thesis, 1959), 73. Michael J. Cohen, *Palestine and the Great Powers: 1945-1948* (Princeton, N.J.: Princeton University Press, 1982), 298. Cited in Cohen, *Truman and Israel*, 170.

30. Cohen, *Truman and Israel*, 170; also Cohen, *Palestine and the Great Powers*, 299.

31. Millis, *Forrestal Diaries*, 323. Also cited in Snetsinger, *Truman, the Jewish Vote*, 72.

32. Andrew Cockburn and Leslie Cockburn, *Dangerous Liaison* (New York: Harper Collins, 1991), 26.

33. Cohen, *Truman and Israel*, 61. Also cited in Cockburn, *Dangerous Liaison*, 25.

34. Millis, *Forrestal Diaries*, 309, 345. In Forrestal's diaries he indicates this consideration in several instances in conversations with high-level Democratic Party officials. One such conversation occurred on September 4, 1947, with Postmaster General Robert Hannegan. Hannegan stated "very large sums were obtained a year ago from Jewish contributors and that they would be influenced in either giving or withholding by what the President did on Palestine" (309). Another similar conversation was held with Senator McGrath on November 26, 1947. Senator McGrath indicated that "Jewish sources were responsible for a substantial part of the contributions to the Democratic National Committee, and many of these contributions were made with a distinct idea on the part of the givers that they will have an opportunity to express their views and have them seriously considered on such questions as the present Palestine question."(345).

35. Millis, *Forrestal Diaries*, 309. Also Snetsinger, *Truman, the Jewish Vote*, 72.

36. Cohen, *Truman and Israel*, 73.

37. Abba Eban, "Dewey David Stone: Prototype of an American Zionist," in *Solidarity and Kinship: Essays on American Zionism, in Memory of Dewey David Stone,* ed. Nathan M. Kaganoff (Waltham, Mass.: American Jewish Historical Society, 1980), 30. Quoted in Cohen, *Truman and Israel*, 73.

38. Millis, *Forrestal Diaries*, 344.

39. Clark Clifford, Memorandum, November 19, 1947, Clifford Papers, Harry S. Truman Library, cited in Cohen, *Palestine and the Great Powers*, 47, cited in Cohen, *Truman and Israel*, 60.

40. See Cohen, *Palestine and the Great Powers*, 48; Stephen D. Isaacs, *Jews and American Politics* (Garden City, N.Y.: Doubleday, 1974), 6; and Zvi Ganin, *Truman, American Jewry, and Israel: 1945-1948* (New York: Holmes and Meier, 1979), 101. Cited in Cohen, *Truman and Israel*, 60.

41. Cheryl Rubenberg, *Israel and the American National Interest* (Urbana, Ill.: University of Illinois Press, 1986), 32-33.

42. Millis, *Forrestal Diaries*, 346,376-77, 410-11. Also cited in Snetsinger, *Truman, the Jewish Vote*, 74.

43. Snetsinger, *Truman, the Jewish Vote*, 77.

44. *New York Times*, 18 February 1948, 1. Cited in Snetsinger, *Truman, the Jewish Vote*, 78-79.

45. *New York Times*, 18 February 1948, 1. Cited in Snetsinger, *Truman, the Jewish Vote*, 80.

46. Snetsinger, *Truman, the Jewish Vote*, 81.

47. Snetsinger, *Truman, the Jewish Vote*,108-09.

48. Rubenberg, *Israel and the American*, 41.

49. Rubenberg, *Israel and the American*, 41-42.

50. Stephen Green, *Taking Sides: America's Secret Relations with a Militant Israel* (New York: William Morrow, 1984), 23.

51. Issacs, *Jews and American Politics*, passim. Cited in Rubenberg, *Israel and the American*, 42.

52. Rubenberg, *Israel and the American*, 43.

53. Green, *Taking Sides*, 76.

54. Leopold Yehuda Laufer, *Dynamics of Dependence,* ed. Gabriel Sheffer, (Boulder, Colo.: Westview Press, 1987), 129-30.

55. Rubenberg, *Israel and the American*, 48-49.

56. Cohen, *Truman and Israel*, 258-59.

57. Steven L. Spiegel, *The Other Arab-Israeli Conflict* (Chicago: University of Chicago Press, 1985), 56.

58. Harry J. Shaw, "Strategic Dissensus," *Foreign Policy*, no. 61 (Winter 1985-1986): 136.

59. U.S. Department of State, *Foreign Relations of the United States, The Near and Middle East, 1952-1954*, Part I (Washington, D.C.: U.S. Government Printing Office, 1986), 9: 130. Also Abraham Ben-Zvi, *The United States and Israel: The Limits of the Special Relationship* (New York: Columbia University Press, 1993), 31-32.

60. Isaac Alteras, *Eisenhower and Israel: U.S.-Israeli Relations, 1953-1960* (Gainesville, Fla.: University Press of Florida, 1993), 26.

61. Israel State Archives, 2400/28, July 31, 1952. Cited in Alteras, *Eisenhower and Israel*, 26.

62. Israel State Archives, 2479/1, February 20, 1952. Cited in Alteras, *Eisenhower and Israel*, 26-27.

63. Green, *Taking Sides*, 90-91; Also see *New York Times*, 23 October 1953, 2. Green cites the various American Zionist groups that condemned the aid cutoff. These were The American Jewish Congress, the American Jewish Palestine Committee, the National Council of Jewish Women, the Labor Zionist Organization of America, the Zionist Organization of America, the Zionist-Revisionists of America, as well as Hadassah. In addition, former ambassador James G. McDonald also condemned the aid cutoff.

64. Ben-Zvi, *United States and Israel*, 45-46. Also Michael Brecher, *Decisions in Israel's Foreign Policy* (London: Oxford University Press, 1974), 192-94. Among the points of agreement between the Johnston Plan and Israel's project was

the diversion of the Yarmuk River as well as part of the Upper Jordan into Lake Tiberias. It also supported the Tel Hai power project.

65. Ben-Zvi, *United States and Israel*, 32. Other sources that discuss this include Spiegel, *The Other Arab-Israeli Conflict*, 56-58; A. F. K. Organski, *The $36 Billion Bargain: Strategy and Politics in U.S. Assistance to Israel* (New York: Columbia University Press, 1990), 32; Mordechai Gazit, "Israeli Military Procurement from the United States," in *Dynamics of Dependence*, ed. Gabriel Sheffer (Boulder, Colo.: Westview Press, 1987), 90.

66. Ben-Zvi, *United States and Israel*, 35-36. Also see, Department of State Position Paper, May 7, 1953, *Foreign Relations of the United States*, 9, pt. 1, 1215-16.

67. For a detailed discussion of the Baghdad Pact and its repercussions see Stephen M. Walt, *The Origins of Alliances* (Ithaca, N.Y.: Cornell University Press, 1987), 58-62. Another interpretation of the Baghdad Pact is that it was brought about as a result of Anglo-American rivalry in the Middle East. It can be further argued that rather than providing an effective counterweight against the spread of Soviet influence, it was designed to enhance American influence in the region at the expense of the British. It can also be pointed out that rather than preserving regional stability, it actually provoked instability. It did nothing to ensure the Iraqi regime, as the revolution of 1958 would seem to indicate, as well as provoked further tensions between India and Pakistan. For a detailed discussion of this interpretation see Ayesha Jalal, "Toward the Baghdad Pact: South Asia and Middle East Defence in the Cold War, 1947-1955," *International History Review* 11, no. 3 (August 1989): 409-33.

68. Rubenberg, *Israel and the American*, 60-65. Discusses the dynamics of this alliance. She argues that the U.S. refusal to let Israel join NATO or the establishment of a bilateral defense treaty emboldened Israel into emphasizing military solutions and reprisal raids. The idea that the Baghdad Pact would broaden American military aid to Iraq was reflected in Israeli government documents. Israel State Archives, February 25, 1955, 2460/10/B; Cited in Alteras, *Eisenhower and Israel*, 126-27.

69. Green, *Taking Sides,* 142

70. Rubenberg, *Israel and the American*, 73. Argues that aid was not actually suspended but only threatened to be suspended. She cites cables back and forth between the United States and Israel. Stephen Green argues that aid was actually suspended for a time. Green, *Taking Sides*, 142. Quoted from "Secret" record of decision re Israel, memorandum for Colonel A. J. Goodpaster, the White House, from Fisher Howe, Director, Executive Secretariat, Department of State, dated November 11, 1956, in White House Central Files, Confidential File, Box 82, Folder: Suez Canal Crisis, Dwight D. Eisenhower Library. See also Ben-Zvi, 67-68; Brecher, *Decisions in Israel's Foreign Policy* (London: Oxford University Press, 1974), 293. The Israeli position was stated in a meeting between Secretary Dulles and Ambassador Eban, *The Foreign Relations of the United States* (1957), 17: 158-65.

71. Rubenberg, *Israel and the American*, 78-79. See also Ben-Zvi, *United States and Israel,* 69-71; Brecher, *Decisions in Israel,* 293.

72. Quoted from Senator Lyndon B. Johnson's letter of February 11, 1957, to Secretary Dulles, *Foreign Relations of the United States* 17:139. Also Ben-Zvi, *United States and Israel*, 69-70.

73. Rubenberg, *Israel and the American*, 78-79. See also Ben-Zvi, *United States and Israel*, 69-71; Brecher, *Decisions in Israel*, 296.

74. David Ben-Gurion, *Israel A Personal Israel* (New York: Funk and Wagnalls

Sabra Books, 1971), 532-34. cited in Rubenberg, *Israel and American,* 83-84.

75. Mordechai Gazit, "Israeli Military Procurement from the United States," in *Dynamics of Dependence,* ed. Gabriel Sheffer (Boulder, Colo.: Westview Press, 1987), 91.

76. George W. Ball and Douglas B. Ball, *The Passionate Attachment: America's Involvement with Israel, 1947 to the Present* (New York: W. W. Norton, 1992), 45.

77. Alteras, *Eisenhower and Israel,* 141.

78. Alteras, *Eisenhower and Israel,* 92.

79. Rubenberg, *Israel and the American,* 51. Regarding nuclear technology see Green, *Taking Sides,* 154.

80. George Ball, "The Coming Crisis in Israeli-American Relations," *Foreign Affairs* 58, no. 2 (Winter 1979-1980): 2.

81. Stephen Green, *Living by the Sword* (Brattleboro, Vt.: Amana Books, 1988), 10. The combat inventory of the Israeli air force at the time of the Six Day War included 65 Mirage IICs, 25 Mysteres, and 25 Super Mysteres. These systems constituted the core of the Israeli air force.

82. Sylvia K. Crosbie, *A Tacit Alliance: France and Israel from Suez to the Six Day War* (Princeton, N.J.: Princeton University Press, 1974), 36; Alteras, *Eisenhower and Israel,* 145.

83. Shimon Peres, *David's Sling: The Arming of Israel* (London: Weidenfeld & Nicolson, 1970), 51; Cited in Alteras, *Eisenhower and Israel,* 145.

84. Alteras, *Eisenhower and Israel,* 145-46; Crosbie, *A Tacit Alliance,* 61. Crosbie also points out that the French-Israeli alliance became so ingrained that the French military had the freedom to transfer any arms it wished to Israel. The major decisions were carried out by the French Chief of Staff, who simply informed the prime minister of what arms were supplied in general. Crosbie, *A Tacit Alliance,* 106.

85. Alteras, *Eisenhower and Israel,* 145. Crosbie argues that there was a great deal of cooperation between the intelligence services of the two countries. She argues that it was in Israel's interest to promote French insecurity about President Nasser and his role in promoting the Algerian uprising, as well as emphasizing the possibility of his upsetting the status quo in the Middle East and sub-Saharan Africa. The Israelis supplied the French with evidence of Egyptian assistance in the Algerian revolution. Crosbie, *A Tacit Alliance,* 58.

86. Ya'akov Tsur, *Prelude a Suez: Journal D'une Ambassade, 1953-1956* (Paris: Cite, 1966), 150. Cited in Crosbie, *A Tacit Alliance,* 56.

87. *Jerusalem Post,* 12 August 1957. Cited in Crosbie, *A Tacit Alliance,* 99.

88. Crosbie, *A Tacit Alliance,* 104-5.

89. In addition to the French there were also indications that the Italians were shipping arms during this period. See Alteras, *Eisenhower and Israel,* 146. More significantly the Federal Republic of Germany also became a supplier of arms to Israel during the 1950s. It has been suggested that this relationship was facilitated by the French, as they participated in shipping German arms to Israel. Crosbie, *A Tacit Alliance,* 102. It was estimated that between 1958-1965 West Germany shipped between $37.5 and $266 million in arms. These were given as grants not as sales. This relationship was confirmed by German Foreign Minister Schroder in *Die Welt,* 26 February 1965. The importance of these arms sales was illustrated by *Maariv,* 22 November 1964. For a thorough account of West German-Israeli relations see Lily Gardner Feldman, *The Special Relationship between West Germany and Israel* (Boston: George Allen and Unwin, 1984), 127.

90. Feldman, *Special Relationship,* 144.

91. "Secret" Department of State telegram 86 from Secretary of State to U.S.

Embassy, Port-au-Prince, dated August 4, 1964, in *Declassified Documents* (Washington, D.C.: Carrolton Press, 1979), 433D Cited in Green, *Taking Sides*, 152-53.

92.Whitman File, Memoranda Series, Box 4, April 26, 1956; Also Marc L. Raphael, *Abba Hillel Silver: Profile in American Judaism* (New York: Holmes and Meier, 1989), 200; Cited in Alteras, *Eisenhower and Israel*, 177.

Chapter 5

The Significance of the American-Israeli Alliance, 1960-1992

The Kennedy Administration: A Shift in Policy

American foreign policy changed during the Kennedy administration as President Kennedy sought to broaden U.S. links to the third world. The emphasis of the Kennedy presidency was to focus somewhat less on security issues and foster more developmental aid to third world states. American economic aid increased during the Kennedy years and was less dependent on the political orientation of the recipients. Among the programs that were initiated by the Kennedy administration were: (1) the creation of the Agency for International Development to better coordinate aid to the Third World; (2) the modification of Public Law-480 which was turned into the Food for Peace Program; (3) the creation of the Peace Corps; and (4) the establishment of the Foreign Assistance Act of 1961 that amended the Mutual Security Act of 1953. Among the policies of the U.S. that gained support in the third world were the voting in the United Nations to end Portuguese rule over Angola in 1961, and in 1963 Washington supported the establishment of sanctions against South Africa.[1]

Kennedy pursued a more activist role in Middle Eastern affairs as he attempted to assist both Israel and the Arab countries. Kennedy sought to build bridges with the United Arab Republic by expanding food aid, as well as recognizing the republican regime in Sanaa while at the same time attempting to get Egyptian troops out of Yemen. Also he assisted Israel with greater sophisticated weaponry, essentially agreeing with Israel on the threats posed to it by the Soviet relationship with Egypt.[2] Kennedy, when he assumed office in 1961, felt that there could be peace in the region if a military balance between the parties were achieved.[3]

During the Kennedy administration the relationship between the United States and Israel underwent fundamental change as a result of political guarantees and military sales. These occurred at about the time that the

French were in the process of scaling back their military support for Israel, and the Soviets were providing increasingly sophisticated military supplies to Egypt, such as the MiG-21 and TU-16. This change in policy was reflected by the sale of HAWK missiles to Israel, which was valued at $21.5 million.[4] President Kennedy justified the selling of the HAWK missiles on several grounds. First, the felt that the HAWK was inherently a defensive system and would cause little criticism in the Arab world. Second, Kennedy viewed the strategic balance as beginning to turn against Israel, which could weaken American interests in the region. President Kennedy was especially concerned about reassuring Israel and trying to forestall them from over compensating for this situation by developing nuclear weapons. Third, it is likely that the Kennedy administration was hoping to use the sale of high-technology weapons to increase American leverage over Israel. Finally, Kennedy had domestic policy motivations, as he did not want to lose Jewish support in the upcoming congressional midterm elections.[5]

Justification for the HAWK Sale by the National Security Bureaucracy

The HAWK sale was justified by the State and Defense Departments for similar reasons as those attributed to President Kennedy discussed previously. A Defense Department memorandum of May 1962 found a valid military reason for the sale of the HAWK the State Department uncharacteristically did not oppose this deal. There were several reasons for this: (1) the HAWK was a defensive weapons systems and it was felt that the Arab reaction would be muted; (2) American-Egyptian relations had improved therefore it was felt that the Egyptians would not vigorously oppose the sale; (3) the State Department, like the Defense Department, thought that the military balance had turned against Israel; and (4) they wanted the United States to send a signal to the Soviets, and their Arab allies, that they would not allow them to flood the Middle East with arms.[6]

The sale of the HAWK missiles were significant for several reasons. First, the size of the sale totaled tens of millions of dollars. Second, it would act as compensation to balance for the delivery of Soviet arms to such Arab countries as Egypt, Syria, Iraq, and Yemen. Third, unlike previous proposals of arms sales to Israel, this sale was supported by all relevant sectors of the government.[7] Fourth, the HAWK sale would require extensive training of Israeli personal in the United States, as well as a spare parts supply pipeline. It was thought that these factors would make Israel dependent on the United States and enable Washington to have more leverage in its dealings with Israel.[8] In addition to the HAWK sale, which was an outright transfer of arms, the United States in 1962 began financing arms sales in secret from West Germany to Israel. When this was discovered in 1965, Washington fulfilled the remaining $80 million worth of equipment on order.[9]

Shortly afterward, American policy makers realized the negative repercussions the HAWK sale had for American interests in the region. "The HAWK sale cost us dearly in terms of goodwill and influence with the Arabs, but did not make Israel more receptive to U.S. efforts to further the Johnson refugee initiative, strengthen UNTSO or maintain silence on implementation of the Jordan waters off-take."[10]

Political Guarantees Made By Kennedy

The issue of military sales takes on even greater significance when coupled with the political guarantees provided by the Kennedy administration. Kennedy promised that the United States would assist Israel in case of attack and he emphasized the special relationship between Israel and the United States.[11] He further expanded on this in 1962 when he privately assured Foreign Minister Golda Meir that Israel and the United States were de facto allies. These guarantees were expanded in various letters to Prime Minister Eshkol to include an acceptance of Israel's definition of its borders, as well as to the amount of water it was entitled to take from the Jordan River.[12]

It was the Kennedy administration that initiated the "special relationship" between the United States and Israel. During this period the restraint on providing Israel with sophisticated armaments, which both the Truman and Eisenhower administrations had taken great pains to avoid, began to disappear. More significant, however, was the expansion of political ties between the two countries. It was President Kennedy, in his discussions with Israeli leaders, who used the term alliance. This alliance was illustrated by the comprehensive political guarantees that were made to Israel. These guarantees did not only include security, but also extended to such specific matters as interpretations of territorial boundaries and water allocation from the Jordan. By essentially agreeing to the Israeli view on these questions, Kennedy made Israeli interests American interests. Thus he initiated the idea of a militarily strong Israel as being essential to American regional interests in the Middle East. Domestic politics was the primary motivation for Kennedy to adopt this view. As indicated earlier, Jews were a core constituency of the Democratic Party, and Kennedy had only narrowly won the presidency in the 1960 election.[13] Future administrations of both parties would expand this policy.

The Johnson Presidency: The Institutionalization of the Special Relationship

Johnson had been a longtime supporter of Israel from his days in the U.S. Senate. His pledge upon assuming the presidency was to carry on Kennedy's policies. This pledge and his long-standing support for Israel gratified supporters of the Jewish state. While in the Senate, Johnson denounced Nasser's nationalization of the Suez Canal as well as pressured the Eisenhower administration against adopting sanctions against Israel.[14]

In addition to Johnson's personal preferences, several of his closest associates were very pro-Israel and certainly influenced Johnson in his support for Israel. Among these were Eugene and Walter Rostow who served as undersecretary of state for political affairs, and national security advisor respectively. In addition there was Walter Goldberg who was ambassador to the United Nations. Others close to the president outside of the national security bureaucracy, but in other influential roles were Abe Fortas, later appointed to the Supreme Court, Clark Clifford, a Washington lawyer and former political advisor in the Truman administration, as well as Arthur Krim and Abe Feinberg, who were wealthy contributors to the Democratic Party.

Arms to Israel

The Sale of Patton Tanks and Skyhawk Jets

Johnson continued and accelerated the process of providing Israel with arms. By 1965 the United States had become the largest supplier of military goods to Israel. This accelerated with the announcement in February of 1966 that America was selling Israel 200 Patton tanks in order to maintain military superiority in the region. Supplying these tanks, as well as other weapons systems, would further bind Israel and the United States at the expense of Washington's relations with Arab states. In addition, American policy makers thought this arms transfer would not give the United States any additional leverage over Israel and would probably make it more difficult for Washington to refuse further requests for arms by Israel: "Our experience with the sale of HAWK missiles suggests that the supply of U.S. tanks to Israel would not assure any greatly increased Israeli cooperation with U.S. initiatives in the Near East."[15]

This was followed up in May by the announcement that Washington had agreed to provide Israel with Skyhawk jet bombers. These planes had a range of 2,000 miles, which gave Israel the ability to strike states outside of its borders such as Libya and Iraq.[16] The United States thus began the process of providing Israel with the military capabilities to attain military superiority in the region that would become a major component of relations between the two countries and a goal of American foreign policy in the region.[17]

Other scholars, however, point out that the increasing amount of arms being provided to Israel was part of American strategy for the region as a whole. They argue the United States was also selling F-5 jets to Morocco and Libya, as well as providing equipment to Tunisia, Lebanon and Saudi Arabia.[18] Analysts maintain that the Skyhawk deal was to balance the Soviet military shipments to Egypt, Syria and Iraq. Also at the same time, the Johnson administration was selling three squadrons of F-104 Starfighter aircraft to Jordan.[19]

While the Skyhawk sale was a turning point in American-Israeli relations it was not intended to establish a precedent. "Israel explicitly recognized that the sale did not constitute a precedent for future U.S. action and further agreed 'to continue to look to Europe for the bulk of its military requirements and not to regard the United States as a major arms supplier.'"[20]

The F-4 Phantom Jet Sale

The Skyhawk sale was followed by an Israeli request to purchase the F-4 Phantom. The pressure by Israel to acquire the Phantom built up in early 1968, but was opposed by both the navy and the air force. They not only disapproved of a possible sale of Phantoms, but also were against the transfer of the Skyhawk as well, being concerned with the effect that these arms transfers would have on American operational effectiveness in Vietnam.[21] Johnson himself was initially reluctant to sell the Phantoms to Israel. The Pentagon concluded that Israel did not need the planes as there was no threat based on strategic grounds. President Johnson was attempting to cultivate relations with the Arab states, especially Egypt, as well as trying to conclude an agreement with the Soviet Union to limit arms sales to the Middle East.[22]

The Phantom introduced a qualitative leap in arms for the region. Its maximum speed is over 1,200 miles an hour and has a range of 1,000 miles. It is considered both an attack bomber as well as a fighter interceptor. In Vietnam the F-4 out-performed the MiG-21, which was the main aircraft used by the Egyptian, Syrian, and Iraqi air forces.[23]

In discussions with American policy makers, the Israelis argued that they wanted the Phantom to keep up with their regional rivals. They stated that by the end of 1967, Egypt, Syria, and Iraq combined had over 500 warplanes. They contrasted this with Israel's own air capabilities, which they stated as 150 planes and, they argued, these were out of date.[24]

Although Johnson was reluctant to commit himself to the sale, the dynamics of domestic politics proved to be overwhelming. Johnson always had been under pressure to provide more support for Israel and the Phantom debate was especially intense. By June of 1968 an effort was made by some members of Congress, led by Senator Stuart Symington (D-Mo), to force the administration to sell the planes to Israel. Senator Symington threaten to kill the Military Sales Bill if the president did not agree to sell the F-4. It should be noted that in addition to providing support for Israel the F-4 was built in the senator's state.[25]

In April of 1968 Representative Bertram Podell (D-NY) had introduced a resolution in the House calling for the sale of the planes and attracted the support of 100 members when the Foreign Assistance Act of 1968 came up. In July, Representative Lester Wolff (D-NY) and Seymour Halperin (R-NY) proposed an amendment that would have required the president to sell at minimum 50 Phantoms as well as replace equipment lost in the 1967 conflict.[26] However, this amendment had problems because in its wording it would have forced the president to perform an action that could have been challenged as an unconstitutional infringement on presidential power.[27]

Conversely, there were some members of the State Department who were reluctant to supply Israel with the F-4 viewing it as too potent of a weapon that would escalate the regional arms race. This group suggested that Israel be offered the F-5, which was a less capable fighter already being sold on the third world market.[28]

The Phantom Jet As a Campaign Issue

In addition to causing problems with Congress the F-4 also became an issue in the 1968 presidential election. In April of 1968 the Republican Coordinating Committee recommended the sale of arms to Israel in order to maintain the balance of power in the region. The committee noted that since the Soviet Union was providing sophisticated arms to the Arabs, the United States should do likewise with Israel, and thus supported the sale of the F-4.[29] Richard Nixon, the Republican Party Presidential candidate, on several occasions expressed his support for the F-4 sale to Israel. In a speech to the B'nai B'rith he stated that

> the balance must be tipped in Israel's favor . . . (we) support a policy that would give Israel a technological military margin to more than offset her hostile neighbors numerical superiority. If maintaining that margin should require that the United States supply Israel with supersonic Phantom F-4 jets we should supply those Phantom jets.[30]

His opponent for the presidency, Vice-President Hubert Humphrey, in an address before the B'nai B'rith convention on September 8, 1968, stated, "The want of strength wets the appetite for war, for aggression . . . Israel must have the means to defend itself, including such items as Phantoms."[31]

The Israeli lobby in the United States was able to bring enormous pressure to bare on President Johnson during 1968. In large part due to American Israeli Political Affairs Committee (AIPAC) pressure, the Congress passed resolutions supporting the sale. The respective platforms of the Democratic and Republican Parties supported the sale as well.[32] In addition to pressuring government institutions, AIPAC and other Jewish organizations also sought to influence the press as well as gain the endorsement of such powerful and prestigious groups as the AFL-CIO, Americans for Democratic Action, and the American Legion to support the sale.[33]

The political pressure became so intense on the president that in conversations with Lucius Battle, the assistant secretary of state for Near Eastern and South Asian Affairs, President Johnson told him he had never experienced such political pressure as with this sale. He stated, "You have to give me more a reason not to do it."[34]

Political as well as regional pressures on Johnson eventually forced him to conclude the sale. The increasing costs of the Vietnam War were causing a domestic backlash. Johnson's popularity was plummeting in general, and in particular with the American Jewish community. Congress also became active in trying to force the sale. These domestic factors along with the French embargo against arms sales to Israel and the Soviets providing aid to the Arabs helped to make the sale a reality. At the same time, he thought that reaction to the sale in the Arab world would be muted as the United States was also selling arms to Jordan.[35]

Significance of the Sale of F-4 Phantom Jets

The American sale of the F-4 was a turning point in its relationship with Israel. The sale gave Israel a significant qualitative edge over the Arab states as it was superior to the aircraft the Soviets were providing to their Arab allies. It provided Arab leaders, such as Nasser, with ammunition to verbally attack the United States.[36]

The sale was important strategically, as the War of Attrition illustrated to Israeli leaders the desirability of possessing a weapon that could carry six tons of bombs deep inside Egypt.[37] In addition, the Israelis had requested the most advanced version of the F-4, the E series, which was capable of delivering nuclear weapons. Premier Eshkol in his discussions with President Johnson insisted that the modifications making the plane nuclear-capable should remain in the Israeli order. A similar request was made by Israeli Air Force Commander Mordechai Hod in his discussions with the Defense Department. This was a point that Weizman had raised in 1965 when this sale was first discussed.[38]

The sale of the F-4 raised the stakes for the United States in the American-Israeli relationship as Washington became firmly identified with Tel Aviv. This was discussed in a conversation between Yitzhak Rabin and Assistant Secretary of Defense Paul Warnke. Mr. Warnke stated that the United States would have preferred not to have become Israel's major arms supplier so as to avoid possible confrontations with the USSR, however, the French decision not to arm Israel had precluded this:

> We will henceforth become the principal arms supplier to Israel, involving more directly the security of the United States. He said that it was not just the agreement to provide fifty Phantoms that was significant it was the sale of the Phantoms plus one hundred Skyhawks and other equipment requested by Israel that marked a distinct change from past policy.[39]

Politically, the sale of the F-4 committed the United States to its special relationship with Israel. It placed Israel on an equal footing with the other major allies of the United States, Great Britain and Germany, and did so in a very visible way. Israel gained prestige as a special American ally, which was something regional opponents had to take into account.[40] The United States did not seek any concessions from Israel in making this sale. Johnson, in part as a result of election year pressure, did not attempt to link the sale with either a withdrawal from the occupied territories or Israeli signing of the Nuclear Nonproliferation Treaty. These were conditions that his secretaries of state and defense were urging him to make.[41]

America-Israel and the 1967 War

The United States actively assisted Israel in gathering and analyzing intelligence during the 1967 war. Units from Ramstein West Germany and Britain were sent to the Negev to conduct surveillance flights and develop the photos. During the first few days of the conflict the function of these units was to gather intelligence on the destruction of the Arab airfields. Once air superiority had been achieved by the Israelis the mission of these units changed to night flights to ferret out Arab troop movements. When the war shifted to the northern front these reconnaissance flights were carried out over Syria as well.[42]

This assistance represented a radical departure from the policy of previous administrations. During the Johnson administration the emphasis of American policy shifted from one of balance, to facilitating Israeli military superiority. This occurred for two reasons: to embarrass the Soviets by winning an overwhelming victory over their allies and to allow Israel to acquire Arab territory and thus hopefully force a peace settlement.[43]

A further benefit from the point of view of conservatives in the American administration was that radical Arab nationalism had been checked. Nasser suffered a blow from which he never fully recovered. The disastrous defeat of 1967 forced Nasser to make a rapprochement with his former rivals, the Saudis, in order to get the funds to rebuild his shattered military. The quid pro quo for this was the withdrawal of Egyptian military forces from Yemen.[44]

However, this benefit was fleeting as the June war ushered in a new round of conflict in the region, the War of Attrition. As a result, the Egyptians became more dependent on the Soviets than had been the case previously, as large amounts of equipment and advisors were sent to Egypt. The result was greater Soviet-American rivalry in the region that was manifested in the October war of 1973.[45] The result of the 1967 war was to intensify regional instability. However, a significant difference was that now the United States was firmly out in front supporting one of the parties, rather than behind the scenes as was the case earlier. It was the 1967 war in which the United States displaced France as Israel's principal ally and military supplier. The De Gaulle government, with other policy goals, decided to end its quasi-alliance with Israel.[46] The freedom of action of the United States was curtailed, which has been the case from this point onward.

Conclusions

It was under President Johnson that the American-Israeli alliance developed fully. Although the Kennedy administration began the process of providing sophisticated armaments to Israel, the HAWK missile was a defensive weapon. The weapons President Johnson agreed to sell to Israel were offensive and assured Israeli military superiority in the region. This commitment was illustrated by the rapid increase of American military aid under Johnson as opposed to Kennedy. In fiscal year 1964 (which was the last year under Kennedy) the United States granted $40 million in aid. In fiscal year 1965 this figure rose to $71 million, and in FY 1966 to $130 million. The purposes of this aid also shifted dramatically. In FY 1964 all the aid was designated as economic. In FY 1965 (the first year of the Johnson administration) 20 percent of aid, $14 million, was military aid. In FY 1966 this figure rose dramatically to 71 percent (91.3 million).[47] The rapid rise in quantity and quality of arms sales can be illustrated by a comparison with FY 1963. In 1963 Kennedy authorized the sale of only five batteries of HAWK anti-aircraft missiles. In FY 1965-1966, during the Johnson administration, the United States sold 250 modified M-48 tanks, 48 A-1 Skyhawk attack aircraft, communications and electronic equipment, as well as artillery and recoilless rifles.[48]

The influences and constraints operating in the Johnson administration were very similar to those in the Truman era. Johnson, like Truman, was under a great deal of domestic pressure to provide these arms from special interest groups, Congress, as well as American presidential electoral politics. In the election of 1968 both political parties and nominees, Richard Nixon and Hubert Humphrey, who was the sitting vice-president, were attempting to use aid to Israel to maximize their political support. Like Harry Truman, Lyndon Johnson was being pressured by certain sectors of the national security bureaucracy against the sale of both the Skyhawk and the Phantom. A fundamental difference between these two administrations, however, was the nature of the Cold War. In 1948 the Cold War was just beginning, while in the mid-1960s the Cold War had been in place for almost 20 years. This was compounded by the conflict in Vietnam that was being justified by the administration in Cold War terms. Therefore, Lyndon Johnson had a perception that Israel could be viewed as a strategic asset in the Middle East in response to the increasing influence of the Soviet Union in certain quarters of the Arab world. This idea took on more importance as the United States increasingly became committed in Southeast Asia and America's ability to intervene militarily in other regions of the world was limited.

In conclusion, the Johnson administration proved a watershed period in American-Israeli relations for the following reasons. First, it was under Johnson that the United States became the principal arms supplier and backer of Israel. Second, President Johnson essentially guaranteed a further escalation of the Middle East arms race by assuring the Israelis that their qualitative edge over the Arab nations would be maintained. Third, the fact that President Johnson did not demand as a quid pro quo Israeli agreeing to the Nuclear Nonproliferation Treaty in return for supplying nuclear capable F-4 Phantoms, gave the impression that the United States was encouraging

Israel's nuclear weapons program. Fourth, the Johnson administration's cooperation in covering up the attack on the *Liberty* further established for Israeli elites that their policies would not imperil American aid. Finally, acquiescing to the Israeli occupation of the West Bank and Gaza, and not using American aid to force Israel to withdraw, led to several new rounds of fighting.[49]

The Nixon Administration

President Nixon had made substantial promises concerning Israel in the 1968 campaign. The Nixon Doctrine that was promulgated in 1969, while being initially directed toward Southeast Asia, had its largest impact in the Middle East. While much has been written concerning the Nixon Doctrine and Iran it is important to remember that Israel also sought and was assigned to play a strategic role in the region by the administration. This contributed to Israel being viewed as a strategic asset that had begun in the Johnson administration.[50]

The Nixon administration was initially disturbed by the intransigence of Israel in negotiations after the 1967 war, as well as the position of the American Jewish community. However, he realized the importance of the Jewish vote in key states and wished to make inroads into this group for himself as well as his party. This reflected the strong interests that domestic policy plays in the formation of American foreign policy.[51]

Nixon at first moved cautiously when it came to arms sales to Israel. The Nixon administration in 1969 consented to the deliveries of 25 Phantom F-4 jets as well as 80 Skyhawk fighters. However, in 1970 the Phantom sale was postponed as it was feared it would jeopardize relations with Egypt and Syria, as a restoration of diplomatic relations were being renegotiated. The event that cemented the Israeli-American alliance in particular for Nixon was the Jordanian crisis of September 1970. Nixon encouraged Israeli assistance to intervene and save King Hussein from the PLO as well as a Syrian invasion. In the end, American and Israeli forces were not needed due to the strong resistance from the Jordanian military as well as splits within the Syrian military.[52]

This relationship was illustrated by the message Nixon sent to Prime Minister Rabin in the aftermath of this crisis:

> The president will never forget Israel's role in preventing the deterioration in Jordan and in blocking the attempt to overturn the regime there. He said that the United States is fortunate in having an ally like Israel in the Middle East. These events will be taken into account in all future developments.[53]

Rabin remarked in reply, "this was probably the most far-reaching statement ever made by a president of the United States on the mutuality of the alliance between the two countries."[54]

This support for Israel was illustrated with the airlift during the 1973 war. It has been argued that the aid provided was not militarily significant as most of it did not get to the front until the fighting was over. However, it did serve as a morale booster and allowed Israeli leaders not to have to worry about conserving supplies. The most significant aspect was that it emboldened the Israelis to seek military victory.[55] The United States provided Israel with 25 percent more equipment than the Soviets provided the Arabs to demonstrate support for Israel, as well as the superiority of American arms.[56] There were also domestic implications should the United States not supply Israel with military supplies. During the 1973 war the Israelis initially felt that the United States was not providing adequate support. The Israeli ambassador in Washington, Simcha Dinitz, threatened that if Washington did not provide a massive airlift of supplies the Israelis would publicly complain. This would have caused problems domestically for an already politically weakened administration as a result of the Watergate scandal.[57] However, it was during the 1973 war that the United States was able to extend some leverage over its ally. The Israelis desired military victory, while the United States was working towards establishing more of a stalemate in order to facilitate its relationship with the Arab states and particularly Egypt. This can account for the American delay in supplying Israel and also not furnishing Israel with satellite intelligence data on Arab troop movements. It seems that American objectives were achieved in the aftermath of the 1973 war. Israeli dependence on the United States was illustrated. In addition, President Sadat was able to justify pursuing a settlement with Israel and a general reorientation toward the United States economically, politically, and strategically.[58] However, as a result of threatened Soviet intervention there was a real possibility of a general conflict between the superpowers. As a result, broader American international interests were threatened, which overrode Israeli considerations. This shows how leverage in an alliance can fluctuate over time and can change temporarily in response to specific situations.

Despite the tensions that arose over the 1973 war and Kissinger's shuttle diplomacy, the American-Israeli alliance was expanded greatly during the Nixon administration. It was during this period that Israel became the single largest recipient of U.S. foreign aid. In 1973 Nixon extended $2.2 billion in grants and loans to Israel. By 1974 aid to Israel had reached $2.63 billion as compared to $350 million in 1972. American aid to Israel stayed at similar levels from then on.[59]

Military ties between the two countries were broadened during the Nixon administration as a result of a number of agreements. The Master Defense Development Data Exchange Agreement was concluded in December 1970, which established the terms and conditions for exchange of technical data on a wide array of military subjects. An agreement for production in Israel of American designed defense equipment was signed in November 1971. The Weapons Systems Evaluation Group was established in November 1973 to collect, organize, and distribute data concerning the comparisons of Soviet versus American and European weapons systems during the October 1973 war.[60]

The Ford Administration

President Ford by and large continued the policies of the Nixon administration. After assuming the presidency in August 1974, Ford ordered the delivery of $750 million in military equipment.[61] However, he also initiated a process of reassessment of American policy toward Israel. During the period from March to September 1975 no new arms sales were concluded, but items already agreed upon were delivered. Ford was responding to what he felt was Israeli intransigence to a total withdrawal from Sinai.[62] As a result, Ford came under tremendous pressure from the pro-Israel lobby, as well as from Congress. In May 1975, 76 Senators signed a letter to Ford urging him to support Israel's request for $2.59 billion in military and economic aid. This frosty relationship lasted until about September 1 when a Sinai agreement was reached. A component of this agreement was an Israeli-American "memorandum of understanding" that agreement provided for an expansion of American military and economic aid, as well as agreeing to supply Israel with the oil it would lose from giving back the Sinai oil fields. The United States also gave political pledges that it would not create initiatives in the Middle East without prior consultation with Israel, and not diverge from Security Council resolutions.[63]

Despite this relatively brief period of tension, the American-Israeli strategic relationship expanded during the Ford administration. In response to Israeli agreement with Egypt on disengagement, the United States expanded aid to the point where Israel was placed ahead of other foreign nations to receive weapons. Rabin stated that he was largely satisfied with Ford's treatment of Israel, as when Ford left office Israel was in a much stronger position militarily. Rabin noted that the tank force had grown 50 percent, the mobile artillery had increased 100 percent, armored personnel carriers by 800 percent, and planes by 30 percent.[64]

The Carter Administration

Carter, like Ford, at least initially sought to use arms sales as leverage over Israel and sought to limit the sale of certain sophisticated armaments in order to gain concessions during his first year in office. Carter, for example, extended $100 million in military credits for Israel's own indigenous armor production development as well as provided new night-fighting equipment. On other points, Carter delayed the selling of Cobra helicopter gunships as well as Israel's request for coproduction of the F-16. When the Israeli government agreed to allow some Palestinian representation in the Geneva talks, the sale of the helicopters was put through.[65]

The second major decision in the Carter administration with regard to strategic relations between the two countries concerned the plane package in 1978. Israeli political leaders felt that this was a form of sanction against Israel for its tough negotiating posture and they felt that the selling of sophisticated aircraft to Saudi Arabia and Egypt were detrimental to Israel's long-term security interests. However, the Israelis were promised and subsequently received additional supplies of military equipment as compensation later on.[66] Arms transfers continued as a result of the Arab-Israeli peace agreement which was concluded in 1978. The 1979 supplemental foreign aid package provided Israel with even more military hardware. This was designed to serve as a replacement for the Israelis giving up the Sinai. This included $3 billion in military aid, $800 million of which was in the form of grants to construct new air bases in the Negev.[67]

Under Carter the strategic relationship between the two countries continued and a greater understanding was achieved between them for cooperation in military development. A Memorandum of Agreement on Principles Governing Mutual Cooperation in Research and Development, Scientist and Engineer Exchange, and Procurement and Logistics Support of Selected Defense Equipment was concluded in March 1979. This permitted Israeli firms to bid on U.S. defense contracts without Buy American Act restrictions and led to higher levels of cooperation in military research and development.[68] In addition, other arms aid was furnished, specifically an acceleration of deliveries of the F-16. However, in areas of direct military coordination between the two countries the Carter administration still kept Israel at arms length. This despite the creation of the U.S. Rapid Deployment Force and the role the Israelis could have conceivably played in providing support. There were very few direct and overt displays of military cooperation between the two countries and they tended to be restricted to ceremonial displays such as port calls by American ships. This changed drastically during the Reagan administration as a new era of strategic cooperation was created between the two countries.[69] In total, the Israelis viewed Carter favorably. When Israel's former Foreign Minister Moshe Dayan summed up American-Israeli relations during the Carter administration, he emphasized that while there were some tensions, President Carter never threatened to slow down economic and military aid to Israel.[70]

The Reagan Administration

The strategic significance of Israel was further heightened with the election of Ronald Reagan in 1980. Reagan, in discussing Israel, stated that Israel was a strategic asset and important ally of the United States. The other major candidates, John Anderson and President Carter, also made similar statements during the campaign.[71] The initial months of the Reagan administration saw some tensions between the United States and Israel as a result of two Israeli actions in June and July of 1981. In June 1981 the Israeli Air Force bombed the Osiraq nuclear facility in Baghdad, which led to a strong American condemnation and the suspension of the delivery of F-16 aircraft, which was only temporary. Probably more significant from the Israeli perspective was the State Department's refusal to label Israeli-American relations as an alliance.[72] Relations were further strained one month later when the Israelis attacked the PLO headquarters in Beirut. However, despite these early problems a large number of political, military, and economic agreements were concluded between the two countries during the 1980s, and American aid vastly increased. A problem for American-Israeli relations occurred early in the Reagan administration with Israel's invasion of Lebanon in 1982. This illustrated the potential repercussions a large power can have in aligning with a smaller state. Israel invaded Lebanon in pursuit of its own security interests, which ultimately would include seeking to destroy the PLO infrastructure that had been established in that country. At the height of this conflict it seemed that Israeli military forces would invade West Beirut in an effort to destroy the PLO command center. This ultimately would entangle the United States and American military forces in the Lebanese civil war through the establishment of subsequent peacekeeping missions, as well as the sending of economic and military aid to Beirut.

The Israeli invasion threatened to weaken relations with the United States as the Begin government violated the restrictions that Washington had placed on the use of American military equipment such as cluster bombs. To protest Israeli actions, President Reagan delayed the sale of 75 F-16 jets to Israel as well as suspended shipments of 4,000 155 mm artillery shells, which are in the same category as cluster bombs. While great publicity was made of these mild punishments, the Reagan administration ruled out placing financial sanctions on Israel. Also during this period other forms of economic and military aid continued. Later that year the United States also delayed the licensing of military technology to Israel. There was some criticism from members of Congress who felt that Israel had gone overboard in Lebanon. Among the members of Congress who criticized Israel were Larry Pressler, Howard Baker, Paul Tsongas, Henry Jackson, Jim Wright, and Alan Cranston, who maintained that Israeli actions could lead to a lessening of ties between the two countries. However, by the end of 1982 Congress voted an economic aid package to Israel that exceeded the amount proposed by the Reagan administration by $475 million. Military aid was also extended by an estimated $635 million more than was requested by the administration. In addition, a proposed arms sale to Jordan was rejected.[73] Therefore the United States, aside from some minor sanctions and criticisms from members of Congress, did not substantively change Israeli policy. Rather, America itself was drawn into the Lebanese civil war on the side of the Christian-dominated Beirut government. This led to the United States incurring the enmity of the Shia and their subsequent attacks on American forces and installations.[74]

The relationship between the United States and Israel continued under Reagan. One of the central tenets of foreign policy during the Reagan administration was ensuring that Israel possessed military superiority. Several agreements were concluded between the United States and Israel during the Reagan years, including agreements that provided: U.S. assistance in developing and supporting Israel's defense and technological industrial base; safeguarding classified information shared by the two countries; and cooperation between NASA and the Israeli Space Agency among others.[75]

The most important agreement concluded between the two countries was the Strategic Cooperation Agreement in 1981 and represented a high point in relations between the United States and Israel. This agreement led to closer military cooperation between the two countries, such as access to Israeli facilities by the United States, greater military aid, a close relationship with regard to military-industrial production, as well as closer economic ties in general by providing for duty free and tax free imports and exports between the two nations. The major provisions of the agreement are: (1) the formation of a joint American-Israeli committee to oversee joint military exercises; (2) the U.S. Rapid Deployment Force was allowed to preposition military equipment in Israel; (3) the United States would resume the delivery of cluster bombs; (4) American financial assistance for Israel to build the Lavi fighter aircraft; (5) American military aid to Israel would be increased $425 million per year; and (6) a trade agreement to be concluded between the two nations that would provide duty free and tax free imports and exports.[76]

Legally this agreement was not a treaty or an alliance. However, it served the same purpose as it bonded America to Israel militarily, politically, and economically. As was illustrated earlier, there was no similar agreement with any Arab state that indicated the unique nature of this relationship.[77]

Although the Strategic Cooperation Agreement seemed impressive on paper, it was not viewed as such by either party. The Israelis were disappointed because their expectations were dashed. There were differences even within the Israeli leadership as to the scope and significance of cooperation with the United States. Prime Minister Begin was seeking the establishment of what he hoped would be a genuine alliance. This he defined as being based on equality between the countries and based on mutual interest. Eventually he hoped that this would lead to a form al bilateral defense treaty. Defense Minister Ariel Sharon saw Israel as being a major component of the defense of the free world. He advocated the use of force and envisioned American support as leading to an increase of Israeli stature and power in the region.[78]

The American position at this time was lukewarm as it did not want to be seen as cooperating too closely with Israel. In addition, Secretary of Defense Caspar Weinberger was not an advocate of close ties with Israel and he was joined in this view by sectors of the Defense and State Departments. This opposition was to last all during the Reagan administration. The reasons cited were that support for Israel could erode American influence in the Arab world, could make the United States vulnerable to ever higher demands for foreign aid, as well as force the Defense Department to compete with Israel for military equipment and supplies.[79]

There were several factors that led to a stark improvement in American-Israeli relations in the aftermath of the U.S. intervention in Lebanon. First, there occurred changes in personnel within both governments, a change of views of certain decision makers, the growing role of the National Security Council in bilateral relations. Second, American policy setbacks in the region led to a reevaluation of how best to achieve American interests there. Third, there was the perception that the Soviet Union was reemerging as a threat to American interests in the region. Finally, domestic pressures were forcing the Reagan administration to seek improvement in American-Israeli relations.[80]

The Strategic Cooperation Agreement was expanded on in 1983, just after the bombing of the U.S. Marine barracks in Beirut. The justification of the Reagan administration increasing aid to Israel was to limit what the American administration perceived as increased Soviet influence in the region. The major provisions of the agreement included: (1) an increase in American military grants to Israel by $425 million per year, some of which would be used to build the Lavi jet; (2) the formation of an American-Israeli Committee to establish joint military planning and exercises, as well as to arrange for the U.S. Sixth Fleet to use Israeli port facilities; (3) the establishment of procedures for prepositioning military medical supplies in Israel for possible use by the U.S. Rapid Deployment Force; (4) the beginnings of negotiations for a free trade agreement in an effort to allow duty and tax free trade between Israel and the United States.[81]

A by-product of this agreement was the establishment of a formal Joint Political-Military Group (JPMG) that would meet every six months. Over the next several years this group established strategic cooperation in a variety of areas. These included: American naval vessels using the Israeli port of Haifa as a port of call; the United States leasing 25 Kfir C-1 fighter jets from Israel to simulate Soviet aircraft in combat training; joint naval maneuvers in the Eastern Mediterranean designed to enhance antisubmarine war fighting techniques; American naval aviators conducting bombing practice in the Negev desert; Israel agreeing to permit the installation of Voice of America transmitters that would beam broadcasts into the southern Soviet Union; and Israel becoming the third foreign nation, after Great Britain and West Germany, to participate in the Strategic Defense Initiative (SDI) program.[82]

This later agreement was brought about in May of 1986 when Israel and the United States completed a Memorandum of Understanding establishing Israel as a participant in the SDI program. Israel thus joined Belgium, Canada, Denmark, France, West Germany, Italy, Japan, the Netherlands, and the United Kingdom in participating in SDI contracts. In the first three years of allied participation in the SDI program, contracts came to $334 million, of which Israel received $174 million, or 52 percent. The other countries with large shares of this program were West Germany with 20 percent, and the United Kingdom with 17 percent.[83]

This helped pave the way for more broad based Israeli-American defense industrial cooperation as in 1987 Israel was eventually designated a non-NATO American ally under the National Defense Authorization Act. This legislation established the process by which the secretaries of state and defense could designate countries that could participate jointly with the United States in research and development programs that were established in 1986 with the NATO countries. In addition to Israel, other countries declared eligible to participate in this program were Australia, Egypt, Japan, and South Korea.[84]

The Bush Administration

During the early years of the Bush presidency, American policy makers still maintained the importance of Israel as a strategic ally in the region. First, it was argued that although the Soviet threat was lessened, it could reemerge in the future. Second, administration officials raised the possibility of regional threats that would require the United States to sustain military operations and therefore a strong Israel would be better able to assist in this. Third, there was the growing realization accompanied by political demands that the defense budget be reduced. American decision makers now began to place an even greater emphasis on exploiting joint cooperation agreements with other countries that would help subsidize research and development costs.[85]

Israel's importance in the minds of American decision makers was reflected in March of 1990 when Secretary of Defense Cheney in a speech to the United Jewish Appeal, sought to refute media speculation that in the wake of the easing of tensions with the Soviet Union, Israel's strategic importance to the United States had declined. In his speech Cheney emphasized that the political changes in the world made America's alliance relationships all the more important.[86] The importance of Israel in the perceptions of American policy makers in light of improved American-Soviet relations was further illustrated in comments made by Undersecretary of Defense Paul Wolfowitz:

> I've heard a lot of nonsense over the last few months about how this crisis demonstrates that with the end of the Cold War, with the Soviet Union gone as a strategic threat, that we no longer need strategic cooperation with Israel. First of all, I would say that any particular crisis only proves what's relevant to that crisis, and as someone said, history has more imagination than the people who write scenarios for us. There have been regional crises in the past

in which the Soviet Union had no role to play where Israel played a crucial role in preserving stability; there may be some in the future.[87]

These statements were also accompanied by concrete measures of support. In September 1990, Secretary of State James Baker announced a supplemental aid agreement to Israel. This aid would include two Patriot missile batteries worth about $114 million, and 15 F-15 aircraft. Ten CH-53 helicopters were also promised, as well as an acceleration of the program to preposition $100 million worth of ammunition to Israel. This agreement was later supplemented by Congress, which approved additional aid worth more than $1 billion. This included the transferring of $700 million of equipment from American military stocks in Europe to be transferred to Israel. In addition Congress authorized the prepositioning of $200 million worth of American equipment in Israel, as well as establishing a stockpile of 4.5 million barrels of fuel worth about $485 million. Also, Congress provided funding to dredge the port of Haifa in order to accommodate American aircraft carriers.[88] A further enhancement of American strategic cooperation took place during the Gulf conflict as the United States and Israel took steps to greater facilitate communications by establishing a "hot-line" between the Pentagon and the Israeli Ministry of Defense. This communications link had three purposes. First, it provided a greater ability for American and Israeli political elites to coordinate their actions. Second, it served to enable the United States to more quickly pass on missile attack warnings to Israel. Third, it established a means by which Israel could communicate with the allied coalition forces in Saudi Arabia.[89]

This cooperation continued after the Gulf War in several significant ways. Favorable comments toward Israel were articulated by General Colin Powell, chairman of the Joint Chiefs of Staff, as well as Secretary of Defense Dick Cheney, who stressed that Israel made positive contributions in the Gulf conflict.[90] These remarks of praise were further accompanied by greater high-level cooperation in certain areas. An agreement was concluded in May of 1991 in which the Israeli Arrow antiballistic missile (ATBM) program would be subsidized by the amount of $300 million, or 72 percent of the total cost of the program. Of greater significance was the program to preposition weapons within Israel in case of future conflicts in the region that would necessitate American military involvement.[91]

Another important development in the strategic cooperation between Israel and the United States was the role that major American military contractors played in facilitating this relationship. In mid-April 1992 the General Dynamics Corporation offered a deal to the Israel Aircraft Industry that would involve the coproduction of the F-16 C/D aircraft. This was done in order to try to beat out the rival of the F-16, the McDonnell Douglas F-18.[92] In March of 1992 the Israel Aircraft Industry was awarded a contract worth $68 million to upgrade and maintain the American F-15s based in Europe. This was significant as the development of innovations would add to the life of weapons systems, which was important in a period of lower defense budgets.[93]

Despite the continued strategic cooperation there were tensions between the Bush administration and Israel. A continual priority for American foreign policy in the region is to maintain regional stability, which means Western access to oil as well as promoting favorable economic activity in general. This proved difficult at times due to the dynamics of the Arab-Israeli conflict, specifically the Israeli occupation of the West Bank and Gaza Strip. After the Gulf War the Bush administration sought to actively promote a settlement of this dispute, which meant putting pressure on Israel not to construct new settlements in the occupied territories. These tensions began with the first meeting between President Bush and Prime Minister Shamir in April 1989. Later on, both governments would feud over the question of Palestinian negotiators as the Shamir government refused to talk to the PLO and vetoed many of the Palestinians that the State Department suggested could compose a possible delegation.

In April of 1990 Washington authorized the granting of $400 million in loan guarantees to finance the absorption of Soviet immigrants. However, unlike previous aid the Bush administration, this package demanded a full accounting of Israeli expenditures on settlements. Israel also received $650 million for repairs and military resupply, which was viewed in part as a reward for Israel not retaliating against Iraq during the Gulf War.

In the aftermath of the Gulf War, Israeli leaders felt that the previous relationship with the United States could continue as before. As a result of their going along with the Americans and not retaliating against Iraq, they felt they could gain further concessions from Washington. A turning point in American-Israeli relations took place with Jerusalem's request for $10 billion in loan guarantees in July of 1991. This was opposed by America in light of the continuing Israeli policy of constructing settlements on the West Bank that threatened to scuttle the upcoming Middle East peace negotiations. After tense negotiations, and despite AIPAC lining up 70 senators in support of the guarantees, both governments decided to postpone this issue for 120 days to allow the Middle East peace conference to move forward.[94]

The subsequent failure of the United States to grant these guarantees weakened relations with Shamir, who sought to campaign on a platform of having stood up to Washington. However, this did not go over well with the Israeli electorate and contributed to the defeat of the Likud party in June of 1992. This was a scenario that pleased American policy makers as they preferred to work with the Labor party.[95]

In August of 1992, on Rabin's first visit to Washington, the Bush administration, anxious to bolster the new Israeli prime minister as well as the president's own political fortunes, agreed to the loan guarantees providing Israel curtail its spending on settlements. This episode, however, did cost President Bush political support, as he lost Jewish votes in the 1992 election. In 1988 the Republican ticket won 27 percent of the Jewish vote, in 1992 the figure was 10 percent.[96] Although it did carry political costs, this was one of the few instances since the Eisenhower administration that the United States was able to successfully use pressure to influence Israeli policy. However, the administration was also assisted by the fact that there were splits within the Jewish community over the policy of continued settlement of the occupied territories, as well as with the policies of the Likud-dominated government in general.

The Israeli Lobby

The pro-Israeli lobby has been one of the most successful lobbying groups in American politics for a variety of reasons. The most significant factor has been the symmetry of the lobby's goals with American elite perceptions. Since the Kennedy administration, American political elites have viewed it in American interests to align with Israel. Second has been the success of the lobby to link support for Israel in the larger context of the Cold War. The third factor was the growing importance of Congress in foreign policy decision making and appropriations, especially as a result of the Vietnam War. Congress is more permeable to influence than the executive branch. Fourth the strength of pro-Israeli sentiments in American public opinion as a result of the Judeo-Christian traditions of the society, reinforced by the generally favorable portrayals of Israel in the American media. This latter point was aided by the ability of pro-Israeli groups to use the media to illustrate their views. The fifth factor was the development and growth of what has been referred to as "Christian Zionism," which emphasizes support for Israel as a religious obligation. Finally, knowledge of the political system enabled pro-Israeli Jewish groups to build coalitions with non Jews.[97]

The Structure and Significance of AIPAC

The American Israeli Public Affairs Committee (AIPAC) is a highly centralized organization as opposed to the Conference of Presidents of Jewish Organizations, which is more loosely organized. While AIPAC does have leaders of other Jewish organizations on its board, its executive director is a salaried professional. The organization has grown in personnel, budget, as well as influence in the last 20 years. In 1981 the organization possessed a staff of 20, by 1989 it employed a staff of 100. In addition, employees are specialized to deal with the American political process, particularly as it relates to Congress, where AIPAC has had the most influence, as well as foreign affairs, communication, and Jewish affairs. Its membership has increased from 11,000 in 1981 to 50,000 in 1984. AIPAC's budget increased from $250,000 in 1973 to $11,000,000 in 1989. Analysts have argued that it has displaced other, more established organizations such as the Conference of Presidents of Jewish Organizations as the leader of the American Jewish community.[98]

This influence was gained as a result of the day to day activities of

AIPAC, particularly in its lobbying of Congress.[99] AIPAC is not a political action committee as it does not give money to candidates. However, officials of AIPAC serve on political action committees (PACs) whose primary purpose is to give money to candidates to influence the political process. A study based on 1986 Federal Election Commission reports showed 51 pro-Israel PACs operated by AIPAC officials or people who hold seats on AIPAC's two major policy making bodies. The study further illustrated that 80 pro-Israel PACs spent more than $6.9 million during the 1986 campaigns.[100] AIPAC's power was illustrated by the end of the 1980s. In the election of 1988, 80 pro-Israeli lobbying groups contributed $6 million to various candidates under the direction of AIPAC.[101]

Successes and Failures of the Lobby

The lobby was weakened as a result of its stinging loss of the AWACS sale to Saudi Arabia in 1981 and intensified its efforts to target those legislators that were deemed to be unfriendly to Israel. In 1982, various Jewish political action committees contributed funding to defeat Congressmen Paul Findley (R-Ill.), the ranking minority member of the House Foreign Relations Committee. Congressman Findley's opponent benefitted from $104,325 distributed from 31 Jewish PACs. In addition, another member of the House Representative Paul McCloskey of California was also defeated after being targeted by AIPAC.[102] The activity of the Jewish PACs escalated during the 1984 elections as these groups cumulatively gave $3.5 million. Slightly over $1.5 million was directed toward the Senate, and of this amount 44 percent was directed at defeating five Republican incumbents who had voted in favor of the AWACS sale. These were Percy (Ill.), Jepsen (Ia.), both of whom lost, as well as Helms (N.C.), Cochran (Miss.), and Humphrey (N.H.), who won. Representative Clarence Long of Maryland, who was also targeted for defeat, was able to win reelection despite the pro-Israeli PACs giving his opponent $155,000.[103]

While much has been written and discussed concerning the activities of AIPAC in the 1980s, it must be understood that even before AIPAC was a strong political force Congress was already very supportive of aid to Israel. The importance of the Jewish vote throughout the history of American-Israeli relations has already been discussed. It has been pointed out specifically, however, that during the period 1969-1976, when the United States took over as Israel's patron, on average 80 percent of the Senate and 86 percent of the House casts votes favorable to Israel in granting aid.[104]

Traditionally, AIPAC's major allies in Congress were a formidable group. In the Senate they were Joseph Biden, Alan Cranston, Dennis DeConcini, Christopher Dodd, Daniel Inouye, Robert Kasten, Edward Kennedy, George Mitchell, Daniel Moynihan, Bob Packwood, Donald Riegle Jr., Paul Simon, and John Warner. In the House the major proponents of AIPAC were Barney Frank, Benjamin Gilman, Stephen Solarz, Tom Lantos, Mel Levine, Larry Smith, Henry Waxman, Charles

Wilson, and Sidney Yates.[105]

Another important constituency group in American politics and society that provide a reservoir of support for Israel is the growing influence of Christian fundamentalism. Many evangelical Christians believe that the establishment of the state of Israel was a partial fulfillment of religious scripture that would herald the Second Coming and the conversion of the Jews to Christianity. The presence of fundamentalist Christians in the pro-Israel coalition illustrates a paradox. The views of this group on social issues tend to clash with liberal American Jews, although they are compatible with the views of the Likud party in Israel. Former Prime Minister Begin welcomed the support of Christian fundamentalists: "I tell you, if the Christian fundamentalists support us in Congress today, I will support them when the Messiah comes tomorrow."[106]

While the lobby has been successful in gaining support for Israel in American society as a whole and specifically within Congress, it has suffered some setbacks in recent years. The most significant of these setbacks was the weakening of the Israeli-American relationship during the Bush presidency. As mentioned previously, economic aid continued but there were demands by the United States to link at least of portion of it to Israeli concessions on the settlements issue. In addition, the Intifada presented Israeli policy in a negative light to the American public. The news images of well-armed Israeli troops shooting children throwing rocks made it more difficult for Israeli supporters in the United States to rely on the theme that Israel was surrounded by threats on all sides.

A more deep-seated problem for the pro-Israel lobby is the differences that were manifested within the American Jewish community. Many Jews felt that during the 1980s AIPAC shifted from simply trying to gain support for Israel to actively promoting the political agenda of the Israeli right, which dominated or at least shared power in Israeli politics from 1977 until 1992. As a result of the Israeli lobby articulating support for the Likud policies of actively promoting settlement of the occupied territories and being unwilling to make territorial concessions, it linked American Jews to policies that a significant number of them disagreed with.[107] The relationship between the Likud and Christian fundamentalist also troubled many American Jewish leaders as it was felt that these Christians were encouraging the Likud government's militaristic policies.[108]

American-Israeli Cooperation in Weapons Production and the Significance for Israel

The Merkava Tank

A significant joint military cooperation program between Israel and the United States was the Merkava (Chariot) tank project. In 1977 the Carter administration agreed to give an additional $107 million in American foreign aid to build this system. Carter emphasized that this was a onetime extension, although when the Israelis decided to expand production from 80 to 100 tanks per year the United States extended another $50 million.[109]

Implications of the Development of the Lavi

The Lavi project was originally conceived in the 1970s. The purpose of constructing the Lavi was that it was envisioned as being a low-cost, low-technology, primarily ground support aircraft. It was envisioned as replacing the A-4 and Kfir in Israeli inventory. However, it evolved into a high-cost multipurpose fighter in the class of the F-16, the purpose of which was to maintain air superiority, and the program suffered from cost overruns and delays. Eventually it was conceived that the Israeli air force would acquire about 300 Lavis.[110] In 1983-1984 the United States began to bankroll this project directly in a 1984 amendment to the Israel aid package which totaled $1.7 billion. This amendment allocated $550 million for the Lavi project and was $150 million more than the Israel Aircraft Industry had requested. Of this $550 million, $300 million was to be spent in the United States and $250 million in Israel. In 1985-1987 an additional $400 million was approved by the U.S. for each year, $250 million to be spent in the United States. In 1988 an additional $450 million was allocated despite skepticism from the Defense Department that this project was feasible.[111] This was a project that had joint American cooperation as several American defense contractors were involved in constructing components of this plane. Among these companies were Grumman, which constructed the wings and tail, Lear Siegler produced some of the avionics, and Pratt & Whitney constructed a new engine especially for the Lavi.[112]

The Lavi had economic and political significance for Israel. Economically, about 18,000 jobs were dependent on the Lavi program and its expenditure was thought to involve $9 billion. In addition, the project would enhance the technological base of the economy while at the same time leading to other industrial spin-offs. There was also the possibility that once the Lavi was demonstrated as being a capable military system it could be exported, which would generate hard currency for Israel and perhaps alleviate the amount of the American subsidy. There were also some significant economic benefits for the United States. The Grumman Corporation and the Israeli Aerospace Industry (IAI)) estimated that it would lead to $1.5 billion worth of spending and 37,000 jobs in the United States. Politically, a successful Lavi program for the Israelis could decrease the dependency on the United States for high-performance air superiority aircraft.[113]

While some American corporations benefitted from the Lavi program the Northrop Corporation charged that it was hurting them. Northrop had developed the F-20 Tigershark fighter, which although viewed as a superior aircraft, was not purchased by the American military as the Defense Department did not wish to produce another aircraft. As a result, Northrop was forced to turn to the export market to salvage this program. The company was blocked from selling this aircraft to Persian Gulf states, the most lucrative region for arms exports, by protests from the pro-Israel lobby who did not want to see this plane in the inventories of the Arab countries. Not being able to sell this plane, the company was forced to absorb substantial research and development costs at the same time as the U.S. government was subsidizing the Lavi program.[114]

The Significance of Israeli Arms Exports

The manufacture of armaments is a significant industry in Israel militarily, politically, and economically. By building up an industrial base in which sophisticated technological products can be produced, Israel is developing and keeping intact assembly lines to safeguard military production in the future. This was one of the justifications for the Lavi. Politically, arms sales were used to enhance Israeli influence and prestige in the third world. Economically, arms sales were extremely significant as they contributed to increasing the industrial base of the country, as well as its technology base. Since 1970 the Israeli arms industry has shown dramatic growth. In the mid 1970s this growth rate was reflected in trade figures. In 1974 arms exports were up 15 percent, in 1975 they increased 80 percent, and 85 percent by 1976. Since the mid 1960s the Israelis had invested 3 percent of their GNP in research and development. As a result of this constant investment in the military industrial sector, 40 percent of industrial exports were military products by 1991. By the mid 1990s this figure was projected to rise to 60 percent and by 1990 Israel was ranked as the sixth largest arms exporter in the world. While one of the goals of Israel was to become as self-sufficient in military production as possible, the more the military industrial complex expanded the greater these industries were dependent on technology imports, a large share of which came from the United States.[115]

Israel, the United States, and Nuclear Weapons

The Israeli desire to possess nuclear technology began shortly after independence in 1949. The Israelis turned to France for assistance because the political elites realized that Israel would not be able to develop its own nuclear capability. Both countries hoped that through cooperation they could broaden their expertise. Cooperation between the two countries was first acknowledged in 1954. The early joint programs the two states developed involved the production of heavy water, as well as the extraction of uranium from low-grade phosphate ores from the Dead Sea.[116] The major emphasis, however, of French-Israeli cooperation was the construction of the Dimona nuclear facility in the Negev desert, which was agreed to in

October of 1957. Originally this facility was a 24 megawatt reactor that had the ability to turn out one Hiroshima-type bomb per year. This facility was running at full capacity within five years, and it is argued that Israel had enough plutonium to produce a bomb as early as 1967.[117]

However, it has been argued that the United States assisted either wittingly or unwittingly in providing assistance. It was during the Eisenhower administration that the U.S. government provided funding for the Weizmann Institute, where much of the research for the Israeli nuclear program was carried out, as both the United States Air Force and Navy provided funding for this institution.[118] It has been suggested by Andrew Cockburn that American support was provided more consciously, as the CIA not only knew the real purpose of the Dimona nuclear facility, but actively provided assistance to the Israeli nuclear program. He argues that this was part of the quid pro quo for Israeli withdrawal from the Sinai, and the fear that the Soviets were about to provide nuclear technology to their Arab allies.[119] Other analysts argue that the distribution of American nuclear technology to Israel and other nations was more involuntary, as part of Eisenhower's Atoms for Peace Program in 1953. The following year the Atomic Energy Act of 1954, which made possible the dissemination of nuclear technology to cooperating nations, authorized the Atomic Energy Commission to negotiate agreements without Senate approval. Under this program 26 American research reactors were built in other nations and the United States gave licenses to foreign companies to build and sell American reactors abroad. It also shipped nuclear materials to other countries, as well as provided nuclear training for foreign nationals. Between 1954-1979 about 13,456 foreign nuclear researchers received training in the United States. Of this number, 3,532 were from nations that did not sign the 1968 Nuclear Nonproliferation Treaty.[120] Under the Eisenhower Atoms for Peace program the United States agreed to provide a research reactor to Israel at Nahal-Soreq, which was in operation by 1960. This facility could not produce nuclear weapons, however it did serve as a training facility for Israeli nuclear researchers. Towards the end of his administration Eisenhower wanted the Dimona facility to be dismantled, but backed off when the Israelis agreed to allow inspections.[121]

The expansion of the military relationship with Israel was carried out by the United States to check Israeli nuclear capabilities. In his meeting with Ben-Gurion in 1962, Kennedy agreed to sell the HAWK missile in return for a promise of limited access by American inspectors to the Dimona reactor.[122]

The issue of Israeli nuclear weapons was used a few years later by Prime Minister Eshkol in an effort to gain offensive weapons systems from the Johnson administration. In discussions with Johnson in 1966, Eshkol offered to delay a decision on constructing a nuclear arsenal if Johnson agreed to provide offensive arms to match the capabilities of the Soviet weapons provided to the Arabs. This was agreeable to President Johnson as it also supported other foreign policy and domestic goals. Johnson viewed the weapons the Soviets were providing to their Arab allies with suspicion and the growth of Arab socialism as a means by which the Soviets were seeking to export the Cold War to the Middle East. Therefore he viewed with favor the establishment of a militarily strong Israel as a pro-Western force in the region. This also served Johnson's interest domestically, as he did not want to engage in a political dispute with Israel over the bomb at a time when he needed to maximize domestic support to both fight the Vietnam War and initiate comprehensive domestic social legislation. As a result Johnson agreed to sell 48 Skyhawk tactical fighters capable of delivering 8,000 pounds of bombs.[123]

In discussions prior to the agreement to sell the F-4 Phantom to Israel, the goal of the Johnson administration was to get the Israelis to agree on a number of policy questions of importance. Among them was support for the Nuclear Nonproliferation Treaty. At the 1968 meeting between President Johnson and Prime Minister Eshkol at LBJ's Texas ranch, Johnson privately agreed to supply the desired planes, he did not, however, receive any commitments for Israeli support on certain important issues.[124]

The Nixon administration fully supported the Israeli nuclear program. Nixon was opposed to the Nuclear Nonproliferation Treaty despite public pronouncements to the contrary. President Nixon issued an order to the bureaucracy know as National Security Decision Memorandum No. 6, which indicated that the United States would not pressure other nations to ratify the Nuclear Nonproliferation Treaty.[125] This support was demonstrated later in 1969 when the United States ended the inspection of the Dimona facility. These inspections had begun in 1962 and were largely meaningless due to the unwillingness of the United States to press Israel, as well as Israeli circumvention of the inspections. In addition, reports indicating Israel's nuclear capability by the State Department in 1971 were suppressed.[126]

A factor that may have influenced the United States in its tolerance of an Israeli nuclear force was its growing power, sophistication, and most importantly range. It was estimated, based on the information provided by ex-Israeli government officials, that Israel possessed 20 nuclear warheads by 1973. Israel also had developed the Jericho I missile launcher that had a range of 700 miles and therefore was able to hit targets in the southern Soviet Union. Israel had also developed a special air force squadron of F-4 fighters that were capable of delivering nuclear bombs, and kept on constant alert. This squadron had enough range to fly a one-way trip to Moscow, but would have to be refueled in midair to return to its base.[127]

The idea of establishing a joint nuclear strategy between the United States and Israel was raised by Israeli representatives during the Carter administration, but Secretary of Defense Brown vetoed the idea even before it got to President Carter. At this time it was still the American position to deny that Israeli nuclear weapons even existed.[128]

Most recently, officials of both nations have expressed concern about other Middle Eastern states, particularly Iran, acquiring a nuclear capability. The former head of the Central Intelligence Agency Robert Gates has stated that Iran is attempting to purchase Western nuclear and missile technology while at the same time trying to lure back Iranian scientists who emigrated in the aftermath of the revolution. He also cited the possibility that Iranian links with the newly independent state of Kazakhstan will allow the Iranians to acquire technology from the former Soviet republic.[129] This was followed six weeks later by Israeli Foreign Minister David Levy officially informing the United States about the threat of Iran acquiring nuclear weapons.[130]

Israeli Relations with the Third World

An important component of the American-Israeli relationship has been and continues to be the assistance that Israel provides in the third world. This received a great deal of attention as a result of the Iran-Contra scandal. It has had implications for both nations, as pro-American states receive additional assistance while Israel has attempted to cultivate alliances in the third world for its own political, economic, and military purposes. This strategy was adopted by Israel as early as 1949. David Ben-Gurion had articulated it as the peripheral strategy where the Israelis would effectively jump over the surrounding Arab states and develop relations with Iran, Turkey, Ethiopia, as well as states in Africa. These relationships include developmental aid as well as security assistance. The strategy was also adopted to illustrate to the United States that Israel had the potential to be a regional power.[131] This section focuses on the more significant bilateral relationships and the implications for the United States.

Iran

The Iranian-Israeli relationship was of benefit to both parties. For Iran it represented what the Shah viewed as positive nationalism and served two important functions the nation. First, it provided Iran with technical expertise for economic development; second, it was to serve as a counterweight to the dangers posed by the increase in Soviet relations with Egypt.[132]

For Israel this alliance also had benefits. It represented a breakthrough from the Arab bottleneck that surrounded Israel and also carried with it the opportunities for political economic and strategic advancement. In the political sphere it represented a breakthrough for Israel. It conformed with Ben-Gurion's view that the Middle East was not simple Arab and Muslim, but rather a multidimensional, multiethnic region.[133]

There were economic and military factors why this relationship was significant as well. These center largely around the issues of oil and military relations. Iran was Israel's primary source of oil up until the revolution of 1978-1979 and this occurred as a result of two factors. The first centered around Iran's need for funds for economic development in the

1950s and as a result they did not discriminate against any purchaser of its oil. The second and most significant reason was Iran's desire to maintain and expand relations with the United States. The Shah felt that American support for Israel as well as the support of pro-Israeli groups in the United States would translate into support for Iran if he became Israel's regional ally.[134] The oil relationship was further expanded after the 1967 war, as the Israelis constructed an oil pipeline from Eilat to the Mediterranean so Iranian tankers could bypass the closed Suez Canal.[135] The emphasis on oil was to have strategic ramifications later on, as before the Israelis concluded the Sinai disengagement agreement of 1975, Prime Minister Rabin obtained a personal assurance from the Shah that Iran would provide the oil necessary to compensate Israel for returning the Sinai oil fields.[136]

The two countries had extensive contacts in the military field. An agreement was concluded in 1977 that provided arms for oil and was valued at $1 billion. The most significant project was the establishment of a joint surface-to-surface missile project between the two countries, capable of carrying a nuclear warhead. The implications for Israel were: the acquisition of badly needed investment capital for its military industries; the securing of a long-range test sight in central Iran; and finally and most significantly the establishing of Iranian-Israeli military cooperation that would constrain Iran from adopting an Arab option.[137]

Other important aspect of Iran-Israeli military cooperation was the assistance Israel provided Iran in modernizing its air force, specifically by the installation of electronic countermeasures on Iranian F-4 and F-14 aircraft that would protect them from antiaircraft weaponry furnished by the Soviets to Iraq. In addition both nations undertook naval cooperation. For Israel this was important to gain financing for naval development, for Iran it was important to safeguard the sea-lanes of the Persian Gulf and Indian Ocean.[138] This type of military cooperation also had economic implications for Israel, as it spurred on industrialization and exports in vital industries such as metals, electronics, and aerospace equipment.[139] Strategically, the two countries also enjoyed good relations. They were united by their opposition to radical Arab nationalism and the spread of Soviet influence in the region. The two states cooperated in supporting pro-Western regimes in the region and the third world as a whole as well as seeking to destabilize what they considered to be radical pro-Soviet states. This point was graphically illustrated with the case of the Kurds of Iraq. Both Israel and Iran cooperated in arming and fueling the Kurdish rebellion designed to destabilize the Iraqi government and tie down the Iraqi military internally.[140]

This relationship continued after the Iranian revolution of 1978-1979 on a reduced scale. In October 1980 the Israeli government sold several thousand dollars worth of tires to Iran for their fleet of F-4 aircraft.[141] This would prove a rehearsal for Israeli involvement in the Iran-Contra Affair. There were two reasons why the Israelis continued the military relationship with Iran and they were similar to the reasons why it was initiated in the 1950s. First, Iran was necessary to block the expansion of the Soviet Union into the Persian Gulf and the Middle East. This was a view Israel shared with the United States. Second, assisting Iran in fighting the war with Iraq served to tie down Iraqi military forces and drain the country economically, while at the same time orienting Arab hostility away from Israel.[142]

Africa

The Israelis have been very active in Africa from the 1950s onward serving as a source of economic aid, technical and developmental expertise as well as providing military aid to friendly African nations. Technical assistance began in 1958 with a budgetary allocation of $94,700 and grew to involve all sub-Saharan African countries. By the early 1960s, 24 official or quasi-official Israeli institutions were involved in the program. Most of the projects emphasized areas of agriculture, youth organization, community development, vocational training, health and medicine, construction management, and public service.[143] Along with these aid programs Israel was able to initiate trade with many states in Africa. Primarily Israel exported food products, clothing, medicines, agricultural machinery, electronic equipment, and office supplies, while importing such raw materials as industrial diamonds from the Central African Republic and Zaire, uranium from Gabon and Zaire, and beef from Ethiopia and Kenya.[144]

Israel was also involved in Africa militarily all over the continent, particularly during the 1960s. Israel trained air force pilots from Uganda, Ethiopia, and Ghana, as well as Nigerian civilian air force ground personnel and established the first naval school in Ghana. In addition, Israeli policemen were sent all over Africa on training missions. By the mid 1960s the Israeli military and technical presence in Africa was formidable. In Ethiopia about 100 military advisers were in the country, involved in training the army and air force. This military mission was second only to the United States. In Uganda the Israelis trained both military and police forces as well as members of the intelligence service; in Sierra Leone they trained the entire army officer corps.[145] In analyzing Israel's relations with Africa, the four countries the Israelis were most involved with were Zaire, Ethiopia, South Africa, and Uganda.

Zaire

Relations between Zaire since 1997, Democratic Republic of the Congo and Israel began in the early 1960s. President Joseph Kasavubu, who succeeded Patrice Lumumba and was supported by the United States, paid a state visit to Israel in 1963. That same year Israel sent advisers to establish a presidential guard as well as hosted 250 Zairian soldiers who were sent to Israel for training. Among these was the army commander and future president of Zaire General Joseph Mobutu.[146]

This relationship continued and expanded in the 1980s. An Israeli military aid plan was made in regards to Zaire in 1981-1982. The four components of this military aid plan were: (1) training and expanding the Special Presidential Brigade; (2) training and expanding the Camaniola Brigade into a division. This unit would eventually form the core of forces monitoring the Angolan border in Shaba province in a program involving the construction of agricultural-security settlements; (3) developing artillery units; (4) training Mobutu's bodyguards and domestic intelligence services.[147]

By 1982 Israel sold $10 million of military supplies to Zaire. Relations deepened with an exchange of visits by Defense Minister Ariel Sharon and his Zairian counterpart Admiral Lomponda. Among the equipment that President Mobutu himself admitted Israel was providing were artillery, mortars, and communication equipment. It was rumored that Israel was also providing patrol boats, pilotless planes, air defense equipment, and a warning system for monitoring border incursions. The most significant aspect of this relationship was the establishment of armed farming settlements along the border of Angola in Shaba province. This is Zaire's wealthiest region, historically only loosely tied to the central government, and it has been the scene of various secessionist movements.[148]

Ethiopia

Ethiopia was considered a key in Israeli strategy. Friendly relations between the two countries began in the early 1950s, civilian trade relations started in 1952, while contacts at higher levels involving strategic relations began in 1958. Common interests developed between the two countries as they perceived themselves as being surrounded by hostile Muslim states. Therefore, their common goals were to check radical Arab nationalism and maintain the territorial integrity of Ethiopia. This involved Israeli assistance in combating the separatist movement in Eritera. An important strategic interest of geographical importance to Israel was to prevent the Bab el Mandeb Straits from being blocked and thus in effect closing the Red Sea and the Straits of Tiran to Israeli shipping. The most significant relationship between the two nations involved Israeli training of the Ethiopian police. It was this Israeli trained force that helped to preserve the monarchy as long as it did, foiling three coup attempts prior to the eventual ousting of the emperor in 1974.[149]

The revolution in Ethiopia, however, did not mean the end of Israeli involvement with Ethiopia. The Israelis provided support to the Mengistu regime in 1989 just prior to its overthrow in an effort to obtain the freedom of Ethiopian Jews. The Israelis agreed to provide captured Soviet equipment, training, and intelligence to the Ethiopian army in return for providing an airlift of Ethiopian Jews to Israel. This policy ran counter to the United States at this time, which was backing Mengistu's opponents. In addition there was some controversy between Washington and Jerusalem over this as the Israelis provided American-made cluster bombs to the Ethiopian government without obtaining permission from the United States.[150]

South Africa

There have been extensive ties between the two countries in military relations that encompass four broad categories: arms transfers, technology transfers, intelligence cooperation, and mutual assistance to their respective nuclear programs.[151] The military cooperation began in 1955 when Israel sold Uzi submachine guns to Pretoria. These weapons have, since 1971, been produced in South Africa under license. In 1962 Israel sold South Africa 32 Centurion tanks. South Africa reciprocated during the 1967 war by selling Israel spare parts for their French military equipment that Paris refused to provide.[152]

The two countries have had a very close working military relationship since the mid-1970s. It is difficult to put a precise dollar figure on this trade, but estimates are that it is worth about $500 million a year to Israel, along with several thousand jobs in the vital industrial sectors. These include actual military sales as well as joint development projects.[153] An example of the items that Israel has provided South Africa include Reshef-class warships equipped with Gabriel surface-to-surface missiles. In addition the Israelis were selling military support equipment such as radar stations, electronic fencing, computers, antiguerilla infiltration alarm systems, and night vision devices.[154]

The two countries have also undertaken joint military projects as well as the sharing of military technology. An example of this were the reports of Israeli-South African collaboration in the construction of an 850-ton guided missile corvette and a nuclear-powered submarine. In addition there have been reports that the two nations are working on developing a advanced version of the Israeli Jericho intermediate range missile.[155] Another example of the two countries sharing technology is the assistance Israel provided for the South Africans to produce their own fighter aircraft, the Cheetah.[156]

Another important component of this relationship is the assistance that Israel has provided South Africa in military training and intelligence. This relationship started in the mid-1960s and has progressed, along with the growth of arms transfers and technology-sharing between the two countries. Reports have indicated that there are as many as 300 Israelis in South Africa training the military, as well as South Africans who travel to Israel to receive military training. In addition it is charged that the Israelis have actively assisted the South Africans in planning and directly participating in military operations in Angola and Namibia during the 1970s and 1980s.[157]

A significant area of cooperation between the two countries has been in the area of nuclear technology. Israel has not been alone in assisting South Africa's nuclear program. It is alleged that other Western countries, specifically France, Great Britain, the United States, and West Germany have also been involved.[158] However, there have been persistent allegations that Israel has played a significant role in South Africa's nuclear development. Reports have suggested that Israel, in return for uranium, has provided South Africa with essential nuclear technology. There are also allegations, which have not been conclusively proven, that the two countries jointly tested a weapon in the southern Indian Ocean in September of 1979.[159]

Uganda

One of the more extensive Israeli relationships in Africa was with Idi Amin's Uganda. This started while Amin was rising through the ranks of Uganda's political and military elite and it was with Israeli assistance, along with the United States and Britain, that he was able to overthrow President Milton Obote in 1971. Obote had been falling out of favor with these powers because of his nationalization of some Western companies, as well as the leftward political shift in his government in general. Israeli security interests were already active in the country, as Tel Aviv was supporting an insurgency in southern Sudan by the Anya-Nya tribe, which was Amin's tribe. This was part of the Israeli peripheral strategy of trying to weaken hostile Arab governments. In addition, the Israelis sold Uganda surplus American tanks in 1970 that Amin, with Israeli advisement, was able to use to pull off his coup. The British also took steps to insure that the coup would succeed by positioning 700 troops in neighboring Kenya. Once Amin took power he reversed the policies of his predecessor by supporting arms sales to South Africa, denationalizing Western companies that were previously taken over by the government, as well as permitting an increased Israeli presence within the country.[160]

Latin America

The Israelis have also sought to expand their military assistance programs to Latin America. This was of special interest to the Begin government in the early 1980s, as it was more than willing to play the role of American proxy in the region.[161]

Israel had found that Latin America was a very good export market for their military goods. Israeli arms exports range from sophisticated items such as electronics, fighter bombers, missiles, and patrol boats, to small arms and ammunition as well as stocks of PLO weapons captured in Lebanon. Most significant has been Israeli technical and advisory support in the region.[162] This was a process that the United States encouraged. During this period, when asked if Washington approved of Israeli activities in Central America, a high State Department official remarked, "Absolutely. We've indicated we're not unhappy they are helping out. But I wouldn't say we and the Israelis have figured out together what to do."[163]

During the 1980s, Israeli assistance was furnished to various governments in Latin America to combat insurgent groups. Among the recipients of aid from Israel were Guatemala, Honduras, El Salvador, and

Costa Rica. While this assistance was small in total, it was considered substantial given the modest size of the military forces in this region. Israel moved into these nations in a big way in the 1970s, supplying military aid to the crumbling regime of Somoza in Nicaragua. It began to intervene on a larger scale in the 1980s to combat the PLO, which was furnishing assistance to Nicaragua, as well as to establish military export markets for the future. It sought to gain markets in part due to American self-imposed limitations on arms transfers due to human rights violations in some of these nations. The United States viewed these Israeli arms sales favorably.[164]

An example of Israel's expanding role in Latin America occurred in 1981. Israel provided support to the government of El Salvador when the Reagan administration wished to extend military aid, but its foreign aid funds had run out. He requested Israel to transfer $21 million in military credits to the government of El Salvador, which was repaid to Israel the following fiscal year.[165] Guatemala was another example. In 1981 Congress blocked military aid to the government, which led Secretary Haig to appeal to Israel to step in and provide support.[166]

While in some cases Israeli activities seemed to be complementing official American policy in Latin America, in other instances it seemed to be working against it, at least the official administration policy. Examples of this include the cases of Argentina, Chile, and Paraguay in which Israel supplied arms and support in contradiction of American foreign policy. Israel continued to supply Argentina with military equipment after the invasion of the Falklands Islands in 1982, and continued to supply Buenos Aires after the war to make up for many of their combat losses.[167] The United States embargoed military sales to Chile in 1977 as a result of that nation's human rights violations. The Israelis, however, maintained their arms link with Santiago and even furnished the Chileans with the technology of manufacturing cluster bombs, a large amount of which were eventually sold by Chile to Iraq.[168] Paraguay was also banned by the United States from receiving military equipment as a result of the country's poor human rights record. Israel, however, continued to supply the army with small arms, despite President Stroessner's infamous history of shielding Nazi war criminals.[169] The Israelis as early as 1983 sought to provide aid to the Contras by furnishing them captured PLO arms from Lebanon. This was part of a larger role that Israel was playing in the region at the request of the United States.[170] This encouragement provided by the United States was related to the conflict between the Republican administration and the Congress over aid to Central America. It was argued that the administration was attempting to develop alternative sources of support for the Contras and friendly Central American countries should Congress vote to cut aid.[171]

Conclusions

The American-Israeli relationship with the third world has been strategically significant for both parties. The United States has sought to use Israel in an effort to provide aid to third world countries. The emphasis of both the United States and Israel has been to assist pro-Western conservative states against external threats as well as internal subversion. This has been justified by the argument that these forces were either directly or indirectly supported by the Soviet Union. Thus the Cold War environment was an important factor in this aspect of bilateral relations. The Israelis gained politically, economically, as well as strategically from these relationships.

The advantages for the United States was that it allowed America to step back from some of these states and allow Israel to take the initiative in providing support. This complemented American geopolitical interests, as well as maintained these countries political, economic, and military orientation towards the West. At the same time, the United States did not have to get involved directly with states that were either international outcasts like South Africa, or where there was domestic pressure against providing American aid such as in parts of Latin America.[172]

The strategic assistance that Israel has provided through arms transfers and the building up of its industrial base has contributed to its growth as a military power, as well as increasing the military strength of the country it assists. Other examples of Israeli assistance to pro-Western states that have also benefitted the United States would include: Argentina before the resumption of American military ties, Chad when under pressure from Libya, as well as Israeli aid to Taiwan, which was politically inconvenient at best for the United States given the emphasis on the development of better relations with the People's Republic of China.[173]

The disadvantages for the United States in the long term was that America was associated further with autocratic regimes. In certain cases conflicts, and certainly oppression, were prolonged. As a result, when political change has occurred in various parts of the third world it has generally taken an anti-Israeli and anti-American tone. Finally, the Israeli connection in American relations with certain countries of the third world has been used to influence decision making within the United States. This was true with regard to Iran and Zaire. One of the reasons why the Shah was interested in cultivating ties with Israel was to gain the support of the Israeli lobby in Washington. Mobutu of Zaire also sought the good offices of pro-Israeli groups to gain additional aid for Zaire from Washington, in return for restoring diplomatic relations with Tel Aviv.[174]

American-Israeli Relations in the Aftermath of the Cold War

The end of the Cold War and the uncertain world map left in its wake has resulted in the speculation that America's own military force posture as well as its alliance commitments will have to undergo change. There was some tension in the American-Israeli alliance during the Bush administration. This centered around the initial refusal of the United States to provide loan guarantees to Israel, and the allegations that the Israelis had illegally shipped American arms and technology to third world countries. In addition there has been some questioning of the utility of the American-Israeli alliance given the potential political problems that would have been caused had Israel intervened against Iraq during the Gulf War. It was thought that if Israel had intervened this would have caused the breakup of the coalition against Iraq. As a result, the Bush administration was forced to engage in sensitive negotiations to ensure that Israel refrained from retaliating against Iraq.

This was illustrated with the establishment of $10 billion in loan guarantees that Congress passed on October 1, 1992 with the support of the Bush administration. Congress has also guaranteed the entire $10 billion loan and provided that Congress could overrule any presidential suspension should Israel use the funds in the occupied territories.[175]

As part of the same bill, Congress also voted Israel an additional $3 billion in grants for economic and military aid. Despite the ending of the Cold War the United States is still building Israel up militarily. This includes supplying it with the most up-to-date American technology. Israel will receive Black Hawk helicopters, along with having $300 million worth of military equipment positioned inside Israel should American military forces have to intervene in the region again. These supplies will include advanced artillery munitions and Patriot antimissile missiles. These systems could be placed at Israel's disposal should there be a need.[176]

In addition, the Israeli role as a strategic partner has been confirmed by the Bush administration. In a meeting between President Bush and Prime Minister Rabin in Maine in August 1992, the President reaffirmed the American commitment to Israel and the vital strategic role that Israel plays in American foreign policy calculations. These same ideas are stated in the Republican Party platform, which was also adopted in August at the party's national convention in Houston, Texas. It read:

> consistent with our strategic relationship, the United States should continue to provide large-scale security assistance to Israel, maintaining Israel's qualitative military advantage over any adversary or coalition of adversaries . . . we will continue to broaden and deepen the strategic relationship with our ally Israel—the only true democracy in the Middle East.[177]

In addition to these statements, the strategic relationship has been in the process of being broadened not only with regard to arms transfers, but also in the development of infrastructure within Israel capable of supporting American military forces. The Israeli port of Haifa is being developed to accommodate U.S. navy vessels for use as a repair facility. Israel Aircraft Industries is also doing the servicing of American F-15s based in Europe.[178]

While the Cold War and the Soviet Union are gone, the strategic connection between American and Israel still exists and is being modified to undertake new challenges. One of the most significant emerging areas of the world, which affects both the Middle East and the United States, is Central Asia and is a region where American and Israel have common interests. The United States has five broad interests with regard to the new states of Central Asia. First, the extent that politics in the Central Asian republics can influence and moderate the politics of the Russian Republic. Second, how these states will impact on the politics and policies of their neighbors. Third, to deter arms proliferation and specifically nuclear proliferation in these emerging nations. Fourth, there are American commercial interests in these new republics, specifically in the exploitation of the oil and gas reserves of Kazakhstan and Turkmenistan respectively. Fifth, there is an American geopolitical interest in insuring the development of stable governments in these nations, specifically since events in Central Asia have repercussions on the Middle East.[179] The last point is the most significant relative to Israel. Both the United States and Israel are alarmed by the increase of Islamic fundamentalism in Central Asia. In particular the opportunities this offers for the growth of Iranian influence.[180]

The Israeli view of this can be observed from the statement of its ambassador to the United States, Zalman Shoval. He pointed out in an interview in March the necessity of strategic cooperation between the United States and Israel in order to combat Islamic fundamentalism in Central Asia:

> Is there not a danger that they will become fundamentalist and anti-Western and present a danger to the Middle East more than the Soviet Union did? Is it wise for the Bush Administration to disregard Israel as a strategic ally at this time? The strategic relationship between the United States and Israel now is as important as it ever was—even more.[181]

There have been reports that both the United States and Israel are jointly cooperating in spreading their influence in Central Asia and developing friendly relations in this region. This is illustrated by reports of a joint American-Israeli agricultural project in Central Asia utilizing American funds and Israeli agricultural and irrigation knowledge.[182]

The demise of the Cold War has not diminished the American-Israeli alliance. Rather, the alliance will be reoriented towards new perceived threats and strategic considerations will remain paramount between the two countries. A significant reason for this is the importance that Israel holds in American domestic politics. Both political parties actively court the Jewish vote; this has been the case since 1948 and was true in the most recent presidential election. American Jews still form a core constituency of the Democratic Party.

The Clinton administration came into office with strong support from the American Jewish community. Many Jews who had been drifting towards the Republican Party in the 1980s, in part due to Ronald Reagan's strong support for Israel, returned to the Democratic fold in 1992 mainly due to the tensions between the Bush administration and Israel over the question of the loan guarantees. While the relationship between the Clinton administration and Israel has been much warmer than was the case in the Bush presidency, the current administration has different priorities, and the mood of the country has shifted as well. The emphasis has been more on domestic reform and the concerns about paying for these programs as well as deficit reduction. Foreign assistance has a lower priority than in previous administrations. Some of the policies that the Clinton administration has enacted towards Israel are: reducing the 1994 payment of the loan guarantees by $437 to reflect the amount that the Israeli government spent on settlement related projects in 1992-1993; pressuring Israel to join the Missile Technology Control Regime, which attempts to limit the spread of ballistic missile technology; and maintaining the offer made by President Bush to link Israel to the American early-warning satellite system in the event of another major conflict in the region, but not before. While the United States was not directly a major actor in the Israeli-PLO negotiations that led to the September 1993 agreement to gradually transfer power in the West Bank and Gaza Strip, Washington did organize a conference to get other nations to contribute funds for aiding the Palestinians in the West Bank and Gaza in which $2.4 billion was pledged. The United States pledged $500 million of this amount to be paid over a five-year period. However, unlike in previous administrations, the political climate was not present to underwrite an Israeli withdrawal from the occupied territories.[183]

American Aid to Israel

Despite the advanced offensive military systems made available to Israel during the Johnson administration, the amount of economic and military aid extended was relatively small. Most of the aid furnished to Israel in the late 1960s and early 1970s was in the form of military and economic loans. In 1969 the United States government granted $30 million in military loans for 1970, and $60 million in economic aid. Regional events, however, were to play a role in the escalation of aid to Israel. In 1970 the Jordanian government attempted to destroy the Palestinian movement within Jordan that had emerged as a challenge to the monarchy. Israeli threats of intervention to forestall possible Syrian intervention was a catalyst to the rapid escalation of American aid to Israel. President Nixon agreed in response to raise the aid level to Israel by $500 million as well as to accelerate the delivery of Phantom jets. Within the next three years the United States extended aid to Israel worth $1.608 billion. This is compared to the $1.581 billion since 1948. Analysts argued that this infusion of aid to Israel allowed the Israelis to increase the amount of funding for the military, as economic aid created the opportunity to challenge those funds that would have been spent on economic aid to the military sphere. By 1971 Israel was spending 20 percent of its GNP on the military. In addition to military and economic aid the two countries began to heighten their strategic cooperation. In December of 1970 the United States and Israel concluded a Master Defense Development Data Exchange Agreement. The significance of this agreement was that it allowed the two countries to share technology information. A follow-on agreement in 1971 initiated the process that allowed Israel to construct American-designed military equipment. As a result of this shared technology the Israelis were able to construct a heat-seeking air-to-air missile, the Shahrir, which was almost identical to the American-manufactured Sidewinder missile. In addition, the United States granted Israel permission to manufacture the J-79 engine for use in the Israeli Kfir jets.[184]

This aid pipeline and cooperation was given further impetus as a result of the airlift during the 1973 war. This proved to be the largest airlift in history up until that time and the United States succeeded in flying in 22,497 tons of military equipment, involving 26,000 thousand military and civilian personnel.[185]

Stages of U.S. Assistance to Israel

From 1948 to the early 1980s Israeli military procurement from the United States passed through four stages. The first encompassed the years 1948-1961 and was characterized by relatively low levels of American aid to Israel, both economic and military. The second stage took place between 1962-1965 in which the Kennedy and Johnson administrations began the process of selling sophisticated armaments to Israel while still maintaining that it did not wish to be Israel's principal arms supplier. The third phase took place during the Johnson administration, 1966-1969, where the United States accelerated the process of providing offensive armaments to Israel. Between the years 1969-1982 the United States extended a vast amount of aid to Israel and provided this aid long term. Between the years 1974-1980 Washington provided on average $1.6 billion a year, $636 million of this figure was in the form of grants. During this period the annual defense imports of Israel were $1.9 billion, 85 percent of which was paid by American grants and loans.[186] See table 5.1 for a detailed illustration.

In addition to military aid the United States was providing a vast amount of economic aid to Israel. Between the years 1970-1984 the total figure for American economic aid was $32 billion, of which $11 billion was in the form of grants.[187]

Aid in total terms was relatively low between the years 1948-1973. While from the mid 1960s to 1973 the United States was involved in transferring sophisticated arms to Israel, it did not extend much in the way of economic or military aid in general. See tables 5.1 and 5.2 for detailed illustrations. Between 1948 and 1973 the United States extended $2.7 billion in economic and military aid. More significant from the standpoint of military and economic aid to Israel were the funds acquired from the contributions of Jewish and non-Jewish supporters worldwide, as well as aid from Jewish charities that amounted to about $2 billion, and about

Table 5.1. U.S. Military Assistance to Israel, 1960-1973
(U.S. dollars in millions)

Year	Loans	Grants	Total
1960	0.5	—	0.5
1961	—	—	—
1962	13.2	—	13.2
1963	13.3	—	13.3
1964	—	—	—
1965	12.9	—	12.9
1966	90.0	—	90.0
1967	7.0	—	7.0
1968	25.0	—	25.0
1969	85.0	—	85.0
1970	30.0	—	30.0
1971	545.0	—	545.0
1972	300.0	—	300.0
1973	307.5	—	307.5
Total	1429.4	—	1429.4

Source: Source: Clyde R. Mark, *Israel: U.S. Foreign Assistance,* CRS Issue Brief, Congressional Research Service (Washington, D.C.: Library of Congress, January 5, 1993), 6-7. Cited in Camille Mansour, *Beyond Alliance: Israel in U.S. Foreign Policy* (New York: Columbia University Press, 1994), 190.

Table 5.2. U.S. Economic Assistance to Israel, 1960-1973
(U.S. dollars in millions)

Years	Loans	Grants	Total
1960	42.3	13.4	55.7
1961	59.6	18.3	77.9
1962	73.0	7.2	80.2
1963	68.6	6.0	74.6
1964	32.2	4.8	37.0
1965	47.3	4.9	52.2
1966	35.9	0.9	36.8
1967	15.1	1.6	16.7
1968	75.0	6.5	81.5
1969	74.7	0.6	75.3
1970	50.7	12.9	63.8
1971	86.5	2.8	89.3
1972	124.9	56.0	180.9
1973	80.5	104.8	185.3
Total	866.3	240.7	2646.3

Source: Clyde R. Mark, *Israel: U.S. Foreign Assistance,* CRS Issue Brief, Congressional Research Service (Washington, D.C.: Library of Congress, January 5, 1993), 6-7. Cited in Camille Mansour, *Beyond Alliance: Israel in U.S. Foreign Policy* (New York: Columbia University Press, 1994), 190.

$2 billion from the sale of Israeli bonds. During this period Israel also received $6 billion in reparations from the Federal Republic of Germany.[188]

Aid from the Reagan Administration

Between 1981-1989 the Reagan administration extended over $27 billion in aid to Israel, of which $23 billion was in the form of grants. This was out of a total of $46 billion that the United States had extended to Israel between the years 1948-1989.[189] The amount of aid was accelerated as a result of the emphasis on grants as the means by which assistance was extended. This occurred early in the Reagan administration as in November of 1981, on a visit to Washington, Prime Minister Shamir and President Reagan agreed on a package in which American aid to Israel would be reduced from $1.7 billion to $1.3 billion, but it was to be extended as a grant as opposed to a loan. In addition, unlike other aid recipients, Israel did not have to spend it all in the United States as 15 percent could be spent in Israeli for Israeli-made weapons. The president promised an additional $910 million as an economic grant as well as agreeing with Congress to extend $550 million to Israel to produce the Lavi fighter. Reagan also indicated his willingness to enter into greater strategic cooperation with Israel and establish duty free trade. For this the United States did not receive any Israeli commitments on such questions as support for the Reagan peace plan, freezing West Bank settlements, or dropping opposition to American arms sales to Jordan.[190] Several reasons why Washington was so forthcoming have been cited, including strategic considerations for the United States in using Israel as a regional ally to block Soviet expansion in the region both directly and indirectly. It can also be argued that Washington was trying to assuage Israel, and its supporters in the United States, as a result of the AWACS sale to Saudi Arabia concluded earlier in the year.

The bilateral aid figures for the United States and Israel between the years 1949-1991 totaled $53 billion in aid and other benefits, the equivalent of 13 percent of all American aid granted during this period worldwide. This figure is even more dramatic when it is considered that from 1979 the amount of aid totaled $40.1 billion, which was equal to 21.5 percent of all American aid during this period.[191]

Conclusions: The Ramifications of the Israeli-American Alliance

Most analysts maintain that the Israeli-American military alliance has benefitted the United States strategically. Several factors of this argument revolve around the enhancement of American military technology, the testing of American equipment under battlefield conditions, such as the F-15 and F-16, the sharing of intelligence specifically on captured Soviet equipment, and the access by the American military to Israeli facilities. A more general strategic benefit of this alliance was the growth of Israel as

Table 5.3. U.S. Military Assistance to Israel, 1974-1990
(U.S. dollars in millions)

Year	Loans	Grants	Total
1974	982.7	1500.0	2482.7
1975	200.0	100.0	300.0
1976	850.0	850.0	1700.0
1977	500.0	500.0	1000.0
1978	500.0	500.0	1000.0
1979	2700.0	1300.0	4000.0
1980	500.0	500.0	1000.0
1981	900.0	500.0	1400.0
1982	850.0	550.0	1400.0
1983	950.0	750.0	1700.0
1984	850.0	850.0	1700.0
1985	—	1400.0	1400.0
1986	—	1722.6	1722.6
1987	—	1800.0	1800.0
1988	—	1800.0	1800.0
1989	—	1800.0	1800.0
1990	—	1792.3	1792.3

Source: Clyde R. Mark, *Israel: U.S. Foreign Assistance,* CRS Issue Brief, Congressional Research Service (Washington, D.C.: Library of Congress, January 5, 1993), 6-7. Cited in Camille Mansour, *Beyond Alliance: Israel in U.S. Foreign Policy* (New York: Columbia University Press, 1994), 190.

Table 5.4. U.S. Economic Assistance to Israel, 1974-1990
(U.S. dollars in millions)

Years	Loans	Grants	Total
1974	72.3	91.3	163.6
1975	96.0	407.0	496.7
1976	410.3	544.9	955.2
1977	277.9	509.6	787.5
1978	272.2	550.4	822.6
1979	358.8	554.2	913.0
1980	591.9	554.1	1146.0
1981	217.4	791.0	1008.4
1982	24.0	821.5	845.5
1983	—	800.6	800.6
1984	—	926.6	926.6
1985	—	1971.7	1971.7
1986	15.0	1920.9	1935.9
1987	—	1235.2	1235.2
1988	—	1234.9	1234.9
1989	—	1239.9	1239.9
1990	400.0	1235.7	1235.7
Total	2735.8	15389.5	18125.3

Source: Clyde R. Mark, *Israel: U.S. Foreign Assistance,* CRS Issue Brief, Congressional Research Service (Washington, D.C.: Library of Congress, January 5, 1993), 6-7. Cited in Camille Mansour, *Beyond Alliance: Israel in U.S. Foreign Policy* (New York: Columbia University Press, 1994), 190.

Table 5.5. U.S. Military Sales Agreements with Israel, 1983-1992 (U.S. dollars in thousands)

Years	Worldwide	Near East and South Asia (NESA)	Israel
1950-1982	106,591,953	52,294,748	9,262,083
1983	14,206,786	4,909,580	2,115,031
1984	12,417,976	3,968,794	93,862
1985	10,403,224	3,664,118	84,949
1986	6,301,880	1,888,027	168,686
1987	6,253,629	1,893,613	100,680
1988	11,394,921	7,097,335	1,362,544
1989	10,485,798	6,665,648	339,745
1990	13,735,480	7,705,460	383,449
1991	22,725,578	16,401,055	367,923
1992	14,983,717	2,974,693	98,001
1950-1992	229,590,942	109,463,071	14,376,954

Source: U.S. Department of Defense. *Foreign Military Sales, Foreign Military Construction Sales, and Military Assistance Facts* (Washington, D.C.: U.S. Government Printing Office, September 1992), 16-17.

**Table 5.6. U.S. Military Sales Deliveries to Israel,
1983-1992 (U.S. dollars in thousands)**

Years	Worldwide	Near East and South Asia (NESA)	Israel
1950-1982	66,136,485	32,510,907	8,032,713
1983	10,606,795	5,787,356	258,962
1984	8,166,927	3,571,866	212,877
1985	7,508,743	3,167,020	475,342
1986	7,236,031	3,397,162	164,206
1987	10,876,542	5,999,925	1,293,515
1988	8,790,663	2,617,805	750,953
1989	6,942,576	1,640,265	230,440
1990	7,438,878	2,354,029	151,238
1991	8,761,831	4,095,119	239,301
1992	9,675,035	4,844,259	696,798
1950-1992	152,140,506	69,985,713	12,506,348

Source: U.S. Department of Defense. *Foreign Military Sales, Foreign Military Construction Sales, and Military Assistance Facts* (Washington, D.C.: U.S. Government Printing Office, September 1992), 16-17.

a regional military hegemon whose influence is felt outside the Middle East. As a result, the United States developed a strong pro-American military force that Soviet decision makers had to take into account in their regional policy. In addition a strong Israel has traditionally given the United States a barrier against what America considers to be radical nationalism in the region, such as Pan-Arabism and the Palestinian movement.[192]

However, the limitations of this view were illustrated during the Persian Gulf War of 1990-1991. The American-Israeli alliance threatened to split the anti-Iraqi coalition that the Bush administration had so carefully constructed. Supporters of Israel had always argued that Israel was a strategic asset to the United States. During this conflict, however, it was exposed as a strategic liability. Washington was forced to allocate diplomatic energy in order to keep Israel out of the conflict militarily. The United States also had to expend military forces in assisting Israel. This included the sending of Patriot missile batteries and crews to defend Israeli cities, as well as diverting elements of American air power from strategic missions to seeking and destroying mobile SCUD launchers in western Iraq.[193] This was a source of controversy between Israel and the United States, and specifically the American military command in Riyadh. The chief of staff of the Israeli air force, General Bin-Nun, claimed that only 3 percent of allied air sorties during the war were to locate and destroy SCUD sites in western Iraq. Out of 110,000 total during the war this amounted to about 3,000. The U.S. military command in Riyadh felt constrained, being under political pressure to divert resources away from the strategic campaign to SCUD hunting. General Schwarzkopf acknowledged that the SCUD priority was interfering with other parts of the military campaign, although it did have strategic implications in keeping Israel out of the war.[194]

In addition to broad strategic cooperation the two countries have also entered into a number of joint arrangements concerning developing systems for intelligence. Israel has worked with many American corporations, such as Boeing, Sylvania, RCA, E-systems, Beechcraft, and 21st Century, in developing these systems. Proponents argue that Israeli participation in these programs saved research and development costs for the United States and developed systems that can be used in other areas. Some examples of the above benefits garnered for the United States were Israeli research and development of sophisticated intelligence gathering systems such as the Guardrail V. This is a small plane designed to gather tactical intelligence.[195]

The sharing of intelligence by Israel with the United States on captured Soviet military equipment has been one of the foundations of the strategic relationship between the two countries. This dates back to the 1956 Suez War when the Israelis allowed American experts to examine captured Soviet military equipment in the Sinai. After the Yom Kippur War six Soviet T-62 tanks were sent to the United States to be examined and were used in training American forces. Examples of American-Israeli cooperation in military development and intelligence gathering occurred during the 1982 Lebanon War. The Israelis were able to upgrade American equipment and develop new tactics to counter Soviet technology by examining the wreckage of MiG-23 and MiG-25 fighter planes shot down during the war. The Israelis were also able to modify artillery shells to pierce the armor of a Soviet T-72, which was the Soviets main battle tank at that time.[196]

A further ramification of this alliance is that American policy makers and military officials have looked upon Israel, and the Middle East in general, as a proving ground for U.S. military technology and tactics.[197] However, it should be noted that it is argued that some American weapons systems were deliberately made to appear to be more effective than they really were. It is alleged that this was the case with the Maverick and the Sparrow (beyond visual range) missiles during the 1973 war. The successes of these systems may have been overstated as a result of inaccurate measures of success, or the use of the system in a false battle environment.[198]

In studying the alliance it can be stated that it has become difficult, if not impossible, to divorce Israeli interests from American interests. The two have essentially become merged, which can be detrimental to both parties, in particular the United States. This linkage of interests is a result of the perceptions in both countries of the importance of the alliance and the necessity of maintaining high levels of military and economic assistance, as well as political cooperation. This is also taken as a given domestically by both nations. In the United States, Israel is significant domestically as pro-Israeli groups have a great deal of influence with Congress. In addition, Israel has traditionally enjoyed the support of large sectors of non-Jewish American public opinion and held the support of interest groups in American society generally not concerned with Middle East issues, such as the AFL-CIO. Therefore this has served to reinforce the concept held by American decision makers that Israel is important strategically for the United States. The foundations of this idea can be traced back to the Kennedy administration and has developed since.

The idea of Israel as a significant American partner has taken hold in Israeli politics as well. Israeli officials have argued that Jerusalem played a critical role in American foreign policy in the region as a strategic asset. Shimon Peres in 1977 stated that "Israel contributed more than any other country to the fact that the West in general and the U.S. in particular have such an impressive bargaining power in our region." Another commentator has argued that the United States can utilize Israel as a base of operations. "We will be sort of another American aircraft carrier out here, a platform from which the Americans can operate."[199]

What has developed in the American-Israeli relationship has been a case of reverse leverage in which the United States has overcommitted to the alliance. The relationship has been predicated on the forging of an extensive military and political relationship that is supported by increasing amounts of American military and economic aid. Therefore any attempt by the United States to significantly cut back on military assistance will result in causing a crisis within the relationship. This will also lead to political costs on the American administration that attempts to initiate such a policy. The end result would be the administration having to spend political capital in fighting Israeli supporters in Congress and in winning over American public opinion in general. Such a move would most likely end up costing the administration support on other foreign policy initiatives, as well as on its domestic agenda. An example of this that was previously discussed was the case of President Johnson and the Phantom sale. Johnson did not want to sell the plane to Israel but felt that as a result of the Vietnam War, the upcoming American presidential election, as well as trying to salvage his domestic agenda, he could not risk a major political fight with Israel and her supporters in Washington.

This factor is true of American alliances in the Middle East in general. Alliances are created for a combination of strategic and domestic factors. Client groups either develop or reinforce around these relationships. Therefore the alliance perpetuates itself despite changing strategic conditions. The test of American support becomes hinged upon the continuation of the high levels of military and economic aid and political support. This was stated by George Ball when he argued, "In the minds of Israeli leaders, the test of American friendship would thus appear to be our unquestioning willingness to continue our heavy subsidy, however aberrant Israeli policies may seem." In supporting this view he makes a point of acknowledging a statement by former Israeli Foreign Minister Moshe Dayan who stated that despite some serious disagreements with the Carter administration, the level of U.S. aid was not diminished.[200]

It is this factor that has served to limit the maneuverability of the United States in general when making alliance commitments. The American-Israeli relationship has developed to the point that American security and Israeli security are virtually synonymous. The idea that Israel is a "strategic asset" has essentially been accepted in both American and Israeli strategic thinking. This led to the development of the idea that Israel is essentially a strategic bargain for the United States. Supporters cite the expense that Washington has incurred in placing its own military forces in various parts of the world directly to perform the same function that Israel performs. They cite the $130 billion that the United States has spent on NATO forces and the roughly $40 billion in the American military commitment to Asia in arguing that aid to Israel is a bargain for the United States.[201] A similar view was expressed by a former American air force intelligence officer Major John Keegan who stated, "it would cost U.S. taxpayers $125 billion to maintain an armed force equal to Israel's in the Middle East, and that "the United States-Israel military relationship was worth five CIAs."[202]

Because of these factors and perceptions, American and Israeli security interests have effectively been wedded. The ramifications for the United States are that any attack on Israel proper would be seen by American decision makers as an attack upon the United States.[203] American policy makers have become locked into the present relationship with Israel and aside from symbolic gestures of displeasure, such as the delaying of certain arms transfers, any type of coercive diplomacy has become virtually impossible. This is a result of the power of Israeli supporters domestically, and the actual and perceived strategic importance that Israel has served in American foreign policy calculations.[204]

Notes

1. For a general discussion of the policies of the Kennedy administration in the third world see David Louis Cingranelli, *Ethics, American Foreign Policy and the Third World* (New York: St. Martin's Press, 1993), 151-57.

2. Stephen Green,*Taking Sides: America's Secret Relations with a Militant Israel* (New York: William Morrow, 1984), 183.

3. Cheryl Rubenberg, *Israel and the American National Interest* (Urbana, Ill.: University of Illinois Press, 1986), 91. Also Gazit argues that Kennedy felt balance of power slipping away from Israel. He felt if the United States did not do anything to rectify it Israel would seek to compensate in ways contrary to American interests such as developing nuclear weapons. Mordechai Gazit, *President Kennedy's Policy toward the Arab States and Israel* (Tel Aviv: Shiloah Center for Middle Eastern and African Studies, Tel Aviv University, 1983), 44.

4. Green, *Taking Sides*, 187.

5. Gazit, *President Kennedy's Policy*, 44. He indicates that the most persuasive argument was the second point listed. Gazit states that the fact that the HAWK was a defensive system is not a very strong argument, as previous administrations could have authorized similar type systems and did not. The last point, Gazit argues, was not very strong as well because Kennedy initiated other actions significant for Israeli security that were not publicized. See also Edward Tivnan, *The Lobby* (New York: Simon and Schuster, 1987), 58.

6. Gazit, "Israeli Military Procurement from the United States," in *Dynamics of Dependence*, Gabriel Sheffer ed. (Boulder, Colo.: Westview Press, 1987), 96.

7. Gazit, "Israel's Military Procurement," 95.

8. Mitchell Geoffrey Bard, *The Water's Edge and Beyond* (New Brunswick, N.J.: Transaction Publishers, 1991), 190.

9. Memorandum, David Klein to McGeorge Bundy, February 17, 1965. This document claims that the United States was unaware of German arms transfers to Israel, but as early as 1960 did discuss the possibility with Germany of selling American tanks to Israel. Memorandum, Robert Komer to President Johnson, April 23, 1965. Indicates that the Germans appreciated the United States taking over the sale. LBJ Library. Cited in Bard, *The Water's Edge*, 193. Also see Robert H. Trice Jr., "Domestic Political Interests and American Policy in the Middle East: Pro-Israel, Pro-Arab and Corporate Non-governmental Actors and the Making of American Foreign Policy, 1966-1971," (Unpublished Ph.D. Diss. University of Wisconsin-Madison, 1974), 132-226.

10. National Security Action Memorandum, *Meeting Israeli Arms Requests*, LBJ Documents, NSAM no. 290, April 28, 1964, Box no. 3, Document no. 2, 4.

11. Gazit, in "Israeli Military Procurement," 91.

12. Michael Brecher, *The Foreign Policy System of Israel: Setting, Images, Process* (New Haven, Conn.: Yale University Press, 1972), 44. Quoted in Rubenberg, *Israel and the American*, 92. She emphasizes the significance of the territorial guarantees as the territorial claims made by Israel were not clearly defined.

13. Andrew Cockburn and Leslie Cockburn, *Dangerous Liaisons: The Inside Story of the U.S.-Israeli Covert Relationship* (New York: HarperCollins Publishers, 1991), 90. The Cockburn's discuss a conversation between Kennedy and Ben-Gurion in which they argue Kennedy stated, "I know I was elected by the votes of American Jews. I owe them my victory. Tell me, is there something I ought to do?"

They state that Ben-Gurion was shocked at this and replied, "You must do whatever is best for the free world."

14. Cockburn and Cockburn, *Dangerous Liaisons*, 190.

15. National Security Action Memorandum, *Meeting Israeli Arms Requests,* 4.

16. Bard, *The Water's Edge*, 195.

17. Rubenberg, *Israel and the American*, 91. As a result of these agreements the $92 million provided in FY 1966 was cumulatively greater than the years 1948-1965. This figure is even more important when one realizes that in the previous fiscal year, 20 percent of all aid to Israel was military, while in fiscal year 1966 the corresponding figure was 71 percent. See Green, *Taking Sides*, 186-87.

18. Bard, *The Water's Edge*, 195.

19. Gazit, "Israeli Military Procurement," 101.

20. National Security Action Memoradum, *Meeting Israeli Arms Requests*, 4.

21. Memorandum, Charles Baird to Assistant Secretary of Defense, Israel State Archives, January 5, 1968, LBJ Library. Cited in Bard, *The Water's Edge*, 200.

22. Bard, *The Water's Edge*, 205.

23. Hedrick Smith, "U.S. Will Start Delivering F-4 Jets to Israel in 1969," *New York Times*, 28 December 1968, 1(A).

24. Department of State Memorandum of Conversation, *U.S.-Israeli Talks*, January 7, 1968, LBJ Documents, 3-4. The Israelis stressed the importance of the Phantoms in part because they doubted the reliability of France delivering French Mirages. Even if these planes were to be delivered they argued that the De Gaulle government would seek to balance by furnishing arms to the Arab states.

25. Bard, *The Water's Edge*, 201.

26. Bard, *The Water's Edge*, 202.

27. I. L. Kenen, *Israel's Defense Line* (Buffalo, N.Y.: Prometheus Books, 1981), 218-19.

28. Cockburn and Cockburn, *Dangerous Liaisons*, 164. Also Stephen Green, *Living by the Sword* (Brattleboro, Vt.: Amana Books, 1988), 13.The potential negative regional repercussions were reflected within the State Department. "We believe the Phantom is not needed by Israel and would risk escalating the arms race." Visit of Levi Eskol, *Israeli Arms Request,* January 3, 1968, LBJ Documents.

29. Kenen, *Israel's Defense Line*, 218.

30. Robert B. Semple Jr., "Nixon Stresses Commitment to Israel," *New York Times*, 9 September 1968, 1. Quoted in Gazit, "Israeli Military Procurement," 104-5 and Bard, *The Water's Edge*, 203.

31. Semple, "Nixon Stresses Commitment," 1(A). Quoted in Bard, *The Water's Edge*, 203.

32. Tivnan, *The Lobby*, 67.

33. Tivnan, *The Lobby*, 66.

34. Tivnan, *The Lobby*, 66.

35. Bard, *The Water's Edge*, 208. Also Gazit, "Israeli Military Procurement," 104.

36. James Reston, "Nasser, in Interview, Says He Is Seeking Soviet Weapons to Thwart Israeli Raids," *New York Times*, 15 February 1970, 1(A). Cited in Gazit, "Israeli Military Procurement," 104. The regional significance of the F-4 Phantom sale was illustrated in various public statements made by President Nasser. See *New York Times* article cited above.

37. Cockburn and Cockburn, *Dangerous Liaisons*, 164.

38. "Secret-Sensitive" Memorandum for the Record by Chairman of the Joint Chiefs of Staff, Earle G. Wheeler, January 24, 1968, National Security File, Country File Israel, Vol. 8, Box 141, LBJ Library. See also *Jane's All The World's*

Aircraft, 1967-1968 (London: Jane's, 1969), 373. Cited in Green, *Living by the Sword*, 11, 19. Green points out that at this time American units were themselves waiting for the newest version of the F-4. The Israelis, therefore, were competing with the American military for these planes.

39. Memorandum of conversation between Yitzhak Rabin et al. and Paul Warnke et al., November 4, 1968, LBJ Library. Quoted in Bard, *The Water's Edge*, 204.

40. Cockburn and Cockburn, *Dangerous Liaisons*, 164.

41. Helena Cobban, *The Superpowers and the Syrian-Israeli Conflict* (New York: Praeger, 1991), 79. See also Steven L. Spiegel, *The Other Arab-Israeli Conflict: Making America's Middle East Policy, from Truman to Reagan* (Chicago: University of Chicago Press, 1985), 159-64; and William B. Quandt, *Decade of Decisions: American Policy toward the Arab-Israeli Conflict, 1967-1976* (Berkeley, Calif.: University of California Press, 1977), 65-68.

42. Green, *Taking Sides*, 204-11. Provides a detailed analysis of American activities. A paradox to these events was the case of the USS *Liberty*, a reconnaissance vessel that was sent to the war zone to gather intelligence. Thirty-four sailors were killed in the attack. It would seem by the accounts of events, and despite Israeli denials, that the Israelis purposely attacked the ship to prevent the United States from becoming aware that Israel was about to undertake military action to seize the Golan Heights near the end of the war. This event did not have much of an impact on American-Israeli relations, as both states have sought to downplay this incident. For a detailed account of the events involving the *Liberty* see Green, *Taking Sides*, 212-42. The impact of the *Liberty* incident was felt even during the most recent Gulf War. A point of contention between the two nations during the Gulf War of 1990-1991 was the pressure the United States placed on Israel not to respond to Iraqi SCUD attacks. The United States refused to release the Identify Friend or Foe (IFF) codes, which would have permitted the Israelis to retaliate without inadvertently attacking American planes, and vice versa. Israeli military officials complained about the lack of military coordination between the two countries. Israeli Air Force Chief of Staff Avihu Bin-Nun, in attempting to persuade American officials to release these codes, stated he feared the possibility of an aerial *"Liberty."* For a discussion of this issue see Yossi Melman and Dan Raviv, *Friends in Deed: Inside the U.S.-Israel Alliance* (New York: Hyperion, 1994), 396.

Despite the close strategic relationship that developed between the two countries, particularly with regards to intelligence and military research and development, there was a lingering resentment in some quarters of the American military as a result of the *Liberty* incident. This is an issue I would like to explore further in the future.

43. Green, *Taking Sides*, 211; Also see Cockburn and Cockburn, *Dangerous Liaisons*, 154.

44. Cockburn and Cockburn, *Dangerous Liaisons*, 153. The reasons for the radical American departure in its policy toward Israel is also illustrated by Ball and Ball. They maintain that the reasons for the American shift were: (1) an Arab defeat would waste the resources the Soviets allocated in building up its Arab allies and also illustrate the weakness of relying on Soviet support. It was felt that this would strengthen the hand of the United States as the player who held the cards in the region; (2) by destroying the military capabilities of the major Arab states the United States hoped that Israeli demands for arms would lessen; (3) some elements within the United States hoped that after a disastrous military defeat that the Arab governments would be overthrown, especially Nasser of Egypt; (4) that an overwhelming Israeli victory would bring stability to the Middle East by forcing the

Arab governments to recognize Israel and draw closer to the United States in an effort for Washington to intercede with Jerusalem. George W. Ball and Douglas B. Ball, *The Passionate Attachment: America's Involvement with Israel 1947 to the Present* (New York: W. W. Norton, 1992), 53-54.

45. Rubenberg, *Israel and the American*, 125.

46. The French had begun to cool to the Israeli connection for several reasons. First General De Gaulle wished to disassociate France from American policy. He felt that the Soviets were getting more involved in the Middle East as a direct consequence of United States involvement in Southeast Asia. Second, he desired to extend France's influence in the Middle East, and particularly to take advantage of a growing arms sales market. Third, President De Gaulle wanted to assure France's oil supplies separately from the other Western powers. Fourth, he wanted French interests to be taken into account by the superpowers. Therefore he wanted to preserve Western influence in the region but at the same time not cede the Middle East to American hegemony. He therefore suspended further arms shipments to Israel a few days before the outbreak of the June 1967 war. For a discussion of French policy see Sylvia K. Crosbie, *A Tacit Alliance: France and Israel from Suez to the Six Day War* (Princeton, N.J.: Princeton University Press, 1974), 190-214.

47. Ball and Ball, *The Passionate Attachment*, 52.

48. Ball and Ball, *The Passionate Attachment*, 52; and Green, *Taking Sides*, 187. Green indicates that this figure of about $92 million in military aid provided in FY 1966 was more than all the military aid extended by the United States to Israel since 1948.

49. Ball and Ball, *The Passionate Attachment*, 65-66. For a discussion over the question of nuclear weapons see also Helen Cobban, "Israel's Nuclear Game: The U.S. Stake," *World Policy Journal* 5, no. 3 (Fall 1988): 425.

50. Rubenberg, *Israel and the American*, 14.

51. George Lenczowski, *American Presidents and the Middle East* (Durham, N.C.: Duke University Press, 1990), 122.

52. Lenczowski, *American Presidents*, 126-27.

53. Yitzhak Rabin, *The Rabin Memoirs* (Boston: Little Brown, 1979), 189. Cited in Lenczowski, *American Presidents*, 127.

54. Lenczowski, *American Presidents*, 189.

55. Spiegel, *The Other Arab-Israeli Conflict*, 255; Quandt, *Decade of Decisions*, 184. There is some debate on this issue as the amount of supplies can be considered significant, although they did arrive relatively late in the conflict. The actual amount of supplies that the United States provided Israel were 40 F-4 Phantom jets and 36 A-4 Skyhawks, as well as 12 C-130 transport planes. The airlift itself began on October 14, after some initial resistance by the Nixon administration, and at its height was bringing in thousands of tons of supplies per day. See Melman and Raviv, *Friends in Deed*, 160-61.

56. Gazit, "Israeli Military Procurement," 111.

57. Paul Findley, *Deliberate Deceptions: Facing the Facts about the U.S.-Israeli Relationship* (New York: Lawrence Hill Books, 1993), 107. Another example also from the 1973 war illustrated the Israeli influence within Congress that occurred over the supplying of the Maverick air-to-land antitank missile. Admiral Thomas Moorer, chairman of the Joint Chiefs of Staff, was initially opposed to supplying airplanes with the Maverick missile as the United States at that time only had one squadron of these planes and Congress would never allow the transfer. The Israeli military attaché Mordecai Gur stated to Admiral Moorer, "You get the airplanes; I'll take care of Congress." Moorer further added, "And he did, I've never seen a

President—I don't care who he is—stand up to them (the Israelis). It just boggles your mind. They always get what they want." See Findley, *Deliberate Deceptions*, 107; Paul Findley, *They Dare to Speak Out* (Westport, Conn.: Lawrence Hill Books, 1985), 161.

58. For a general discussion of this view see Melman and Raviv, *Friends in Deed*, 160-63.

59. Lenczowski, *American Presidents*, 139-40.

60. Green, *Living by the Sword*, 222-23.

61. Gazit, "Israeli Military Procurement," 112.

62. Lenczowski, *American Presidents*, 149-50.

63. Lenczowski, *American Presidents*, 152. Lenczowski cites Rabin, as well as Ismail Fahmy, *Negotiating for Peace in the Middle East* (London: Croom Helm, 1983). This is also discussed by George W. Ball, "The Coming Crisis in Israeli-American Relations," *Foreign Affairs* 58, no. 2 (Winter 1979-1980): 240.

64. Gazit, "Israeli Military Procurement," 114-15. See also Rabin, *Rabin Memoirs*, 505.

65. David Pollock, *The Politics of Pressure* (Westport, Conn.: Greenwood Press, 1982), 235-36.

66. U.S. House International Relations Committee, *U.S. Arms Policy and Recent Sales to Europe and the Middle East, Hearings before the International Relations Committee*. 95th Cong., 2nd sess., 1978, 20; Also see Pollock, *The Politics of Pressure*, 239.

67. Pollock, *The Politics of Pressure*, 242-43. Also see U.S. House of Representatives, Foreign Affairs Committee, *Documents 1979, House Foreign Affairs Committee*. 96th Cong., 1st sess., 1979, 29. U.S. House of Representatives Foreign Affairs Committee, *Supplemental 1979 Middle East Aid Package for Israel and Egypt, Hearings and Markup, House Foreign Affairs Committee*, 96th Cong., 1st sess., 1979, 157. For documents on the military, political, and oil supply guarantees provided to Israel by the United States see also U.S. Department of State, *American Foreign Policy, Basic Documents, 1977-1980* (Washington, D.C.: U.S. Government Printing Office, 1983), 684-85. For documents on American assistance to Israel for the construction of air bases in the Negev see Brown letter to Weizman, *American Foreign Policy, Basic Documents*, 667. For the Memorandum of Understanding Regarding the U.S. Supplying Oil to Israel see *American Foreign Policy, Basic Documents*, 699-700, and 713-15. Also see Karen L. Puschel, *U.S.-Israeli Strategic Cooperation in the Post-Cold War Era: An American Perspective* (Boulder, Colo.: Westview Press, 1992), 27.

68. Green, *Living by the Sword*, 223.

69. See Melman and Raviv, *Friends in Deed*, 228-30.

70. George Ball, "The Coming Crisis in Israeli-American Relations," 247.

71. Ronald Reagan, "Recognizing the Israeli Asset," *Washington Post*, 15 August 1979, 25(A). Then governor Reagan stated, "The fall of Iran has increased Israel's value as perhaps the only remaining strategic asset in the region on which the United States can truly rely."

72. *Jerusalem Post International Edition*, 21-27 June 1981, 1. Cited in Puschel, *U.S.-Israeli Strategic Cooperation*, 38.

73. For a comprehensive discussion on American policy during the 1982-1983 Israeli intervention in Lebanon see Abraham Ben-Zvi, *Alliance Politics and the Limits of Influence: The Case of the U.S. and Israel, 1975-1983* (Tel Aviv: Jaffee Center for Strategic Studies, April 1984, Paper #25), 41-57; Also see, "Reagan Sends Aid, Troops to Lebanon," *Congressional Quarterly Almanac* 38 (Washington, D.C.: Congressional Quarterly Inc., 1982), 167-71.

74. This is discussed by Leon Hadar, *Quagmire: America in the Middle East* (Washington, D.C.: Cato Institution, 1992), 76.

75. Green, *Living by the Sword*, 223-24. Provides a summary of the more significant agreements concluded between the United States and Israel during the Reagan administration.

76. U.S. Department of State, *Department of State Bulletin* 82, no. 2058 (January 1982): 45-46; Also see Lenczowski, *American Presidents*, 261.

77. Lenczowski, *American Presidents*, 261-62.

78. Puschel, *U.S.-Israeli Strategic Cooperation*, 41-43.

79. Puschel, *U.S.-Israeli Strategic Cooperation*, 41, 73-75. Discusses the tensions within the Reagan administration between individuals and sectors of the bureaucracy, and even within certain departments. She notes that the secretary of the navy, while being within the Defense Department, was enthusiastic about close cooperation with Israel to give the American Sixth Fleet access to the port of Haifa. Also significant, she points out, was that President Reagan himself seemed to have been genuinely supportive of Israel. This was especially evident heading into the 1984 election as his domestic advisors were advocating closer relations with Israel for electoral purposes.

80. Puschel, *U.S.-Israeli Strategic Cooperation*, 65. Regarding these personnel changes, Puschel identified them as the removal of Ariel Sharon as Israeli Defense Minister and his replacement by Moshe Arens, and the decline in influence in foreign affairs, and the subsequent removal, of Prime Minister Begin in favor of Yitzhak Shamir. For the Americans the replacement of Alexander Haig by George Schultz eventually contributed to the betterment of relations as within a year his views of Israel had fundamentally shifted (66-67).

81. Ball and Ball, *The Passionate Attachment*, 139.

82. Helena Cobban, *The Superpowers and the Syrian-Israeli Conflict* (New York: Praeger, 1991), 88. Also see Harry Shaw, "Strategic Dissensus," *Foreign Policy*, no. 61 (Winter 1985-1986): 129. The use of Haifa as a port was of special interest to Navy Secretary John Lehman. The port of Haifa offered the Navy a high quality naval repair facility as well as the opportunity to take on fresh supplies and offer personnel shore leave. This would involve the U.S. spending $200 million in Israel in using the port of Haifa. In addition to having access to a naval port in the region Secretary Lehman also was interested in joint weapons projects such as a naval missile. Cited in Puschel, *U.S.-Israeli Strategic Cooperation*, 77, 88. Also see Steven Spiegel, "U.S. Relations with Israel: The Military Benefits," *Orbis* 30, no. 3 (Fall 1986): 487. Among the systems that Spiegel discusses as being under development were a ship-to-ship missile, electronic decoy devices, submarines, and a corvette (the SAAR 5). In regards to facilities in the Negev, see Puschel, *U.S.-Israeli Strategic Cooperation*, 89 which discusses various instances when American personnel participated in training exercises.

83. Dore Gold, *Israel As an American Non-NATO Ally: Parameters of Defense Industrial Cooperation in a Post-Cold War Relationship* (Boulder, Colo.: Westview Press, 1992), 25; cited from *Armed Forces Journal*, January 1990, 24. See also Ball and Ball, *The Passionate Attachment*, 261 who argue that the Reagan administration had two reasons for including Israel in the SDI program. The first was to assist Israeli industrial development and the second was to attempt to use Israeli participation in order to get the pro-Israeli lobby to support the SDI.

84. Gold, *Israel As an American Non-NATO Ally*, 25. This legislation came about as a result of the initiative by Sam Nunn (D-Ga) in 1985. The purpose of this amendment was to achieve weapons standardization within NATO by establishing a process to begin collective weapons development. For a further discussion of the

Nunn amendment see Marvin Leibstone, "U.S. Defense Imports," *Military Technology*, March 1989, 41; and *Armed Forces Journal*, December 1986, 20. Cited in Gold, *Israel As an American Non-NATO Ally*, 25.

85. Puschel, *U.S.-Israeli Strategic Cooperation*, 103.

86. Puschel, *U.S.-Israeli Strategic Cooperation*, 104; Cheney's comments cited in *ADL Bulletin* (September 1990): 6-7.

87. Undersecretary of Defense Paul Wolfowitz, *USIS Press Clips*. NXE 309, December 19, 1990, 106; Cited in Pushell, *U.S.-Israeli Strategic Cooperation*, 104-5.

88. See testimony of James Baker, House Foreign Affairs Committee, October 18, 1990, *USIS Press Clips*, October 18, 1990, 20-21; also *Wall Street Journal*, October 23, 1990, A13 and *Jerusalem Post*, October 31, 1990, 10. Cited in Puschel, *U.S.-Israeli Strategic Cooperation*, 120-21.

89. Puschel, *U.S.-Israeli Strategic Cooperation*, 125; Also see *New York Times*, 5 March 1991, 5.

90. See remarks made by General Colin Powell to AIPAC, March 19, 1991, *USIS Press Clips*, NXE 203, March 19, 1991, 75. Defense Secretary Cheney made his remarks before Jewish leaders on March 6, 1991, *USIS Press Clips*, NEA 313, 30. Cited in Puschel, *U.S.-Israeli Strategic Cooperation*, 145.

91. See *International Herald Tribune*, 1-2 June 1991, 1; as well as *Jerusalem Report*, 6 June 1991, 6. Cited in Puschel, *U.S.-Israeli Strategic Cooperation*, 145.

92. *Ma'ariv*, 14 April 1992. Cited in Gold, *Israel As an American Non-NATO Ally*, 47.

93. Gold, *Israel As an American Non-NATO Ally*, 76-77.

94. Melman and Raviv suggests that Shamir was hoping that in attending the conference Washington would grant the guarantees. After the conference, however, these guarantees were still not forthcoming. Then in February of 1992 Secretary of State Baker stated that the guarantees would only be given if Israel did not begin the construction of new settlements and would be reduced by the amount that Israel was spending on maintaining its existing settlements. See Melman and Raviv, *Friends in Deed*, 430-31, 436.

95. Melman and Raviv, *Friends in Deed*, 435-36.

96. Melman and Raviv, *Friends in Deed*, 442-43.

97. Rubenberg, *Israel and the American*, 15.

98. Camille Mansour, *Beyond Alliance: Israel in U.S. Foreign Policy* (New York: Columbia University Press, 1994), 240.

99. Tivnan, *The Lobby*, 215.

100. John Fialka, "Political Contributions from Pro-Israel PAC's Suggest Coordination," *Wall Street Journal*, 24 June 1987, 1.

101. CBS correspondent Mike Wallace "Sixty Minutes," 23 October 1988. Cited in Richard H. Curtiss, *Stealth PACs: How Israel's American Lobby Seeks to Control U.S. Middle East Policy* (Washington, D.C.: American Educational Trust, 1990), 97.

102. John Fialka and Brooks Jackson, *The Wall Street Journal*, 26 February 1985. Curtiss, *Stealth PACS*, 37. Mansour, *Beyond Alliance*, 250-51. For a discussion of the Israeli lobby and Congress see Paul Findley, *They Dare to Speak Out* (Westport, Conn.: Lawrence Hill and Company, 1985), 84-113.

103. Fialka and Jackson, *The Wall Street Journal*, 26 February 1985; Curtiss, *Stealth PACS*, 54; Findley, *They Dare to Speak Out*, 39.

104. Mansour, *Beyond Alliance*, 254.

105. Ball and Ball, *The Passionate Attachment*, 216-17.

106. Thomas Friedman, *From Beirut to Jerusalem* (New York: Anchor Books, 1989), 486; also Ball and Ball, *The Passionate Attachment*, 203. See also Mansour, *Beyond Alliance*, 271. Discusses the significance of the political role of Christian fundamentalists on the right wing of the Republican Party and their influence on the foreign policy of the Reagan administration. Among the influences Mansour cites besides support for Israel are the demonization of the Soviet Union. For a personal account of the fundamentalist view of Israel and the influence on politics see Grace Halsell, *Prophecy and Politics: The Secret Alliance between Israel and the U.S. Christian Right* (Chicago: Lawrence Hill Books, 1986).

107. Tivnan, *The Lobby*, 242-43. He also points out that it was the policies of the Likud that encouraged the development of right-wing extremism within Israel with the development of the Kach movement and Gush Emunium. These are movements that many American Jews do not support. It should be noted that there are Jewish groups on the left, such as the New Jewish Agenda and the New Israeli Fund, who will disagree and challenge the Israeli government, although they may lack the resources and name recognition of AIPAC. See Tivnan, 264-65.

108. See Melman and Raviv, *Friends in Deed*, 360-61.

109. U.S. General Accounting Office, *Foreign Assistance Analysis Cost Estimates for Israel's Lavi Aircraft*, (Washington, D.C.: U.S. National Security and International Affairs Division, January 31, 1987), 45. Cited in Ball and Ball, *The Passionate Attachment*, 264. They also discuss a request made by Ariel Sharon in May of 1982 for a further $250 million per year in FMS credits for in-country use for the Merkava, as well as other projects. This request, however, floundered as a result of the invasion of Lebanon.

110. Among the sources that discuss the Lavi are U.S. General Accounting Office, *U.S. Assistance to the State of Israel*, June 24, 1983, 55. Also, Duncan L. Clarke and Alan S. Cohen, "The United States, Israel and the Lavi Fighter," *Middle East Journal* 40, no. 1 (Winter 1986): 17.

111. Ball and Ball, *The Passionate Attachment*, 268.

112. U.S. GAO, *U.S. Assistance*, 57; Clarke and Cohen, "The United States, Israel," 17; Also see Ball and Ball, *The Passionate Attachment*, 267.

113. Clark and Cohen, "The United States, Israel," 18-19; Also see Ball and Ball, *The Passionate Attachment*, 268. They argue that one of the primary motivations for Israel to press ahead with the Lavi project was to alleviate unemployment in a key sector of the economy. For a good discussion on the significance of the Israel Aircraft Industry (IAI) see Alex Mintz, "The Military-Industrial Complex: The Israeli Case," *Journal of Strategic Studies* 6, no. 3 (September 1983): 115. Ball and Ball, *The Passionate Attachment*, 264. Discusses a marketing brochure put out by the IAI in which plans were outlined to sell over 400 Lavis to Argentina, Chile, South Africa, and Taiwan. The goal of the Israelis was to acquire 17 percent of the developing nations market in export aircraft by the year 2000.

114. Ball and Ball, *The Passionate Attachment*, 266. Also Clarke and Cohen, "The United States, Israel," 27. Northrop officials also publicly argued that the Lavi could eventually emerge as a competitor to the F-20. However a company official confidentially admitted that this was not the case. General Dynamics officials also expressed a concern that the Lavi could compete in export markets with the F-16.

Ultimately, the Lavi project was canceled. Ball and Ball discuss the costs to the United States as being, in addition to the funds expended, 6,000-8,000 jobs lost in addition to those jobs lost at Northrop. For Israel, the costs was the loss of 3,000-4,000 jobs, as well as increased tensions within the Israeli military since the Lavi was viewed as a white elephant by its opponents. Ball and Ball, *The Passionate Attachment*, 266-67.

115. David Schoenbaum, *The United States and the State of Israel* (Oxford: Oxford University Press, 1993), 303; See also GAO, *U.S. Assistance*, 43. See also Aaron S. Klieman, *Israel's Global Reach: Arms Sales and Diplomacy* (New York: Pergamon Press, 1985), 58; Aharon Klieman and Reven Pedatzur, *Rearming Israel: Defense Procurement through the 1990s* (Boulder, Colo.: Westview Press, 1991). Stewart Reiser, *The Israeli Arms Industry* (New York: Holmes and Meyer, 1989). Clarke and Cohen, "The United States, Israel," 21. Cites arms trade figures in the 1980s. Ralph Sanders, *Arms Industries: New Suppliers and Regional Security* (Washington, D.C.: National Defense University, 1990), 50-65. Discusses the significance of arms exports to the country, as well as the development of the Israeli arms industries, specifically the IAI.

116. Crosbie, *A Tacit Alliance*, 98-121. Discusses the specifics of French-Israeli nuclear cooperation, as well as other military aspects of the alliance.

117. Louis Toscano, *Triple Cross: Israel, the Atom Bomb, and the Man Who Spilled the Secrets* (New York: Birch Lane Press Book, 1990), 97-98. In addition, Toscano also describes the methods by which the Israelis used to obtain the needed uranium to run the facility. The man in charge of the Israeli nuclear program during this period was Shimon Peres. He established a special intelligence agency known as the Science Liaison Bureau to acquire the needed raw materials to run the program. Heavy water and small amounts of uranium were purchased. There are allegations that large amounts of uranium were diverted over a period of years from an American company, the Nuclear Materials and Equipment Corporation of Apollo, Pennsylvania. In addition it is alleged that Israeli agents stole 200 tons of uranium from a ship sailing from Antwerp in 1968. For a discussion of the diversion from the Pennsylvania company see also Green, *Taking Sides*, 157-59. Also for a general discussion of French-Israeli cooperation and the exposing of the Dimona facility as a nuclear plant see Schoenbaum, *The United States and the State*, 126-27.

118. Cockburn and Cockburn, *Dangerous Liaisons*, 89.

119. Cockburn and Cockburn, *Dangerous Liaisons*, 87.

120. For a discussion of Atoms for Peace and the Atomic Energy Act of 1954 see William Badar, *The United States and the Spread of Nuclear Weapons* (New York.: Pegasus, 1968), 18, 22-23, 26, 40; For a description of the specifics of the dissemination of nuclear technology see David Hoffman, "Aliens Gain U.S. Atomic Arms Lore," *Philadelphia Inquirer*, 19 May 1979. Cites figures from a report by the U.S. Congress, General Accounting Office. Also statement by Fred C. Ikle, Director of the Arms Control and Disarmament Agency, September 18, 1974. Cited in Shai Feldman, *Israeli Nuclear Deterrence: A Strategy for the 1980s* (New York: Columbia University Press, 1982), 195-96.

121. Schoenbaum, *The United States and the State*, 126-27; also see Peter Pry, *Israel's Nuclear Arsenal* (Boulder, Colo.: Westview Press, 1984), 8-9.

122. Schoenbaum, *The United States and the State*, 89-90. Also Seymour Hersch, *The Samson Option Israel's Nuclear Arsenal and American Foreign Policy* (New York: Random House, 1991), 109-11. Hersch discusses ways the Israelis circumvented these inspections as to render them meaningless.

123. Hersh, *The Samson Option*, 139.

124. Spiegel, *The Other Arab-Israeli Conflict*, 160, 453. Cites individuals who were present who confirmed that this guarantee was made. It was obvious to American decision makers that the Israelis were keeping their options open with respect to nuclear weapons and delivery systems. U.S. policy makers believed that Israel could utilize nuclear weapons at fairly short notice. Also, Israel had contracted with a French company to purchase surface-to-surface missiles that were

nuclear capable. See *Memorandum for the President. Military and Economic Assistance to Israel: The Arab-Israel Arms Race and Status of U.S. Arms Control Efforts,* May 1, 1967, LBJ Documents.

The Johnson administration's desire to get Israel to except international norms covering nuclear materials was reflected also with International Atomic Energy Agency (IAEA) controls. "Israel's reluctance to accept IAEA controls also adds to our suspicions. We can't make Israel an exception because we're making sixty or so other clients toe the IAEA line." R. W. Komer, *Memorandum for the President,* May 28, 1964, LBJ Documents.

The other issues that Johnson was interested in getting Israeli support besides the Nuclear Nonproliferation Treaty (NPT) were: support for the war in Vietnam, Israeli flexibility for the UN-sponsored Middle East peace negotiations, as well as not annexing the occupied territories. See *New York Times,* 9 January 1968, 1(A). Cited in Green, *Living by the Sword,* 12.

125. Hersh, *The Samson Option,* 209-10.

126. Hersh, *The Samson Option,* 210-11, 213.

127. Hersh, *The Samson Option,* 215-16. For a further discussion on Israeli nuclear delivery systems see Helena Cobban, "Israel's Nuclear Game: The U.S. Stake," *World Policy Journal* 5, no. 3 (Summer 1988): 421. She cites evidence that the Israelis were developing an upgraded missile, the Jericho II, which was eventually projected as having a range of 900 miles. In addition she discusses the capabilities of the F-15 and F-16, as well as Israeli refueling capabilities that would put the Soviet Union well within range of the Israeli nuclear force. As an example of Israeli effectiveness in this regard, she cites the examples of the Israeli raid on the Iraqi nuclear reactor in 1981, and the attack on the PLO headquarters in Tunis in 1985. Both operations required midair refueling. Cobban also discusses Israeli-Soviet nuclear dynamics. She maintains that an Israeli strategic calculation to build up its nuclear forces to potentially threaten the Soviets was an effort to reinforce Soviet reluctance to build up the military forces of the Arab states, which could lead to global nuclear war, (419).

128. Cobban, "Israel's Nuclear Game," 269-70.

129. Statement of Robert Gates, Federal News Service Transcripts, May 1992, Cited in Geoffrey Aronson, "Hidden Agenda: U.S.-Israeli Relations and the Nuclear Question,"*The Middle East Journal* 46, no. 4 (Autumn 1992): 627.

130. *Ha'aretz,* 19 June 1992, cited in Geoffrey Aronson, "Hidden Agenda: U.S.-Israeli Relations and the Nuclear Question," *The Middle East Journal* 46, no. 4 (Autumn 1992): 627.

131. Benjamin Beit-Hallahmi, *The Israeli Connection* (New York: Pantheon Books, 1987), 189. Aaron Klieman, *Israel's Global Reach* (New York: Pergamon-Brassey, 1985), 158. Also see Uri Bialer, "The Iranian Connection in Israel's Foreign Policy, 1948-1951," *Middle East Journal* 39, no. 2 (1985): 292-315.

132. Sohrab Sobhani, *The Pragmatic Entente: Israeli-Iranian Relations, 1948-1988* (New York: Praeger Publishers, 1989), 19.

133. Sobhani, *The Pragmatic Entente,* 35. Also Samuel Segev, *The Iranian Triangle* (New York: The Free Press, 1988), 35-36. Cockburn and Cockburn, *Dangerous Liaisons,* 99.

134. Sobhani, *The Pragmatic Entente,* 53.

135. Beit-Hallahmi, *The Israeli Connection,* 10. Sobhani, *The Pragmatic Entente,* 65.

136. Sobhani, *The Pragmatic Entente,* 118.

137. Sobhani, *The Pragmatic Entente*, 131. Cobban discusses Israeli plans to further enhance the strategic value of Project Flower. She points out that Foreign Minister Dayan stated that this missile would be nuclear capable. The chief of the navy, Rear Admiral M. Barkai, expressed interest in this project being expanded to make the missile capable of being launched from submarines. See Cobban, "Israel's Nuclear Game," 421. She cited as a source for this CIA documents that were seized from the takeover of the American embassy in Tehran.

138. Sobhani, *The Pragmatic Entente*, 132-33.

139. Sobhani, *The Pragmatic Entente*, 146. For a discussion on the importance of the arms industry to the Israeli economy see Aaron Klieman, *Israel's Global Reach*, 53-69.

140. Sobhani, *The Pragmatic Entente*, 47. Also see Cockburn and Cockburn, *Dangerous Liaisons*, 105. Discusses CIA support for the Kurds and its importance.

141. Klieman, *Israel's Global Reach*, 159. He cites as his source *Time Magazine* article 25 July 1983.

142. Klieman, *Israel's Global Reach*, 160.

143. Olusola Ojo, *Africa and Israel: Relations in Perspective* (Boulder, Colo.: Westview Press, 1988), 18.

144. Ethan A. Nadelmann, "Israel and Black Africa: A Rapprochement?" *The Journal of Modern African Studies* 19, no. 2 (June 1981): 190-91. Nadelmann derives this information from Golda Meir's memoirs, 281.

145. Stuart Schaar, "Patterns of Israeli Aid and Trade in East Asia: Part I," AUFS, *East Africa Series* 7, no. 1 (New York: American Universities Field Staff, 1968): 7. Jacob Abel, "Israel's Military Aid to Africa, 1960-1966," *Journal of Modern African Studies* 9, no. 2 (1971): 179. Quoted in Olusaola Ojo, "Israeli-South African Connections, Afro-Israel Relations," *International Studies* 21, no. 1 (January-March 1982): 20-22. It is argued that the Israelis were involved in the coup which brought Idi Amin to power in 1971, and initially he was very friendly to Israel. At the same time the Israelis were also active with the CIA in promoting a secessionist movement within southern Sudan in an effort to weaken the central government. See Cockburn and Cockburn, *Dangerous Liaisons*, 113-14; also Nadelmann, "Israel and Black Africa," 203.

146. Cockburn and Cockburn, *Dangerous Liaisons*, 112.

147. Beit-Hallahmi, *The Israeli Connection*, 59.

148. Klieman, *Israel's Global Reach*, 155.

149. Beit-Hallahmi, *The Israeli Connection*, 52; Also see Nadelmann, "Israel and Black Africa," 193-94. He points out also the historic links between the royal family and Amharic elite with the biblical Hebrews.

150. Ball and Ball, *The Passionate Attachment*, 289-90. Israel at first denied the sale, and then later claimed that these cluster bombs were Israeli-made. See *Israeli Foreign Affairs* 6, no. 1 (January 1990): 6. Cited in Ball and Ball, *The Passionate Attachment*, 290. Also see Jan Perlez, "Ethiopian-Israeli Accord Eases Jewish Emigration," *New York Times*, 5 November 1989, 4. The newspaper reported that 3,000 Israelis were in Ethiopia providing assistance to the government.

151. Ojo, "Israel-South African Connections," 129.

152. Ball and Ball, *The Passionate Attachment*, 290-91.

153. Joel Peters, *Israel and Africa* (London: British Academic Press, 1992), 156. See also Yossi Melman and Dan Raviv, "Has Congress Doomed Israel's Affair with South Africa?" *Washington Post*, 22 February 1987, 1(C).

154. Peters, *Israel and Africa*, 158. He cites Richard Adams, *The Unnatural Alliance* (London: Quartet Books, 1984), 111, 122, as well as *The Economist*, 5 November 1977.

The Israeli Galil rifle, which has become the standard weapon, is also produced under license in South Africa. Another significant military system provided by Israel is reconnaissance Drone aircraft. In addition to its own equipment the Israelis have also shipped American-made M-113A armored personnel carriers and 106 mm recoilless rifles. There were also reports that Israel was constructing gunboats for the South African navy, as well as training naval personnel and supplying South Africa with Kfir jets. See Ball and Ball, *The Passionate Attachment*, 291; Ojo, "Israeli-South African Connections," 46; also see *New York Times*, 8 August 1976.

155. Peters, *Israel and Africa*, 159. Cites for naval collaboration see Adams, *The Unnatural Alliance*, 123-24; for the Jericho missile cites see *Jerusalem Post*, 21 June 1989, and *Israeli Foreign Affairs*, July 1989.

156. Jane Hunter, "Israel and South Africa: Comrades in Arms," *Middle East International* (July 25, 1986): 13-14; Quoted in Peters, *Israel and Africa*, 159.

157. Peters, *Israel and Africa*, 159. He cites as sources *The Sunday Times*, 15 April 1984. Hunter, "Israel and South Africa," 13-14. *New York Times*, 14 December 1981. Richard P. Stevens and Abdelwahab Elmessiri, *Israel and South Africa: The Progression of a Relationship* (New York: North American, 1977), 68.

158. For a comprehensive discussion of German collaboration with South Africa in the nuclear field see Zdenek Cervenka and Barbara Rogers, *The Nuclear Axis: Secret Collaboration between West Germany and South Africa* (New York: Times Books, 1978).

159. *Africa Confidential*, 4 August 1978. Quoted in Ojo, "Israel and Black Africa," 132. Concerning the alleged nuclear test see also Peters, *Israel and Africa*, 160. Beit-Hallahmi, *The Israeli Connection*, 134. Provides a comprehensive overview of Israeli-South African relations, in particular focusing on military cooperation. Also see Ball and Ball, *The Passionate Attachment*, 290-92.

160. Cockburn and Cockburn, *Dangerous Liaisons*, 110-15. They also discuss the penetration of Uganda by Israeli intelligence even after Idi Amin adopted more radical positions.

161. Beit-Hallahmi, *The Israeli Connection*, 203; See also Edward Cody, "Sharon to Discuss Arms Sales in Honduras," *Washington Post*, 7 December 1982, 19; and "Salvador, Israel Set Closer Ties," 17 August 1983, 1.

162. Bishara Bahbah, *Israel and Latin America: The Military Connection* (New York: St. Martin's Press, 1986), 71.

163. Leslie Gelb, "Israelis Said to Step Up Role As Arms Suppliers to Latins," *New York Times*, 17 December 1987, 11(A). Also see Klieman, *Israel's Global Reach*, 169.

164. Leslie Gelb, "Israelis Said to Step Up," 1.

165. Bahbah, *Israel and Latin America*, 167-68. See also *New York Times*, 21 July 1983.

166. For a discussion of this see Cockburn and Cockburn, *Dangerous Liaisons*, 218; Ball and Ball, *The Passionate Attachment*, 286-87. Knesset member General Matityahu Peled in speaking about Israeli policy towards Central America stated, "In Central America, Israel is the 'dirty work' contractor for the U.S. administration. Israel is acting as an accomplice and arms of the United States." Cited in Cockburn and Cockburn, 218.

167. Ball and Ball, *The Passionate Attachment*, 289; also see Beit-Hallahmi, *The Israeli Connection*, 101-4.

168. Ball, and Ball, *The Passionate Attachment*, 289; Beit-Hallahmi, *The Israeli Connection*, 98-101. Beit-Hallahmi discusses the major sales to Chile and their significance. He points out that Israel supplied the Reshef patrol boat, which has become the primary ship in the Chilean navy. In addition, he points out that Israel

has assisted Chile in establishing its own domestic aircraft industry, as well as providing it with other types of military equipment. The Israelis were also involved with providing weapons to the Chilean police forces, notably a specialized crowd control vehicle equipped with four water canons. For a discussion of the supplying of cluster bomb technology to Chile and the subsequent sale of these bombs to Iraq see "Bomblets Away," *Time Magazine* 124, no. 9 (August 27, 1984): 34.

169. Ball and Ball, *The Passionate Attachment*, 288-89; also Beit-Hallahmi, *The Israeli Connection*, 103-4. Beit-Hallahmi cites that Paraguay's voting record in the UN is the most favorable to Israel of any country in the world. In addition, President Stroessner, like the Shah of Iran and President Mobutu of Zaire, has attempted to curry favor with the United States and soften criticism of his regime by emphasizing his Israeli link.(CBS interview with Mike Wallace, *60 Minutes*, 5 January 1986).

170. Philip Taubman, "Israel Said to Aid Latin Aims of U.S.,"*New York Times,* 21 July 1983, 1(A).

171. Taubman, "Israel Said to Aid Latin Aims," 1(A). See also Bahbah, *Israel and Latin America*, 167, and Klieman, *Israel's Global Reach*, 170.

172. Klieman, *Israel's Global Reach*, 169. Beit-Hallahmi, *The Israeli Connection*, 196. R. Zelnick, "U.S.-Israeli Relations after the Pollard Affair," *Christian Science Monitor*, 27 December 1985, 11.

173. Klieman, *Israel's Global Reach*, 170. Also see Cockburn and Cockburn, *Dangerous Liaisons*, 98-124. Gives accounts of Israeli aid with American assistance to various pro-Western leaders and nations.

174. For Iran see Sobhani, *The Pragmatic Entente*, 54, 119. In regards to Zaire see Cockburn and Cockburn, *Dangerous Liaisons*, 123.

175. Donald Neff, "America's Unconditional Hand-outs to Israel," *Middle East International*, no. 435 (October 9, 1992): 3.

176. Neff, "America's Unconditional Hand-outs to Israel," 3-4.

177. Nasser Aruri, "The U.S.-Israeli Special Relationship after Shamir and the Cold War," *Middle East International*, no. 433 (September 11, 1992): 21.

178. Aruri, "The U.S.-Israeli Special Relationship," 21-22.

179. Graham E. Fuller, *Central Asia: The New Geopolitics* (Santa Monica, Calif.: Rand Corporation, 1992), 77-78.

180. For a discussion of Islamic fundamentalism in Central Asia see Steven Erlanger, "An Islamic Awakening in Central Asian Lands," *New York Times*, 9 June 1992, 1(A). For a discussion of the competition between the United States and Iran in this region see Thomas L. Friedman, "U.S. to Counter Iran in Central Asia," *New York Times*, 6 February 1992, 3(A).

181. Statement by Israeli Ambassador Zalman Shoval. Appeared in Thomas L. Friedman, "U.S. and Israel at Sea," *New York Times*, 22 March 1992, 1(A).

182. Aruri, "The U.S.-Israeli Special Relationship," 22.

183. For a brief discussion of Israeli-American relations during the first part of the Clinton Administration and the Israeli government's response see Melman and Raviv, *Friends in Deed*, 444-60. The changing political mood within the United States is also discussed by Leon Hadar. He discusses the development within the American left, specifically within the African-American community, of greater sympathy for the Palestinian cause, criticism for Israel as a result of its ties to apartheid South Africa, as well as disillusionment with the amount of assistance rendered to Israel that could have been used for domestic social programs and aid to other nations, particularly in Africa. See Leon Hadar, *Quagmire: America in the Middle East* (Washington, D.C.: Cato Institute, 1992), 81. The tensions between supporters of Israel and the African-American community in the United States is

also discussed in Findley, *They Dare to Speak Out*, 136-38. Also cited by Hadar.

184. Cockburn and Cockburn, *Dangerous Liaisons*, 169-70. For aid figures see Clyde R. Mark, "Israel: U.S. Foreign Assistance Facts," *Congressional Research Service* (July 1990); for aid and its affect on the Israeli economy and military Expenditure see also Schoenbaum, *The United States and the State*, 187. In 1971 Israel received $545 million, 1972, $300 million, and 1973, $307.5 million. In 1973 Israel spent about 30 percent of its GNP on military expenditures while improving its overall economic development. These figures also cited in Quandt, *Decade of Decisions*, 163.

185. Cockburn and Cockburn, *Dangerous Liaisons*, 174.

186. Gazit, "Israeli Military Procurement," 84-85. Also see A. F. K. Organski, *The $36 Billion Dollar Bargain: Strategy and Politics in U.S. Assistance to Israel* (New York: Columbia University Press, 1990), 161. He identifies the four stages of the escalation of American assistance to Israel between 1948-1985.

187. Gabriel Sheffer and Menachem Hofnung, "Israel's Image," in Gabriel Sheffer ed. *Dynamics of Dependence* (Boulder, Colo.: Westview Press, 1987), 25.

188. Tivnan, *The Lobby*, 221.

189. Ball and Ball, *The Passionate Attachment*, 109; U.S. Agency for International Development, *Overseas Loans and Grants and Assistance from International Organizations Obligations and Loan Authorizations, July, 1945-September 30, 1988* (Washington, D.C.: U.S. Government Printing Office, 1989), 18.

190. Mansour, *Beyond Alliance*, 228.

191. U.S. Government, Statement of Robert Byrd (D-W.Va.), *Congressional Record*, 102 Cong., 2nd sess., April 1, 1992. Also Clyde R. Mark, "Israel: U.S. Foreign Assistance Facts," *Congressional Research Service*, updated July 5, 1991; Cited in Paul Findley, *Deliberate Deceptions: Facing the Facts About the U.S.-Israeli Relationship* (Brooklyn, N.Y.: Lawrence Hill Books, 1993), 111.

192. Beit-Hallahmi, *The Israeli Connection*, 196. The importance of Israel was discussed by analysts in regard to potential Soviet operations in the Eastern Mediterranean. The relinquishing of the Sinai Peninsula in 1982 has enabled the Israelis to concentrate most of their naval forces along the Mediterranean coast of Israel. These forces, coupled with the Israeli air force, gives Israel the range to dominate 250-300 miles into the Eastern Mediterranean. See Steven Spiegel, "U.S. Relations with Israel," 493-94.

193. Leon T. Hadar, *Quagmire*, 85. This view was also commented on within Israel as the commentator Akiva Eldar in the newspaper *Ha'aretz* stated, "On the face of it, the American taxpayer [has] the right to ask his representatives why they are shelling out $3 billion to a country that, in the moment of truth, turns out to be nothing but an empty vessel." Jackson Diehl, "Israel Fears Sideline Role Jeopardizes Its Ties to U.S.," *Washington Post*, 16 August 1990. Cited in Hadar, *Quagmire*, 85. For a comprehensive discussion of the negotiations involving the United States and Israel during this period as well as the furnishing of intelligence on Iraq by Israel to the United States prior to the Gulf War see Melman and Raviv, *Friends in Deed*, 378-98.

194. Melman and Raviv, *Friends in Deed*, 398-402. They argue that Schwartzkopf felt personally that the SCUDs deserved a lower priority as they were not strategically significant militarily. Melman and Raviv further argued that some critics within Israel felt that the Bush administration purposely wanted the SCUD search to have a low priority to remind Israel of its dependence on the United States in order to win political concessions later on for Middle East peace initiatives. Melman and Raviv, 399-400. However, this is speculation and certainly there were

heavy stakes involved. If the damage and casualties had been heavier within Israel the Shamir government would have been under enormous pressure from within the government and military, as well as from the general public to intervene. This would have potentially been a strategic nightmare for the Bush administration.

195. Steven Spiegel, "U.S. Relations with Israel: The Military Benefits," *Orbis* 30, no. 3 (Fall 1986): 477. Spiegel argues that this program alone saved the U.S. Army $70 million. Another development of the Israelis was an intelligence balloon, at a cost of $100 million, which the United States used to gather intelligence on Cuba. He further cites an expert who states that 60 percent to 70 percent of high technology intelligence equipment developed by Israel is used by the United States. Spiegel also emphasizes the savings in research and development costs for the United States by Israeli designs that are then sold to the United States, as well as Israeli purchases with special features that are then made available to American military forces. Examples of the former include various types of mine and obstacle-clearing equipment, as well as helicopter air filters. Specifics of the latter were conformal fuel tanks for the F-15, leading edge slats for the F-4E Phantom, the external fuel tank for the M-113A, and bomb racks for the F-16 among others. Spiegel, "U.S. Relations with Israel," 482-83.

The development of joint weapons systems has proven less successful. Dore Gold maintains that aside from a few systems, joint United States-Israel cooperation has not been very beneficial as they do not involve brand-new systems but rather upgrade existing systems. He states that the only true brand-new systems that have been produced are the Multi-Mission Optronic Stabilized Payload developed with the U.S. Navy, and the Arrow missile produced in conjunction with the American SDI program. See Gold, *Israel As an American Non-NATO Ally*, 27.

196. Gold, *Israel As an American Non-NATO Ally*, 479. Also see Benjamin S. Lambeth, *Moscow's Lessons from the 1982 Lebanon Air War*, R-3000-AF, (Santa Monica, Calif.: Rand Corporation, 1984), 13; and Mansour, *Beyond Alliance*, 6. In addition to the intelligence garnered from examining Soviet equipment, analysts point out that the knowledge gained by the Israelis of Soviet tactics was a result of engagements between Israeli and Soviet pilots during the War of Attrition. See Edward Bernard Glick, *The Triangular Connection: America, Israel, and American Jews* (London: Allen and Unwin, 1982), 154.

Other analysts take issue with Spiegel's assessment concerning the benefits of the Israeli ability to defeat the Soviet-built equipment used by the Syrians in 1982. Helena Cobban points out that the Soviet-built SAM-6s, which the Syrians had deployed in Lebanon, were 15 years old. More significantly, she argues in jamming these missiles the Israelis compromised technology to the Soviets that could be used against NATO. Cobban, *The Superpowers and the Syrian-Israeli Conflict*, 97.

197. Puschel, *U.S.-Israeli Strategic Cooperation*, 15. She cites an example during the War of Attrition in which the Israeli air force, flying Western-style aircraft, were able to illustrate the limitations of the Soviet antiaircraft systems defending Egypt. See also Chaim Herzog, *The Arab-Israeli Wars* (New York: Vintage Books, 1984), 196.

198. Cockburn and Cockburn, *Dangerous Liaisons*, 178-79. Based on interviews with former American military officers, Cockburn suggests that the success of the Maverick was due to its use against what were defined as Egyptian command headquarters. These "headquarters" were tents in a perimeter in the desert about the size of a football field. A "hit" was defined as a Maverick landing within this perimeter, without measuring what actual damage it caused. The Sparrow system posed a problem as it could not distinguish between friendly and hostile aircraft and as a result it was only of limited utility in actual combat when many planes were in

the air. The Israelis were able to indicate the success of the Sparrow by grounding their air force for one evening except for one plane equipped with the Sparrow. Therefore the pilot was sure of hitting a hostile aircraft. USAF Colonel James Burton, Ret. stated that this was a way of placating the American air force and justifying the continuation of this weapons system.

199. Shimon Peres, "The Minister and the Real Danger," *Yediot Aharonot,* 28 September 1979; H. Goodman, "A Mutual Dependence," *Jerusalem Post,* 25 May 1984. Quoted in Beit-Hallahmi, *The Israeli Connection,* 195.

200. George Ball, "The Coming Crisis in Israeli-American Relations," 247.

201. Beit-Hallahmi, *The Israeli Connection,* 197. He cites S. Maoz, "Strategic Bargain," *Jerusalem Post,* 4 April 1986 and H. Goodman, "A Mutual Dependence," *Jerusalem Post,* 25 May 984. Also see Organski, *The $36 Billion Bargain.*

202. E. A. Winston, "Worth Five CIAs," *Newsweek,* 2 January 1985. Cited in Beit-Hallahmi, *The Israeli Connection,* 198.

203. Green, *Living by the Sword,* 225. Rubenberg, 51, traces the development of the American-Israeli alliance and makes the argument that the growth of this alliance has fostered the growth of Israeli militarism that has served to destabilize the Middle East. Also see Ben-Zvi, *Alliance Politics and the Limits of Influence,* 58, argues that between 1975-1983 American decision makers suffered from a lack of maneuverability in the relationship with Israel due to both regional issues as well as domestic constraints that impeded the adoption of any significant degree of coercive diplomacy.

204. For a general discussion of commitment and leverage in American alliance politics see Bruce Jentleson, "American Commitments in the Third World," *International Organization* 41, no. 4 (Autumn 1987): 667-704. For a discussion on the American-Israeli alliance specifically see Thomas R. Wheelock, "Arms for Israel: The Limit of Leverage," *International Security* 3, no. 2 (Fall 1978): 123-37.

Chapter 6

The Origins of the American-Saudi Alliance

The Establishment of Modern Saudi Arabia

The origins of Saudi Arabia can be traced to a political-religious alliance that was established in the mid-eighteenth century between Sheikh Muhammad Abdel-Wahab, who preached a strict interpretation and reform of Islam, and the Al-Saud, the rulers of Dariyah in central Arabia. There were three attempts at establishing a Saudi state in Arabia. The first began in 1745 and ended in 1818 when Egyptian troops loyal to the Ottoman sultan-caliph defeated the Al-Saud. The second Saudi state ended in 1891 when the Al-Saud were defeated by an alliance between their traditional rivals, the Al-Rashids and the Ottomans. The third Saudi state began in 1902 when Ibn Saud retook Riyadh.[1]

The borders of the modern day nation-state of Saudi Arabia were established between 1925-1936. In 1925 Ibn Saud's forces conquered the Hejaz region, which includes the major cities of Mecca, Medina, and Jedda, from the Hashemites. The establishment of the mandate system in which Britain acquired control of TransJordan and Iraq prevented Ibn Saud from adding additional territory in the north. Despite some tensions with the British in the mid-1920s, British-Saudi relations stabilized by the latter portion of the decade as Ibn Saud consolidated his control over the kingdom by destroying the Ihkwan military forces with British assistance. The Kingdom of Saudi Arabia was formally proclaimed in 1932. The borders of the state were more firmly established by the mid-1930s, as the Saudis stabilized their northern frontiers by signing treaties with the British supported kingdoms of Iraq and TransJordan between 1933-1936. The border with Yemen was fixed after the 1934 conflict between Saudi Arabia and Yemen. As a result of this conflict, which resulted in an overwhelming victory for Saudi Arabia, Saudi control was extended to the Asir region.[2]

The Origins of Saudi-American Relations: The Importance of Oil

The Development of the Saudi Oil Industry

The early relations between the United States and Saudi Arabia were established as a result of oil. The foundations of an extensive relationship were formed between the two countries in 1933 when King Abd al-Aziz granted an oil concession to the Standard Oil Company of California. The company had been active in neighboring Bahrain as it established the Bahrain Petroleum Company in 1930 and discovered oil in 1932. King Abd al-Aziz was motivated to grant the concession to an American company as it offered better financial terms than the British. Another concern of Ibn Saud was that he did not want the British to gain predominate influence within Saudi Arabia. The original concession consisted of 360,000 square miles, which was later extended by 80,000 square miles. The Standard Oil Company combined with the Texas Oil Company in 1936 to better exploit this concession. The partnership of these companies in Saudi Arabia was renamed the California Arabian Standard Oil Company (CASOC). Oil was discovered and developed in commercial quantities by 1938. By 1940 geologists estimated that the oil reserves in Saudi Arabia exceeded the reserves of the United States.[3]

The Importance of Oil during World War II

Oil's significance was graphically illustrated during World War II. After Pearl Harbor, Admiral Chester W. Nimitz, commander of the Pacific Fleet, observed that victory would depend on the Allies having beans, bullets, and oil. By 1945, however, Nimitz changed the order of these priorities to oil, bullets, and beans. This was reflected by the changing nature of warfare, which required more gas and oil consumption to feed the modern mechanized forces. This was illustrated by the daily gasoline consumption of American forces in Europe which was 14 times the total amount of gasoline sent to Europe between 1914 and 1918. By 1945, seven billion barrels of petroleum had been required to fuel the allied war effort.[4]

Saudi Arabia had assumed a strategic position during the war because of its oil, which was especially important to the U.S. Navy. This was illustrated in May of 1945 when President Truman authorized the navy to develop a billion-barrel oil reserve in Saudi Arabia. Although this project was ultimately not established, the Arabian American Oil Company (ARAMCO) supplied 80 percent of its inventory to the American navy by 1946.[5]

A key element in American-Saudi relations was the further development of the country's oil industry during the early postwar period. Saudi oil production leaped from four to five million barrels per year in the period of 1939-1945 to 21 million barrels per year in 1945. In 1946 production continued to increase to 60 million barrels. This rise in oil wealth necessitated a greater amount of economic and military planning that was done with the assistance of American officials in ARAMCO.[6]

Oil production would eventually increase to 200 million barrels by 1949, which produced about $50 million in revenues. The growth of Saudi oil production continued at about a 9 percent increase per year until 1970. This revenue provided the impetus for the Saudis to initiate policies of economic and military modernization that were announced in July of 1947. These were largely drawn up by a combination of ARAMCO executives, American government officials, and Point Four advisory teams.[7]

The oil company officials sought to pressure the American government into supporting Ibn Saud and the company management reported to Washington concerning British involvement in Saudi Arabia. They contrasted the British position in the country with the American position and the potential benefits which the United States could acquire if it aided Ibn Saud.[8]

Initially, the United States did not support Saudi Arabia directly during the war, but rather channeled American aid through Great Britain. Cal-Tex executives feared that the U.S. government was not adequately exploiting its opportunity to influence Ibn Saud, and was instead reinforcing the British position in the kingdom. The company felt that to ensure its position in the kingdom, lend-lease aid had to be extended to Saudi Arabia by the American government directly. A major figure in the Roosevelt administration who was sympathetic to the appeals of the oil companies was Secretary of the Interior Harold Ickes. Ickes became an advocate of granting aid to Saudi Arabia and also supported easing restrictions on the oil companies by the extension of tax benefits, the suspension of antitrust laws, and raising the ceilings on crude oil. It was evident at the onset of the war that the United States would have to supply the bulk of the oil to the Allies. In February 1943 President Roosevelt agreed to extend lend-lease aid to Saudi Arabia. In an effort to gain greater control and access over oil in June of 1943 Ickes, along with Secretary of the Navy Knox and Secretary of War Henry Stimson, proposed the outright purchase of Middle East oil concessions. President Roosevelt agreed with this assessment and established an interdepartmental committee composed of the State, War, Navy, and Interior Departments to form the Petroleum Reserves Corporation (PRC). The purpose of this organization was to acquire ownership of petroleum reserves outside the United States with a special emphasis on Saudi Arabia. The president of the board of directors was Harold Ickes.[9]

The latter goal was opposed by the major oil companies active in Saudi Arabia, California Standard Oil and Texas Oil, as the Saudi concession was the linchpin of their distribution network for Asia. They also maintained that the Saudis would view this as a threat and would serve as a basis for Britain and the Soviet Union to demand similar terms in other areas. Further, they argued, this would make other nations hesitant to grant concessions to American companies that could hurt the U.S. strategic position as well as the fortunes of the oil industry in the long run.[10]

The first major project which the PRC embarked on was a pipeline that sought to link the Saudi oil fields to the Eastern Mediterranean. This would have increased American government involvement in the concession and was opposed by many of the smaller companies who felt they would be shut out of this lucrative area. The technical mission that was sent to the region reported that the emphasis of world oil production was shifting from the Western Hemisphere to the Persian Gulf. The mission concluded that the proven reserves of the region were 26 billion barrels.[11]

During the war there were tensions between the United States and Great Britain concerning oil. The pipeline project of the PRC provoked controversy in Great Britain as it was felt by the British that the United States was trying to gain paramount control over Middle Eastern oil. While there was a split within the British government over the desirability of greater American access to Middle Eastern oil, this issue was aggravated by a proposal put forth by the Truman Committee, which suggested that Britain transfer some of its oil concessions over to the United States. This provoked a great deal of controversy between the two governments and was only settled by an exchange of notes between Roosevelt and Churchill in which they each promised that they did not have ambitions toward the others oil concessions.[12] This had been a point of contention between the two countries since the early 1930s when the United States first established a position in the Middle East. The original Red Line Agreement did not apply to Saudi Arabia or Kuwait. The United States felt that the British were using their position to advance the claims of the Anglo-Persian Oil Company (APOC) to the detriment of American companies. Eventually an agreement was reached in which the APOC and the Gulf Corporation agreed to form a company to administer the Kuwaiti concession jointly.[13]

Although oil from Saudi Arabia was a fraction of total world supplies in 1948, the disruption of this source could have forced the United States to supply Europe's oil needs, as well as institute rationing domestically. Saudi oil was considered essential to facilitate the European Recovery Program in order to strengthen Western Europe against Soviet influence.[14]

The wartime demands, as well as Ibn Saud's quest for greater royalties, led ARAMCO to increase productivity over 100 times from the prewar levels. This, however, posed a problem as ARAMCO markets could not absorb all of this production. The company management ultimately decided that rather than infringe on the markets of the other companies, which would have violated cartel agreements, it was necessary to include other companies in ARAMCO. This would allow Saudi oil more market outlets.[15] These companies were given an added benefit in the 1950s as the tax laws were amended so that the royalties paid to the government of Saudi Arabia by ARAMCO were deducted from the companies' U.S. taxes.[16] Thus, ARAMCO increased its royalty payment to Saudi Arabia, which gave the kingdom added resources; the company was able to claim that it was a Saudi tax, which they were able to deduct from its U.S. tax obligations. This provided a means by which aid could be funneled to the Saudis without congressional approval through the royalties paid by ARAMCO. Between

1950 and 1951 the taxes ARAMCO paid to the United States went from $30 million to $5 million, while the payments to the Saudi government rose to $110 million from $44 million.[17]

In the five years after World War II, Saudi oil revenues increased from $10.4 million in 1946 to $165 million by 1951. By 1965 these revenues would increase to $650 million. The rise in oil revenues for the kingdom was facilitated by the new agreement giving the company more revenues, as well as the Anglo-Iranian oil crisis that led to Saudi Arabia becoming the largest oil producer in the region between the years 1950 to 1955.[18]

In addition to royalties derived from oil, Saudi Arabia also benefitted from construction projects built by ARAMCO. In 1950 the TAPLINE pipeline was completed at a cost of $200 million, linking the oil fields of eastern Arabia to the Mediterranean. The company also constructed a 360-mile railway at a cost of $160 million from Dhahran, on the Persian Gulf, to Riyadh. ARAMCO officials also provided legal and logistical support in their border conflict with Oman over the Buraimi oasis.[19]

Security Ties between the United States and Saudi Arabia: 1945-1960

In addition to oil, American policy makers became interested in Saudi Arabia for its political as well as its strategic importance. American decision makers hoped to utilize Ibn Saud's political importance in the Arab and Muslim worlds by virtue of his position as guardian of the Holy Places. American military planners were interested in using Saudi Arabia as a logistical base for overflight rights and basing facilities.[20]

The official U.S. presence in the kingdom was established in 1943 when a military mission was sent to Saudi Arabia. The function of these advisors was to assist Saudi officials in planning. A more significant strategic and political development for the United States was the construction of the air base at Dhahran. This base became the main facility in the Gulf during the war, and in the postwar period provided a major link between Europe and Asia. While American lend-lease assistance was granted in mid-1943 it became apparent that the Saudis would need additional aid in early 1944. Saudi oil revenues were not enough to cover the kingdom's expenses and with the threat to the Middle East having been eliminated by 1944, the British were reducing the subsidies that they paid to Ibn Saud. The United States quickly rushed in to fill this gap. Secretary Hull recommended to President Roosevelt that the United States assume 50 percent of the subsidies to Ibn Saud. The officials felt that if the Saudis relied on Britain too much the British would demand oil concessions. The State Department was especially active in pressing the case that the stability of Saudi Arabia was an important national interest to the United States. In December 1944 they argued that, an American national interest, basically strategic in character, existed in Saudi Arabia. Saudi Arabia was strategically located and its vast oil reserves should be safeguarded and developed in order to supplement Western Hemisphere oil reserves. In addition, the military urgently desired to construct certain facilities in Saudi Arabia to aid in the prosecution of the war.[21]

The State Department recommended that the president should ask Congress to appropriate money for foreign aid, as well as to recommend to the Export-Import Bank to grant development loans to Saudi Arabia. In the short term, the military could construct projects such as airfields and roads, as well as training missions. These recommendations were approved by President Roosevelt on January 8, 1945.[22]

It was during the 1950s that the military relationship between the two countries reached a higher level, as the United States began to replace Great Britain as a source of military support for the regime. This occurred as a result of disputes between London and Riyadh concerning the British position in South Arabia and Oman. American involvement in the Middle East was facilitated by the almost financial bankruptcy of Great Britain after World War II. Great Britain was a recipient of the Marshall Plan and shortly thereafter was forced to relinquish its traditional sphere of influence in the Eastern Mediterranean when in 1948 it had to ask America to take over its security commitments to Greece and Turkey. The United States also took the lead in pressuring the Soviets to withdraw from Iran in 1946. Thus Britain's traditional role in the region was gradually giving way to the United States. The debacle of the 1956 Suez War further eroded British influence in the region as it was perceived as a fading power seeking to hang on to its empire at all cost. The withdrawal of Great Britain from the region was finally accomplished when the last vestiges of the British presence left the Persian Gulf in 1971. This paved the way for the development of regional powers such as Saudi Arabia and Iran while leading to a growth in American influence. The rise in oil prices fueled massive arms sales and other purchases by these countries from the United States.[23]

The preponderance of British influence in the region had been a concern for Ibn Saud prior to World War II. Part of his rationale for granting oil concessions to American companies was to weaken British influence and decrease the opportunities that Britain had to pressure him. Saudi Arabia had also approached Germany prior to the war for the purchase of arms as well as the possibility of setting up an ammunition factory. However, neither of these projects were carried out.[24]

Ibn Saud favored closer relations with the United States in order to acquire American support against several threats to his regime. Although the king was a virulent opponent of Zionism, which caused some tensions with the United States, he feared communism more. As a result he was deeply wary of potential gains for Soviet influence in the region. The king also felt threatened by the Hashemites in Jordan, and their possible irredentist claims on Saudi territory. Ibn Saud was cautious of the traditional alliance between Great Britain and the Hashemites as illustrated by the close relationship that

Britain had with the Hashimite kingdoms of Jordan and Iraq. He was suspicious that the British might try to encourage border incursions by the Hashimites in an effort to put pressure on the Saudis. Part of the wartime cooperation with the United States saw America promise to maintain the territorial integrity and political independence of the kingdom. By 1948 Ibn Saud was quietly inquiring about entering into a formal alliance with the United States.[25]

By 1949 oil production served to enhance the strategic importance of the kingdom. Oil field security, along with the suspicion of Soviet-sponsored regional instability, became dominant interests for the Saudis as well as for the United States. From early on in the Cold War, American-Saudi interests were on a duel track that consisted of securing the oil fields and containing Soviet expansion.[26] The oil industry and access to oil also had become important for the United States. By the end of the 1950s the majority of the top 10 American corporations were oil companies and the United States consumed more than 60 percent of world production.[27]

The Importance of Dhahran Air Base and American Military Aid

In 1948 Secretary of Defense James Forrestal informed Secretary of State George Marshall that the American Joint Chiefs of Staff had concluded it was essential to upgrade the American strategic position in Saudi Arabia by expanding the number of personnel at the base.[28]

Security ties between the United States and Saudi Arabia were steadily enhanced throughout the 1950s. In 1951 the first formal defense agreement was concluded between the two countries. This agreement provided for an extension of American access to the Dhahran air base as well as establishing a permanent military mission in the country. This was followed on later by a further five-year extension for the Dhahran facility that was concluded in 1957. In return, Washington granted the Saudis a $180 million-increase in economic and military aid.

Additionally, in 1958 the United States provided a grant of $25 million under the Foreign Assistance Act and $50 million in military assistance over a five-year period. America also agreed to aid in the doubling of the Saudi army from 15,000 to 30,000 men and furnishing this force with modern arms such as M-41 light tanks, M-47 medium tanks, artillery, and F-86 Sabre jets. The United States also encouraged the Saudis to develop a modern navy and air force as independent services. The acquisition of the Sabre jets by the kingdom led to an expansion of the American military mission in the country as well as to the development of a close working relationship between the Royal Saudi Air Force and the U.S. Air Force.[29]

It was the opinion of members of the State Department that it was necessary to give Ibn Saud additional military grants in aid. They recommended to the president that this aid be extended under Section 202 of the Mutual Security Act of 1951. The official position of the Department of State was:

(1) the strategic position of Saudi Arabia makes it of direct importance to the defense of the Near East Area, (2) such assistance is of critical importance to the defense of the free nations, and (3) the immediately increased ability of the recipient country to defend itself is important to the preservation of the peace and security of the area and to the security of the United States.[30]

Despite the improvements in American-Saudi relations during the late 1950s the use of Dhahran by the American military was becoming a problem for Saudi Arabia in inter-Arab relations. President Nasser of Egypt, as well as the new government of Abd al-Karim Qasim in Iraq made Dhahran a political issue against the Saudis.[31] For the United States, Dhahran had diminished in strategic importance by the early 1960s. The development of Intercontinental Ballistic Missiles (ICBM) made overseas Strategic Air Command(SAC) bases obsolete. In April of 1962 the formal American base rights to Dhahran were terminated.[32]

Implications of Saudi Foreign Policy for the United States: The Baghdad Pact and Relations with Egypt

The Implications of the Baghdad Pact on Saudi Arabia

Although a complex military, political, and economic relationship between the two countries was being formed during the early Cold War period, there were also strains in the relationship. An important source of tension between the two countries was the unwillingness of the Saudis to enter into, or endorse, the American-sponsored Baghdad Pact in 1955. The Saudis felt that this was a manifestation of Western imperialism and responded by forging closer relations with both Egypt and Syria.[33]

The refusal of Saudi Arabia to participate in the Baghdad Pact illustrated a fundamental difference between Saudi and American foreign policies. The United States, particularly in the 1950s, emphasized more formal security arrangements linking its respective regional allies by establishing broad treaty organizations. The Saudis, however, preferred a more informal relationship with implicit guarantees of American support that would be based over the horizon. The Saudis did not want to become involved directly in superpower confrontation or basing-treaty arrangements that would limit their ability to maneuver diplomatically in the region.[34]

Saudi-Egyptian Relations: 1955-1962

During the 1950s Saudi Arabia had extensive ties to Egypt as a result of Nasser's hostility to the Hashemites. A mutual defense pact was concluded with Egypt in 1955. This was later expanded to include Yemen in the

Tripartite Jeddah Pact. In 1957 Saudi Arabia, Egypt, Syria and Jordan concluded the Treaty of Arab Solidarity. A primary purpose of this agreement was for the former three nations to provide financial assistance to Jordan to make up for the loss of aid from Great Britain, as the Anglo-Jordanian treaty was in the process of being terminated. In addition, the Saudis agreed to provide Egypt with oil at a subsidized price by accepting payment in Egyptian pounds, which when compared with other customers, meant Egypt was paying about one-third the price.[35]

Relations between Egypt and Saudi Arabia began to break down for a variety of reasons. Tensions were caused as a result of Nasser's popularity in the Arab world that even extended to Saudi Arabia. In a visit to Saudi Arabia in September 1956 to meet with King Saud and President Kuwately of Syria, huge crowds came out to greet President Nasser to the consternation of King Saud.[36] The Saudis ignored Nasser's proposal to participate in a federation with Egypt and Syria. In January 1957 Saud visited the United States and agreed to support the Eisenhower Doctrine as a means of constraining the spread of Nasser's influence within the Arab world. He also received additional economic and military assistance as a quid pro quo for extending American usage of the Dhahran air base for five more years as well as providing assistance to King Hussein of Jordan in dismissing the pro-Nasserite government by placing Saudi troops based in Jordan at the king's disposal. Saud also attempted to block the formation of the United Arab Republic (UAR), and there were accusations that he was involved in formulating an assassination plot against Nasser.[37] The ultimate breakup of the UAR in 1961, along with Egyptian involvement in Yemen beginning in 1962, nearly brought about conflict between the two countries.

The Eisenhower Doctrine and American-Saudi Relations

The Purpose of the Eisenhower Doctrine

The Eisenhower Doctrine established in January of 1957 was done in response to several factors. The policy came on the heels of the Suez Crisis of 1956 in which the United States forced Britain, France, and Israel to withdraw from Sinai and cease hostilities against Egypt. The United States was alarmed by its breach with Great Britain as well as a fear that the Soviets would attempt to exploit regional conditions to enhance their influence in the area. President Eisenhower proposed three main provisions of a joint congressional-executive declaration, which has become known as the Eisenhower Doctrine. First, to maintain the stability of the region the nations of the Middle East had to be stronger economically. Therefore $200 million was requested by the executive branch for foreign aid to be used at the discretion of the president. Second, this resolution gave the president greater flexibility to use already approved funding to assist any nation with military aid. Third, the United States would guarantee the independence and territorial integrity of nations being threaten by another state or states allied with the Soviet Union. This would be done by the use of American armed forces.[38]

The U.S. strategy assumed that the Arab states would be content with an informal Western (American) control, provided that the more overt vestiges of Western colonialism were removed from the region. It also assumed that as a quid pro quo for encouraging its European allies to withdraw directly from the Middle East, and extending economic and military aid, the Arab states would accept being a junior partner in the American global containment strategy. Another premise of the Eisenhower doctrine was that the Arab states viewed communism as a significant threat and feared the expansion of Soviet influence.[39]

The Saudi Role under the Eisenhower Doctrine

The Eisenhower Doctrine looked to Saudi Arabia to provide leadership in the Arab world and illustrate a pro-Western model for other Arab states. King Saud was viewed by some policy makers as the ideal choice to play this role as an anti-communist leader who could provide legitimacy for the American role in the Middle East. This legitimacy derived in large part from his position within the Islamic world as the guardian of the Holy Places. The ambassador to Saudi Arabia George Wadsworth in congressional testimony illustrated the American position concerning Saudi Arabia:

> We are recognizing that Saudi Arabia is a stabilizing force in the area, and we state in those terms for the first time to my knowledge, that it is our policy to continue to contribute to the strengthening of the Kingdom; we want to build up something strong which will resist this nebulous force of aggression which we sense building up.[40]

King Saud, however, had his own motivations for going along with U.S. policy. He wanted to use an agreement to extend the American access to the air base at Dhahran to acquire additional economic and military aid. This was ultimately granted for $180 million. King Saud was also able to smooth relations with the Hashimite monarchies of Jordan and Iraq at the behest of the Eisenhower administration.[41]

It would seem therefore that the objectives of American foreign policy were satisfied at this stage of the relationship. The United States was taking the lead in building up the kingdom's armed forces which, along with the commercial contacts involving oil, provided for a higher level of interaction between the two states. This gave the United States a certain amount of influence over the regime, particularly at the expense of the British. In addition, American containment goals were satisfied with the beginnings of a formal treaty relationship, as well as access to the important air base at Dhahran.

The Conflict in Yemen and the Impact on American-Saudi Relations

The attempt by army officers to overthrow the Imam of Yemen drastically increased tensions in the Arab world and provided an arena for superpower competition on the Arabian Peninsula. The coup in Yemen occurred in September of 1962 after the death of the tyrannical Imam Ahmed and the proclamation of his son, Mohamad al Badr, the new Imam by the sheikhs and ulema. While Yemen was an autocratic monarchy dominated by the Imam, whose core of support were the Zaydi Shia tribes of the north, during the 1950s the country had flirted with support for Nasser. Yemen was officially, although loosely, part of the United Arab States with Egypt and Syria and many military officers were trained in Egypt. The Imam had also maintained relationships with the Soviet Union and the People's Republic of China that included some small-scale arms purchases. Yemen, however, was an extremely backward, isolated country. The Imam Yahya, who ruled from 1918-1948, attempted to cut Yemen off from the rest of the world as a way of preserving the country's independence, closing the country to foreigners, including diplomats. The central government had little authority, as the tribes were autonomous from the state and frequently fought each other. In addition, the country had deep social and regional divisions that were reflected in the opposition to the government. Under the control of the monarch, there were no modern state institutions.[42]

There were several plots to overthrow the Imam. Dissent came from within the royal family as some princes wanted to assert their claims on the throne at Mohamad al Badr's expense. The more significant plots, however, were from the army. The chief architect of the coup was Lieutenant Ali Abdul al Moghny who had received training in Egypt and was in communication with the Egyptian charge d'affaires, Abdul Wahad. Lieutenant Ali Abdul al Moghny was able to convince Brigadier General Abdullah Sallal, who himself was conspiring against the Imam in another coup plot, to join him on the night of the rebellion by promising him the presidency. Mutinous army troops attacked and leveled the Imam's palace, but he escaped and fled to the north where he rallied the tribes.[43]

Soon after the coup Egypt began to send military forces to support the new republican regime. The first of these arrived on October 5, 1962. By October 21 there were 1,000 Egyptian troops in Yemen. These initial deployments were meant to be more symbolic to illustrate support for the republicans. However, as it became apparent that the Imam was successful in rallying the northern tribes and that resistance would be formidable, the Egyptians were forced to increase their commitment substantially. Within a short period of time they would have to take over the prosecution of the war. The first Egyptian offensives against the royalists began in February 1963 under the command of the head of the Egyptian military, Abd al-Hakim Amr, and involved 20,000 troops.[44]

For the Saudis the coup in Yemen, and especially the vast Egyptian presence in the country, posed a number of potential threats to the country. It threatened to transform North Yemen from what had been a friendly, militarily weak state, to a regime that articulated a hostile ideology and also potential irredentist ambitions. An immediate threat to the Saudis was the opportunity that the Egyptians had to use North Yemen as a base to destablize Saudi Arabia through both overt and covert intervention. These fears seemed to be realized in November 1962 when Egyptian naval and air forces conducted raids on Saudi bases near the border. In addition, arms were dropped on the road between Mecca and Jidda for opponents of the Saudi regime.[45]

The monarchy attempted to take steps to forestall possible border incursions by the Egyptians or their republican allies. They ordered a general mobilization of the army, as well as moving three squadrons of jets and antiaircraft weapons close to the border. The Saudi troops at the border were joined by a small Jordanian force.[46]

King Saud attempted to encourage support for the royalist government in several ways. These included pressing the Imam's claims in the international community in general, and particularly with the United States, as well as in the Arab world and in international organizations. On a visit to the United States in October 1962, Crown Prince Faisal was able to raise the question of Yemen with members of the Senate Foreign Relations Committee, as well as with President Kennedy in a private talk. During Crown Prince Faisal's discussions with President Kennedy he was able to lay out the Saudi position with regard to Yemen. He argued that the republican regime in Yemen was dependent on Egyptian military support, and that since Imam al-Badr had survived the coup and was able to rally many of the tribes to his banner, the royalists should be considered the legal government of Yemen.[47]

The Saudis rallied support in the Arab world for the royalist's position. Among the Arab states that supported the Imam were Jordan, Lebanon, and Kuwait. In the U.N. the Saudis were successful in blocking the recognition of the republican government. Within the Arab League they sought to prevent the republicans from being seated as the official government of Yemen, but in this they were not successful.[48]

In addition to trying to block the spread of Egyptian influence in the Arabian Peninsula, the Saudis were concerned about the close relations between the republican government in Sanaa and the Soviet Union. These fears were heightened with President al-Sallal's visit to the Soviet Union to conclude a treaty of friendship. The provisions of this treaty included: (1) an increase in Soviet economic and technical support to Yemen; (2) an increase in the number of Soviet advisors; (3) further arms shipments that would include tanks and planes; (4) soviet development of infrastructure that would include the construction of schools and paved roads, as well as a new harbor at al-Hudaydah.[49]

The Yemeni civil war did cause tensions in the American-Saudi relationship. The war occurred during a time when the United States was attempting to mend relations with Nasser of Egypt. The Kennedy administration's recognition of the republican government in 1962 caused a great deal of consternation in Riyadh.[50] However, despite this disagreement the United States did send a squadron of aircraft to the kingdom in a show of support when King Faisal appealed for support after Egyptian airplanes attacked villages in Saudi Arabia.[51]

These tensions passed quickly as Saudi Arabia was confronted by the more immediate threat of radicalism in the Arab world. A legacy of the Yemeni civil war, however, was that the Saudis had to develop stronger military capabilities than they had previously desired. As a result, the American-Saudi military link expanded.[52]

The conflict also had implications for Saudi internal politics. A number of commoners urged recognition of the republican regime, while several Saudi military personnel defected to Egypt. This splits were even reflected within the royal family. A group of younger princes who advocated constitutional reform, led by Amir Talal ibn Abd al-Aziz who was dismissed from a cabinet position in 1961, fled to Cairo where they criticized the regime. Saud gave some aid to the royalists but his policy appeared to be indecisive. Prince Faisal returned from the United States and assumed a prominent role in government. He instituted needed reforms that served to modernize but not democratize the state. With regard to Yemen, Faisal continued the policy of aiding the royalists, but at a level so as to avoid coming into direct conflict with Nasser.[53]

Saudi Arabian Political Development

The Struggle for Succession after Ibn Saud

Another significant implication for American-Saudi Arabian relations was the internal struggles within the royal family. This was reflected in the conflict between King Saud and Prince Faisal that ultimately resulted in Saud being removed from his position in favor of Faisal. This transition illustrated that it was necessary for the monarch to retain the support and confidence of the senior princes.

King Saud was unable to consolidate his position within the royal family. He could not maintain relations with his brother Prince Faisal who was prime minister, as well as the other senior princes. Saud sought to ally himself both with the conservative tribal leaders and ulema, who were against rapid modernization, and the emerging middle class and younger princes who wanted more modernization and rather substantial political reforms. Saud, however, was not a competent ruler and by the late 1950s the Saudi elite had cleavaged along three lines. The first were those princes and tribal elites who supported King Saud. The second were the senior princes who supported Prince Faisal and his plans for reforms and gradual modernization. The third group was a collection of liberal princes led by Prince Talal who favored rapid modernization, a constitutional monarchy, as well as closer relations with Nasser. In 1958 the royal family essentially deposed Saud, although he was left with the title of king, in favor of Prince Faisal, who assumed the role of prime minister with full political authority.[54]

In an effort to get the kingdom's finances in order he began an austerity campaign that led to the cutting of subsidies to the Bedouins as well as increased unemployment due to greater urbanization. This led to a degree of conflict between Faisal and the liberals, who while initially enthusiastic about him felt he was not moving fast enough to establish political reforms. There was also dissatisfaction within the armed forces as some officers held pro-Egyptian views. Institutionally, there was hostility against the reduction of the armed forces budget and the freezing of force levels. The military was dissatisfied with the weakening of the armed forces in general, favoring the more tribal oriented, and politically reliable, National Guard. The result of this policy was to keep the armed forces deliberately weak so they could not challenge the regime.[55]

King Saud and his supporters made a comeback in 1960, as he was able to dismiss Faisal and appoint a cabinet in which the liberal princes were prominently represented. However, after Saud left the country for medical treatment in 1962, Faisal and his supporters were able to gain control. Saud was eventually deposed officially in 1964. Faisal embarked on a policy of repression and neglected his promises of introducing constitutional reforms. There were arrests of suspected opponents in the intelligentsia, as well as leftist and Shia dissidents in the Asir and the Eastern Province. In addition, new antistrike laws were established in 1964 that provided for 10-15 years imprisonment.[56]

Faisal's Pattern of Rule

The achievements of Faisal's reign were the development of the Saudi economy, which enhanced Saudi prestige and leadership in the Arab and Islamic worlds, and closer ties with the United States.[57] King Feisal increased the oil wealth of the kingdom and sought to pursue modernization and developmental policies that resulted in increased urbanization. The number of students also increased. By 1970, 7,000 students were in higher education with 500,000 students in other levels.[58]

In 1969-1970 there were charges of an alleged coup attempt involving military officers and senior technocrats who were suspected members of the National Liberation Front. In addition, several hundred Shias were arrested on suspicion of membership in the Baath party. Most of the military officers came from the air force, which was grounded for several weeks thereafter. Faisal had a carrot-and-stick approach for dealing with the elites: those who could not be coopted were crushed.[59]

King Faisal's rule was defined by relying on senior members of the royal family as well as technocrats who he slowly brought into decision making positions. However, the promise of establishing a constitution and an assembly were ignored. The technocrats who were given political positions were appointed to the Council of Ministers, where they had more of an influence on domestic and budgetary matters. Foreign policy decisions were controlled by the senior princes, with some consultation with younger members of the royal family and selected military officers and ministers.[60]

Another important group in the Saudi elite is the ulema. The Saudi family has sought to placate the ulema by consulting them on major issues and identifying with them. The ulema are important in domestic politics, as they set the standards of social behavior, have influence over the educational system, as well as keep Saudi politics in general in an Islamic orientation. The Saudis have sought to use the ulema to legitimize their position internally as well as internationally. This has been particularly evident during crises within the regime, such as the deposition of King Saud in favor of Faisal, the assassination of King Faisal in 1975, as well as the takeover of the Grand Mosque in Mecca. The family has sought to gain approval of the ulema to cover subsequent actions, and use the ulema to gain approval of developmental policies in general, such as the introduction of telephones and radios, which it was argued could be used to spread the Koran.

The royal family has deftly managed to identify the ulema so closely with the regime that any criticism of the rule of the Al Saud is portrayed as a challenge to Islam itself.[61]

The Development of American-Saudi Military Relations, 1965-1977

The military relationship between the United States and Saudi Arabia began to escalate in the mid 1960s as the Saudis acquired more and better quality American armaments. In 1965 Saudi arms purchases totaled $341 million and increased each year thereafter. This was a dramatic jump from the $87 million that had been spent in the years 1950-1964. In addition, during the 1960s American advisors made various suggestions in the development of the Saudi military, such as advising the Saudis to mechanize their army in stages to make maximum use of equipment.[62]

The military relationship was reinforced at this time as a result of several factors. The Saudis were disillusioned with the policies of their alternative military suppliers, Britain and France. The relationship between France and Saudi Arabia was strained as a result of French involvement in Algeria, as well as the close military ties which existed between France and Israel. A more serious threat to Saudi Arabia however was the conflict the kingdom was engaged in with Egypt. This conflict had two dimensions. The first was direct and concerned the backing of rival factions in the war then raging in North Yemen. The second dimension concerned the pitting of the two rival leaders against one another: Egypt, led by Nasser, as the leader of the radical-socialist faction, and Saudi Arabia, led by Faisal, as the leader of the religious-conservative grouping.[63]

The Development of the Saudi Air Force and Air Defense Capabilities

An American air defense survey team completed a study in November 1963, in the wake of the outbreak of the civil war in North Yemen. This survey recommended to the Saudis that they acquire surface-to-air missiles, an air defense radar net, and three squadrons of supersonic aircraft in groups of twelve. The aircraft that these American advisors had in mind was the Northrop F-5, or the Lockheed F-104.[64] The efforts to improve Saudi air defenses was complicated by the difficulties that Great Britain was having in meeting its balance of payments deficits, which made it seem unlikely that the British would be able to purchase the F-111 aircraft. A deal was worked out between Secretary of Defense McNamara and British Air Minister Roy Jenkins where the United States agreed to assist Britain in obtaining $400 million worth of exports so the British could afford the F-111. This was done by formulating a joint Anglo-American air defense package that would have the British sell three squadrons of F-52 Lightning aircraft, an air defense center, as well as five sector-operations centers, early warning radar and communications equipment, as well as provide a five-year maintenance and training program. The cost of this program would amount to between $275 and $400 million. The United States would supply to Saudi Arabia 150 Raytheon Hawk surface-to-air missiles and associated missile batteries at a cost of $126 million.[65]

This Raytheon contract had a long life, as in 1968 the Saudis contracted to purchase an additional half-battery of HAWK missiles as well as additional training and construction services for $52 million. In 1974, Saudi Arabia placed an order for improved HAWKS (I-HAWK) surface-to-air missiles for an initial cost of $270 million. When the contract was finally concluded in 1977 it was worth $1 billion.[66] In addition to the HAWK missiles, they contracted in 1968 with the United States to purchase AIM-9E and modification kits for the F-86 fighter. In the spring of 1969 they purchased eight T-33 training jets.[67]

In addition to the air defense improvements outlined above, other American military assistance efforts included the construction of a network of military bases in the country by the U.S. Army Corps of Engineers. In 1966 the United States also sponsored a $100 million program to provide combat vehicles for the Saudi armed forces.[68]

In the late 1960s the Saudis improved their airlift capabilities dramatically by purchasing four Lockheed C-130 transport aircraft. In 1965 they purchased four of these planes and awarded Lockheed a management service contract. By 1969 the Saudis had purchased four additional planes deploying them into two transport squadrons.[69]

The Growth of the Saudi Army

It was during this period that the Saudi armed forces went through complex changes, as Saudi Arabia was given the opportunity by the United States to rapidly expand its military capabilities, while the dramatic increase in oil prices gave the monarchy the means to accomplish this. In the period from 1971-1980 Saudi military purchases from the United States alone totaled over $34 billion dollars.[70] In addition, the Saudis purchased military hardware from France and to a lesser extent Britain. Among the programs the Saudis initiated during this period were major modernization programs for its Army and National Guard. During this period the Saudis embarked on a major modernization program to build up their ground forces into an effective fighting force. In the late 1960s and early 1970s, they adopted a system where they relied on American and French supplied armaments. In 1974 Saudi Arabia and France concluded a major arms purchase that gave the Saudis 50 AMX-30 tanks to add on to the 200 they had purchased in 1973, 200 AML-60/90 armored cars, 500 AMX-10P infantry carriers, and AMX-30 SP antiaircraft guns.[71] In addition, the Saudis purchased an enormous amount of equipment from the United States such as M60 tanks and armored personnel carriers. The growth of Saudi military purchases increased dramatically during the 1970s. In 1970 the Saudis spent $45 million on American arms and related services. This figure rose to $1.15 billion by 1973, and $2 billion in 1974. This is illustrated by tables and graphs 6.1 and 6.2. By the end of the decade the Saudis had made over $6 billion in agreements for arms, training, and construction.[72]

The Modernization of the National Guard

Another component of the ground forces of the Saudi military is the National Guard, whose purpose is to safeguard the regime. Recruits in this force have been drawn from tribes that have demonstrated loyalty to the Al-Saud family. In an effort to enable the National Guard to deal effectively with the internal security of the nation, the Saudis requested the United States to develop a program that would assist in the modernization of this force. This led to a detailed joint modernization plan with America agreeing to provide the equipment and training needed for the National Guard to become an effective military force. This agreement was officially approved in 1975.[73] It called for a government-to-government contract worth about $330 million. One company that was included as a part of this agreement was the Vinnell Corporation, which was concluded at a cost of $77 million. Vinnell was given the task to train four of the twenty battalions of the National Guard. In addition, as a part of this arrangement the guard was sold Cadillac Gage V-150 armored cars and Vulcan antiaircraft guns. In order to

**Table 6.1. U.S. Military Sales Agreements with Saudi Arabia,
1968-1977 (in thousands of U.S. dollars)**

Year	Near East and South Asia (NESA)	Saudi Arabia
1950-1967	3,067,667	2,269,411
1968	460,068	13,969
1969	360,110	4,214
1970	265,537	65,090
1971	857,293	15,861
1972	1,284,807	330,709
1973	3,076,241	688,607
1974	8,737,616	2,017,145
1975	6,113,517	1,977,085
1976	9,615,184	5,806,950
1977	8,526,215	1,894,732
1950-1977	42,364,264	14,993,500

Source: U.S. Department of Defense. *Foreign Military Sales, Foreign Military Construction Sales, and Military Assistance Facts* (Washington, D.C.: Data Management Division DSAA, 1978), 1.

**Graph 6.1. U.S. Military Sales
Agreements with Saudi Arabia, 1968-1977**

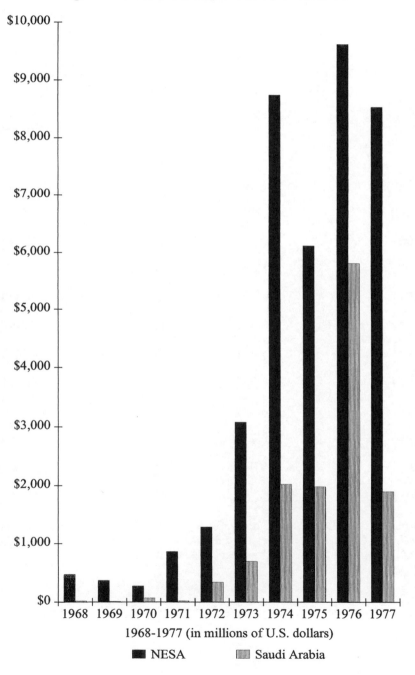

1968-1977 (in millions of U.S. dollars)

■ NESA   ▦ Saudi Arabia

**Table 6.2. U.S. Military Sales Deliveries to Saudi Arabia,
1968-1977 (in thousands of U.S. dollars)**

Year	Worldwide	Near East and South Asia (NESA)	Saudi Arabia
1950-1967	5,595,199	415,233	121,487
1968	986,707	149,721	36,856
1969	1,277,235	253,428	32,856
1970	1,363,860	489,260	51,937
1971	1,450,621	557,541	144,049
1972	1,360,867	484,366	59,646
1973	1,365,473	538,520	86,159
1974	2,956,089	1,775,101	254,971
1975	3,328,438	1,958,631	342,239
1976	5,258,716	3,357,200	1,027,640
1977	6,898,061	5,055,864	1,617,423
1950-1977	31,841,274	15,034,865	3,774,494

Source: U.S. Department of Defense. *Foreign Military Sales, Foreign Military Construction Sales, and Military Assistance Facts* (Washington, D.C.: Data Management Division DSAA, 1978), 4.

Graph 6.2. U.S. Military Sales
Deliveries to Saudi Arabia, 1968-1977

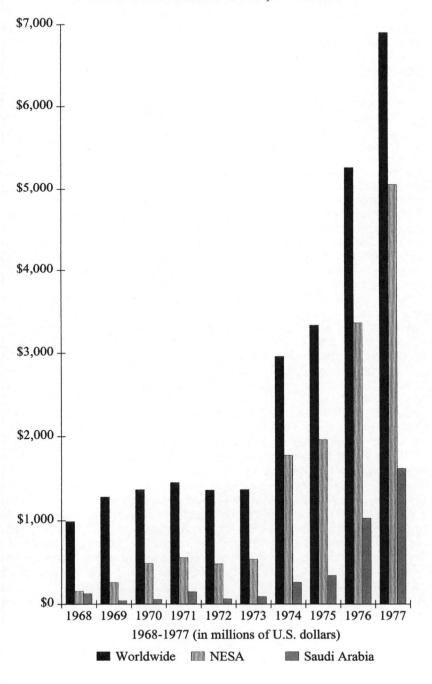

1968-1977 (in millions of U.S. dollars)

■ Worldwide   ▦ NESA   ▨ Saudi Arabia

facilitate this training 1,000 ex-serviceman were sent as advisors.[74] The scope of this project was expanded in 1976 to include the creation of the National Guard Academy and additional training to place the guard on an equal footing with the army.[75]

The Construction of the Saudi Navy

In addition to their ground forces the Saudis were also very eager to develop credible naval and air forces. A big step toward the development of the Saudi Navy occurred in 1972 when America and Saudi Arabia agreed on a modernization plan called the Saudi Naval Expansion Plan (SNEP) had its origins in 1968 when the Saudis asked the United States to submit a study on the feasibility and force requirements of naval expansion. The team ultimately recommended the construction of bases at Jubail and Jidda, a headquarters facility at Riyadh, a modest force consisting of 12 vessels, and that maintenance and repair performed by contract personnel. The Saudis wanted a more ambitious program and proposed a 25-ship force; eventually a force of 19 was agreed upon. The program of constructing a Saudi navy under the SNEP program was to be placed under the United States Military Training Mission (USMTM), with the supervision of the base construction under the authority of the U.S. Army Corp of Engineers.[76]

The purpose of this plan was to expand the Saudi navy from a largely coastal force, equipped with mainly patrol and torpedo boats along with hovercraft, to a force that could have a blue-water capacity. This modernization plan called for the Saudis to procure four 700-ton guided missile patrol boats, nine 300-ton guided missile patrol boats, four MSC-322 coastal minecraft, and other smaller craft. In addition, the Saudis were to purchase Harpoon surface-to-surface missiles, 76 mm rapid-fire guns, MK-46 torpedoes MK-92 fire-control systems, and AN/SPS surface search radar. The United States also agreed to assist the Saudis in constructing and designing their naval facilities, as well as providing both American naval personnel and civilians under contract to train and advise the Saudi navy.[77]

These American advisors were primarily based at the important Saudi naval installations of Jiddah, Jubail, and the main training base at Dammam. There have been some significant problems with the naval advisory missions. First was the lack of training of some of the advisors. Second, the United States Navy was not accustomed to operating the heavily armed, highly technical, smaller vessels that the Saudis acquired.[78] The Saudi navy also had problems in absorbing the equipment it purchased and had to depend a great deal on air support, as well as over-the-horizon support from Western naval forces. Eventually the Saudis hoped to be able to deploy naval forces on both coasts with major bases at Jiddah on the Red Sea, and Al Qatif and Jubail on the Gulf. In addition, the Saudis are planning on having bases at Ras Tanura, Dammam, Yanbu, and Ras al Mishap.[79]

The Role of the U.S. Army Corps of Engineers

Given the Saudi goal of building up the nation's infrastructure as a way of developing militarily, the role of the U.S. Army Corps of Engineers (COE) has been indispensable. A large part of the reason why the COE was so important in American-Saudi relations was due to the high regard it was held in by King Faisal. Most of the COE activity in the kingdom was negotiated by the Agreement for the Construction of Military Facilities, which was concluded on May 24, 1965. The Corps of Engineers was charged with planning and supervising the construction of Saudi military facilities. Among the major projects the COE worked on were the construction of three major military cities: Khamis Mushayt, which was completed in 1971 at a cost of $81.4 million; Tabuk on the Jordanian border, completed in 1973 at a cost of $81 million; and King Khalid military city near the Iraqi border, which was estimated to cost more than $7.8 billion. Construction projects were so extensive that a new port on the Gulf, Ras Al Mish'ab, had to be constructed to accommodate the needs of the COE. Other Corps of Engineers projects included the headquarters of the Ministry of Defense and Aviation, the Royal Saudi Air Force, and King Abd al-Aziz Military Academy. In addition, the Corps of Engineers was assigned broad responsibilities in developing the infrastructure to accommodate the development of the Saudi military detailed earlier.[80]

The value of military construction in the American military relationship with Saudi Arabia was significant. By 1977 military construction in Saudi Arabia accounted for 60 percent of the value of military sales orders from the United States. This is illustrated in tables and graphs 6.3 and 6.4. This construction was managed by the U.S. Army Corps of Engineers. This was viewed by American policy makers as a way of advancing not only American political influence in the kingdom but also the commercial interests of American contractors and businessmen. This view was articulated in a U.S. government report which stated:

> Construction accounts for over 60 percent of the value of U.S. military sales orders to Saudi Arabia and is managed by the U.S. Army Corps of Engineers. Indications are that the Corps role will expand and continue for several years. Such involvement can increase U.S. influence in Saudi Arabia and provide increased opportunities to U.S. contractors and businessman.[81]

Saudi Arabia and Iran both invested heavily in American arms during this period, but the Saudis were willing to spend more on construction, infrastructure, and services than the Iranians were. During the 1970s the Iranians tended to invest 70 percent of their military purchases from America in equipment and munitions. The Saudis, on the other hand, were the opposite as 70 percent of their military purchases were directed to creating and further developing their military infrastructure.[82] Thus when they did receive new military equipment the Saudis were in a better position to make more efficient use of it. However, in the short-term they continued

Table 6.3. U.S. Military Construction Sales Agreements to Saudi Arabia, 1973-1982 (in thousands of U.S. dollars)

Year	Worldwide	Near East and South Asia (NESA)	Saudi Arabia
1950-1972	606,128	605,293	603,949
1973	1,033,885	1,027,000	1,027,000
1974	562,782	562,782	562,204
1975	4,679,691	4,679,691	4,679,676
1976	5,454,677	5,454,677	5,453,707
1977	677,922	647,672	647,672
1978	667,869	667,869	667,400
1979	1,024,211	1,023,584	1,021,000
1980	1,551,801	1,551,800	1,551,800
1981	879,596	879,596	877,400
1982	1,870,331	1,865,699	1,845,699
1950-1982	18,978,893	18,965,663	18,937,506

Source: U.S. Department of Defense. *Foreign Military Sales, Foreign Military Construction Sales, and Military Assistance Facts* (Washington, D.C.: U.S. Government Printing Office, September 1982), 13-14.

Graph 6.3. U.S. Military Construction Agreements to Saudi Arabia, 1973-1982

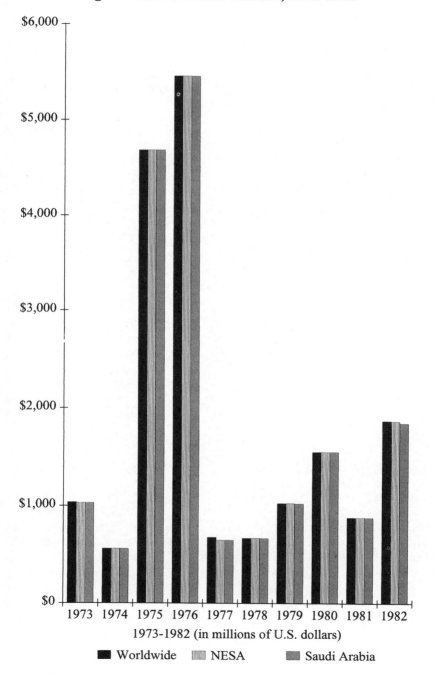

1973-1982 (in millions of U.S. dollars)

■ Worldwide   ▥ NESA   ▨ Saudi Arabia

**Table 6.4. U.S. Military Construction Deliveries to
Saudi Arabia, 1973-1982 (in thousands of U.S. dollars)**

Year	Worldwide	Near East and South Asia (NESA)	Saudi Arabia
1950-1972	259,965	259,130	257,786
1973	146,900	146,900	146,900
1974	120,283	120,283	120,283
1975	139,838	139,168	138,859
1976	471,635	465,727	465,465
1977	483,919	483,893	483,892
1978	1,239,901	1,239,493	1,239,471
1979	1,518,557	1,518,502	1,515,508
1980	1,459,015	1,458,592	1,458,534
1981	1,570,921	1,570,783	1,570,783
1982	1,947,953	1,947,857	1,946,887
1950-1982	9,358,886	9,350,327	9,344,367

Source: U.S. Department of Defense. *Foreign Military Sales, Foreign Military Construction Sales, and Military Assistance Facts* (Washington, D.C.: U.S. Government Printing Office, 1982), 15-16.

Graph 6.4. U.S. Military Construction Deliveries to Saudi Arabia, 1973-1982

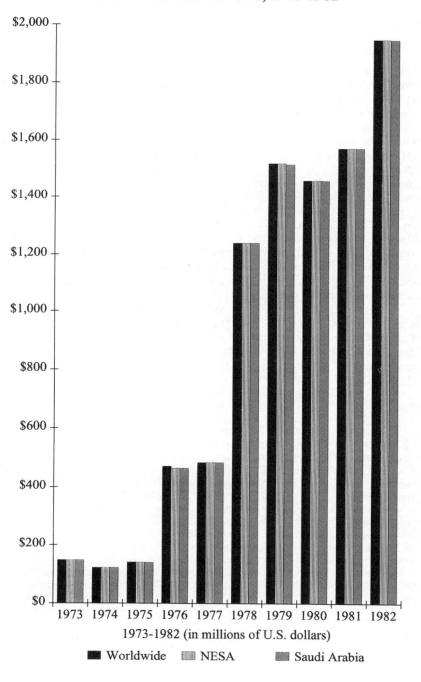

1973-1982 (in millions of U.S. dollars)

■ Worldwide   ▥ NESA   ▨ Saudi Arabia

to lag behind the Iranians in overall military strength.

Conclusion

The formation of the American-Saudi alliance had its origins in maintaining Western access to oil. After World War II, Saudi oil became significant for both economic and strategic reasons, as its market share rapidly expanded. This became significant as Saudi Arabia provided a large percentage of the oil that was essential to rebuild industry in Europe. In the early postwar period, Western Europe was considered essential for American economic, political, and strategic interests. Economically it was important to revitalize Western Europe in order to create a market conducive for American exports. Politically and strategically it was important to rebuild Western Europe in order to build up these areas to resist the spread of Soviet influence.

However, in the calculations of American decision makers, Saudi Arabia became important for other factors. They were generally supportive of American foreign policy initiatives and the Saudi monarchy provided a counterweight to radical forces in the region by aiding other pro-Western governments. The United States looked to Saudi Arabia to provide political leadership in the Arab world and to use the monarchy's religious legitimacy as a means of gaining support for American policy in the region.

Militarily, Saudi Arabia was weak, but under American auspices, was beginning to embark on a program to upgrade its armed forces. Although their power projection capabilities were severely limited, the kingdom's emphasis on building up military infrastructure could have served to accommodate Western military forces should the need have arisen.

Notes

1. Bahgat Korany, "Defending the Faith Amid Change: The Foreign Policy of Saudi Arabia," in *The Foreign Politics of Arab States*, eds. Bahgat Korany and Ali E. Hillal Dessouki (Boulder, Colo.: Westview Press, 1991), 316. Also see James P. Piscatori, "Ideological Politics in Saudi Arabia," *Islam in the Political Process*, ed. James P. Piscatori (New York: Cambridge University Press, 1983), 56-58.

2. Anthony Cordesman, *The Gulf and the Search for Strategic Stability* (Boulder, Colo.: Westview Press, 1984), 92. See also R. Hrair Dekmejian, *Islam in Revolution* (Syracuse, N.Y.: Syracuse University Press, 1985), 137-39.

3. Bruce Kuniholm, *The Origins of the Cold War in the Near East* (Princeton, New Jersey.: Princeton University Press, 1980), 179-80. Also Irvine H. Anderson, "Lend-Lease for Saudi Arabia: A Comment on Alternative Conceptualizations," *Diplomatic History* 3, no. 4 (Fall 1979): 414. Note that the partnership of the California and Texas Oil Companies was referred to as Caltex for the marketing of oil in Asia and Africa. In 1944 the name of this company was changed to the Arabian American Oil Company (ARAMCO).

4. Aaron David Miller, *Search for Security* (Chapel Hill, N.C.: University of North Carolina Press, 1980), 122.

5. Malcom C. Peck, "Saudi Arabia in United States Foreign Policy to 1958: A Study in the Sources and Determinants of American Policy," (Unpublished Ph.D. dissertation, Fletcher School of Law and Diplomacy, Tufts University, April 1970), 210-11.

6. Cordesman, *The Gulf and the Search*, 93-95.

7. Cordesman, *The Gulf and the Search*, 93.

8. Michael B. Stoff, *Oil, War, and American Security* (New Haven, Conn.: Yale University Press, 1980), 56-57. Also see Fred Halliday, "A Curious and Close Liaison: Saudi Arabia's Relations with the United States," *State, Society, and Economy in Saudi Arabia*, Tim Niblock ed. (New York: St. Martin's Press, 1982), 125. Discusses pressure from the oil companies on the Roosevelt administration, culminating with President Roosevelt's declaration that the defense of Saudi Arabia was in American national interests. See also David S. Painter, *Oil and the American Century: The Political Economy of U.S. Foreign Oil Policy, 1941-1954* (Baltimore, Md.: Johns Hopkins University Press, 1986), 37.

9. Kuniholm, *The Origins of the Cold War*, 181-82. State Department officials also expressed concern about the potential expansion of British influence at the expense of the United States. Miller, *Search for Security*, 206-7.

10. Painter, *Oil and the American Century*, 42-43.

11. Painter, *Oil and the American Century*, 52.

12. Painter, *Oil and the American Century*, 54-56.

13. Peck, "Saudi Arabia in United States," 60.

14. Miller, *Search for Security*, 203, 208. Initially, oil supplies to Europe came from the Caribbean. This was eventually replaced by Middle East oil, which ultimately supplied 80 percent of the oil required for the European Recovery Program by 1951. The availability of Saudi oil held further significance as it would enable the United States to conserve its own domestic supplies as well as Western Hemisphere oil in general. This was important as America became a net oil importer in 1948. See Peck, "Saudi Arabia in United States," 216-17.

15. Stoff, *Oil, War*, 195-96. As a result, Jersey Standard and Socony-Vacuum, whose operations were primarily based in the Western Hemisphere and who needed access to oil reserves to sustain their markets, joined ARAMCO in 1946.

16. Halliday, "A Curious and Close Liaison," 131.

17. Fred Halliday, *Arabia without Sultans* (New York: Vintage Books, 1975), 63.

18. J.C. Hurewitz, *Middle East Politics: The Military Dimension* (Boulder, Colo.: Westview Press, 1982), 248.

19. Halliday, *Arabia without Sultans*, 63.

20. Miller, *Search for Security*, 205-6.

21. U.S. Department of State, *Foreign Relations of the United States* (Washington, D.C.: U.S. Government Printing Office, 1944) 5: 757-58; (1945) 8: 847. Cited in Painter, *Oil and the American Century*, 88.

22. Painter, *Oil and the American Century*, 88-89.

23. For a discussion of the decline of Britain in the region and the implications for the United States see Leon T. Hader, *Quagmire: America in the Middle East* (Washington, D.C.: Cato Institute, 1992), 44.

24. Peck, "Saudi Arabia in United States," 80. Both Japan and Germany had approached Ibn Saud about acquiring concessions in the country during the 1930s on terms more favorable than that agreed to with CASOC, but were rejected by Ibn Saud. The Saudis did receive some arms from Italy in the late 1930s, and did receive a shipment of 4,000 rifles from Germany in 1939. See Cordesman, *The Gulf and the Search*, 93-95.

25. Miller, *Search for Security*, 201.

26. David Long, *The United States and Saudi Arabia: Ambivalent Allies* (Boulder, Colo.: Westview Press, 1985), 34.

27. Stephen J. Randall, *United States Foreign Oil Policy: 1919-1948* (Montreal: McGill-Queen's University Press, 1985), 259-60; See also Miller, *Search for Security*, 203.

28. Benson Lee Grayson, *Saudi-American Relations* (Washington, D.C.: University Press of America, 1982), 77.

Malcom Peck argues that from 1945 to 1951 the use of Dhahran was an outgrowth of World War II. However, with the growth of American containment policy and the impact of the Korean War, American policy makers came to view Dhahran as essential to American security with the justification that it was a significant turnaround for American bombers in the event of conflict with the Soviet Union. See Peck, "Saudi Arabia in United States," 227.

29. Michael Collins Dunn, "Soviet Interests in the Arabian Peninsula: The Aden Pact and Other Paper Tigers," *American-Arab Affairs*, no. 8 (Spring, 1984): 97, 104-5; Also see Deborah J. Gerner, "Consistencies and Contradictions: U.S. Foreign Policy toward Saudi Arabia and the Arab States of the Gulf, 1945-1973," Paper presented at the annual meeting of the American Political Science Association, Washington, D.C. (September 1-4, 1988), 7.

Long gives the figures as: 116 tanks (of which the U.S. would sell immediately 18 M-47s and 18 M-41s), 10 propeller training aircraft, 8 T-33 aircraft, 12 F-86 aircraft, and 2 naval vessels. These arms transfers and grants were part of the 1957 extension agreement for American access to Dhahran. See Long, *The United States and Saudi Arabia*, 39.

30. U.S. Department of State, *Walter B. Smith Undersecretary to Harold E. Stassen Director for Mutual Security*, Letter, DeClassified Documents, no. 000788, (Washington, D.C: Carrolton Press, 1990), 1.

31. Long, *The United States and Saudi Arabia*, 39.

32. Long, *The United States and Saudi Arabia*, 39-40. He also discusses the attempt by King Saud, in an effort to reap political capital, to preempt the American announcement that it was giving up the base, and how the United States made the announcement unilaterally in an effort to beat the Saudis to the punch.

33. Deborah J. Gerner, "Consistencies and Contradictions," 7.

34. Cordesman, *The Gulf and the Search*, 102-3. Provides a detailed discussion of Saudi aims and goals.

35. David Holden and Richard Johns, *The House of Saud: The Rise and Rule of the Most Powerful Dynasty in the Arab World* (New York: Holt, Rinehart, and Winston, 1981), 190.

36. Mordechai Abir, *Saudi Arabia in the Oil Era* (Boulder, Colo.: Westview Press, 1988), 80. He cites a source that states that not only did the crowd cheer President Nasser when he arrived in Dhahran, but also that stones were thrown in the direction of the royal party and banners were displayed denouncing the royal family. *Al-Dustur*, 4 February 1979, 4. Cited in Abir, 80.

37. Abir, *Saudi Arabia in the Oil*, 80-81. Also see Holden and Johns, *The House of Saud*, 190-92. Discusses American opposition to Nasser and U.S. encouragement to Saud to go against him. There were charges that Nasser was implicated in a plot to assassinate Saud. See Nadav Safran, *Saudi Arabia: The Ceaseless Quest for Security* (Ithaca, N.Y.: Cornell University Press, 1988), 83-84.

38. William R. Polk, *The Arab World* (Cambridge, Mass.: Harvard University Press, 1980), 331. Also see Long, *The United States and Saudi Arabia*, 111.

39. L. Carl Brown, *International Politics and the Middle East* (Princeton, N.J.: Princeton University Press, 1984), 179.

40. U.S. Senate Committee on Foreign Relations and the Committee on Armed Services, *The President's Proposal on the Middle East (Eisenhower Doctrine), Hearings* on S. J. Res. and H. J. Res. 117, pt. 2. 84th Cong., 1st sess., 1957, 665. Quoted in Long, *The United States and Saudi Arabia,*112. Policy makers argued that Saud would be an important counterweight to Nasser. See Colonel A. J. Goodpaster 1956, "Memorandum of Conference with the President." November 21, Declassified Documents, 1987. Cited in Gerner, "Consistencies and Contradictions," 8.

41. Long, *The United States and Saudi Arabia,* 112-13.

42. For a good, concise discussion of these conditions see Saeed M. Badeeb, *The Saudi-Egyptian Conflict over North Yemen, 1962-1970* (Boulder, Colo.: Westview Press, 1986).

43. For a detailed account of the events leading up to the coup and the various intrigues, as well as the primary role the Egyptians had in setting in motion these events See Dana Adams Schmidt, *Yemen: The Unknown War* (New York: Holt, Rinehart, and Winston, 1968). Also see Edgar O'Ballance, *The War in the Yemen* (Hamden, Conn.: Archon Books, 1971). For a chronology of Egyptian opposition to the Imamate see Badeeb, *The Saudi-Egyptian Conflict,* 34-35.

44. F. Gregory Gause III, *Saudi-Yemeni Relations: Domestic Structures and Foreign Influence* (New York: Columbia University Press, 1990), 59.

45. Gause, *Saudi-Yemeni Relations,* 59-60. Also see Robin Bidwell, *The Two Yemens* (Boulder, Colo.: Westview Press, 1983), 198.

46. Badeeb, *The Saudi-Egyptian Conflict,* 54.

47. Badeeb, *The Saudi-Egyptian Conflict,* 56.

48. Badeeb, *The Saudi-Egyptian Conflict,* 56-57.

49. Badeeb, *The Saudi-Egyptian Conflict,* 68.

50. William B. Quandt, *Saudi Arabia in the 1980's: Foreign Policy, Security, and Oil* (Washington, D.C.: The Brookings Institution, 1981), 49. The Saudis felt that this recognition without requiring the Egyptian forces to withdraw sent the signal that Nasser could intervene wherever he wanted in the Arab world. See Badeeb, *The Saudi-Egyptian Conflict,* 62; See also Gause, *Saudi-Yemeni Relations,* 60.

51. Thomas L. McNaugher, "Arms and Allies on the Arabian Peninsula," *Orbis* 28, no. 3 (Fall 1984): 518. Gause points out, however, that this demonstration of American support was confined to flying over the major cities of Saudi Arabia and not near the border with Yemen. Gause, *Saudi-Yemeni Relations,* 60. However, this by itself was significant as Halliday points out defections from the Saudi Air Force forced it to be grounded. Halliday, *Arabia without Sultans,* 79.

52. Michael Collins Dunn, "Soviet Interests in the Arabian Peninsula," 13.

53. Gause, *Saudi-Yemeni Relations,* 61. Among the reforms Faisal instituted was an abolishing of slavery, the setting up of a Judicial Council, and extensive economic reforms in order to put the kingdom's finances in order, which had been mismanaged under Saud. In addition he promised to establish a constitution, which he ultimately never did. With regard to Yemen, Faisal did not establish a royalist air force, which would have had to have been based in Saudi territory, as well as not supplying the royalists with many heavy armaments. Further, he promised the Arab League that Saudi forces would not cross the border. See also O'Ballance, *The War in the Yemen,* 108-9; and Safran, *Saudi Arabia: The Ceaseless,* 97-98.

54. Abir, *Saudi Arabia in the Oil,* 66-68.

55. Abir, *Saudi Arabia in the Oil*, 82-84.

56. Abir, *Saudi Arabia in the Oil*, 97-98.

57. Quandt, *Saudi Arabia in the 1980s*, 77-78.

58. Abir, *Saudi Arabia in the Oil*, 113.

59. Abir, *Saudi Arabia in the Oil*, 114-18. Provides a concise, comprehensive discussion of the opposition movements and Faisal's response.

60. Quandt, *Saudi Arabia in the 1980s*, 86-87.

61. Quandt, *Saudi Arabia in the 1980s*, 88.

62. Cordesman, *The Gulf and the Search*, 127-28.

63. Cordesman, *The Gulf and the Search*, 132-33.

64. Long, *The United States and Saudi Arabia*, 45; See also Safran, *Saudi Arabia: The Ceaseless*, 119.

65. Long, *The United States and Saudi Arabia*, 45. Also see Anthony Sampson, *The Arms Bazaar: From Lebanon to Lockheed* (N.Y.: Viking Press, 1977), 174-81. Also see U.S. House Committee on International Relations, Subcommittee on Investigations, *The Persian Gulf, 1975: The Continuing Debate on Arms Sales. Hearings* before the Special Subcommittee on Investigations, Committee on International Relations, House of Representatives, 94th Cong., 1st sess., 1976. The aftermath of this three-way arrangement was that the British faced other budgetary problems and as a result never purchased the F-111. See Sampson, *The Arms Bazaar,*164.

66. Holden and Johns, *The House of Saud*, 360. Also Long, *The United States and Saudi Arabia*, 46.

67. Long, *The United States and Saudi Arabia*, 46.

68. Safran, *Saudi Arabia: The Ceaseless Quest*, 119.

69. Long, *The United States and Saudi Arabia*, 48.

70. Halliday, *Arabia without Sultans,* 137.

71. Cordesman, *The Gulf and the Search*, 170.

72. Quandt, *Saudi Arabia in the 1980s*, 52.

73. Cordesman, *The Gulf and the Search*, 178.

74. Holden and Johns, *The House of Saud*, 360. It was thought that this arrangement facilitated a greater CIA presence in the kingdom.

75. Cordesman, *The Gulf and the Search*, 179. See also U.S. Senate, Committee on Foreign Relations Committee, *"U.S. Arms Sales Policy."* 94th Cong., 2nd sess., 1976, 54-75. The price tag for the Vulcan antiaircraft guns was $12.4 million, the National Guard Headquarters cost $158 million. Also these sources indicate that 200 Vinnell advisers were assigned to the country.

Long, *The United States and Saudi Arabia* identifies two instances in the 1960s when the National Guard proved significant. The first occurred in 1964 when Faisal replaced Saud as king, the guard faced down Saud's supporters. The second incident took place in 1967 when the guard was called out to quell riots in the Eastern Province in the aftermath of the Arab-Israeli war, whose targets were various American facilities, such as an ARAMCO compound, the American Consulate, and USMTM center at Dhahran. See Long, *The United States and Saudi Arabia*, 52-53.

76. Long, *The United States and Saudi Arabia*, 51.

77. Cordesman, *The Gulf and the Search*, 174-75.

78. Anthony H. Cordesman, *Western Strategic Interests in Saudi Arabia* (London: Croom Helm, 1987), 138.

79. Cordesman, *Western Strategic Interests*, 157.

80. For a concise, comprehensive account of the COE in Saudi Arabia see Cordesman, *The Gulf and the Search*, 128-32. Also Long, *The United States and Saudi Arabia*, 48-50.

81. U.S. General Accounting Office, *Perspectives on Military Sales to Saudi Arabia*, (Washington, D.C.: U.S. Government Printing Office, 1977), 11.

82. Cordesman, *The Gulf and The Search*, 159-62.

Chapter 7

The Strategic Implications of the American-Saudi Alliance

The Nixon Doctrine and the Implications for Saudi Arabia

Up until the late 1960s America had been comforted by the fact that there was a substantial British presence in the Gulf to insure the status quo. In 1968 the British government decided to withdraw its military forces from the Gulf by the end of 1971 and all the states that were under its control would be granted their full independence. This was viewed by America as a serious threat to the stability of the region as the traditional dominant Western power would no longer be present. American policy makers viewed this as a disruption of the status quo and the possible destabilization of the pro-Western regimes in the Gulf. In order to compensate for this the Nixon Doctrine was announced on Guam in November of 1969.

This doctrine stated that the United States would honor its treaty obligations and provide economic and military assistance to friendly nations who would provide the armed forces necessary to preserve the status quo in the region from the threat of outside powers, the Soviet Union, and more importantly from internal revolution within these individual states. Thus America would assist these nations to preserve the status quo that would correlate with its foreign policy goals. The Nixon Doctrine was a "twin pillar policy," as America counted on Iran and Saudi Arabia to provide regional security. Iran was looked upon as the main military pillar, since it possessed the armed forces and population to enable itself to be a credible military power in the region. Saudi Arabia, although it received substantial amounts of military equipment, was looked upon as more of a stabilizing influence due to its financial resources and influence it held in the Arab and Islamic worlds.[1]

Several factors in the American-Saudi relationship became significant in the late 1970s and early 1980s: (1) domestic pressures in Saudi Arabia for a more restricted policy on oil production may complicate economic relations; (2) Saudi concern over the Palestinian issue and East Jerusalem will complicate relations; (3) a greater sensitivity for the Saudi position in the region; (4) the likelihood that the Al Saud family will remain in power for the foreseeable future, but no guarantee that the family will remain in power indefinitely; (5) executive divisions within the Saud family will result in the reassessment of United States-Saudi relations whenever a succession occurs; (6) other American policy goals complicate American-Saudi relations; (7) the Saudis perceive the military relationship with the United States to be the principal test of America's political commitment to the Kingdom.[2]

The Buildup of the Saudi Armed Forces, Implications for the United States

The Development of the Saudi Air Force in the 1970s: The F-5 Sale

The close military ties between the United States and Saudi Arabia during the 1970s was characterized by an emphasis on building up the Saudi air force as a means of deterring a hostile power from attacking the country, as well as defending the oil fields. Politically this was also of note as the royal family had always been wary of building up significant ground forces for fear of possible coup attempts. Economically, as a result of the oil shocks of the 1970s, Saudi Arabia had the resources to purchase the most up-to-date weapons systems from the United States. It was during the 1970s that the Saudis embarked, with American arms sales and planning, on a very ambitious plan to build up their air force.

In May of 1971 the Saudis made a formal request to purchase 20 F-5As along with equipment, spare parts, and training for Saudi pilots. The F-5 had been designated an export fighter for sale to friendly third world nations as an inexpensive but quality fighter jet.[3] The Saudis followed by purchasing 20 F-5E Tiger fighters. This gave the Saudis greater access to American military and contractor support, as they were able to use training facilities in the United States while increasing the number of American military and civilian support personnel in Saudi Arabia.[4]

Joint American-Saudi Air Force Planning: The Significance of The Peace Hawk Program

In 1974-1975 American-Saudi cooperation increased with the

development of a series of analyses by the United States and Saudi Arabia. Called the Peace Hawk studies, they examined the air threat to Saudi Arabia and how this could be defended against, as well as Saudi defense modernization needs. The purpose of the studies was to create a comprehensive plan for Saudi military modernization.[5]

The Peace Hawk VII study produced a four-volume examination of Saudi defense requirements for improved ground-based command control and communications facilities. The study recommended a comprehensive network of bases and an integration of Saudi Air defenses, linking bases, ground-based defenses, and fighters similar to NATO's Air Defense Ground Environment System (NADGE), and the North American Air Defense (NORAD) in the United States.[6] Several American defense contractors derived great benefits from the relationship between the United States and Saudi Arabia as Northrop became the main subcontractor to the Saudi Arabian air force modernization program in 1976. As a result, American advisors in Saudi Arabia working for Northrop increased from 450 in 1975 to 1,800 by 1980. The American military also provided training facilities for Saudi air force personnel in the United States such as at Lackland Air Force Base in Texas.[7]

The Regional Implications Leading to the Arms Sales of 1978-1981

The period from 1978-1981 was a pivotal period of American-Saudi relations for a variety of reasons. The end of detente with the Soviet Union, the revolution that overthrew the Shah of Iran, as well as the continuing strategic and economic importance of oil led to closer relations between America and Saudi Arabia and mended the tensions caused earlier in the decade by the oil embargo. There were a number of smaller crises in the region that fostered greater American-Saudi cooperation. These included the civil war in the People's Democratic Republic of Yemen (PDRY), the border conflict between the PDRY and the Yemen Arab Republic (YAR), the Soviet invasion of Afghanistan, as well as the Iran-Iraq War. The Saudi goal regarding Yemen was to prevent the unification between North and South, as well as to destabilize the Marxist republic of South Yemen since it was viewed as a source of instability in the region. The Iran-Iraq War posed other problems for Saudi Arabia. The possible strategic benefit was that it tied down both countries who were aspiring for regional hegemony in a brutal conflict that drained their resources. However, it posed a threat since not only could the war spill over into the Gulf, but the side that emerged victorious could also be emboldened to try to make further gains. The end result of the conflict would seem to confirm this, as Iraq was able to gain the upper hand, with American support, at the end of the conflict. As a result, this contributed to the regional climate where Baghdad felt strong enough to initiate a new round of hostility against Kuwait.

There was also controversy within the relationship as a result of the

Saudi role in OPEC, their refusal to support the Camp David Accords, and accusations by Israeli supporters that the Saudis were a front line confrontational state. The latter criticism occurred when the Saudis wished to purchase sophisticated armaments during this period. While the growth of the military relationship during these years seemed to symbolize this alliance, it also increased tensions between the two countries. The importance of these arms transfers overshadowed all other facets of interaction between the two countries and Saudi-American relations were defined by two arms sales concluded in this period: the sale of the F-15 in 1978 and the Air Defense Enhancement package in 1981.[8]

The Significance of the 1978 F-15 Sale

Reasons Why the F-15 Was Selected

The sale of the F-15 was part of a package that included sales to Egypt and Israel, put together to make it more politically acceptable. The rest of the package included the sale of 50 F-Es, although Egypt had requested 120. Israel received 35 F-15s, and 75 F-16s, 20 more F-15s than had been requested. In large part this was to placate congressional support and compensate for the sale of the F-15s to Saudi Arabia.

A second reason for purchasing a new generation of fighter aircraft was based on the joint Peace Hawk threat assessment study, which recommended that a new system be procured by the early 1980s to replace the Lightnings previously purchased from Britain. For the Saudis the sale of the F-15 became a "litmus test" of their relationship with the United States, as well as the American commitment to the security of the Gulf. A team from Saudi Arabia studied the F-14, F-15, F-16, and F-18 and they eventually selected the F-15 for purchase. The advantages of this plane were that it was a twin-engine craft, was less technical than the F-14, and also had a greater ability for upgrading than the F-16.[9]

Other technical advantages of the F-15 were that it had an advanced radar that could provide long-range detection, as well as an effective fire-control system. The radar system had an excellent look-up and look-down radar system, and a shoot-down potential that would be ideal for defending the oil fields. The mission turnaround time for the F-15 was 12 minutes, offering the Saudis the opportunity to establish high sortie rates to compensate for lesser numbers of aircraft.[10] In addition, the F-15 could fly at an altitude and velocity that could match the Soviet MiG 23 and 25.[11]

For the United States the potential sale of the F-15 also carried certain benefits. First, the sale of the F-15 would lower the unit costs per plane, which would result in a savings for the U.S. Air Force. Second, and more politically significant, the F-15 was an air superiority fighter (defensive fighter). Therefore it was felt that it would not pose a threat to Israel, as opposed to the F-16, which is primarily an attack plane. While this sale was agreed to by the Ford administration, no action was to be taken until after the 1976 election. The Carter administration in confirming this sale promised that the F-15s would lack critical attack capabilities. These included certain avionics as well as providing that there would be no linkages to an early warning radar system, no long-range fuel pods or bomb racks, as well as fewer hard spots on the airframe to limit the capacity for offensive operations. In addition, the Saudis promised that the planes would not be based at Tabuk, in the northwestern part of the country, which was the Saudi air base closest to Israel.[12]

The F-15 As a Litmus Test

The Saudi leadership attached a high political importance to this sale. The monarchy felt that they had been a moderating influence in the region against political radicals, as well as those nations who advocated for steep oil price increases within OPEC. The sale of this aircraft also raised important alliance questions, as Saudi Arabia viewed it as illustrating that the United States considered it a worthy ally.[13]

This latter point was complicated by the fact that during the 1970s the United States had proceeded to sell every nonnuclear military system to Iran that the Shah requested. If the United States denied this sale, the Saudis would view it as the United States favoring one Persian Gulf ally over another.[14]

Secretary of Defense Brown, in hearings before Congress, emphasized the importance of the sale politically. He stated, "I do not recommend this sale solely on military ground, however although the military need is clear. I recommend it also because I know it is important to American-Saudi relations and the American position in the Middle East."[15]

The American sale of the F-15 to Saudi Arabia illustrated the desirability on the part of top American policy makers to sell sophisticated armaments to Saudi Arabia. Secretary of State Kissinger argued that this sale was desirable, over the objections of some within the bureaucracy who felt that the aircraft was too sophisticated for Saudi defense needs, in order to create an interdependent relationship that the United States could exploit to increase its leverage.[16]

These ideas were further articulated in a U.S. General Accounting Office report on the proposed sale of the F-15 that stated that

> the sale of 60 F-15s to Saudi Arabia is fully consistent with U.S. national interests. This sale should not have a significant impact on the Middle East arms balance or pose a threat to Israel but rather it would act as a stabilizing influence by providing the Government of Saudi Arabia an improved means of defending their natural resources and geographical boundaries while allowing the U.S. a measure of control over the use of this means.[17]

In congressional testimony concerning the F-15, Secretary of Defense

Brown stated that Saudi Arabia required air defense aircraft. He further stated that if the United States does not sell the aircraft to Saudi Arabia, the Saudis will turn to other countries such as France for similar systems. Secretary Brown noted that the French F-1 Mirage fighter had a superior air-to-ground capability than the F-15, which would allow the Saudis to conduct offensive operations that would be more of a threat to Israel:

> If the U.S. refuses to sell F-15 to Saudi Arabia it has the funds and the ability to buy aircraft from others. My own judgment is that the Saudis would have no lack of prospective vendors. In particular the French have now an aircraft the Mirage F-1 which although not as advanced as the F-15 does have substantial air defense capability. Moreover it has substantial air to ground capability which the F-15 does not.[18]

Military Threats to Saudi Arabia

The sale was also supported by policy makers as necessary to counterbalance military threats to Saudi Arabia. In justifying the transaction Secretary Brown discussed the threats to Saudi Arabia in the region, specifically noting the supplying of Soviet arms to allies such as Iraq, the People's Democratic Republic of Yemen, and Ethiopia. He stated that Iraq possessed over 400 aircraft. The PDRY had over 100 Soviet supplied aircraft in its inventory, as well as giving the Soviets access to harbor and air facilities in the PDRY. In addition, the Soviets were in the process of sending $1 billion in military aid to Ethiopia.[19]

The F-15 was justified for a variety of reasons, all of which are similar over different administrations in the United States. In testimony before Congress, Secretary of Defense Harold Brown articulated the threats posed to Saudi Arabia by radical regimes in the region backed by the Soviet Union. He pointed out that Iraq possessed an air force of over 400 planes and the PDRY had almost 100 planes in its inventory. He emphasized the Soviet supply link with Ethiopia, as well as the direct Soviet presence in close proximity to Saudi Arabia in Aden and naval operations in the Red and Arabian Seas.[20]

The Saudis placed a great deal of symbolic value on the sale of the F-15. In addition to the enhancement of the capabilities of the Saudi air force, the sale was also being considered at a time when it seemed anti-Western forces were making gains throughout the region and the Saudis were perceived as vulnerable. Two weeks before the Senate vote, the president of Afghanistan, Muhammad Daoud, was overthrown by a military coup which placed into power Nur Muhammad Taraki and set Afghanistan on a Marxist political orientation. In addition, in the Horn of Africa the Ethiopians, who had realigned themselves with the Soviets and benefitted from the presence of Cuban troops, were in the process of routing the Somalis and Eriterans in June. Finally, in the PDRY the pro-Saudi president, Rubai Ali, was overthrown and executed in an internal coup within the Yemen Socialist Party (YSP) which lead to the growth in influence of the pro-Soviet Abdul (Fattah) Ismail.[21]

The Saudis sought to play up the threats to their own regime as well as the threats to Western interests in the region as a whole. King Khalid wrote a letter stating that the Saudis needed the F-15 in order to combat communist expansion in the region. The Saudi foreign minister also at this time criticized the Carter administration for not being more aggressive in combating the Cubans in Africa.[22]

The Saudis sought to emphasize the regional threats facing their regime. The reason that the Saudis valued the arms was not simply for the technology itself, which could have been obtained from other suppliers, but the implicit guarantee that came along with these weapons. Their view of the F-15 sale, and American arms sales in general, was the translation of American support for the regime. On the surface it would seem that this factor would give the U.S. leverage over the Saudis both from a practical as well as a psychological dimension. The practical issue is that the United States could threaten to withdraw military assistance, like spare parts, and training that would then make these armaments virtually useless. From the psychological end, the fear of abandonment by its ally could have enhanced American leverage over the Saudis. However, the opposite was the case. American policy makers felt that by not selling the Saudis arms it would seem that the United States was abandoning them, and this could affect the American relationship with other states as well.

Importance of the F-15 to the United States

Some significant political factors for the United States concerning the sale of F-15 was the necessity of American advisors to maintain the system, particularly in the initial stages of procurement. In addition there were concerns regarding the security of the system. These questions were raised in a Senate report commissioned to study the sale of the F-15:

> The report questions whether Saudi Arabia with 100 trained fighter pilots and a limited ground personnel, could cope with the F-15. It says 'well over 300 American technicians will be needed to help absorb the aircraft.' It also expresses concern 'that either the aircraft itself or its manuals would be stolen and transferred to unfriendly countries.' The authors of the study Hano-Bimmendijk and William Richardson, says arms sales officials 'admitted that they had given no thought to the physical security of the F-15.'[23]

The sale of the F-15 also had an impact on the U.S. defense budget, which would benefit the U.S. Air Force:

> A government source said the Air Force is seeking to sell the F-15 to the Saudis because a major sale would accelerate production and help reduce costs. The F-15 has a cost problem and to a degree it makes sense to lessen the cost said a source. F-15 costs between $12.2 and $17 million per plane.[24]

Another benefit of the sale would be to cement ties to a major oil producer and important player in Mideast peace negotiations. It was also argued that the willingness of the United States to sell the Saudis the F-15 would bolster Saudi Arabia's position in the Mideast, as well as America's standing in the Arab world.[25]

The Economic Ramifications for the United States of Not Selling the F-15

The possible repercussions that the Saudis could enact should the sale of the F-15 be denied were retaliation in the form of increased oil prices and or production cutbacks; a demand for payment of oil in currencies other than cheap American dollars, such as Swiss francs, German marks, or Japanese yen; and a selling off of some Saudi investments in the United States that total $60 billion in American dollars. This was out of a total of $100 billion invested overseas. Saudi Arabia was the single biggest supplier of foreign oil to the United States, which was expected to increase in coming years.[26]

This was articulated by Sheikh Yamani, the Saudi oil minister, who linked the purchase of F-15 jets to Saudi support for the dollar and oil production. Yamani emphasized Saudi support for the dollar, at a certain disadvantage to Saudi Arabia, and the benefits that accrued for the United States as a result. He stated that if the sale were denied, the Saudis might reevaluate the benefits of continuing this special relationship.[27]

It can be argued that for the Saudis, a quid pro quo for selling them the F-15 was their continued stabilization of the American dollar. During 1978 Saudi Arabia resisted pressure from other OPEC states to substitute another currency for the dollar. In addition, during 1978 the Saudis invested more heavily in the United States by purchasing additional American government securities, while at the same time lengthening the average maturity of the American bonds they held to about five years.[28] Therefore, American policy makers were forced to calculate the potential effects on the U.S. economy should the sale of the F-15 not go through and the Saudis decided to divest themselves of some of their American holdings.

The Saudi Lobbying Efforts for the F-15 and the Role of American Business

The Saudis invested $365,000 in an advertizing campaign in an effort to counter pro-Israeli groups lobbying against the sale. Prince Bandar bin Sultan, the son of the Saudi Defense Minister, along with the Saudi ambassador Ali Alireza, led the Saudi lobbying effort. Saudi Arabia also retained the services of a public relations firm recommended by John West, the American ambassador to Saudi Arabia. The lobbying effort hinted that if the sale of the F-15 was not forthcoming the Saudis would drop their opposition to extremist demands coming from within OPEC to raise oil prices, as well as turn to France for purchase of a comparable plane.[29]

The Saudis hired the public relations firm of Cook, Reuf, Spann, and Weiner in order to lobby for congressional approval. Former American government officials were also lobbying for the sale, notably Frederick Dutton, a former assistant secretary of state for congressional relations, and J. William Fulbright, a former chairman of the Senate Foreign Relations Committee.[30]

These former government officials were joined by American business interests who had present or perceived future commercial ties in the Kingdom:

> American businesses with now and future interests in Saudi Arabia-Bechtel Corp., Computer Sciences Corp., to name a pair have sent their people around to quietly whisper to legislators about the urgency of approving the airplane sale to the Saudis.[31]

Conclusions

It was argued by American decision makers that it was imperative for the United States to remain on friendly terms with Saudi Arabia in order to preserve its interests in the region: "While some risk is obviously involved one analyst notes that without cooperation from the Saudis the task of protecting American's strategic interests would become 'very close to impossible' in the Middle East."[32]

Another strategic implication for the sale of the F-15 was the potential it offered for increasing the strategic position of the United States in the region. The United States was seeking to build major military bases for $1.5 billion to handle the F-15 program. This was viewed by American decision makers as improving the deterrent capabilities of the Saudi air force.[33]

Administration officials pushing the sale accepted that symbolism as well. They acknowledged that denying a relatively small number of an advanced American fighter bombers to the Saudis, who have been assured by three American presidents that they could have such a plane, would do enormous strategic damage to the special relationship the United States and Saudi Arabia have established.[34]

In conclusion, both parties misread the outcome of the F-15 sale. The Saudis overreacted when the sale was approved, seeing it as a major turning point in American-Saudi relations, representing a more evenhanded policy toward Saudi Arabia. For the Saudis it seemed to justify their strategic orientation toward the United States and the opposition of radicals within the Arab world. American decision makers in turn felt that they had expanded a great deal of political capital to get the sale through and that Saudi Arabia should be more forthcoming in the future. This caused greater misunderstandings when the AWACS sale was considered.[35]

The Air Defense Enhancement Package (AWACS)

The Components of the Package

As a part of Saudi military modernization plans, as well as to complement the purchase of the F-15 in 1978, Saudi Arabia and the United States negotiated the American-Saudi Air Defense Enhancement Package in 1981. The centerpiece of this sale revolved around five E-3A AWACS aircraft. These planes are among the most sophisticated aircraft in the world and serve as an early warning detection system. Such planes were ordered by the Shah but were never delivered. There was some opposition in the United States, about selling sophisticated equipment to a nation in such a volatile region. In the end, however, the sale was approved. Included in this defense package were ground command and control equipment and six to eight KC 707 or KE-3A tanker planes for midair refueling worth $2.4 billion. This would include two years of spare parts, training, maintenance, and support. The package also included 101 conformal fuel tanks giving the F-15s greater range worth $110 million, and 1,177 AIM -9L air-to-air missiles costing $200 million. This would include 42 months of contractor training, maintenance, and logistics support. The total cost of this package was $8.5 billion and provided for 130 American military advisors, as well as 809 American defense corporation employees.[36]

The ground-based defense component of this sale was named Peace Shield. The awarding of the Peace Shield contract was made in 1985 to a consortium led by the Boeing Corporation. This initial contract was worth $1.18 billion and the entire system when fully in place would cost about $3.7 billion. Other major subcontractors on this program were: Westinghouse (displays and software), ITT (communications, engineering and long-haul communications), and General Electric (radar installation services).[37] The main purpose behind the Peace Shield program was to establish: an integrated network of control centers; 17 modified AN/FPS-117 ground-based radars that were based on the "SEEk Igloo" radars in use by the air force in Alaska.; upgrading the centralized Command Center already established in Riyadh; construction of two countrywide base operations centers to coordinate air activities; creation of five sector command and operations centers; improved integration with Saudi Arabia's already existing air defense structure such as the HAWK missiles and the Shahines. The Air Defense Enhancement Package, and specifically its AWACS component, caused a major political battle in the first year of the Reagan administration. Aside from its strategic, political, and economic significance it served as a test of the American-Saudi relationship in the early 1980s similar to the F-15 sale three years earlier.[38]

The Strategic Rationale for AWACS

The AWACS sale was justified for strategic reasons. The long borders of the country, the terrain, as well as the small number of ground forces led to a great deal of emphasis placed on air defense. The total area of the country is 85,000 square miles and the most vulnerable area for Saudi defenses is the oil fields and facilities on the Gulf. The core area of defense extends from the offshore oil field of Safaniya to Ras Tanura and Berri on the Gulf coast down to the Shawar oil field. This extends for 250 miles and covers about 10,000 square miles.[39]

In addition to improving Saudi Arabia's defense capabilities there were more specific strategic and political reasons for the American sale of AWACS. An important benefit for the United States was that Saudi Arabia agreed to have joint training between the U.S. Air Force and U.S. Navy and the Saudi air force, would aid in the projection of American power in the region. Supporters of the sale argued that the improvement of Saudi military capabilities reduced the need to have American forces intervene directly in the region. If American intervention was necessary the provisions of the Air Defense Enhancement Package would give the United States the opportunity to deploy as many as two wings of about 140 fighter planes to support Saudi Arabia and the smaller Arab states of the Gulf as it also provided for the construction of basing and service facilities, refueling capabilities, spare parts, and ammunition depots. Another advantage of this sale was that it would enhance the development of Saudi military infrastructure as well as develop stockpiles of military equipment that would be available to American forces.[40]

Importance of a Regional Defense Network

A significant factor for the United States was that the AWACS sale would be an important step in the formation of a regional air defense network. AWACS would put into place the command and control system for the infusion of American forces in the region. In addition, the United States and Saudi Arabia agreed that the AWACS would be capable of air attack and intelligence capabilities that the United States had assured Israel it would not provide.[41] The AWACS sale was also considered important to provide frontline defense for the oil facilities, as well as a stockpile and staging area for American forces should they be needed.[42]

The Political Considerations of the AWACS Sale

Secretary of State Alexander Haig stated that a veto of the sale would create bad feelings for Washington in the Arab world. This would cause Arab states to doubt American promises of commitment, and limit the ability of the United States to forge a consensus against the Soviet Union.[43]

Testifying before Congress, Secretary Haig laid out the basic strategic rationale for the sale. First, the sale of AWACS would result in information sharing arrangements. This would provide American forces with increased intelligence concerning instability in the Persian Gulf. In addition, the support for developing infrastructure could assist the United States in future troop deployments. Second, the plane would enhance the ability of the Saudis to defend the country, and especially the oil facilities. Third, it would demonstrate political support on the part of America for Saudi Arabia, and illustrate how valued the Saudis are as allies by the United States. Finally, a secure Saudi Arabia firmly allied to the United States could better serve as a source of moderation in the region.[44]

This view of the Saudi role in containment was reflected by Senator Charles Percy (R-Ill.), the chair of the Senate Foreign Relations Committee. In his support for the sale he emphasized the presence of the Soviets in Syria, Iraq, Afghanistan, and the Horn of Africa.[45] Percy further noted the comparison between the selling of the AWACS to Saudi Arabia and the F-5 aircraft to Egypt, maintaining that the F-5 sale had helped Sadat to trust the United States and contributed to peace negotiations with Israel. He stated that a failure by the United States to support the sale would affirm the perception that the Arab nations would not be treated as full regional partners.[46]

Implications of Not Selling AWACS to Saudi Arabia

James Buckley, undersecretary of state for security assistance, argued that the sale was necessary for Saudi Arabia to defend itself against its regional adversaries. In addition, he stated that the sale would encourage military and technical collaboration between the two countries and thus would require a substantial American presence while this system was deployed. Failure to sell the AWACS, he warned, could result in the Saudis purchasing the British Nimrod. This would cause a loss of American prestige and the weakening of the U.S. presence in the country. Congressmen Pritchard maintained that while the British Nimrod could not compare technically to the AWACS, the United States would have no influence in maintaining or deploying this system. Representative Hyde justified his support of the sale by stating that the moderate forces in the Middle East had to be reinforced. He indicated that the AWACS sale would reinforce the position of moderate Saudi Arabia in the region.[47]

Supporters of the sale also raised the point that if the Saudis purchased the Nimrod, the British might not be willing to disengage from the program should the Saudis use the system against Israel. Moreover, should the sale be rejected the Saudis might not trust the United States and America would lose influence over shaping Saudi foreign and military policy.[48]

In addition to the British, there was a strong possibility that the failure of the AWACS sale would result in other European countries, specifically France, gaining market share. The French were hoping to sell military equipment to Saudi Arabia as a way of easing their trade deficit with the kingdom that was $3 billion in the first six months of 1981. This was chiefly a result of French dependence on Saudi oil.[49]

Significance of American Advisors for the AWACS Program

The number of American advisors involved in the AWACS program was 480 American corporate contractors and 25 U.S. Air Force personnel up until 1985. Also 270 American contractors would be needed for the KC707 program and it was estimated that 35,000 separate items of spare parts would be required to maintain the system. It was felt that this would establish American leverage over the program.[50]

In addition to leverage over the program it was felt that the sale could benefit the industrial base of the country by keeping an important production line in operation. It would also further tie Saudi Arabia with major American defense contractors.

> The AWACS aircraft will require an immense support network of parts and services which will ensure dependency upon and, to some extent, effective control by the United States. Not only does this enhance the American industrial base, but it will foster a closer defense cooperative effort between Saudi Arabia and the United States.[51]

However, it can be pointed out that this could cause potential problems for American-Saudi relations by adding to the already large number of Americans in the country. It was estimated that there were over 40,000 Americans in the country, which when taking into account the Saudi population was seven times more than the ratio of Americans in Iran during the 1970s. There were about 1,500 U.S. government personnel working on security projects as well as 3,000 contractor employees.[52] Another potential liability was the response of the Israelis to the enhanced Saudi capabilities. In congressional testimony it was stated that the Israelis would have to divert some of their forces to guard against the potential of a Saudi attack, while in the worst case scenario might actually engage in a preemptive strike on Saudi facilities. In addition, this could place the Saudis under greater pressure to engage in a new round of fighting with their greater military capabilities.[53]

Importance of AWACS to Saudi Arabia: Implications for the United States

The Saudis viewed AWACS as an important source of prestige and placed a high value on acquiring the system. The Saudi finance minister pointed out that while acquisition of the system would give the Saudis an enhanced status in the region, failure to acquire it would conversely cause the Saudis to lose credibility.[54]

This could also have a bearing on the internal support for the regime. Analysts argued that this delay was having ramifications on internal Saudi politics; the loss of prestige in not acquiring AWACS coupled with the perceived lack of confidence by the United States in the monarchy could result in possible challenges to the regime. More immediately, however, it was argued that if the AWACS agreement was canceled the Saudis would turn to other sources for similar systems, and this would impact negatively on both American and Israeli security interests. He also stated that failure to supply AWACS would lead to a weakening of interests and prestige of the faction within the Saudi leadership, which supported closer ties to the United States.[55]

Sheik Yamani, the Saudi oil minister, openly speculated that a failure on the part of the United States to sell AWACS would result in strained relations with the United States. Saudi Arabian Oil Minister Sheik Ahmed Zaki Yamani denied any direct link between AWACS and oil, but he said congressional rejection of the planned sale of the radar planes would produce bitter feelings among Saudi leaders.[56]

Other top Saudi officials articulated similar viewpoints should the AWACS sale be denied. The defense minister, Prince Sultan, indicated that if the United States did not provide these systems the Saudis would purchase comparable systems elsewhere. The Saudi foreign minister, Prince Saud, stated that the failure of Washington to provide AWACS would raise questions about the course of American-Saudi relations.[57]

Executive-Legislative Relations and AWACS

Anti-AWACS groups had the early advantage in the political process of denying the sale. The Reagan administration made several political errors in introducing the AWACS sale for congressional approval. First, the administration did not want to introduce the AWACS package early in the legislative session, as it could have distracted from the President's domestic agenda. Second, the lobbying effort was headed by the national security advisor, who did not have much experience in dealing with Congress. Third, the Reagan administration underestimated congressional opposition, as well as the power and organizational skills of pro-Israeli lobbying groups. Fourth, the administration felt that Prime Minister Begin would be defeated and that his successor would not oppose the sale as strongly. Finally, Israeli officials were permitted to lobby without much opposition.[58]

The AWACS sale provoked a great deal of politicking between the administration and the Congress. The administration sought to use unrelated issues in order to bargain with undecided senators or attempt to change votes. It was reported that Senator DeConcini (D-Ariz.) was promised that if he voted for the sale that President Reagan would not actively campaign for his Republican opponent in the upcoming election. Senator Charles Grassley (R-Ia.) stated that a White House staff member offered that his choice for U.S. Attorney in the northern district of Iowa would be expedited in return for the senator's support for AWACS. Senator

S. I. Hayakawa (R-Calif.) linked his vote on AWACS with the sale of fighter planes to Taiwan. Further, Senator Robert Byrd (D-W.Va.) was likewise promised certain unspecific considerations.[59] Senator John Melcher (D-Mont.) was promised that the administration would reconsider plans to eliminate federal funds for an experimental coal-burning plant in Butte. Senator Slade Gorton (R-Wash.), eight days prior to the vote, received $26 million for renovating a public health hospital in Seattle.[60]

The most dramatic vote switch was Senator Roger Jepsen (R-Ia.) who had been an early opponent of the sale. However, Jepsen was persuaded to change his vote by personal and patriotic appeals by President Reagan as well as the threat of tough political sanctions. Jepsen had been elected as an underdog candidate in 1978 and White House officials felt that he owed the party and its president for their support. More significantly, the White House organized pressure from Jepsen's political backers in Iowa. In an effort to sweeten the arrangement it was charged that the White House promised that the MX missile system would be based in Iowa.[61] Other senators were punished when they did not vote the way the Administration wanted them to. Senator Rudy Boschwitz (R-Minn.) was penalized with a closing of a military base in his state.[62] The AWACS sale was important also for the administration with regard to domestic issues by bolstering the president's popularity. It would also illustrate that he could deal with Congress. From a military standpoint it was argued by Pentagon officials that it was important to protect the oil fields of Saudi Arabia, which supplied 25 percent of American oil imports. "A defeat, proponents of the sale say, would not only fray U.S.-Saudi relations but also would raise questions around the world about Mr. Reagan's ability to deliver on his commitments."[63]

AWACS supporters, particularly within the Republican party in Congress, maintained that if the administration lost the AWACS sale it would lead to a crisis of confidence and confusion in American intentions from U.S. allies, as well as the Soviet Union:

> But the consequences of a defeat on the AWACS sale go far beyond U.S.-Saudi ties. Doubts about Mr. Reagan's ability to carry through his commitments would be particularly disturbing to U.S. allies: a defeat also would seem sure to raise new concerns in Moscow about whether Mr. Reagan would be any more successful than Mr. Carter in winning Senate approval of the arms control treaty the administration intends to begin negotiating next February or March.[64]

Republicans in Congress asserted that it was important to support the president. Charles Percy, the chairman of the Senate Foreign Relations Committee, argued that it was essential that the president not lose the AWACS vote as this would damage the credibility of the president to conduct foreign affairs, and that the Arab states would consider themselves second-class allies.[65] Other commentators linked President Reagan's success or failure on AWACS with his legislative agenda as a whole:

If Reagan wins, he maintains momentum that will help his legislative initiatives. Also, to a degree, he will have won a battle with Congress over who makes U.S. foreign policy. If he loses he will lessen his clout on Capitol Hill and, to some extent, decrease the prospects for his proposals.[66]

Therefore, as a result of the politics around the AWACS sale it not only became a question of the credibility of American commitments, but also of the presidency as an institution. It was argued that if the Air Defense Enhancement Package was rejected, American pledges of assistance would lose value and American influence in the Arab world would decrease.[67] President Reagan stated this view clearly:

If the AWACS sale does not go through he said, how do I then go forward with this quiet diplomacy of trying to bring the Arab states into a peacemaking process in which they can sit there and say, Well, we don't know whether you can deliver yourself or not. You're not the fellow that's in charge, Congress is.[68]

Economic Benefits

The economic benefits of the AWACS sale for the companies involved were significant. The Boeing Corporation stated that without the order 400 employees would have lost their jobs by the following June. The Saudi order extended production of AWACS through 1986, which kept 1,500 people working two more years.[69]

AWACS also had a direct economic benefit for the U.S. government and specifically the air force. There is speculation that the air force was interested in moving ahead with the sale for two reasons. The first was a strategic rationale, as without any high mountain tops the Saudis needed an ability to have a 24-hour surveillance capability to protect the strategic oil region. Second was that the Saudi acquisition of AWACS, which would cost $1 to $2 billion, would be money saved by the defense department.[70]

Conclusions

In justifying this sale, the president advanced the argument that the Saudis would obtain similar types of military equipment should the United States agree or not to sell AWACS. He stated that the United States needed the goodwill of the Saudis to advance American interests in the Middle East and contribute to the peace process.[71] Therefore, he argued this sale was essential to ensure that the Saudis would continue to play the role of a strong, secure, regional pro-Western state that the earlier Eisenhower administration had envisioned.

The counter argument to this was that the building up militarily of Saudi Arabia ultimately impeded American objectives in the Gulf. As a result of these sales, Saudi Arabia was able to acquire a veto over American policy because vested interest in the United States would not want to jeopardize the economic, political, and strategic benefits that these military ties provided for the United States.[72]

The consensus in American government circles was that the Air Defense Enhancement Package would better facilitate American policy and power projection capabilities in the region. It was maintained that one prime reason for this package would be the expansion of Saudi facilities and the prepositioning of compatible equipment to better facilitate an American force buildup should it be necessary:

> In essence, the associated infrastructure needed to support U.S. AWACS aircraft deployments to Saudi Arabia—if requested in times of emergency— would already be in place. With compatible facilities and trained U.S. and Saudi personnel already in place, the opportunities for a successful defense of the Persian Gulf region are markedly improved.[73]

National Security Advisor Richard Allen summarized the arguments in favor of the sale. First, it would enable the Saudis to better defend the oil fields, and the important implications this would have for the West. Second, enhance the effectiveness of the American military should it have to be deployed in the Middle East. Third, it would provide security for the other Gulf states by cementing the foundations of greater American-Saudi defense cooperation. Fourth, it would serve to rebuild confidence in the United States as a credible partner in maintaining the stability of the region.[74]

Business and AWACS

In addition to the executive branch, American businessmen were lobbying members of the Senate and this was particularly true of American corporations who did business with Saudi Arabia. Many of these were also important American defense contractors or oil companies. Among the most prominent business lobbyist was Boeing Aircraft. E. H. Boullioun, president of the commercial aircraft division of Boeing Aircraft, on September 15, 1981, sent a mailgram to 1,600 subcontractors and vendors asking them to lobby for the sale. In addition, senators charged that other major American corporations such as Bechtel, Mobil, and Pratt and Whitney were lobbying for the sale.[75]

Other business leaders who lobbied extensively in the form of mailgrams and magazine columns were Harry Gray, chief executive officer of United Technologies, and George David, president of Otis Elevator. Gray and David cited the importance of Saudi Arabia to Western interests. They pointed out Saudi restraint on oil prices, Saudi purchases of $5.7 billion in American goods, and supporting 250,000 jobs in the United States. These remarks were also taken up by Joseph Alibrandi, president of the Whittaker Corporation in a Newsweek column.[76]

Many of these business interests were tied into the campaigns of freshmen Republican senators and were located in southern states where defense interests are very prominent. Many of these senators in the days before the vote changed their minds or decided to vote for the sale. Brown and Root sent position papers in support of the sale to senators, mainly from the south where Brown and Root has facilities, in support of the sale.[77]

On winning the AWACS vote, President Reagan stated the implications of the victory:

> he asserted that the Senate action, 'will not only strengthen Saudi-American relations, but will also protect our economic lifeline to the Middle East, win favor among moderate Arab nations and most important, continue the difficult but steady progress toward peace and stability in the Middle East.'[78]

Saudi Arabia's Regional Foreign Policy

In addition to attempting to build up a credible military posture, the Saudis sought to establish a strong, assertive foreign policy that would reflect their regional interests and thus, at least indirectly, the interests of America. For Saudi Arabia, the Arab world, and specifically the Arabian Peninsula and the Gulf, are the main emphasis of foreign policy. The Saudis have traditionally tried to maintain the status quo in the region and have emphasized three major threats in the region that can upset this status quo. These are the spread of Soviet influence, the Arab-Israeli conflict, and the inability of many Arabs to achieve their aspirations economically, due to lack of domestic opportunities and resources, and politically as a result of the creation of Israel, which denied statehood to the Palestinian people.[79]

The Saudis have traditionally practiced three strategies in an effort to deal with these threats. First, to actively combat and roll back Soviet influence in the region. Second, to strengthen Saudi defenses so as to offer a credible deterrent. Third, promote stability and the status quo in the region by trying to resolve regional disputes, notably the Arab-Israeli conflict. Riyadh has stated that the resolution of this issue is essential, as continuing hostility with Israel carries with it the potential of endangering Saudi relations with the United States. It would also give strength to radical forces in the region who opposed the Saudi monarchy. Another strategy that the Saudis have embarked on is to encourage Muslim nations to reinforce Islamic values and practices. This further adds to the legitimacy of the monarchy in the Islamic world.[80]

The Saudis have sought to use their financial clout in order to enhance their position and subsequently reduce Soviet influence in the region. In particular, Saudi Arabia has been active in extending economic aid, which by the mid-1970s accounted for 8 percent of its gross national product. In 1978 Saudi Arabia granted $5.5 billion in foreign aid, which translated to 8.45 percent of GNP.[81]

The Saudis have used foreign aid in order to achieve several goals. These are to support Arab states in general, and specifically those frontline states opposing Israel, notably Egypt and Syria. The confrontational states bordering Israel-Egypt, Syria, and Jordan- received $841.6 million in 1976, which was doubled in 1977. Aid to these states is a way that the Saudis gain credibility in the Arab-Israeli conflict within the Arab world as a whole, as well as internally within the country. This avoids direct participation that could threaten the Saudi state physically as well as imperil the special relationship the Saudis have with the United States. The second way foreign aid is used is to assist regional powers in order to curtail the spread of Soviet and communist influence. Third, to assist Muslim states in reinforcing Islamic values. Most of the foreign aid from Saudi Arabia, 96 percent, was granted to Islamic countries, three-quarters of which were Arab states.[82]

Saudi Aid to Africa

Throughout the 1970s Saudi Arabia had adopted a very anticommunist, antiradical foreign policy in the region. Among the more important initiatives in Saudi policy during this period was the providing of financial assistance to Egypt after the latter's break with the Soviets in the early 1970s.[83] In addition the Saudis, like the Iranians, gave aid and support to Somalia in its conflict with Ethiopia. This was illustrated in February 1978 when over 30 ships carrying arms and supplies to the Somali forces arrived in Somalia, most of this financed by Saudi Arabia. During this period the Saudis extended $200 million in aid for the purchase of arms. In addition, the Saudis extended $400 million to compensate for the expulsion of Soviet advisors.[84] The Saudis also facilitated the transit of Eastern European weapons, purchased by middlemen in Switzerland, which were airlifted to Somalia via Jeddah.[85]

The Saudis encouraged the United States to supply aid to Somalia, as well as sent aid to the rebels in Eritrea fighting the government in Addis Ababa.[86] The Saudis supported the Eritreans in part because they wanted to keep the pro-Soviet government in Addis Ababa off balance.[87] This helped set the stage for a large American involvement in Somalia. In August 1980 the United States extended $45 million in military sales and credits in return for the right of the United States to use Somali facilities and airlifted arms in 1982 to aid Somalia in its conflict with rebels supported by Ethiopia. The United States also raised the amount of Military Assistance Program (MAP) aid from $15 million to $40 million annually and increased both economic and developmental aid to $35 million and $42 million annually. Additionally, the United States spent $110 million to upgrade the air and harbor facilities at Berbera, as well as provide the Somalis with antiaircraft equipment for villages in the contested Ogaden region.[88]

The Saudis had also shown a willingness to assist pro-Western forces outside of the region. They offered assistance to Zaire (now the Democratic

Republic of the Congo), and to The National Union for the Total Independence of Angola (UNITA) in Angola.[89] Saudi aid to Zaire was significant due to Congress's refusal to appropriate $50 million to support Zaire's President Mobutu in a 1976 confrontation with the Soviet-supported government in Angola. In 1977 the Saudis aided Mobutu's hold on power by providing the finances for Moroccan troops to be airlifted into Zaire to put down a revolt in Shaba province.[90]

The Saudis, along with the Egyptians, urged the United States to give support to the government of Sudan. The result was an American arms sale of 12 F-5 jets, 2 trainers, and 10 F-5Es at a cost of $75 to $80 million. The Saudis were expected to pay for the planes. This was in response to the Sudan expelling its Soviet advisors in May of 1977.[91]

Saudi support for conservative forces also extended to Central America. Combating the Sandanista government in Nicaragua was a primary foreign policy goal of the Reagan administration. The Boland amendment passed by the U.S. Congress in October of 1984 eliminated funding for the Nicaraguan contras from October 1984 to December 1985. The exact language of the amendment was as follows:

> No appropriations or funds made available pursuant to this joint resolution to the Central Intelligence Agency, the Department of Defense, or any other agency or entity of the United States involved in intelligence activities may be obligated or expended for the purpose or which would have the effect of supporting, directly or indirectly, military or paramilitary operations in Nicaragua by any nation, group, organization, movement or individual.[92]

This led the Reagan administration to solicit funding from pro-American, conservative regimes and Saudi Arabia was one of the states that contributed financially to supporting the contras during this period. In June 1984, Saudi Ambassador Prince Bandar informed National Security Advisor Robert McFarlane, after a conversation a few days earlier in which the White House aide had informed the ambassador that the administration would probably lose the vote on contra funding, that his government would contribute $1 million a month to the contras for the rest of 1984. Ultimately, this was extended into early 1985 and totaled $8 million. The Saudis again contributed to the contra cause in 1985 after a state visit by King Fahd in which the Saudi monarch was treated to a meeting with President Reagan in the family residence portion of the White House in addition to the customary Oval Office meeting. This was meant to indicate that the United States held the Saudi ruler in high regard and was considered a sign of the closeness in relations between the two countries. Shortly after this, the Saudi ambassador informed McFarlane that Riyadh would contribute $2 million per month to the contras for the year 1985. The two Saudi contributions amounted to $32 million for the contras.[93]

Saudi-Iranian Relations

Despite the fact that Iran and Saudi Arabia were to become key components of American foreign policy in the Middle East during the 1970s, there were tensions between the two countries during the early part of the decade. The Saudis were suspicious of the Shah's intentions for a variety of reasons. They fully understood the Shah's ambitions as wanting Iran to be the regional hegemon taking over the traditional British position in the region. This would threaten Saudi interests in the Arabian Peninsula. They also feared the military buildup that accompanied these goals, which was being encouraged by the United States. These fears were fueled by the Iranian takeover of three islands in the Persian Gulf, Abu Musa and Greater and Lesser Tumb, belonging to the UAE in 1971. On the surface, this provoked a crisis between Iran and its neighbors, with the Shah arguing that this was a defensive measure by Iran to better provide security in the Gulf. Many Arabs, however, viewed it as an occupation of Arab soil. The seizure of these islands involved has often been discussed in terms of a simple power grab by the Shah, even though it involved complex negotiations involving Iran, Britain, and some of the various Arab sheikdoms in the Gulf. When Britain announced its intention to withdraw from the Persian Gulf, the Shah sought to use Iran's claim to Bahrain to reinforce his position in the Gulf by obtaining concessions from the British. In an effort to accomplish this, the Shah withheld support for the British-sponsored Arab Federation because of its initial inclusion of the Bahrain islands. The Iranian Foreign Ministry strongly denounced it on July 8, 1968 stating that it was a manifestation of imperialism.[94]

The next year the Shah sought to make concessions on the issue of Bahrain in order to solidify Iran's position in the Persian Gulf. In January of 1969 at a press conference in New Delhi, he proposed that the issue of Bahrain be settled by a U.N.-administered vote as to whether the population preferred union with Iran or independence. However, he warned that Iran would not except a British unilateral granting of independence. If this occurred, Iran would not recognize it as an independent state, nor the Arab Federation should Bahrain become a member. It seemed apparent that the Shah felt he would eventually have to give up Iran's claim to Bahrain, but this was a way of extracting concessions from the British, gaining the support and good will of conservative Arab states when this was finally accomplished, as well as mollifying criticism of this policy within Iran by appealing to the principles of the United Nations as a way of replacing nationalistic aspirations.[95]

This was followed by the development of Iranian relations with other states of the Persian Gulf. Examples of this include an agreement concluded with Kuwait in July of 1970 in which the two countries agreed on demarcating the continental shelf. It was at this time that the Kuwaiti foreign minister expressed his country's support for Iranian policy in light of the impending British withdrawal. In addition, the Shah resumed diplomatic relations with Egypt in August of 1970 as well as extended diplomatic recognition to Qatar, which became independent in September of 1971 outside of the United Arab Emirates (UAE) federation.[96]

The settlement of the islands question involved negotiations between Britain and Iran. The Iranians sought to pressure Britain by withholding recognition of the British-sponsored Arab Federation unless the issue of the island was settled in Iran's favor. This had potentially serious political implications, as it was viewed that the Federation's survival depended on both Saudi and Iranian recognition.[97] An agreement was eventually concluded with the emirate of Sharja over the status of Abu Musa 24 hours before Iranian forces moved in on November 30, 1971. The major provisions were: (1) that Sharja held sovereignty over the islands that would be illustrated by the flying of its flag over official installations and inhabitants remaining under Sharja's jurisdiction; (2) Buttes Oil and Gas Company would conduct oil exploration in the waters off Abu Musa, the proceeds of which would be equally divided between Iran and Sharja; (3) Iranian forces would occupy agreed upon points on the island; (4) Sharja would receive one-and-a-half million pounds sterling a year for nine years from Iran. These payments would be halted when Sharja's oil revenue reached three million pounds sterling annually.[98] At the same time, Iranian forces also occupied the islands of Greater and Lesser Tumbs that had been under the jurisdiction of the emirate of Ras al-Khaima. Although no agreement was reached with Ras al-Khaima, Iranian government officials claimed that it was aware of the Iranian occupation. On December 2, 1971, the UAE was officially formed, encompassing the emirates of Abu Dhabi, Dhabi, Sharja, Ajman, Fujaira, and Umm al-Qaywayn; Ras al-Khaima would join later. The UAE was recognized by Iran the same day.[99] Arab reaction was universal in its disapproval of Iran's actions and several Arab states such as Algeria, Iraq, Libya, and South Yemen asked that Iran be sanctioned by the UN and the Arab League. However, other Arab states such as Egypt and Saudi Arabia, while not supporting Iranian actions, refused to severely criticize Tehran. As a result the proposal advanced by Iraq within the Arab League for Arab states to sever relations with Iran failed.[100]

The Shah's behavior in OPEC also went against Saudi interests, as he was one of the price hawks who advocated large increases in the price of oil in an effort to gain capital for the economic and military development of Iran. The Saudis, as well as the smaller sheikdoms of the Arabian Peninsula, thought that these price hikes were extreme and threatened to upset the economies of the industrialized countries, which would in turn threaten their interests.

By the mid-1970s the tensions between Iran and Saudi Arabia eased, as the two nations found common ground in promoting conservative foreign policies designed to maintain the status quo in the region. This joint cooperation was reflected in aiding other pro-Western regimes. Among the states that both Iran and Saudi Arabia cooperated in assisting were North Yemen, Zaire, Somalia, as well as Oman. In addition, they both sought to destablize radical states such as South Yemen, the People's Democratic

Republic of Yemen (PDRY). Another example of cooperation between the two countries was their support both nations extended to Kuwait against the attempt by Baathist Iraq to gain port concessions. The Saudis also supported Iranian attempts to subvert the Iraqi government and force it to make concessions on the Shat al-Arab dispute. Both states opposed the radical forces present in the region such as the Popular Front for the Liberation of the Occupied Arabian Gulf (PFLOAG), and provided assistance to Sultan Qabus of Oman in defeating the Dhofar rebels who had the support of the PDRY.[101]

The Saudis have sought to support North Yemen, the Yemen Arab Republic (YAR), against the PDRY, and have attempted to destabilize the PDRY. In addition, Riyadh sought to control North Yemen through its support of the northern tribes that have a history of autonomy and hostility to the central authorities in Sanaa.[102]

The Saudis alternated from military confrontation with the PDRY to attempting to bribe it. The Saudis promised $25 million for the South Yemen Five-Year Plan while pledging $100 million for other projects if the PDRY ceased supporting radical movements in the region.[103] The Saudi policy towards the two nations led to hostility and conflict between North Yemen and South Yemen. While it can be argued that this policy has contributed to instability in both countries and has at times threatened to spread conflict outside of Yemen, it has fitted in with the general goals of Saudi foreign policy. A goal of the Saudi monarchy is to support conservative forces in the region, and by working against what they view as radicalism in Yemen, as well as other areas, Riyadh feels it is ensuring the long-term, pro-Western, conservative orientation of the Arabian Peninsula.

Saudi Arabia and North Yemen

Saudi Arabia viewed North Yemen as significant from both a strategic and economic perspective. Strategically, North Yemen affected Saudi Arabia in three ways. The Saudis viewed North Yemen as significant to the politics of the Arabian Peninsula and especially viewed events there as affecting the internal security of Saudi Arabia. This was one of the prime reasons that the Saudis assisted the royalists during the Yemeni civil war. The Saudis were also concerned with the policies of North Yemen in the region, as well as internationally.[104]

The two countries had a significant economic relationship, as the Sanaa government was dependent on Saudi Arabia economically. By the early 1980s, 500,000 Yemenis were working in Saudi Arabia and their remittances helped to fuel the demands for consumer goods for the country as a whole. Second, the Saudis have contributed a substantial portion of the government's budget and military expenses since the end of the civil war, as well as contributed to various development projects in Yemen that helped to stimulate economic activity there.[105] Their view of North Yemen has been shaped by the fear of Soviet influence.[106] However, the YAR has not marched in lock step with Saudi Arabia. While it was considered to be pro-Western, it did not seek a close alignment with the United States and did not support totally the Saudi desire to contain the spread of communism.[107] North Yemen maintained relations with both the United States and the Soviet Union and received aid from both. The United States had been concerned about developments in Yemen going back to the 1950s due to the independent foreign policy of the Imam. Yemen had purchased arms from the Soviet Union and received Soviet advisors, as well as established trade relations. The United States hoped that Saudi Arabia could exert influence on the government of Yemen to limit Soviet influence.[108]

The Soviets had been an early backer of the republican government, supplying economic and military aid through the Egyptians. Initially, after the republican coup, Moscow's influence in the country was limited due to the substantial Egyptian presence. Soviet military aid only began to arrive in large numbers to enforce the USSR-YAR friendship treaty of 1964 after President al-Sallal was ousted in 1967. In mid-November, 24 MiG-19 planes arrived along with Ilyushin bombers and small arms supplies.[109]

Relations between North Yemen and the United States improved during the 1979 border war with South Yemen. The United States agreed to supply $300 million of emergency military equipment during the 1979 border war, with the Saudis paying the bill. This aid included F-5E fighter-bombers, M-60 tanks, and 100 armored personnel carriers.[110] The Saudis sought to control North Yemen and limit the amount of American influence in the country by having American aid channeled through Saudi Arabia as they were paying the costs. The Saudis attempted to exert their leverage on the YAR after the 1979 border war in which the president of North Yemen sought to reach a compromise with the National Democratic Front (NDF). The Saudis felt that if this occurred they would lose influence in the country. They also sought to prevent President Salih from dealing directly with the United States by restricting the American arms supply that had been allocated for the YAR. In large part as a result of this pressure, President Salih in March of 1980 broke off plans to bring the NDF into the government and ceased further arms purchases from the Soviet Union.[111]

The YAR did pose concerns for Saudi Arabia for several reasons. First, the large number of Yemeni laborers in Saudi Arabia could provoke a source of internal instability. Second, the possible mixed loyalties of tribes in the Asir, which prior to 1934, was ruled by the Yemeni Imams. Third, the fact that Yemen's population is about as large as Saudi Arabia and a very poor country. Finally, the YAR had shown that it would deal with the Soviets when it suited its interests.

The Significance of South Yemen

Another source of concern was the Marxist-Leninist government of South Yemen, People's Democratic Republic of Yemen (PDRY). By the end of the 1970s South Yemen had become dependent on Soviet economic and military assistance. This included economic aid, technical assistance, military and police training, as well as Soviet arms. This resulted in a dramatic expansion of Soviet and Eastern-bloc advisors in the country. By 1980 there were 1,500 Soviet economic advisors in South Yemen, and their presence was essential in operating its infrastructure, specifically airports, communications, harbors, etc. In addition, there were other Eastern-bloc advisors notably East German and Cuban.[112] The PDRY has also been active in supporting anti-Western states in the region, notably Ethiopia and Libya, when the three nations signed a cooperative alliance and exchanged military observers and intelligence.[113] The importance of the PDRY to the Soviet Union was illustrated by the military bases and other facilities that the Soviets had access to. In the 1970s, as the Soviet navy was expanding its scope of operations, Aden was seen as an important base between the Black Sea and the Pacific.[114]

Saudi Arabia sought to block the PDRY and to influence its policy, trying to constrain the nation by extending aid to countries such as North Yemen and Oman, while at the same time building up its own military capabilities. It is argued that one of the reasons the Saudis ceased to support the royalists in North Yemen was to cultivate the republican government as a possible ally against the south, and create a buffer against possible PDRY attack. Under King Faisal in the 1970s, the Saudis armed dissidents from the PDRY and in cooperation with the Saudi military made armed incursions into South Yemen that were repulsed. The offering of incentives have also been used from time to time, as the Saudis have tried to bribe the PDRY. After King Faisal's assassination, his successors at times attempted to establish relations with Aden. In March 1976 Saudi Arabia granted $100 million in grant aid to the PDRY in addition to a proposal for a pipeline to carry Eastern Arabian oil to the South Yemeni coast. In May of 1976 formal diplomatic relations were established between the two countries. However, within two years this policy ended as the South Yemeni President Salim Rubay Ali was deposed and later executed. One of the reasons cited for this was his close relationship with the Saudis and his attempt to exploit them for his own political advantage, which alienated him from others in the leadership.[115] The Saudi monarchy has viewed the unification of Yemen along with the attempt at establishing democratic elections as being a possible threat to their regime. The signing of the unity pact occurred in May of 1990, which was followed by the ratification of the constitution in 1991 and parliamentary elections in 1993. This period, lasting roughly four years, introduced a time of democratic politics that featured the establishment of political parties, a free press, and the ability to dissent publicly. However, other conditions for unification were not settled, notably the integration of the military. Eventually, disagreements and politics between the Yemeni Socialist Party (YSP) and the General People's Congress (GPC) ultimately led to tensions. This erupted into open conflict in April of 1994 when the YSP and other allied parties seceded from the union, declaring the formation of the Democratic Republic of Yemen on May 21, 1994. The Saudis who had previously been opponents of the YSP, when the PDRY was still in existence, became their supporters during this conflict. They provided political support when prewar tensions were mounting, as well as sought to aid them diplomatically once fighting had broken out. The Saudi diplomatic initiatives included getting the U.N. Security Council to call for a ceasefire, calling for a halt to arms shipments, as well as sending a U.N. negotiator. The Gulf Cooperation Council (GCC) also condemned the north and claimed that Sana was being supported by Iraq.[116] Therefore it could be argued that the Saudis were promoting instability, as well as impeding democracy, as they helped to fuel the splits between the north and south that led to civil war. However, considering that Yemen was one of the few states to openly back Iraq during the Gulf War, this was probably something that Washington could overlook.

The Soviet Union and Iraq

A particular area of concern for Saudi Arabia and the United States was the growth of Soviet influence in Iraq. Between 1971 and 1975 the Soviets delivered more than $1.7 billion worth of arms. However, the Soviets did not gain much in the way of tangible advantage. Once relations with Iran were stabilized as a result of the 1975 Algiers Accord, the Iraqis began to distance themselves from the Soviet Union. As the number of Soviet exports to the country declined, it fell from being Iraq's largest trading partner in 1973 to fourth in 1975. In addition, the Iraqis shipped Soviet arms and spare parts to Egypt, as well as resumed their feud with Syria. By late 1975 France was displacing the Soviet Union as Iraq's leading arms supplier. Internally, the Iraqi government was able to suppress the Kurdish rebellion, despite a Soviet arms embargo, as well as crack down on the Iraqi Communist Party.[117]

The Algiers Accord and the weakening of Iraqi-Soviet ties saw Baghdad seek to establish friendly relations with the other states of the Gulf. This was particularly true with regard to Saudi Arabia. The Saudis had been the acknowledged leader of the Arab states of the Gulf. Despite some tensions in the early 1970s, the Saudis had developed a complementary relationship with Iran, which was directed against Iraq. For the Iraqis to increase their stature in the Gulf it was important to cultivate good relations with Saudi Arabia. In 1975 Saudi Arabia and Iraq settled their border dispute, which involved dividing the oil wealth from the desert neutral zone.[118]

The Algiers Accord, while ending tensions between Iran and Iraq for a time, posed somewhat of a strategic dilemma for Saudi Arabia. The cooperative relationship between Saudi Arabia and Iran in the early 1970s was a check on Iraqi ambitions to assert authority in the region. After 1975 the three countries had a limited cooperation in Gulf security matters. The Saudis used Iraqi opposition to derail the Shah's proposal to establish a regional collective security pact. At the same time, the Saudis used Iranian opposition against Iraq's plan to establish a series of bilateral security treaties that would have placed Iraq in the superior position.[119]

The Iranian revolution in 1978-1979 changed the strategic calculations in the region. The Gulf states, including Saudi Arabia, became very concerned lest the Iranian revolution spread to the Arab side of the Gulf. The potential of this was manifested to the Saudis with the Shia riots in the Eastern Province in late 1978, early 1979. As a result of these fears, Iraq was able to forge an Arab entente against Iran as relations between Iraq and revolutionary Iran rapidly began to deteriorate. The Saudis were reluctant to see Iran and Iraq in open conflict as they felt the possibility of the war spreading, thus offering new opportunities to the Soviet Union to expand its influence. Iraq was able to forge a consensus amongst Saudi Arabia, Jordan, and the Arab states of the Gulf to support Iraqi military actions against Iran to achieve the following goals: supporting Iraqi territorial claims in the Shat al Arab region; forcing Iran to return islands seized in the Gulf by the Shah's government; and probably most important to inflict a significant military defeat on Iran so it could not support activities to subvert its neighbors. These states wanted to keep the objectives of the war limited, which meant not widening the conflict or having a sustained Iraqi occupation of Khuzistan.[120]

The Saudis had been concerned about the revolutionary government in Iran for a variety of reasons. Riyadh was threatened by the propaganda emanating from Tehran attacking the Gulf monarchies as dominated by corrupt rulers who served the interests of the West and were against Islam. In addition, they were concerned about the impact the revolution and Iran's propaganda would have on the Shia minority in Eastern Saudi Arabia. However, after the outbreak of hostilities the Saudis at least publicly tried to be neutral although from the beginning they were providing material support for Iraq. This included loaning Baghdad the sum of $10 billion by the end of 1981, as well as facilitating Iraqi trade by allowing her to use Saudi ports. The total aid given by the Arab Gulf states to Iraq during the course of the war was estimated at between $35-$50 billion. Saudi Arabia also contributed indirectly to Iraq financially by allowing the construction of a pipeline through Saudi territory to facilitate the sale of Iraqi oil.[121] Despite the support given to Iraq by Saudi Arabia and most of the other Arab rulers of the Arabian Peninsula, these states probably preferred if the war continued at a low level. This would keep both major regional powers tied up and they could not think about expanding their interests at the expense of the other states. The Saudis were able to use this conflict in part to argue for the creation of the GCC, with themselves as the defacto leader of this grouping.

Saudi Relations with Afghanistan

Another country that affected Saudi security was Afghanistan. Outside powers for over a century were seeking to control Afghanistan. During the 1970s the Soviets were in the process of consolidating their control over Afghanistan and took over the task of advising Afghan internal security forces from Turkey by 1963. Also, between 1956-1970 the Soviets trained over 7,000 Afghan officers compared to 600 trained by the United States.[122]

Afghanistan went through a great deal of political change during the 1970s. The monarch, King Zahir Shah, was overthrown in 1973 by his cousin Daud. Daud in turn was killed in a coup in April 1978 by the newly reunited Marxist party of Afghanistan. The Marxist Party of Afghanistan had broken into factions that competed for influence: the Khalq (People's Party), led by Noor Mohammed Taraki, and Parcham (the Red Banner), led by Babrak Karmal. The Marxist Party quickly split apart again after the coup along the above lines. The Khalq faction, the more radical socialist group, initially emerged victorious with its leader Noor Mohammed Taraki heading the government. The Soviets sought to reinforce their position in the country by sending more military aid such as T-62 tanks, MI-24 assault helicopters, and MiG-23 fighter planes. There were conflicts within the Khalq faction between Taraki and Hafizullah Amin who emerged in 1979 as the prime minister. This ultimately caused a power struggle in which Taraki was killed. The Soviets were not in favor of Amin as they felt his policies were too radical and he proved unable to contain the guerrilla movement. As a result, the Soviets used their formidable presence in the country to stage a military coup that placed Babrak Karmal, the leader of the rival Red Banner faction and a more moderate socialist, in power.[123]

It is recognized today that the Soviet invasion of Afghanistan was an attempt to restore stability to a country on the southern periphery of Soviet Central Asia and to eliminate one faction of the Communist Party at the expense of the other who the Soviet leadership felt could better contain the Islamic insurgency. At the time, both the United States and Saudi Arabia viewed the Soviet invasion of Afghanistan as a first step towards the Persian Gulf. There was speculation that this would be a prelude to a Soviet invasion of Iran, or a first step towards the dismemberment of Pakistan and the gaining control of bases on the Gulf and Indian Ocean directly by Soviet forces. The Soviet presence in Afghanistan, the political instability in the PDRY, which saw the radical faction of the Yemeni Socialist Party gain power, the assassination of President Ghashmi of the YAR, gains made by Ethiopia in the Horn of Africa, as well as social and political instability within Saudi Arabia itself, led the Saudi royal family to feel threatened on several fronts.[124] Officially, the Saudis condemned the Soviet invasion and sought to mobilize support throughout the Third World, but notably within the Islamic Conference Organization. In a meeting of this body in January 1980 the Saudis pressed the organization to condemn the Soviet Union, as well as not recognize the Kabul government. This episode worked well for the Saudis for a number of factors. First, they wanted to illustrate their Islamic credentials, particularly in light of the recent Mosque takeover in Mecca. Second, they wanted to reassure their smaller Gulf partners that they were capable of undertaking major foreign policy objectives. Third, they wanted to criticize Syria and other Arab countries who were cooperating with the Soviet Union, and who in turn criticized the Saudis for their alignment with the United States while America was giving support to Israel.[125] Covertly, the Saudis began to cooperate with the United

States to send aid to the Afghan resistance.[126] The regional states that assisted the United States in providing aid to the Afghan rebels during the Soviet occupation were Pakistan, Saudi Arabia, and Egypt. Pakistan served as a key staging area providing bases and material support for many of the various mujahidin groups. Egypt was providing surplus Soviet bloc equipment to the rebels. Saudi Arabia from the beginning was matching the United States in funding the resistance. In the period 1980-1982 this was estimated at between $20-$30 million each from the United States and Saudi Arabia. This figure increased steadily during the 1980s. In 1983 Washington extended about $50 million and the estimated total figure by mid-1984 for American aid to the mujahidin was $325 million.[127]

Saudi Arabia and Pakistan

An important implication of the Soviet invasion of Afghanistan was the strengthening of Saudi relations with Pakistan. The idea of Saudi-Pakistani strategic cooperation was first considered in the 1950s by King Saud. This idea, however, lost its appeal to the Saudis when Pakistan joined the Baghdad Pact. However, Pakistanis did serve in the Saudi armed forces on an individual basis. In 1980 the Saudis agree to subsidize Pakistani arms purchases in return for security assistance. This eventually led to the discussion of the stationing of Pakistani troops in Saudi Arabia.[128]

At the same time, the United States began to reestablish a military and political relationship with Pakistan. The American-Pakistani alliance had hit a low during the Carter administration when an offer of $400 in military credits was rejected. In 1981 the Reagan administration concluded a multi-billion dollar military and economic aid package to Pakistan. This provided the first modern military equipment that Pakistan would receive in years. Among the arms that Pakistan has acquired under the agreement in the years 1982-1983 were: 100 M-48 A5 tanks; 75 M-113 APC's; 24 M-901 TOW vehicles; 100 TOW missiles; 10 AH-1S attack helicopters; 75 M-198 towed 155 mm howitzers; 100 M-109A2 self propelled artillery weapons; and most importantly, 40 F-16 attack fighters.[129]

This Pakistani military buildup had significance for Saudi Arabia, as the nations cooperate in security matters and Pakistani forces are stationed in Saudi Arabia. It could be concluded that America was attempting to give Pakistan the role that had previously been filled by the Iranian army, of being a regional police force. Although this force was not as well equipped as the Shah's army, it did have extensive combat experience. It is this experience coupled with improved armaments that would allow Pakistan to assist Saudi Arabia and the Gulf states in repelling small-scale external as well as internal threats to the ruling elites.[130]

The Foreign Policies of the United States and Saudi Arabia: Complements and Tensions

.The formation of the Gulf Cooperation Council (GCC) enhanced Saudi Arabian regional security and promoted American interests in the region. The council, made up of Saudi Arabia, Kuwait, UAE, Bahrain, Qatar, and Oman, was established to coordinate the security of these states from both internal and external threats. The GCC has given the Saudis a vehicle that they can use to exert regional leadership and yet promote cooperation with its small, but strategically important, neighbors. These nations, by grouping together, serve as a counterweight to promote the status quo in the region. The GCC also provides a good vehicle for America to contribute aid, as it benefits a number of countries simultaneously and serves to meet Saudi security needs as well as American geostrategic goals in the region.[131]

The Saudis, to a certain extent, lost trust with the United States in the late 1970s as a result of policies of the Carter administration. Among the positions that rankled the Saudis was the American unilateral abrogation of the mutual defense treaty with Taiwan when the United States exchanged diplomats with the People's Republic of China. In addition, the Saudis had to prod the unwilling Carter administration to support Somalia in its conflict with Ethiopia. Of greater significance for the Saudis was the unwillingness, in their view, of America to give tangible support to the Shah of Iran during the Iranian revolution. This gave the Saudi royal family pause in relying on American support. "Saudi leaders, in the wake of what happened in Taiwan and Iran, tell visitors they consider American pledges of support less reliable than before."[132]

Despite these tensions, however, the American-Saudi relationship flourished during this period. The foreign policy goals of Saudi Arabia were complementary with those of the United States. The goal of American foreign policy in the Middle East since World War II has been to maintain access to oil for the West; the containment of the Soviet Union; expanding of export markets in the region; maintenance of regional stability by supporting conservative pro-Western nations; and finally, support for Israel. When comparing Saudi foreign policy in the region and the third world as a whole, the Saudis fit the first four of these American aims. Saudi Arabia is the most important state within OPEC and although it has participated in price increases it has advocated that these increases be gradual. In addition, the country has become a big export market for the United States of both military and nonmilitary goods. Finally, the Saudis are anticommunist and opposed to pro-Soviet regimes as well as leftist movements in the Middle East and the third world in general. The Saudis sought to maintain the status quo by providing assistance to pro-Western states such as Jordan, Oman, Somalia, Zaire, as well as the smaller monarchies of the Gulf.[133]

However, while the American-Saudi relationship was substantial it was being built on weak foundations. The foundation of this alliance relationship, especially during the 1970s and 1980s, rested on the United

States providing arms sales and military support to the Saudis. While all of the reasons cited above by Secretary Haig were used to justify the American alliance with Saudi Arabia, they can also be interpreted as providing leverage for Riyadh over Washington. Frequently these considerations were cited by American policy makers as reasons why Saudi Arabia was critical to maintaining American interests in the region. Therefore, the consensus in Washington was that failure to acquiesce to Saudi arms requests would lead to the Saudis not being as interested in safeguarding Western interests in the Middle East as well as the third world as a whole. This illustrates that leverage in an alliance relationship can work both ways. Many American policy makers have been slow to realize this as they have consistently viewed military alliances as promoting U.S. leverage over the regional power.

The Impact of the Carter Doctrine and the Rapid Deployment Force on American-Saudi Relations

The fall of the Shah forced the United States to reorient its strategy towards the Persian Gulf for several reasons. First, from the perspective of American policy makers, the Iranian revolution posed a threat to American interests and the stability of the Persian Gulf. The United States viewed Iran as an anti-status quo regime. However, American decision makers failed to take into account in formulating policy towards Iran the extent that American actions and support for the monarchy since 1953 contributed towards formulating these attitudes. Second, to continue the previous policy, Washington needed a local actor with a strong military force in the region, which Saudi Arabia could not accomplish as it did not possess a strong ground capability. Third, the general view of American policy makers was that the entire region was becoming unstable. Fourth, this view was symmetrical to the general deterioration of American-Soviet relations.[134]

As a result of these factors, plus sagging public opinion, the Carter Doctrine was initiated. It stated that the United States would defend its interests in the Persian Gulf by any means necessary. These interests were defined as defending its major allies and ensuring Western access to oil. The emphasis of the Carter administration was to develop, or reorient, military forces to counter a Soviet attack in the region. The Reagan administration held similar views of the threats to American interests in the region. However, it implemented them differently by focusing more on developing indigenous military forces in the region, prepositioning equipment, and building up base facilities to enable the deployment of American forces should the need arise.[135] Another important factor implicit in the Carter Doctrine was to prevent the emergence of a powerful regional actor who would threaten American interests. In retrospect, it was in this latter application that the military forces allocated and infrastructure developed were used to contain Iraq in the Gulf War of 1990-1991.

The Rapid Deployment Force was constructed in 1980-1981. In 1980 the United States negotiated base facilities with nations in the region. By mid-1980 agreements had been concluded with Kenya, Somalia, and Oman, and Egypt promised cooperation, although there was no formal agreement.[136] These bases provided naval ports, airfields, staging points, and supply depots for the American forces and included: (1) in Kenya, the airfield and port at Mombasa, as well as the airfields at Nairobi and Nanyuki; (2) in Somalia, access to the ports and airfields at Mogadishu and Berbera, just opposite Aden; (3) in Egypt, the airfield and port at Ras Banas and the airfield at Etzion; (4) access to the strategic facilities in Oman at the mouth of the Gulf. These facilities are the airfields and ports at Seeb and Khasab-Goat Island. In addition the United States has access to airfields at Thumrait, Salaleh, and Masirah. Also figuring into the American basing scheme are the airfields at Ezurum, Batman, and Mus in southern Turkey, as well as the Lajes air staging point in Portugal. Finally, the United States itself maintains a strategic base on Diego Garcia Island in the Indian Ocean.[137]

The military forces allocated for the Middle East were upgraded in October 1981 when the Rapid Deployment Force was designated a separate unit from the Readiness Command. In 1983, this force was designated one of the six U.S. multiservice integrated force commands, designated the United States Central Command (USCENTCOM), whose area of operations was designated as Southwest Asia and Northeast Africa. The forces allocated to this command were two Army airborne and one mechanized division, three Navy Aircraft carrier led battle groups, seven tactical fighter wings, and two strategic bomber squadrons, as well as Special Forces trained in counterinsurgency tactics such as the Rangers and Green Berets.[138]

Historically, the monarchy has not viewed the establishment of an American military presence on the Arabian Peninsula favorably. The Saudis have preferred to stockpile weapons and provide support facilities while politically keeping American military forces as an over-the-horizon presence. In 1979, in the aftermath of the fall of the Shah, Secretary of Defense Brown made a formal offer to establish an American presence in Saudi Arabia. However, Saudi Arabia could not afford to have the United States establish a permanent presence on its soil as this would delegitimize the monarchy with most of the Arab world and would also have jeopardized its relations with the other powerful Arab countries, such as Iraq. This problem was demonstrated when at the end of the year the Saudis broke diplomatic relations with Libya over the latter's criticism of American military relations with Saudi Arabia. A similar crisis was narrowly averted with Syria over the same issue.[139]

The question of American access to facilities in Saudi Arabia has, however led to a certain amount of tension between the two nations, as the Saudis are unwilling to overtly commit themselves to allowing American forces to use Saudi territory to intervene in the Middle East. But this has only been minimal, as the military relationship between the two countries, and specifically the volume and sophistication of the arms transfers, have resulted in de facto bases available for American forces should the need have arose. As a result of these transfers, a large quantity of support equipment had already been pre-positioned in Saudi Arabia, such as spare parts, facilities for repair and maintenance, fuel, and munitions. Also located in the country are important infrastructure facilities to accommodate the American forces, such as runways, ammunition storage facilities, and hardened port facilities.[140]

American-Saudi Economic Relations

Saudi Arabia is important in international finance and greatly influences the American economy. This was reflected in the investment holdings made by Saudi Arabia in the United States. By 1978, during the period of the F-15 sale, the Saudis had invested $30 billion in Treasury bonds as well as $10 billion in American industry in general. Should the Saudis have switched to another currency this could have had a negative consequence for the U.S. economy.[141] By the late 1970s Saudi Arabia was supplying 25 percent of American oil needs. At the same time, 85 percent of its financial reserves were held in dollars. In addition, it was estimated that the Saudis had $59 billion dollars invested in the United States, $35 billion in government security, and $24 billion in other investments.[142] Another economic benefit for the United States was Saudi influence within OPEC. As a result of its huge production capacity, Saudi Arabia dominates OPEC and traditionally they have followed a policy of keeping oil prices stable and maintaining the status quo within the organization. In the late 1970s other OPEC nations, such as Kuwait, were trying to substitute the dollar as the currency of OPEC and also wanted to end the 1978 price freeze. The Saudis rejected this and at the same time in order to boost confidence in the dollar, purchased U.S. Treasury securities while increasing the maturity of the United States bonds they held by 5 years.[143]

During the 1970s and early 1980s, Saudi trade with the United States increased. In 1974 Saudi-American trade stood at $2.6 billion in 1974 and advanced to $8.6 billion in 1976. In 1978 Saudi-American trade stood at $10.2 billion and in 1981 trade was $22.8 billion. The average for the years in between was $19.1 billion. This was accounted for by higher prices for oil, as well as higher imports by the Saudis, going up on average to $6.1 billion from $4.3 billion in 1978.[144]

American-Saudi trade was significant by the mid-1980s the trade balance had shifted in favor of the United States. America imported about $73 billion worth of oil from Saudi Arabia between 1974-1984 and exported $48 billion worth of goods and services to the country. In 1982 the Saudis imported $39 billion worth of goods and exported $50 billion. In 1983, however, Saudi Arabia imported $7.9 billion worth of goods from the United States and exported $3.8 billion. This left the Saudis a trade deficit of $4.1 billion to the United States.[145]

To illustrate the significance of the American share of the Saudi market, in 1976 Saudi imports totaled $28 billion, 25 percent of these were from the United States. It is estimated that this supported 165,000 American workers in addition to the 28,000 Americans who were working in Saudi Arabia.[146]

Saudi Arabia has become an important trading partner for the United States. By the late 1970s Saudi Arabia had become the seventh largest market for the United States for goods, services, and technology, excluding military sales. It is also the most rapidly expanding market for American exports. In 1979, Saudi imports of American goods was estimated at $25 billion and has been increasing at a 25 percent rate per year. While American trade with Saudi Arabia ran into deficit because of imports of petroleum from Saudi Arabia, this was made up by American earnings on services in general, gains for oil companies, and military sales. Also during the 1970s, between 1974-1978 there was an average capital inflow to the United States from Saudi Arabia of $5.1 billion per year. The flow of Saudi funds into the American market was $5.22 billion in 1974, $3.55 billion in 1975, 4.477 billion in 1976, $3.172 billion in 1977, and 1.539 billion in 1978.[147]

American trade with the other countries of the Arabian Peninsula was also significant and growing in the early 1980s. In 1980, United States exports to the Arabian Peninsula was $7.653 billion, this figure grew to $9.380 billion in 1981, and $11.066 billion in 1982.[148] In 1982 exports of industrial products, which includes military goods, exceeded $9 billion. In addition, the Saudis also purchased $500 million in agriculture products. Over 650 American companies were operating in Saudi Arabia, with 60,000 employees and their dependents.[149]

From 1978 to 1981 trade grew from $10.2 billion to $22.8 billion. Much of this increase was attributed to the rise in oil prices. The United States averaged $11.6 billion in oil imports from Saudi Arabia between 1978-1981, as compared with less than $6 billion in 1978. However, Saudi imports also rose during this period from $6.1 billion compared to $4.3 billion in 1978.[150] The importance of Saudi Arabian trade with the United States was reflected by Joseph F. Alibrandi, president of the Whittaker Corporation, in congressional hearings. He pointed out the fact that the United States in the late 1970s and early 1980s was suffering from several years of trade deficits, which exceeded $30 billion. In the 1970s the American share of trade in the industrialized world fell from 15.4 percent to 12.1 percent. In dollar value, America fell behind Japan, and was even with West Germany. He pointed out that trade with Saudi Arabia was essential because it strengthened the American economy, provided jobs for Americans, as well as recycled petrodollars back to the United States.[151]

An important step that the two countries took to facilitate bilateral trade occurred in 1974 with the formation, by a joint communiqué issued by

Secretary of State Kissinger and Prince Fahd, of a Joint Commission for Economic Cooperation. The purpose of this commission was to promote cooperation in industrialization, trade, training programs, agricultural development, as well as facilitate scientific and technological development. The commission was to be headed jointly by the American Secretary of the Treasury and the Saudi Minister of Finance and National Economy.[152] The goal for the United States in establishing this agreement, besides giving the Saudis an incentive to raise oil production, was to serve as a model for economic cooperation between America and the Arab world as a whole. It was to assist the Saudis in planning to expand their industrial capacity, which would then lead to a rise in Saudi imports of goods and technology from the United States. In order to facilitate these objectives the agreement provided for the establishment of an economic commission between the two countries. In preparation for this commission, several working groups were established to deal with such issues as: (1) Saudi economic development, in which the first priority was the examination of ways to use flared gas from oil wells to expand fertilizer production; (2) examination of the importance of skilled training and study of the expansion of the Saudi university system focusing on science and technical training; (3) development of specialized cooperative projects dealing with such fields as solar energy and desalination; (4) the examination of ways to improve agriculture in the Kingdom. In addition, the two countries were to consider setting up a council to facilitate private business contacts.[153]

The Saudi Arms Request of 1985

The military links between the two countries continued throughout the 1980s, although at times the relationship was constrained by American domestic political factors. Political tensions between the United States and Saudi Arabia occurred in 1985 over another arms transaction, the sale of additional F-15 fighters to Saudi Arabia. The purpose of the sale of additional F-15s, as well as other systems, was to enhance the capabilities of the Saudi air force.

The systems the Saudi requested were: (1) the upgrading of previously purchased F-15s to the Multistaged Improvement Program at a cost of $250 million; (2) purchase of 40 additional F-15s with eight others to be stored in the United States as a reserve at a cost of $2.8 billion; (3) the purchase of 980 AIM 9L air-to-air missiles for the F-15 and 630 AIM 9P4 for the F-5 at a total cost of $145 million; (4) 800 portable Stinger surface-to-air missiles for the Saudi Air Defense Corps to defend Saudi infrastructure at the cost of $89 million; (5) 100 Harpoon Missiles designed the give Saudi Arabia a maritime defense, which can be equipped to the F-15 and would cost $106 million; (6) to develop a heliborne lift capability by purchasing 12 unarmed Blackhawk helicopters with an option to purchase 12 more.

This would cost $267 million.[154]

There were a number of justifications for the F-15 plane package. It provided superior air combat technology and would compensate for Saudi Arabia's limited ground forces. The sale would demonstrate American support for Saudi Arabia, which provided credibility and a logistical base for USCENTCOM, as well as enhance Saudi prestige and reinforce its position of leadership among the Arab States of the Persian Gulf. Finally, the sale would illustrate balance between Israel and Saudi Arabia in American foreign policy. This would likewise enhance the Saudi position in the Arab world.[155]

The United States denied the sale for several reasons. First, pro-Israeli groups mobilized opponents in Congress. A major policy fight could have jeopardized domestic policy initiatives such as tax and budget reforms. The administration did not wish to antagonize Jewish-American voters, who had been swinging toward the Republican Party, in an effort to try to maintain Republican control of the Senate in the 1986 elections. This reflected a clash between national security advisors and domestic policy advisors. The foreign policy advisors pressed for the sale based on conceptions of American national interests. The domestic policy advisors were more concerned with maintaining Republican control of Congress in order to advance a conservative legislative agenda.[156] The sale illustrated confusion between the bureaucracy, the State and Defense Departments and the executive branch. The White House was looking to postpone the sale while the State and Defense departments were preparing to submit the arms proposal to Congress prior to November 1986. This sent mixed signals to the Saudis. The delays on the part of the United States resulted in the Saudis turning to Britain and France as possible alternative suppliers. Both countries actively sought arms sales to Saudi Arabia when it looked like the American sale would not be concluded. In early 1986 the Saudis decided to purchase an arms sales package from Great Britain that centered around the Tornado jet. Originally, the Saudis were thinking of purchasing only 48 Tornado aircraft, however the sale eventually increased to 132 aircraft. In addition to the 48 attack versions of the Tornado that had initially been discussed, the British sold the Saudis 24 air defense versions of the aircraft, as well as 30 HAWK aircraft, and 30 Swiss-built Pilatus PC-9s. The later two aircraft were trainers. These additional systems escalated the price of the sale from $4 billion to $7 billion and threatened to shift the dependency of the Saudi air force to Britain. Another aspect of this sale was the British agreement to accept payment in oil. A deal was concluded in which the Shell Transport and Trading Company and British Petroleum were to work with ARAMCO for three years to develop ways to market the oil needed to cover the costs of these planes.[157]

The Reagan administration tried to compensate for the initial failure in 1985 by proposing what was described as a mini arms sales package in 1986. This included 995 AIM-9L air-to-air missiles ($98 million), 671 AIM-9P4 air-to-air missiles ($60 million), 100 Harpoon air-to-sea missiles ($107 million), and 200 Stinger man-portable surface-to-air missile launchers and 600 reload missiles ($89 million). The total value of this package was $354 million. The opposition to this sale was very intense, particularly from pro-Israeli groups. The administration itself badly mismanaged the lobbying efforts by trying to downplay the sale in order to diffuse opposition. The opposition forced the Stinger portion of the sale to be canceled. In June of 1986 the sale was approved by a single vote in the Senate. The questioning of Saudi Arabia and the advisability of having it as an ally, which occurred in public as well as in the Congress, did much to strain relations between the United States and Saudi Arabia.[158]

However, while the United States was not the sole supplier of armaments to Saudi Arabia, the military links between the two countries still remained strong. In addition, due to recent developments it appeared that the United States was interested in reinforcing this relationship. This was evidenced by the announcement in 1989 of the decision to sell 300 M1-A1 battle tanks to the Saudis. It is estimated that the value of this sale was between $700 million and $1 billion.[159] Saudi Arabia had also expressed interest in purchasing other weapons systems, such as the F-18 fighter bomber, as well as other air defense systems.[160]

The Gulf War also provided a strategic rationale for escalating the American arms relationship with Saudi Arabia. The Saudi share of arms agreements and deliveries were a significant share of American worldwide and regional figures throughout the 1980s. This is illustrated in tables and graphs 7.1 and 7.2. However, in 1990-1991 these figures escalated tremendously. In 1990 the Saudi percentage of arms agreements was over 40 percent of the total arms agreements concluded by the United States. In 1991 this figure was almost 60 percent. The statistics for Saudi arms agreements and deliveries during 1990-1991 was over half the total of American arms sales and deliveries for the region as a whole. Saudi Arabia also made up a large proportion of American military construction sales and deliveries for this period. This is evident in tables and graphs 7.3 and 7.4.

Arms transfers to Saudi Arabia have also taken on important domestic political incentives, for much the same reason that Iran did in the 1970s. These include easing the American trade deficit in general, as well as seeking to propel American-Saudi bilateral trade. Another significant factor in decision making on these sales is the maintenance of employment in key economic sectors of the American economy. American public officials have sought to exploit this electorally. This occurred in the 1992 presidential election, as both President George Bush and Governor Bill Clinton advocated arms sales as a way of scoring political points in electorally key states.[161]

Table 7.1. U.S. Military Sales Agreements with Saudi Arabia, 1983-1992 (in thousands of U.S. dollars)

Years	Worldwide	Near East and South Asia (NESA)	Saudi Arabia
1950-1982	106,591,953	52,294,748	21,885,948
1983	14,296,786	4,909,580	769,602
1984	12,417,976	3,968,794	2,618,874
1985	10,403,224	3,664,118	2,473,306
1986	6,301,880	1,888,027	712,860
1987	6,253,629	1,893,613	654,617
1988	11,394,921	7,097,335	1,876,054
1989	10,485,798	6,665,648	1,183,798
1990	13,735,480	7,705,460	5,658,094
1991	22,725,578	16,401,055	13,511,215
1992	14,983,717	2,974,693	974,185
1950-1992	229,590,942	109,463,071	52,118,552

Source: U.S. Department of Defense. *Foreign Military Sales, Foreign Military Construction Sales, and Military Assistance Facts* (Washington, D.C.: U.S. Government Printing Office, September 1992), 2-3.

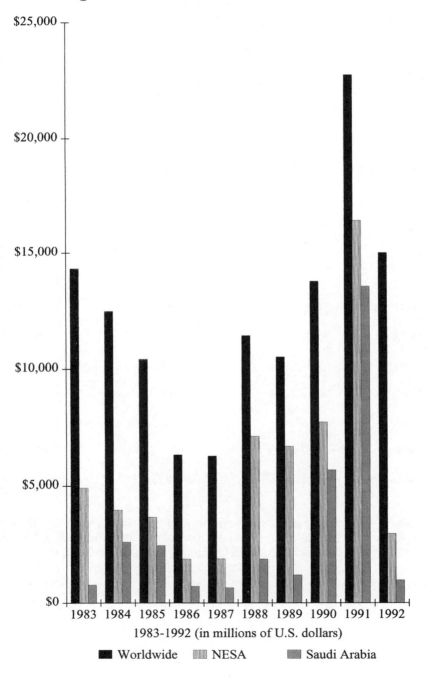

Graph 7.1. U.S. Military Sales Agreements with Saudi Arabia, 1983-1992

1983-1992 (in millions of U.S. dollars)

■ Worldwide   ▥ NESA   ▨ Saudi Arabia

**Table 7.2. U.S. Military Sales Deliveries
to Saudi Arabia, 1983-1992 (in thousands of U.S. dollars)**

Years	Worldwide	Near East and South Asia (NESA)	Saudi Arabia
1950-1982	66,136,485	32,510,907	8,826,766
1983	10,606,795	5,787,356	3,660,736
1984	6,166,927	3,571,866	2,102,524
1985	7,508,743	3,167,020	1,363,942
1986	7,236,031	3,397,162	2,226,108
1987	10,876,542	5,999,925	3,155,254
1988	8,790,663	2,617,805	970,460
1989	6,942,576	1,640,265	629,186
1990	7,438,878	2,354,029	890,468
1991	8,761,831	4,095,119	2,834,299
1992	9,675,035	4,844,259	2,474,571
1950-1992	152,140,506	69,985,713	29,134,314

Source: U.S. Department of Defense. *Foreign Military Sales, Foreign Military Construction Sales, and Military Assistance Facts* (Washington, D.C.: U.S. Government Printing Office, September 1992), 16-17.

Graph 7.2. U.S. Military Sales
Deliveries to Saudi Arabia, 1983-1992

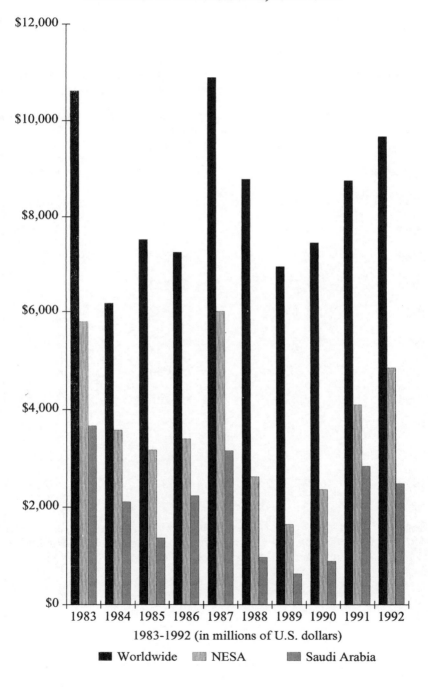

1983-1992 (in millions of U.S. dollars)

■ Worldwide   ▥ NESA   ▨ Saudi Arabia

Table 7.3. U.S. Military Construction Agreements with Saudi Arabia, 1983-1992 (in thousands of U.S. dollars)

Years	Worldwide	Near East and South Asia (NESA)	Saudi Arabia
1950-1982	14,727,610	14,711,766	14,683,778
1983	21,850	16,404	16,404
1984	404,479	398,023	362,658
1985	957,656	944,099	927,660
1986	69,230	32,862	6,000
1987	129,892	117,898	—
1988	209,518	134,802	18,700
1989	79,373	65,684	—
1990	551,272	528,599	470,754
1991	743,479	737,307	389,626
1992	188,031	166,371	45,323
1950-1992	16,082,395	17,853,815	16,920,903

Source: U.S. Department of Defense. *Foreign Military Sales, Foreign Military Construction Sales, and Military Assistance Facts* (Washington, D.C.: U.S. Government Printing Office, September 1992), 10-11.

Graph 7.3. U.S. Military Construction Agreements with Saudi Arabia, 1983-1992

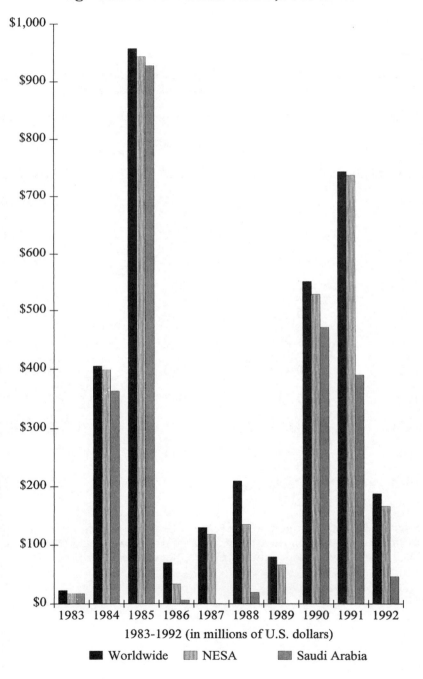

1983-1992 (in millions of U.S. dollars)

■ Worldwide ▥ NESA ▨ Saudi Arabia

Table 7.4. U.S. Military Construction Deliveries to Saudi Arabia, 1983-1992 (in thousands of U.S. dollars)

Years	Worldwide	Near East and South Asia (NESA)	Saudi Arabia
1950-1982	9,046,217	9,037,658	9,031,698
1983	2,160,428	2,155,513	2,153,170
1984	1,475,290	1,473,117	1,470,812
1985	922,394	915,589	901,117
1986	573,824	560,499	547,027
1987	265,165	250,248	242,546
1988	411,013	387,048	359,646
1989	390,499	376,490	346,602
1990	347,738	337,983	263,093
1991	414,074	402,857	274,549
1992	341,627	333,356	222,774
1950-1992	16,348,269	16,230,360	15,813,034

Source: U.S. Department of Defense. *Foreign Military Sales, Foreign Military Construction Sales, and Military Assistance Facts* (Washington, D.C.: U.S. Government Printing Office, September 1992), 24-25.

Graph 7.4. U.S. Military Construction Deliveries to Saudi Arabia, 1983-1992

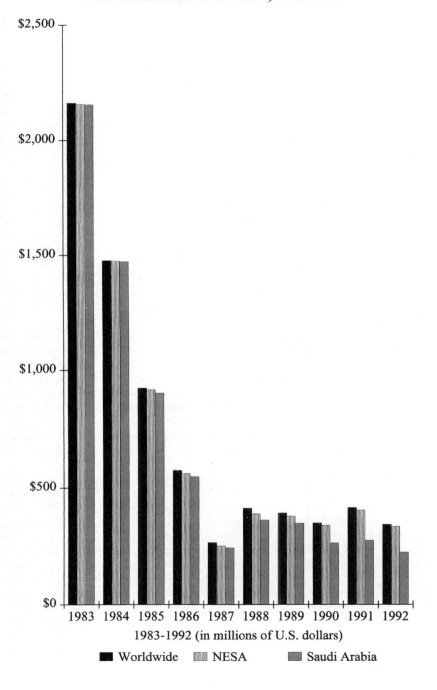

1983-1992 (in millions of U.S. dollars)

■ Worldwide   ▦ NESA   ▨ Saudi Arabia

The Importance of Oil in American-Saudi Relations, 1973-1985

From October 1973 to the mid-1980s, Saudi oil policy passed through four phases. Phase I occurred from October 1973 to September 1974 and was in response to the 1973 Arab-Israeli war and the American resupply of Israel. Saudi Arabia imposed an embargo on oil to the United States and cut back its production by 25 percent, a response that led to a dramatic increase in oil prices. After the price rise, however, the Saudis sought to modify its effects by arguing for lower prices within OPEC and even planned to auction off oil as a way of bringing prices down. The second phase occurred from September 1974 to December 1978. During this period, the Saudis sought to meet market demand and at times this led to conflicts with other OPEC members as the Saudis sought to keep oil at a stable price. Phase III began in December 1978 and ended in July 1979. During this period various factors contributed to a rapid increase in prices. One of the main reasons was the Iranian revolution, which curtailed Iranian production, coupled by two sharp production cuts by Saudi Arabia. Phase IV began in July 1979 to the mid-1980s. The Saudis used their position in the oil market as they increased and decreased production to keep the price of oil stable. This manipulation of oil production prevented a third oil price shock as a result of the Iran-Iraq war.[162]

The first phase of Saudi oil policy led to cutbacks in production and the rapid rise of the price of oil. The organizational structure to bring this about was put in place in 1967 when the Arab members of OPEC formed the Organization of Arab Petroleum Exporting Countries (OAPEC). The goals of OAPEC as defined by Saudi Oil Minister Yamani were to: (1) facilitate the use of oil to serve the interests of member countries, as well as Arab countries in general; (2) provide for joint development of oil resources in the member states; and (3) establish means by which the producer and consumer nations could broaden their contacts economically and politically.[163]

During this period there was pressure on OAPEC, particularly Saudi Arabia, to use oil to force the United States to reduce its support for Israel. Prior to the 1973 war the Saudis indicated that they would consider using oil as a weapon to influence American policy.[164] The oil embargo was triggered by the 1973 Arab-Israeli war and was pursued on three strategies: reduced oil production, embargoes on countries considered friendly to Israel, and a rise in oil prices generally. A fourth option, the nationalization of foreign oil companies, was held in reserve and was not adopted collectively; the only major Arab oil producer advocating this policy was Iraq. On October 17, 1973, OAPEC voted to cut back oil exports and production by five percent from the September 1973 levels, as well as by an additional five percent each month until the Israelis withdrew from Arab territories. On November 7 these cutbacks were increased to 25 percent.

Subsequently, the United States extended $2.2 billion in military aid to Israel, which brought about a total embargo by Arab oil producers against America, as well as Canada, the Netherlands, Portugal, Rhodesia, South Africa, and South Yemen.[165]

As the Saudis sought to reduce world oil prices during Phase II they concluded several bilateral agreements with the United States. The most important was concluded on June 8, 1974, as Saudi Deputy Prime Minister Fahd signed an agreement with Henry Kissinger providing for extensive military and economic cooperation. This provided for an easing of tensions between the two countries as a result of the oil embargo the previous year. In return, it called for the Saudis to cooperate in supplying the energy needs of the United States and its allies.[166]

In January 1979 the United States attempted to shore up relations with Saudi Arabia in the aftermath of the Iranian revolution. During a visit to Saudi Arabia, Secretary of Defense Brown proposed extensive plans to expand Saudi-American military and economic relations. Unofficial reports stated that Secretary Brown offered the Saudis the establishment of American bases as well as the stationing of American military forces in Saudi Arabia. In return, the United States hoped to get from Saudi Arabia assurances that the Saudis would increase oil production, further support the dollar by maintaining investments in the United States, and support the attempts by the administration to resolve the Arab-Israeli conflict.[167]

During the first half of the 1980s Saudi Arabia's importance to the United States was illustrated by the amount of oil it held. The United States imported 20 times more oil from Saudi Arabia than the other Gulf countries. The Saudis control 25 percent of the world's oil reserves and can if they so choose produce as much as 10 million barrels per day. Their importance was illustrated during 1985 when the Saudis were exporting about 3 million barrels per day to make up for shortfalls in the world market caused by the Iran-Iraq War.[168]

This reflected the importance of Saudi Arabia to the West, as they were, and still are, the most important state in OPEC given the amount of oil reserves and production capabilities that they control. They have traditionally kept the organization from establishing profit-maximizing prices and have cut oil prices several times in order to bring stability into the market.[169]

While generally being forthcoming on the price of oil, the Saudis have at times broken with the United States over other issues. They have given military support in all the Arab-Israeli wars, except 1956, as well as stationed troops in Jordan until 1975. In addition, they participated in military maneuvers with other Arab states, the purpose of which was to train for a future outbreak of hostilities. The Saudis also were supporters of the PLO and participated in the Baghdad Conferences of 1978 and 1979, which were to block a resolution of the Arab-Israeli conflict. They also criticized and cut off aid to Egypt after President Sadat's unilateral attempt to seek a separate peace treaty with Israel.[170]

Internal Politics of the Saudi State and the Effects on the American-Saudi Alliance

The Mosque Uprising in 1979

Two major shocks occurred within Saudi Arabia in late 1979 and early 1980 that threatened the foundations of the regime. These were the takeover of the Grand Mosque in Mecca in 1979 and the Shia riots in the Eastern Province in December 1979 and February 1980. The Mecca incident was the result of a group of religious-political dissidents who were inspired by their view of the corruption of the Saudi political-religious leadership, as well as the belief in a Messianic vision that is not present in Sunni Islamic belief. The leader of this group was named Juhayman bin Muhammad bin Sayf al-Utaiba. He was a former National Guard noncommissioned officer whose family had been prominent in the Ikhwan movement of the 1920s. Juhayman had attended the Medina theological college where he was a student of the very conservative religious leader Shaykh bin Baz. However, Juhayman eventually broke with him and established his own following. Prominent among his followers were members of the Utaiba tribe, opponents of the Saudis, descendants of the Ikhwan who fought Ibn Saud in the 1920s, and foreigners. Juhayman began preaching in Riyadh in 1978 and persuaded his followers that a bedouin theology student named Muhammad ibn Abdallah al-Qahtani was the expected Mahdi. In November of 1979, 400-500 armed followers of Juhayman barricaded themselves in the Grand Mosque and resisted Saudi forces for two weeks before the remnants of this force, including Juhayman, surrendered on December 3 after a pitched battle in which the Saudi military retook the Mosque, fighting room by room.

The Saudi leadership delayed at first in sending in the military forces as the Mosque was the holiest shrine in Islam and the ensuing battle risked the shedding of blood as well as the destruction of large portions of the structure. Before the Saudi leadership authorized the use of force they obtained a fatwa from the ulema. Although the fatwa denounced the rebels for their uprising and for using weapons in the Kaba, it did not cite the rebels for heresy. Among the ulema who concurred with the fatwa were ultraconservative religious leaders opposed to modernization, notably Sheikh Abd al-Aziz, the mentor of Juhayman.[171]

The second major disturbance during this period was the Shia riots in the Eastern Provinces in late 1979 and early 1980. The Shia community of Saudi Arabia is concentrated in the Eastern Province known as Hasa. It is estimated that more than one-third of the population of this province are Shia and includes 95 percent of the city of Qatif and half of the Hufuf district. The total Shia population in Saudi Arabia varies, depending on the study, from 200,00 to 440,000. The more accurate figure was probably closer to 350,000.[172]

The Wahhabis view the Shia as deviating from Islam as a result of their practice of saint worship, shrines, and the belief in imams. A central component of the Wahhabi religious ideology is the belief in the doctrine of tauhid, which means the oneness of God. Thus the Shia practice of saint worship and the belief in imams is viewed as interposing other beings between God and humans. In the Wahhabi view this weakens the distinction between God and human beings. Therefore the Wahhabi equate Shiaism with polytheism, or shirk. Historically, the Shia were perceived as unbelievers and their persecution was justified as they were subject to jihad. The conflict between the Wahhabi and the Shia dates back to the late 18th century. In the 1790s the Saudis destroyed all Shia mosques and shrines in the Hasa when that area was taken over by the first Saudi state. In 1801 the Saudis raided Kerbala and destroyed the Shia shrines there.[173]

In 1927 Ibn Saud, in order to placate the Ikhwan, supported a fatwa that would essentially have forced the Shia to convert to Wahhabism or face exile. However, after Ibn Saud's break with the Ikhwan shortly thereafter, he never enforced this and his policy was that the Shia could practice their own traditions in private. The Shia started to become more integrated into the state as the discovery of oil gave them more employment opportunities. However, the Shia were still excluded from much of Saudi society. The Iranian revolution raised the religious consciousness of a segment of the Shia population. Ostensibly, the Shia riots began as a result of the banning of the Ashura demonstrations commemorating the martyrdom of the third imam, Husayn. However, the more fundamental question was the second-class status that the Shia had as citizens, as well as the lack of attention that the Eastern Province received from the central government in terms of budgetary and developmental projects. After 1980 the Saudis sought to remedy this by devoting more emphasis on the development of Hasa. King Khalid visited the province and it figured prominently in the Third Five-Year Development Plan, which included greater expenditures for public health, education, and infrastructure.[174]

Conclusions

Strategic Advantages of the American Arms Relationship with Saudi Arabia

During the 1970s the Saudis sought to modernize all sectors of its military forces. This fitted in with the American policy of bolstering and making militarily strong regional allies to guard its interests in the region. This consisted of ensuring a secure source of oil to the West and containing the growth of Soviet influence in the southwest Asia-Indian Ocean area. Another factor, due to the Nixon Doctrine and the encouraging of these various military modernization programs, was that in the mid-1970s Saudi

Arabia became the second largest purchaser of American military equipment next to Iran.[175]

However, by the latter portion of the decade the only service that could pose a credible threat to a regional adversary was the Royal Saudi Air Force (RSAF). The modernization programs in the other services suffered from a lack of cohesive planning and improper training. The Saudi army remained weak and undermanned due to the diversification of its arms sources. As a result, different training and maintenance programs were required. In addition, various Saudi units were stationed throughout the 1970s in Jordan, Syria, and Lebanon, which further inhibited proper training. The National Guard suffered from similar weaknesses, with the added fact that it tended to recruit along tribal lines from groups deemed most loyal to the Saud family. This inhibited its effectiveness. The Saudi navy, likewise, was weak as it expanded too rapidly causing severe logistical, procurement, and training difficulties.[176]

Although Saudi Arabia, like Iran, was a boon for the American arms industry it could not play the role of a regional military power. This was inhibited in part by the internal dynamics within the nation itself, as well as the problems caused by the military buildup. Thus, while the Saudis remained a good customer for American defense contractors, its role in the view of American policy makers, at least in the military dimension, was secondary to Iran.

During this period Saudi Arabia benefitted American interests in the region. First, the arms buildup brought about new commercial relationships between the two countries. By building up Saudi armed forces the United States was further enhancing its influence in the kingdom. The drawback of this policy was that the United States was becoming more militarily involved with Saudi Arabia, while the Saudi military was not improving by any great lengths. Had the Saudis been drawn into any type of conflict this would have necessitated active American involvement. Another drawback in the relationship with Saudi Arabia was that the status of the alliance began to depend on American military aid and arms sales. This served to foreshadow the nature of the future military relationship between the United States and its regional allies as more far-reaching and meaningful contacts became subordinate to the emphasis on large-scale arms sales.

In analyzing American-Saudi relations during the 1980s, it appears that the relationship has, on the whole, been a beneficial one for the United States, particularly in the political sphere. As stated previously, the GCC has given the Saudis a means by which to exercise regional leadership by formulating coherent political and military strategies with its like-minded neighbors. This gives the United States at least a form of indirect influence over the policies of the other Gulf states.

The military relationship has taken on a new phase as Saudi Arabia came to replace Iran as the leading American military ally in the Persian Gulf. For the United States this had certain advantages and the first of these is economic. The Nixon Doctrine emphasized American arms sales abroad, particularly to the Middle East, to keep domestic production lines open, as well as ease American balance-of-payments deficits. Arms exports to the Middle East, specifically to Iran and Saudi Arabia, enabled American aerospace production lines to not only survive, but to produce at nearly full capacity. This was at a time when the American defense budget was being sharply reduced at the end of the Vietnam War.[177]

This not only served to benefit American industry but the American military as well. There is a conception on the part of American policy makers, particularly military officers, that a vibrant aerospace industry is essential for national security.[178] Therefore, it is necessary to keep these production lines open and at full capacity in order to keep the potential for production in existence, as well as the fostering of technical innovation that is the cornerstone of any armaments industry. In addition, these goals could be extended in one form or another to other defense industries.

This policy goal is evident in more recent American decisions regarding arms sales to Saudi Arabia. Part of the justification for the sales is that if the United States does not sell to the Saudis another country will. It appeared that the proposed sale of the M1-A1 tank was motivated by the desire of American policy makers to keep the General Dynamics tank production line open in order to produce upgraded models in the years ahead.[179]

Another economic benefit was the effect the increasing arms sales to the oil-rich countries of the Middle East would have in easing the American balance-of-payments deficits that were caused by the dramatic rise in oil prices. It is charged that this played a part in American decision makers evaluation of the utility of arms sales to the Middle East.[180]

In addition, the United States' arms relationship with Saudi Arabia has provided access to Saudi political and military elites as a result of the various military advisory groups present within Saudi Arabia. There have also been a number of joint planning studies done between the militaries of both countries that have allowed the United States to gain a certain degree of influence over the defense policy of the country.

Another benefit that these arms sales provided for the United States was the establishment of an informal means for power projection in the region that has been enhanced as a result of the prepositioning of equipment, and the improvements in infrastructure as a result of these arms transfers.

Finally, American arms sales to Saudi Arabia served two purposes regionally in the aftermath of the Iranian revolution. It provided indirect support to the smaller states of the Persian Gulf who were allied with Saudi Arabia by allowing the Saudis to extend a defense umbrella over these nations. These arms transfers served as a possible deterrent to the extension of the Iran-Iraq War to the Arab side of the Persian Gulf.

Disadvantages of the American-Saudi Arms Relationship

The emphasis on arms sales as the primary pillar of support of the American-Saudi relationship carried with it the danger of having arms sales directing the relationship. This would be at the expense of American interests in the region, since by fueling regional arms races the United States would be planting the seeds of instability in the region. This could lead to regional instability and the inability of the United States to achieve its stated goals mentioned earlier. The emphasis on arms sales and the tensions that the debate causes, which was illustrated when the U.S. Congress rejected the sale of additional F-15s in 1986, undercuts the more important strategic consensus that the two nations shared. In addition, this threatened more meaningful political and commercial (nonmilitary) contacts.

Second, the emphasis on arms transfers to help American industry should not be the major determinant for a sale. This perpetuates the view by American defense contractors and military officials that the country is a surplus market, much like Iran was viewed under the Shah. As a result, this could lead to the sale of weapons with little or no strategic value for either party. There are indications that the United States may be heading in this direction, as was illustrated earlier. It is important for the United States to consider the effects that a close military relationship with Saudi Arabia will have on the internal politics of both the country and the region as the perception of too great a reliance on the United States could result in the delegitimation of the Saudi royal family both internally and regionally.

In conclusion, during the 1970s the Saudis sought to modernize all sectors of its military forces. This fitted in with the American policy of bolstering and making militarily strong regional allies to guard its interests in the region. This consisted of ensuring a secure source of oil to the West and contain the growth of Soviet influence in the southwest Asia-Indian Ocean area. Due to the Nixon Doctrine and the encouraging of Saudi military modernization programs in the middle 1970s, Saudi Arabia became the second largest purchaser of American military equipment after Iran.[181]

Although Saudi Arabia and Iran both invested heavily in American arms during this period, the Saudis were willing to spend more on construction, infrastructure, and services than the Iranians were. It can be observed that throughout the 1970s, 70 percent of the Iranian military purchases from America was in equipment and munitions. The Saudis allocated 70 percent of their military purchases to creating and further developing their military infrastructure.[182] Thus, when they did receive new military equipment the Saudis were in a better position to make more efficient use of it. However, in the short-term they continued to lag behind the Iranians in overall military strength.

Despite this factor, however, the implications of the modernization programs on the Saudi armed services was such that by the latter portion of the 1970s the only service that could pose a credible threat to any potential regional adversary was the Royal Saudi Air Force (RSAF). The modernization programs in the other services suffered from a lack of cohesive planning and improper training. The Saudi army remained weak and undermanned due to the fact that its arms sources were diversified and thus needed different training and maintenance programs. In addition, various Saudi units were stationed throughout the 1970s in Jordan, Syria, and Lebanon that further inhibited proper training. The National Guard suffered from similar weaknesses, with the added fact that it tended to recruit along tribal lines from groups deemed most loyal to the Saud family. This inhibited its effectiveness. The Saudi navy, likewise, suffered as it expanded too rapidly causing severe logistical, procurement, and training difficulties.[183]

Therefore, although Saudi Arabia, like Iran, was a boon for the American arms industry, it could not play the role of a regional military power as it was inhibited in part by the internal dynamics within the nation itself as well as the problems caused by the military buildup. Although the Saudis remained a good customer for American defense contractors, its role in the view of American policy makers, at least in the military dimension, was secondary to Iran.

During this period Saudi Arabia benefitted American goals for the region. First, the arms buildup brought about new commercial relationships between the two countries. By building up Saudi armed forces the United States was further enhancing its influence in the kingdom, while at the same time attempting to build up Saudi Arabia as a regional power. The drawbacks of this policy was that the United States was becoming more militarily involved with Saudi Arabia while the Saudi military was not improving by any great lengths. Therefore, had the Saudis been drawn into any type of conflict this would have necessitated active American involvement. This was illustrated with the Persian Gulf War of 1990-1991. The Saudis were not in a military position, despite having purchased large quantities of the latest American equipment, to deter Iraq from attacking Kuwait or evicting them after the fact. The United States was forced to intervene to first protect Saudi Arabia, and then to drive the Iraqis out of Kuwait. While the Saudis did contribute military forces, it was essentially an American operation.

Another drawback in the relationship was that Saudi Arabia, like the American alliance with Iran, began to take on more military characteristics. While this was to be expected given the security implications of American interests in the region, it served to foreshadow the nature of the future military relationship between the United States and its regional allies, as more far-reaching and meaningful contacts became subordinate to the emphasis on large-scale arms sales. In conclusion, the emphasis on arms sales as the primary support pillar of the American-Saudi relationship carried with it the danger of having them direct the relationship. This could lead to regional instability and the inability of the United States to achieve its stated goals mentioned earlier. The emphasis on arms sales and the tensions that the debate causes, which was illustrated when the U.S. Congress rejected the sale of additional F-15s in 1986, undercuts the more important strategic consensus that the two nations shared. This also threatened more meaningful political and commercial (nonmilitary) contacts.

Finally, it is important for the United States to be aware of the basic political, economic, and social problems facing not only the Middle East, but other regions as well, and not base its foreign policy towards the Third World solely on maintaining security. If these other basic issues are not addressed, regional and systemic insecurity will grow, regardless of how militarily strong a particular country is. The policy of basing a foreign policy on large-scale arms transfers could result in the inability of American decision makers to consider alternative policies and approaches in dealing with regional problems. As a result of this, the United States would be unable to react to events in the Third World in a timely manner. This occurred during the Iranian revolution, as the strategic commitment made to the Iranian monarchy led to confusion among American decision makers in dealing with this event. As a result, any chance that Washington might have had in maintaining relations with the revolutionary regime were dashed.

Notes

1. Charles G. MacDonald, "U.S. Policy and Gulf Security," in *Gulf Security into the 1980's*, Robert G. Darius, John W. Amos, and Ralph H. Magnus eds. (Stanford, Calif.: Hoover Institution Press, 1984), 99.

2. U.S. House of Representatives Committee on International Affairs, Subcommittee on Europe and the Middle East, *Saudi Arabia and the United States: The New Context in an Evolving Special Relationship,* Staff Report by Richard M. Preece, 97th Cong., 1st sess., August 1981, 7, 69-70.

3. David Long, *The United States and Saudi Arabia Ambivalent Allies* (Boulder, Colo.: Westview Press, 1985), 47.

4. Anthony Cordesman, *The Gulf and the Search for Strategic Stability* (Boulder, Colo.: Westview Press, 1984), 163.

5. Cordesman, *The Gulf and the Search*, 164. See also U.S. Senate Committee on Foreign Relations, *U.S. Arms Sales Policy*, 94th Cong., 2nd sess., 1976, 2, 10, 62.

6. Cordesman, *The Gulf and The Search*, 279.

7. Cordesman, *The Gulf and the Search*, 163-65.

8. Long, *The United States and Saudi Arabia*, 59.

9. Long, *The United States and Saudi Arabia*, 60-61.

10. Cordesman, *The Gulf and the Search*, 207. Cordesman points out that the Saudis had problems with maintenance engine performance problems and that the F-15 was difficult to maintain without a large stock of spare parts.

11.United Press International, "Saudi Arabian F-15s Purchases Being Discussed," *Washington Post*, 6 January 1978, 2.

12. Long, *The United States and Saudi Arabia*, 60-61; David Holden and Richard Johns, *The House of Saud: The Rise and Rule of the Most Powerful Dynasty in the Arab World* (New York: Holt, Rinehart, and Winston, 1981), 487. See also Shahram Chubin, *Security in the Persian Gulf 4: The Role of Outside Powers* (Totowa, N.J.: Allanheld, Osmun, and Company, 1982), 49. In addition to the previously discussed restrictions, he states that the Saudis also agreed not to transfer the F-15 or allow third country nationals to train on them. In addition, the Saudis promised that they would not acquire additional combat aircraft to supplement the F-15.

13. Robert Keatley and Karen Elliott House, "Israel, Saudi Arabia and the F-15," *Wall Street Journal*, 4 May 1978, 20; and Robert Kaiser, "Vance Told Most of Senate Panel Opposed Sale of F-15 to Saudis," *Washington Post*, 26 January 1978, 7.

14. Richard Burt, "Senate Study Sees a U.S. Dilemma in Saudi Jet Sale," *New York Times*, 23 March 1978, 13.

15. U.S. House of Representatives Committee on Foreign Affairs, *Proposed Sale of AWACS and F-15 Enhancement to Saudi Arabia, Hearings*, before the Subcommittee on International Security and Scientific Affairs, and Subcommittee on Europe and the Middle East, 97th Cong., 2nd sess., 1982, 19, 21. See also Adeed I. Dawisha, "Internal Values and External Threats: The Making of Saudi Foreign Policy," *Orbis* 23, no. 1 (Spring 1979): 142-43. For a discussion of the number of advisors required to maintain this program see U.S. Senate Committee on Foreign Relations, *Proposed U.S. Sales of Fighter Aircraft to Saudi Arabia, Egypt, and Israel, Hearings*, before the Committee on Foreign Relations, 95th Cong., 2nd sess., 1978, 47. The importance of advisors to the F-15 program was illustrated by the chairman of the Joint Chiefs of Staff when stated that the peak period for integrating the F-15 into the Saudi Air Force would take 2 years, 500-600 civilian technicians, and 40 military personnel.

16. Andrew J. Pierre, *The Global Politics of Arms Sales* (Princeton, N.J.: Princeton University Press, 1982), 182. The most important factor was the political implications. The Saudis wanted the F-15 as a way to get a commitment from the United States. The actual plane itself, as well as the infrastructure and training, would require an American commitment for the next two decades. The Saudis felt that the planes would serve as a guarantee of American support for the Saudi regime.

17. U.S. General Accounting Office, *Critical Factors Affecting Saudi Arabia Oil Decisions* (Washington, D.C.: U.S. Government Printing Office, May 12, 1978), 33.

18. Senate Committee, *Proposed U.S. Sales of Fighter Aircraft*, 48. This sentiment was echoed by Secretary of State Cyrus Vance. He stated, "First, let me tell you I think if we delay the requests and let's just start with Saudi Arabia and Egypt that the likelihood is that they are going to turn elsewhere to have those needs met," (101). Vance also pointed out the importance of Saudi Arabia to the U.S. economy as a result of their financial investments and oil policy. See Robert Kaiser, "Top Aides Grilled on Jets," *Washington Post*, 4 May 1978, 1.

19. Senate Committee, *Proposed U.S. Sales of Fighter Aircraft*, 19; See also statement by Senator John Glenn, (D-Ohio), who pointed out the strategic significance of the Strait of Hormuz through which comes 85 percent of Japan's oil, 70 percent of Western Europe's oil, and 18 percent of American oil imports (55).

20. Senate Committee, *Proposed U.S. Sales of Fighter Aircraft*, 19

21. Holden and Johns, *The House of Saud*, 487-88.

22. Editorial, "A Special Relationship," *Wall Street Journal*, 17 May 1978, 22. Argument was advanced that the Saudis specifically had to be concerned with the buildup of Iraqi military forces that were primarily supplied by the Soviet Union. See Graham Hovey, "U.S. Plans First Jet Sale to Cairo, Reduces Israeli Order for Craft; Saudis Get 60; Debate is Expected," *New York Times*, 15 February 1978, 1. The Saudis were also concerned about the defense of their oil fields in the Eastern Province from attacks by Iran. See Pranay B. Gupte, "Saudis Expect US to Agree on F-15s." *New York Times*, 22 February 1981, 11.

23. "Senate Study Sees a U.S. Dilemma in Saudi Jet Sale," *New York Times*, 23 March 1978, 13.

24. Bernard Weinraub, "U.S. Weighing Sale of F-15s to Saudis," *New York Times*, 20 July 1977, 1.

25. Bernard Weinraub, "Pentagon Asks Sale of F-15 to Saudis," *New York Times*, 31 August 1977, 1(A).

26. Geoffrey Godsell, "U.S.-Saudi Fighter Deal: Stakes High for All," *Christian Science Monitor*, 10 April 1978, 1. See also, Associated Press, "Saudi F-15 Wouldn't Alter Power Balance GAO Finds," *Washington Post*, 5 May 1978, 26. The economic links between the two countries included $5 billion in trade and one-tenth of America's oil needs. See Don Oberdorfer, "Saudis Warn U.S. against Delaying Jet Fighter Sale," *Washington Post*, 15 March 1978, 1.

27. Peter Osnos and David Ottaway, "Yamani Links F-15 to Oil, Dollar Help," *Washington Post*, 2 May 1978, 1.

28. John K. Cooley, "Saudi Reprieve for Dollar," *Christian Science Monitor*, 6 March 1978, 3.

29. Holden and Johns, *The House of Saud*, 486.

30. Godsell, "U.S.-Saudi Fighter Deal," 1.

31. Richard Harward and Ward Sinclair, "Lobbying for Warplane Brings Saudis Out of Isolation," *Washington Post*, 7 May 1978, A14.

32. John Dillin, "Saudis Growing Role Prompted F-15 Deal," *Christian Science Monitor*, 23 February 1978, 1.

33. Associated Press, "U.S. Plans Bases for Saudi F-15," *Washington Post*, 25 October 1979, 3(A).

34. Jim Hoagland and J. P. Smith, "Saudi Arabia and the United States: Security and Interdependence," *Survival* 20, no. 2 (March-April 1978): 83. This argument was also made by a State Department official in seeking to justify the sale. "Saudi Arabia has told the United States in strong terms that a substantial delay in the projected sale of F-15 jet fighters would force it to turn elsewhere for advanced warplanes a State Department official said yesterday. The American commitment to meet Saudi Arabia's legitimate defense needs with F-15s was made in 1975 by President Ford and in 1976, and reaffirmed by President Carter in 1977 and 1978. The United States and Saudi Arabia have come to share a special relationship on a broad range of basic matters including $5 billion in trade this year and Saudi supply of almost one-tenth of the oil now being used by Americans." See Oberdorfer, "Saudis Warn U.S.," 1.

35. Long, *The United States and Saudi Arabia*, 61-62.

36. Cordesman, *The Gulf and the Search*, 306; Also Anthony H. Cordesman, *Western Strategic Interests in Saudi Arabia* (London: Croom Helm, 1987), 180.

37. Cordesman, *Western Strategic Interests*, 189.

38. Cordesman, *Western Strategic Interests*, 189-90.

39. Cordesman, *The Gulf and the Search*, 281.

40. Cordesman, *The Gulf and the Search*, 325-27. Provides a comprehensive discussion of the strategic advantages for the United States in terms of power projection capabilities. Also Cordesman points out that this sale builds on previous Saudi weapons system acquisitions, as well as requires American support to maintain these systems.

41. Scott Armstrong, "Saudis AWACS Just a Beginning," *Washington Post*, 1 November 1981, 1.

42. Michael Getler, "Arms and the Mideast: Experts Fear AWACS Impact on Stability," *Washington Post*, 9 May 1981, 1.

43. Richard Whittle, "Instability and Soviet Pressure Seen As Persian Gulf Threats," *Congressional Quarterly* 39, no. 2 (October 17, 1981): 2009.

44. U.S. Senate Committee on Foreign Relations, *The AWACS and F-15 Enhancements Arms Sales Package to Saudi Arabia, Hearings* before the Committee on Foreign Relations, 97th Cong., 1st sess., 1981, 12. Testimony of Secretary of State Alexander Haig. President Reagan himself advanced a similar theme by emphasizing the importance of the sale in increasing stability of the region against the Soviet threat, and that Saudi Arabia should not become another "Iran." Cited in Richard L. Strout, "Senate Tug of War: Both Sides Strain for the Winning Edge," *Christian Science Monitor*, 27 October 1981, 1. Also Secretary of Defense Caspar Weinberger stated that the approval of the AWACS sale would encourage other Arab states that the United States can be counted on. See Godrey Sperling, "AWACS Flies for Reagan, Saudis," *Christian Science Monitor*, 29 October 1981, 1.

45. David Maxfield, "Senate Panel Deadlocks on Mideast Plane Sales; Fight Moves to Floor," *Congressional Quarterly* 36, no.19 (May 13, 1978): 8.

46. Richard Whittle, "Reagan Loses AWACS Votes, but Picks Up Some Support among Senate Republicans," *Congressional Quarterly* 39, no. 2 (October 17, 1981): 2007-08.

47. House Committee, *Proposed Sale of AWACS*, 1981, 40, 65, 148-49.

48. U.S. Senate Committee on Foreign Relations, *Disapproval of the Proposed Sales to Saudi Arabia of E-3A Airborne Warning and Control Systems,* Hearings before the Foreign Relations Committee. 97th Cong., 1st sess., 1981, 16.

49. Edward Cody, "Fahd Warns Senate, Praises Reagan on Handling of Saudi AWACS Deal," *Washington Post,* 29 September 1981, 1.

50. U.S. Senate Committee on Foreign Relations, *The Proposed AWACS/F-15 Enhancement Sale to Saudi Arabia,* Staff Report, 97th Cong., 1st sess., 1981, ix.

51. U.S. Senate Committee on Armed Services, *Military and Technical Implications of the Proposed Sale of Air Defense Enhancements to Saudi Arabia,* Hearings before the Committee on Armed Services, 97th Cong., 1st sess., 1981, 23.

52. Senate Committee, *The Proposed AWACS/F-15 Enhancement*, 1981, 55.

53. Senate Committee, *The Proposed AWACS/F-15 Enhancement*, 1981, 34.

54. Senate Committee, *The Proposed AWACS/F-15 Enhancement,* 1981, ix. See also Geoffrey Godsell, "Political Dogfight in U.S. Leaves Long-Range Diplomatic Trail," *Christian Science Monitor*, 27 October 1981, 1.

55. U.S. House of Representatives Committee on Appropriations, *Proposed AWACS F-15 Enhancement Equipment and Sidewinder AIM-9L Missile Sales to Saudi Arabia, Hearings* before the Subcommittee on Foreign Operations, of the Committee on Appropriations, 97th Cong., 1st sess., 1981, 14, 18. Testimony of Alvin Cottrell. Karen House, "Rejecting AWACS Poses Risks," *Washington Post*, 9 October 1981, 26.

56. Youssef M. Ibrahim, "Yamani Says If Saudis Don't Get AWACS Bitter Feelings toward U.S. Would Result," *Wall Street Journal*, 29 September 1981, 4. See also Gerald F. Seib, "U.S. Plan to Sell AWACS Planes to Saudis," *Wall Street Journal*, 20 April 1981, 3.

57. United Press International, "Saudis May Seek Arms Elsewhere," *Washington Post,* 19 September 1981, 2.

58. Cordesman, *The Gulf and Search*, 331.

59. Albert R. Hunt, "Some Senators Say They Were Promised White House Favors to Vote for AWACS," *Wall Street Journal*, 14 October 1981, 4. In a regional appeal the Agriculture Department announced that the plan to institute user fees for cotton warehouse inspection would be dropped as a gesture for positive votes on the AWACS. This was especially designed to appeal to southern senators. See The Federal Triangle, "AWACS Wheeling-Dealing Reaches the Grass(ley)

Roots," *Washington Post*, 9 October 1981, 29(A).

60. Albert Hunt, "Reagan Letter to Crucial Senator Seeks to Turn Tide of Battle Over Arms Sale," *Wall Street Journal*, 21 October 1981, 2. See also Steven Roberts, "Recipe for a White House Victory: Arm-Twisting, Flattery, and Aura," *New York Times*, 29 October 1981, 1.

61. Albert Hunt, "How Pressure and Horse Trading Won AWACS for Reagan," *Wall Street Journal*, 29 October 1981, 1. See also Sinclair Ward and Lee Lescaze, "Senator Jepsen Does a Flip," *Washington Post*, 28 October 1981, 1.

62. Roberts, "Recipe for a White House Victory,"1(A).

63. Karen Elliott House, and Albert R. Hunt, "Early Warnings: His Handling of AWACS Stands to Hurt Reagan at Home and Abroad," *Wall Street Journal*, 2 October 1981, 1.

64. House and Hunt, "Early Warnings," *Wall Street Journal*, 2 October 1981, 1. See also Drew Middleton, "AWACS Deal: U.S. Credibility at Stake," *New York Times*, 26 October 1981, 3(A). Proponents of the sale argued that not only would a rejection of the sale jeopardize American-Saudi relations but would also negatively affect President Reagan's credibility in international circles as being unable to deliver on his commitments. House and Hunt, 1.

65. Whittle, "Reagan Loses AWACS Votes," 2007.

66. Godfrey Sperling Jr., "Reagan Puts his Prestige on the Line," *Christian Science Monitor*, 27 October 1981, 10.

67. Drew Middleton, "AWACS Deal: U.S. Credibility at Stake," *New York Times*, 26 October 1981, 3.

68. Bernard Gwertzman, "President Says U.S. Should not Waver in Backing Saudis," *New York Times*, 18 October 1981, 1(A).

69. Associated Press, "400 Layoffs Averted at AWACS Producer," *Washington Post*, 29 October 1981, 47; Also Lee Lescaze, "Persuader Speaks Softly," *Washington Post*, 29 October 1981, 7.

70. Rowland Evans and Robert Novak, "The Air Force Worked Too Fast," *Washington Post*, 24 April 1981, 27.

71. Albert Hunt, "Reagan Triumph Appears Possible in Senate," *Wall Street Journal*, 28 October 1981, 3.

72. J. B. Kelly, "The Arming of Saudi Arabia," *Wall Street Journal*, 21 October 1981, 26.

73. U.S. Senate Committee on Armed Services, *Military and Technical Implication of the Proposed Sale of Air Defense Enhancements to Saudi Arabia*, 97th Cong., 1st sess.,1981, 23.

74. Richard V. Allen, "Why the AWACS Sale Is Good for US," *Washington Post*, 20 September 1981, 1(C).

75. Lee Lescaze, "President, Hill Allies Make a Nice Save," *Washington Post*, 30 October 1981, 13.

76. Hebart Rowen, "Press Behind AWACS Was Crass Business Greed," *Washington Post*, 8 November 1981, 1(F).

77. Thomas B. Edsall, "Conservatives, Corporation Aided AWACS," *Washington Post*, 1 November 1981, 11.

78. Henrick Smith, "Reagan's Day: Fortunes Soar at Home and Abroad," *New York Times*, 29 October 1981, Section II, 12.

79. Saeed M. Badeeb. *The Saudi-Egyptian Conflict over North Yemen, 1962-1970* (Boulder, Colo.: Westview Press, 1980), 100. For a concise historical discussion of the development of Saudi foreign policy see Long, *The United States and Saudi Arabia*, 3-8. For a more historical study of Saudi foreign policy under Ibn Saud see Jacob Goldberg, *The Foreign Policy of Saudi Arabia* (Cambridge,

Mass.: Harvard University Press, 1986).

80. U.S. House of Representatives Committee on Foreign Affairs, *Saudi Arabia and the United States: The New Context in an Evolving Special Relationship,* Hearings before the Subcommittee on Europe and the Middle East, 97th Cong., 1st sess., 1981, 6.

81. Badeeb, *The Saudi-Egyptian Conflict,* 101. He cites as a source the Organization for Economic Cooperation and Development Assistance Committee, *Development Cooperation Efforts, 1982 Review.*

82. Dawisha, "Internal Values and External Threats," 139.

83. Dawisha, "Internal Values and External Threats," 139.

84. Dawisha, "Internal Values and External Threats," 140.

85. Holden and Johns, *The House of Saud,* 477.

86. William Quandt, "Riyadh between the Superpowers," *Foreign Policy,* no. 44 (Fall 1981): 49-50

87. Samuel M. Makinda, *Superpower Diplomacy in the Horn of Africa* (New York: St. Martin's Press, 1987), 39. See also William B. Quandt, *Saudi Arabia in the 1980s: Foreign Policy, Security, and Oil* (Washington, D.C.: The Brookings Institution, 1981), 43-45. Another factor was Eritrea, which has a large Muslim population. Makinda notes that because of Arab aid to Somalia and Eritrea, Israel became a significant backer of Ethiopia. Israel assisted Ethiopia militarily after Haile Selassie's overthrow and this continued even during the Ogaden War. This is an example of American allies working against each other.

88. U.S. State Department, *Congressional Presentation: Security Assistance Programs, FY 1984* (Washington, D.C.: U.S. Government Printing Office, 1985), 285-87. Cited in Cordesman, *The Gulf and the Search,* 797.

89. Quandt, "Riyadh between the Superpowers," 49.

90. Jim Hoagland and J. P. Smith, "Saudi Arabia and the United States: Security and Interdependence," *Survival* 20, no. 2 (March-April 1978): 80-81.

91. Bernard Gwertzman, "U.S. in Policy Shift, Now Willing to Sell Sudan Combat Jets," *New York Times,* 23 December 1977, 1(A).

92. Theodore Draper, *A Very Thin Line: The Iran-Contra Affairs* (New York: Hill and Wang, 1991), 24.

93. Draper, *A Very Thin Line,* 80-82. It is unclear if any kind of quid pro quo was given by the United States for Saudi aid. While as a rule, administration officials did not specifically ask for contributions from the Saudis or other countries, they made it known that this was something that these countries might be interested in participating in. Draper, however, does cite Robert McFarlane's acknowledgement that by getting the Saudis involved the United States was leaving itself open to being obligated to the Saudis at some future date. The administration tried to keep these contributions a secret from Congress as well as the public. In addition, various government officials such as Secretary of State Shultz and CIA Director Casey were not informed at this time about the additional resources. Draper provides a detailed description of Saudi involvement with the contras, and its implications, (80-84).

94. Rouhollah K. Ramazani, *Iran's Foreign Policy 1941-1973: A Study of Foreign Policy in Modernizing Nations* (Charlottesville, Va.: University Press of Virginia, 1975), 410-14.

95. Ramazani, *Iran's Foreign Policy,* 415.

96. Ramazani, *Iran's Foreign Policy,* 420-22.

97. Rouhollah K. Ramazani, *The Persian Gulf: Iran's Role* (Charlottesville, Va.: University Press of Virginia, 1972), 59.

98. Ramazani, *The Persian Gulf,* 61.

99. Ramazani, *Iran's Foreign Policy 1941-1973*, 424-25; Also Ramazani, *The Persian Gulf: Iran's Role*, 61-62.

100. Ramazani, *Iran's Foreign Policy*, 425. He emphasizes in particular the importance of Egypt in muting the criticism of Iran and forestalling any kind of meaningful sanctions.

101. Cordesman, *The Gulf and the Search*, 155-57; See also Barry Rubin, *Paved With Good Intentions* (New York: Penguin Books, 1980), 140-41.

102. Christopher Van Hollen, "North Yemen: A Dangerous Pentagonal Game," *Washington Quarterly* 5, no. 3 (Summer 1982): 138; See also F. Gregory Gause, *Saudi-Yemeni Relations: Domestic Structures and Foreign Influence* (New York: Columbia University Press, 1990), 154.

103. Dawisha, "Internal Values and External Threats," 140.

104. Badeeb, *The Saudi-Egyptian Conflict*, 96.

105. Badeeb, *The Saudi-Egyptian Conflict*, 94.

106. Badeeb, *The Saudi-Egyptian Conflict*, 96.

107. Badeeb, *The Saudi-Egyptian Conflict*, 104.

108. U.S. Department of State, Briefing Memorandum, January-February, 1957, no. 00894, in *Declassified Documents* (Washington, D.C.: Carrolton Press, 1988), 5.

109. Mark Katz, *Russia and Arabia: Soviet Foreign Policy toward the Arabian Peninsula* (Baltimore, Md.: Johns Hopkins University Press, 1986), 25-29.

110. Holden and Johns, *The House of Saud*, 501; and Kenneth Bacon, "Carter Speeds Arms Flow to North Yemen to Confront Soviets and Comfort Saudis," *Washington Post*, 6 January 1978, 2.

111. The following sources discuss these events in detail: Nadav Safran, *Saudi Arabia: The Ceaseless Quest for Security* (Ithaca, N.Y.: Cornell University Press, 1988), 387-94; Also see David B. Golub, *When Oil and Politics Mix: Saudi Oil Policy, 1973-1985* (Cambridge, Mass.: Harvard University, Center for Middle Eastern States, 1985), 35; Gregory Gause, *Saudi-Yemeni Relations*, 154-56; See also Cordesman, *The Gulf and the Search*, 472.

112. Cordesman, *The Gulf and the Search*, 59.

113. Cordesman, *The Gulf and the Search*, 784.

114. Katz, *Russia and Arabia*, 85.

115. Robert W. Stookly, *South Yemen: A Marxist Republic in Arabia* (Boulder, Colo.: Westview Press, 1982), 101-2.

116. Sheila Carapico, "From Ballot Box to Battlefied: The War of the Two 'Alis'," *Middle East Research and Information Project* 24, no. 5 (September-October 1994): 24-27.

117. Cordesman, *The Gulf and the Search*, 890.

118. Oles M. Smolansky and Bettie M. Smolansky, *The USSR and Iraq* (Durham, N.C.: Duke University Press, 1991), 197. Regarding the settling of the border issues see, Edmund Ghareeb, "Iraq in the Gulf," in *Iraq in Transition: A Political, Economic, and Strategic Perspective*, Frederick W. Axergard ed. (Boulder, Colo.: Westview Press, 1986), 70.

119. Safran, *Saudi Arabia: The Ceaseless Quest*, 137-38, 230-31.

120. Claudia Wright, "Implications of the Iraq-Iran War," *Foreign Affairs* 59, no. 2 (Winter 1980-1981): 281, 285.

121. Dilip Hiro, *The Longest War: The Iran-Iraq Military Conflict* (London: Grafton Books, 1989), 75-76. Figure of $10 billion cited from *Middle East Economic Digest*, April 2, 1982. Also Shahram Chubin and Charles Tripp, *Iran and Iraq at War* (Boulder, Colo.: Westview Press, 1988), 152-54.

122. Cordesman, *The Gulf and the Search*, 921.

123. Jiri Valenta, "The Soviet Invasion of Afghanistan: The Difficulty of Knowing Where to Stop," *Orbis* 24, no. 2 (Summer 1980): 204-5. Gives a good description of Soviet involvement in the coup and the internal struggles within the Afghan Communist Party.

124. Holden and Johns, *The House of Saud*, 487-88.

125. Safran, *Saudi Arabia: The Ceaseless Quest*, 407, 233-34; and Holden and Johns, *The House of Saud*, 537.

126. Cordesman, *The Gulf and the Search*, 35.

127. Joe Stork, "The CIA in Afghanistan: 'The Good War,'" *Middle East Research and Information Project* 16, no. 4 (July-August 1986): 12-13. Stork cites sources that indicate American aid to the Afghan mujahidin began prior to the Soviet invasion of 1979. The Saudis and Egyptians were consulted by National Security Advisor Brzezinski in September of 1979 concerning the civil war in the country. Stork indicates that by 1983 the group within the American administration who were arguing for a projected war to "bleed" the Soviet Union won out over those who favored a political settlement.

128. Safran, *Saudi Arabia: The Ceaseless Quest*, 363. Discusses pros and cons of the Saudi-Pakistani strategic relationship.

129. Cordesman, *The Gulf and the Search*, 927; Also see Bernard Weinraub, "Reagan Asks $9.2 Billion in Foreign Military Aid for Next Year," *New York Times*, 5 February 1983, 3(A).

130. Cordesman, *The Gulf and the Search*, 348. Discusses Pakistani presence in Saudi Arabia. States that they are officially classified by the United States as training brigades, and have the combat strength of reinforced battalions. Reports range between 7,000-20,000 Pakistanis deployed in Saudi Arabia. This number could facilitate a greater deployment should it be needed.

131. Bruce Kuniholm, *The Persian Gulf and U.S. Policy* (Claremont, Calif.: Regina Books, 1984), 113.

132. Harry B. Ellis, "Saudis Trust in U.S. Shaken," *Christian Science Monitor*, 5 July 1979, 1. During the late 1970s the Saudis wanted the United States to do more in the region to stem what the Saudis view as gains by the Soviets through their allies. See Kenneth Bacon, "U.S. to Supply Weapons to Two Saudi Allies," *Wall Street Journal*, 12 February 1979, 3.

133. It should be noted that at times the Saudis have conflicted severely with American policy, such as the 1973 oil embargo as well as the breaking of relations with Egypt in the aftermath of Camp David. In addition there is the obvious clash with the United States in that the Saudis do not have any relations with Israel.

134. J. E. Peterson, *Defending Arabia* (New York: St. Martin's Press, 1986), 146.

135. Peterson, *Defending Arabia*, 146-47.

136. Peterson, *Defending Arabia*, 152-53.

137. Cordesman, *The Gulf and the Search*, 835. Cordesman derived this list from various sources.

138. Daniel Volman, "Commanding the Center," *Middle East Research and Information Project* 14, no. 6-7 (July-September 1984): 49; also see Cordesman, *The Gulf and the Search*, 808, and Peterson, *Defending Arabia*, 154. For specific force compositions and numbers of personnel. Also see William Olson, "An Alternative Strategy for Southwest Asia," in *U.S. Strategic Interests in the Gulf Region*, William Olson ed. (Boulder, Colo.: Westview Press, 1987), 207.

139. Cordesman, *The Gulf and the Search*, 253; Also see Holden and Johns, *The House of Saud*, 501.

140. Thomas L. McNaughter. "The Limits of Access: Projecting U.S. Forces to the Persian Gulf," in *U.S. Strategic Interests in the Gulf Region*, William J. Olson ed. (Boulder, Colo.: Westview Press, 1987), 180.

141. Andrew Pierre, *The Global Politics of Arms Sales*, 85; See also Sidney Weintraub, "Saudi Arabia's Role in the International Financial System," *Middle East Review* 10, no. 4 (Summer 1978): 18.

142. Dawisha, "Internal Values and External Threats," 141. Cites Paul Martin, "Getting Stronger, 'the best base America has ever had' in Saudi Arabia," *Times of London*, 21 February 1977, 10.

143. John K. Cooley, "Saudi Reprieve for Dollar," *Christian Science Monitor*, 6 March 1978, 3.

144. Safran, *Saudi Arabia: The Ceaseless Quest*, 295-96, 399.

145. Cordesman, *Western Strategic Interests*, 38.

146. Steven Rattner, "Saudis Aren't Hoarding All the Money," *New York Times*, 29 May 1977, 2-3.

147. House, Committee, *Saudi Arabia and the United States*, 43.

148. Aburdene, Odeh, "U.S. Economic and Financial Relations with Saudi Arabia, Kuwait and the United Arab Emirates," *American-Arab Affairs*, no. 7 (Winter 1983-1984): 77.

149. Long, *The United States and Saudi Arabia*, 95.

150. Safran, *Saudi Arabia: The Ceaseless Quest*, 398. He cites as his sources, International Monetary Fund, *Direction of Trade Yearbook*, and U.S. Department of Defense, *Foreign Military Sales, Foreign Military Construction Sales, and Military Assistance Facts* (Washington, D.C.: Government Printing Office, 1982).

151. U.S. House of Representatives Committee on Governmental Operations, *Federal Response to OPEC Country Investments in the United States, Hearings* before the Subcommittee on Commerce, Consumer, and Monetary Affairs, Committee on Governmental Operations, 97th Cong., 2nd sess., 1982, 2-3.

152. Bonnie Pounds, "The U.S.-Saudi Arabian Joint Commission: A Model for Bilateral Economic Cooperation," *American-Arab Affairs*, no. 7 (Winter 1983-1984): 61; Also Long, *The United States and Saudi Arabia*, 92; for a complete text of the agreement see "Chronology," *The Middle East Journal* 38, no. 3 (Summer 1979): 305-07.

153. Bernard Gwertzman, "'Milestone' Pact Is Signed by U.S. and Saudi Arabia," *New York Times*, 9 June 1974, 1(A).

154. Cordesman, *Western Strategic Interests*, 198.

155. Cordesman, *Western Strategic Interests*, 199.

156. Cordesman, *Western Strategic Interests*, 210. This arms sale represented a classic conflict between domestic and foreign policy. Foreign policy advisers such as George Shultz and Caspar Weinberger argued for the sale. Cited various articles in newspapers: *Washington Post*, 24 January 1985, A18; *Chicago Tribune*, 28 January 1985, I-1; *Washington Times*, 29 January 1985, 1(A); and 30 January 1985, 6(A).

157. Anthony H. Cordesman, *The Gulf and the West: Strategic Relations and Military Realities* (Boulder, Colo.: Westview Press, 1988), 291-92. For a discussion on this later agreement involving the marketing of oil see also various journalist accounts cited by Cordesman. Among them *Sunday Times*, 15 September 1985; *New York Times*, 16 September 1985; and *Financial Times*, 21 December 1984, and 16 September 1985.

158. Cordesman, *Western Strategic Interests*, 217-19. Provides a good discussion of the political process of finally getting the sale through by the narrowest of margins.

159. Thomas L. Friedman, "U.S. Tells Israel It Plans to Sell Saudis 300 Tanks," *New York Times*, 29 September 1989, 1(A).

160. Robert Pear, "Saudis Seen As Top Mideast Buyer of U.S. Arms," *New York Times*, 3 February 1989, 3(A).

161. William D. Hartung, *And Weapons for All* (New York: HarperCollins, 1994), 272-94. Discusses various examples. Both Governor Clinton and President Bush advocated the sale of the F-15 (McDonnell Douglas) to the Saudis. President Bush also allowed the F-16 (General Dynamics) to be sold to Taiwan. This went against a previous American policy of limiting arms sales to that country. These cases are discussed more fully in chapter 8.

162. Golub, *When Oil and Politics Mix*, 3-4.

163. Sheikh Rustum Ali, *Saudi Arabia and Oil Diplomacy* (New York: Praeger, 1976), 93-94.

164. See Tareq Y. Ismael, *The Middle East in World Politics: A Study in Contemporary International Relations* (Syracuse, N.Y.: Syracuse University Press, 1974), 236; and *Christian Science Monitor*, 6 July 1973. Cited in Ali, *Saudi Arabia and Oil Diplomacy*, 95.

165. Abulaziz H. Al-Sowayyegh, "Saudi Oil Policy during King Faisal's Era," in *King Faisal and the Modernization of Saudi Arabia*, Willard A. Beling ed. (Boulder, Colo.: Westview Press, 1980), 209-10. Discusses the reasons why a majority of OAPEC, including Saudi Arabia, decided on the moderate course of action. Among the reasons cited were that OAPEC did not want to irrevocably break relations with the United States felt a gradual reduction of supply would be more effective, providing revenues that could be contributed to build up Arab military forces and limiting the effects on neutral/friendly nations. See also *International Herald Tribune*, 30 June 1974. Discusses countries on a list to be embargoed, as well as those nations said to be on a "friendly list."

166. Golub, *When Oil and Politics Mix*, 22.

167. Golub, *When Oil and Politics Mix*, 34. See also *Washington Post*, 6 May, 1979.

168. Zalmay Khalilzad, "U.S. Strategic Concerns: Deterrence Dilemmas in the Gulf Region," in *The Middle East in Global Strategy*, Aurel Braun ed. (Boulder, Colo.: Westview Press, 1987), 233.

169. Alexander Bligh and Steven E. Plaut, "Saudi Moderation in Oil and Foreign Policies in the Post-AWACS-Sale Period," *Middle East Review* 14, no. 3-4 (Spring-Summer 1982): 25-31. Also see John Y Cooley, "OPEC Disarray Sets Stage for Sharp Drop in Oil Prices," *Christian Science Monitor*, 17 September 1985, 3. For a complete discussion concerning Saudi oil price policy see Dankwart A. Rustow, *Oil and Turmoil: America Faces OPEC and the Middle East* (New York: W.W. Norton, 1982), 194-203. He argues that the Saudi price strategy is to advocate for steady smaller increases as opposed to dramatic increases all at once.

170. Bligh and Plaut, "Saudi Moderation in Oil," 27.

171. Mordechai Abir, *Saudi Arabia in the Oil Era: Regime and Elites; Conflict and Collaboration* (Boulder, Colo.: Westview Press, 1988),152. Abir argues that the Saudi regime was in trouble during this period, as there was a significant level of dissatisfaction with the corruption and lifestyles of much of the Saudi royal family. The reason that the rebels were opposed and condemned was their target was the holiest shrine in Islam. Cited sources that stated that King Khalid and Prince Fahd acknowledged that had the rebellion occurred in Jeddah, or had attacked the royal palace, the outcome might have been different. William Quandt takes a different approach, and while he acknowledges that there were some who might have supported the rebellion had the target not been the Grand Mosque, he

argues that for the most part the country was calm and there were no demonstrations of support. Quandt, *Saudi Arabia in the 1980s*, 95.

172. Jacob Goldberg, "The Shi'i Minority in Saudi Arabia," in *Shi'ism and Social Protest*, Juan R. I. Cole and Nikki R. Keddie, eds. (New Haven, Conn.: Yale University Press, 1986), 230-31. The Shia population of the Eastern Province are Twelver Shia, there are smaller populations of Zaidi Shia (Fivers) in Asir on the Yemeni border.

173. For a concise history of these conflicts see Goldberg, *The Foreign Policy of Saudi Arabia*, 232-33.

Author's Note: The term Wahhabi is a Western designation for the religious movement that had its origins in the 18th century. The devotees of this movement refer to themselves as Muwahiddun, those who believe in monotheism. See John L. Esposito, *Islam and Politics*, 4th edition (Syracuse, N.Y.: Syracuse University Press, 1984), 37.

174. Goldberg, *The Foreign Policy of Saudi Arabia*, 241-44; Quandt, *Saudi Arabia in the 1980s*, 96-97; and Abir, *Saudi Arabia in the Oil Era,* 156-58.

175. Cordesman, *The Gulf and the Search*, 164.

176. Cordesman, *The Gulf and the Search*, 165-80.

177. Michael T. Klare, "The Political Economy of Arms Sales," *Society* 2, no. 6 (September-October 1974): 47.

178. James R. Kurth, "Why We Buy the Weapons We Do," *Foreign Policy*, No. 11, 1973, 64.

179. Thomas L. Friedman, "U.S. Tells Israel," 1(A).

180. Michael T. Klare, *American Arms Supermarket* (Austin, Tex.: University of Texas Press, 1984), 118.

181. Cordesman, *The Gulf and the Search*, 164.

182. Cordesman, *The Gulf and the Search*, 159-62.

183. Cordesman, *The Gulf and the Search*, 165-80.

Chapter 8

Conclusions

American Alliances and the Cold War

During the Cold War the United States viewed each new alliance as another vote against communism and the Soviet Union. Hans Morgenthau viewed this as a collector's approach to alliance formation as the United States sought to align with as many states as possible. This added an ideological dimension to the global competition between the United States and the USSR. This intensified global competition, since if a state did not align with America it was viewed as a potential enemy. It became very difficult to revise this policy domestically because of the ideological implications surrounding it.[1]

The ideological dimension of these cases was significant in providing justification for their integration in the American alliance framework. Iran and Saudi Arabia were considered legitimate allies from an ideological standpoint, as they were both anticommunist states seeking to contain the Soviet Union as well as implementing development strategies which benefitted the United States. As a result, the Shah and the Saudi royal family were considered by American policy makers and the press as being "modernizing monarchies." Israel fit into the American alliance framework ideologically as it has a Western-model parliamentary form of government and a competitive electoral system.

There were three major factors in the belief system of American policy makers during the early Cold War period. First, the competition with the Soviet Union was viewed as a zero-sum conflict. Second, the international system had become polarized, and policy makers believed that those states that were not aligned to the United States ran a greater risk of succumbing to Soviet pressures. Third, the international system was very unstable, so a defeat in one area could have a ripple effect in other regions. These beliefs helped to shape the perception of the threats facing the United States and how American foreign policy should deal with them. Several views of alliances were formed by these beliefs. First, the United States placed a great emphasis on peripheral interests, ensuring that they did not come under control of anti-Western elites, local communist movements, or the direct control of either the USSR or China. Second, the United States pledged and enacted policies to defend many small countries that critics have labeled overcommitment. Third, these beliefs encouraged policy makers to view different areas of the world as having a similar interest for the United States. Fourth, American alliance commitments were viewed as interdependent. Therefore, a weakening of American credibility in one country could impact negatively on the U.S. position throughout the international system. Finally, these beliefs fostered policies that emphasized military deterrence and framed American-Soviet relations almost solely in military terms. This was at the expense of other means to limit conflict and tensions with its opponents.[2]

This latter view was summed up by Alan Tonelson. He stated in discussing commitment theory that

> every American failure—no matter how important or unimportant on it own terms—allegedly stirs allied and neutral doubts about American determination to protect any of its interests, no matter how vital, and especially about their own security, despite American pledges. And the temptation to tilt toward Moscow would grow considerably.[3]

Tonelson discusses the lack of formulating a clear idea of specific interests by American decision makers. This led to a universal approach to foreign policy in which interests were unlimited, resulting in a policy that did not make a distinction between secondary and primary interests. This caused a disproportionate amount of political, economic, and military resources placed in areas that were not vital to the United States. Tonelson sums this up by stating:

> America's lack of well-defined priorities has also left Washington at the mercy of weak, often repugnant regimes and of worthier but nonetheless free-riding allies. In addition, it has undermined the confidence of its allies and the respect of its adversaries that is generated by a clear sense of purpose.[4]

In the post-World War II period, American goals in the region have been contradictory. Support for Israel has to a certain extent caused political tensions in America's relations with several Arab states. Most significantly, the emphasis on maintaining what American policy makers define as regional stability, which essentially means the keeping in power of authoritarian regimes at the expense of encouraging more popular, broad-based nationalist regimes, helps to perpetuate a cycle of poverty and despotism that serves to promote terrorism and violence.

The Formulation of American Alliance Policy

The Origins of Containment

United States postwar foreign policy was influenced by differing interpretations of American decision makers and shaped by domestic political factors. There was a division among American political elites between those who held an internationalist outlook as opposed to those who focused on traditional American interests. They wanted to keep America's orientation centered on Europe as a means of facilitating the reconstruction of the international system. The nationalists felt that American interests were more oriented toward Asia. The emphasis on global commitments strategy was a compromise between these two policy views. This was largely forged by John Foster Dulles and, although these views crossed party lines, it was primarily a compromise within the Republican Party in Congress.[5]

The Europe-first internationalists included major decision makers within the Truman administration such as Dean Acheson, George Marshall, and George Kennan. They emphasized maintaining American control of the core industrial areas of Western Europe and Japan. However, they found it difficult to differentiate between what they labeled as core areas and the periphery.[6]

The early postwar American alliances were made to protect and rebuild industrial centers important to the United States. This included Western Europe, Japan, Australia, and New Zealand, which were considered essential to maintaining American military, economic, and political power.[7] The American postwar policy of rebuilding Western Europe and Japan caused Moscow concern. This, along with America taking over traditional British interests in various parts of the world, such as the Middle East, led the Soviet Union to be suspicious of U.S. policy. These were areas that they had interests in as well.[8]

The rebuilding of Europe and Japan required the reindustrialization of these states and it was essential that there be a secure cheap supply of oil available. As a result, Iran and Saudi Arabia became more important for American interests and was a primary factor for American involvement in the Azerbaijan crisis in 1946. The Soviet Union was aiding an insurgency in the Iranian provinces of Azerbaijan and Kurdistan in an effort to place pressure on Tehran to grant an oil concession similar to the one the British enjoyed in the south. The United States supported Iran in its political conflict with the Soviet Union. American policy makers wanted to maintain Western control over Iranian oil reserves and viewed Iran as an important buffer to safeguard the major U.S. oil holdings in Saudi Arabia.

The alliance system established by Eisenhower and Dulles continued Truman's policy of cultivating a worldwide alliance network. During the 1950s the United States augmented NATO and its Pacific defenses by constructing complementary alliances such as SEATO, and CENTO, which extended the American alliance system across Asia and through the Middle East.[9]

However, the inability of Great Britain to maintain the role that she held prior to the war led the United States to take over these commitments to fulfill its great power role. Domestically, the administration felt that it needed to take a stand against the Soviets given the postwar settlement and the unwillingness of the Soviets to hold elections in the territories of Eastern Europe that the Red Army controlled. In order to aid pro-American countries on the periphery that affected the core areas of U.S. interests, it became necessary to exaggerate to Congress and the American public the ramifications of not extending aid. This occurred in the spring of 1950 with the establishment of NSC-68. This was authored by Dean Acheson and Paul Nitze to justify extending American aid to pro-Western states.[10] Iran and Saudi Arabia both would become recipients of American aid based on this view of containment. This laid the groundwork for the reorientation of these alliances in the 1970s. The perceptions of American policy makers changed due to the greater strategic importance that became attached to these alliances and as a result, the United States lost control over these relationships.

The Expansion of American Security Commitments

This policy was further perpetuated in various studies and policies of the United States. The National Security Council in 1953 developed the "Basic National Security Policy," which concluded that "If our allies were uncertain about our ability or will to counter Soviet aggression, they would be strongly tempted to adopt a neutralist position."[11] This justified policy makers' fears that if the United States allowed its client in Saigon to fall it would result in allies in other areas of the world abandoning the United States. This was summed up by Secretary of State Dean Rusk when he stated: "America's alliances are at the heart of the maintenance of peace, and if it should be discovered that the pledge of America was worthless, the structure of peace would crumble and we would be well on our way to a terrible catastrophe."[12]

An alternative explanation of American policy in Vietnam was the desire to stifle third world nationalism. If Vietnam was allowed to succeed in frustrating the will of the dominant Western power this could be an example for other countries. This seems to have been a common thread running through American foreign policy, regardless of which party was in control of policy. In the Middle East, the United States was opposed to Nasser shortly after he took power as a result of the nationalist forces he threatened to mobilize in the region, as well as the third world as a whole.

American alliance commitments have escalated in the postwar period particularly during the Carter and Reagan years. President Carter advanced American alliance commitments in the Middle East. This was illustrated by the Camp David peace accords where the United States extended financial and security commitments to both Israel and Egypt. This included the presence of American personnel in the Sinai to ensure the peace as well as guarantee that the United States would make up any oil shortages for Israel. In addition, the United States responded to the Iranian revolution and the Soviet invasion of Afghanistan by establishing the Carter Doctrine. This stated that the United States would resist any attempts by outside powers (USSR) to gain control of the Persian Gulf by any means necessary. The Carter Doctrine was accompanied by additional security commitments and arms sales to countries in the Arabian Peninsula and Persian Gulf.[13]

Ronald Reagan intensified and restated the importance of American security commitments in containing the Soviet Union. In an address to the American Legion, President Reagan stated, "Maintenance of our alliance partnerships is a key to our foreign policy."[14] An important factor in emphasizing American alliances was the building up of American power to confront potential Soviet threats. This was articulated by Secretary of State George Schultz in 1983. "The United States cannot defend its interests by operating out of the United States and Europe alone. We need the cooperation of countries in the Third World to grant transit, refueling, and base rights."[15]

During this period Israel and Saudi Arabia became more important in order to project American military power. It was during the Reagan administration that strategic cooperation with Israel expanded greatly. The American political leadership was enthusiastic about this, primarily because of the potential political benefits for the Reagan administration and the Republican Party in general. However, elements of the American military were skeptical about the utility of strategic cooperation with Israel as this potentially threatened American geostrategic relations with the Arab world. The military buildup in Saudi Arabia during the 1970s and 1980s featured an emphasis on developing military infrastructure and prepositioning equipment.

The history of American alliances and military bases fits a pattern. The United States contributed economic and military aid to build up the recipient country as well as extend its deterrent capabilities to ward off threats to its ally. In return, the United States was furnished with bases as well as military support from its ally, which included the formation of joint strategy.[16]

As a result they are better able to define and reinforce the interests that they each deem significant. In addition, the establishment of a military presence in a region creates a deterrent to the expansion of the other power. Should the rival power seek to acquire military bases in that region it could provoke tensions and/or conflict. It has to decide what interests are at stake and how important they are before it attempts to establish a presence in a region that is dominated by its rival.[17]

The importance of American military bases in the third world has changed because of the development of military technology. For a good portion of the postwar period, the United States needed bases from which its bombers and missiles could reach the Soviet Union due to the limitations in the range of these delivery systems. Bases were also considered essential to monitor any strategic arms treaty with the Soviet Union. As a result of improved weapons technology and spy satellites, these bases are no longer needed for these purposes. Another factor limiting the utility of American military bases is that countries have responded to nationalist appeals and interests of their own to limit the use of these facilities by the United States.[18] It would seem that the rationale for military bases is not as extensive as it once was. This is particularly true in light of the downsizing of the military, as many facilities that were previously considered as cornerstones of American security such as Subic Bay in the Philippines have been closed. The Gulf War did illustrate for proponents the value of prepositioning military equipment as well as building up the facilities of friendly governments in the event of a regional military contingency.

Despite the lessening of American dependency on the third world for strategic military purposes, it is becoming more important economically. By the late 1980s it was estimated that developing countries accounted for about 40 percent of American exports and imports. More significantly, the Less Developed Countries (LDCs) account for a higher percentage of American exports than the developed countries. It was estimated that if the Third World could go back to the growth figures before the debt crisis of the early 1980s, then by the year 2000 about 50 percent of U.S. exports would be going to developing nations.[19] The emphasis on maintaining favorable trade balances had been an important component in justifying the expansion of the American alliance with Iran a decade earlier. During the period of the mid to late 1980s it continued to be a pertinent issue in the American-Saudi alliance.

The Nixon Doctrine and the Growth of American Arms Transfers As a Component of United States Security Policy

American foreign policy shifted during the Nixon administration in response to the Vietnam War and the inability of the United States to fulfill the vast network of security commitments that had been constructed after World War II. This had a significant aspect on American alliance policy in the Middle East, particularly towards Iran and Saudi Arabia. The Nixon Doctrine would fundamentally change the American relationship with these states. The assumptions of the Nixon Doctrine was that the international system had changed. This resulted in the system shifting from bipolarity to conditions of multipolarity involving several major powers. As a result, it was necessary for the United States to lessen many of its overseas commitments, justified on the basis that nations were becoming more affluent. Countries like Iran and Saudi Arabia were better able to provide for their own defense needs. It was also argued that this was more efficient and cost effective for the United States. The purpose of the Nixon Doctrine was to create balances of power within regions that would lessen the need for long-term American military involvement. The implementation of the Nixon Doctrine was to facilitate and encourage the building up of the conventional power of regional allies. The United States would provide a nuclear deterrent, as well as the supplying of American air and naval power while sponsoring various military assistance programs. The ultimate strategic goal of the United States was to reduce its conventional military forces and the defense budget in general. American forces were to be geared to fighting one-and-a-half wars, a large war in Europe or Asia and a smaller insurgency elsewhere. Prior to the Nixon Doctrine, the United States had planned for contingencies of fighting major wars in Europe and Asia, as well as a smaller conflict at the same time.[20] The Nixon Doctrine reinforced the process by which the United States ceded control of the Iranian and Saudi alliances to those countries. These relationships became predicated on the United States supplying ever greater quantities of sophisticated armaments. Constituency groups within the American government and the private sector developed vested interests in implementing these alliances in this way.

Arms transfers and military assistance have been an important aspect of American foreign policy in the postwar international system. The Vietnam War was a watershed period in American history, illustrating the limitations of American foreign policy. As a result, the Nixon Doctrine sought to minimize American troop presence while at the same time maintaining American interests. These policies were followed to a large degree by succeeding administrations despite differences in political parties. President Carter attempted to limit American arms transfers abroad, seeking to link them to human rights and democratization. However, while there were some limited successes, the attempts at restraint during the Carter administration did not succeed. This was partly due to limitations placed on the administration by a bureaucracy geared toward facilitating arms transfers. Second, Carter himself exempted strategically important countries, like Iran, from the linkage of military assistance to human rights and political reforms. Carter's overall policy differed from the Reagan administration in which foreign affairs was governed by principals of realpolitik and not human rights. During the Reagan years, American security assistance and arms transfer programs accelerated.[21]

The major criticism of American security assistance is that it is ineffective because it does not take into account changing regional requirements. Rather, the same allies are supported over the years with little modification, despite evolving systemic, regional, and domestic considerations.[22]

A problem with reforming American security assistance and arms transfer programs in particular is that they are politically motivated. This was illustrated in the 1992 election as arms transfers became an issue in the presidential election. In the summer of 1992 President Bush, fearing a faltering in the polls, attempted to gain campaign points by allowing

General Dynamics to sell 150 F-16s to Taiwan, worth $6 billion. This sale ended the American policy of limiting arms sales to Taiwan established under the Reagan administration. It effectively channeled government support to key industries in an electorally important state, as the F-16 was manufactured in Fort Worth, Texas. Texas was shaping up as a state the Republicans had to carry in order to have a chance of retaining the White House. The same strategy was adopted by Governor Bill Clinton as he declared his support for the sale of F-15s to Saudi Arabia on a campaign stop in St. Louis, Missouri, the headquarters of the McDonnell Douglas Corporation.[23]

The history of American arms transfers policy was summed up by William Hartung when he stated:

> With the exception of a few promising moments during the Carter administration, arms transfers have steadily gained favor throughout the postwar era as a convenient, all-purpose foreign policy instrument used by Democratic and Republican presidents alike. Selling arms to win friends and bolster allies has come to be seen as a no-lose proposition, a cheap and efficient way to exert U.S. military influence without risking the soldiers' lives or taxpayers' dollars that direct U.S. intervention would entail. The dangers inherent in transferring advanced military technology to a series of dictatorial, frequently unstable regimes in the Third World have generally been overlooked by U.S. policymakers preoccupied with larger strategic goals, such as combating the Soviet Union and its allies and keeping the Third World safe for United States investment and trade.[24]

In addition, American arms sales also provided such economic benefits as maintaining employment levels in key industries in significant states electorally, assisting in America's balance of payments, subsidizing research and development costs, and lowering the overall unit price of the military item being sold, which enables the American military to purchase it for less.

This was especially pertinent with regard to the cases of Iran and Saudi Arabia. It appears that economic factors played a strong part in the decision making process regarding arms transfers to these nations, although they were justified on strategic military rationales. These arms programs supported the interests of important economic and political groups within American domestic politics. This caused a process of reverse leverage in which the regional powers were able to gain control over these alliances by exploiting the U.S. political system and fostering relationships with segments of the American political, economic, and military elite.

The Justification of American Alliance Policies and Their Implementation: Iran, Israel, Saudi Arabia

It can be argued that these alliances did enhance American national interests as traditionally articulated by U.S. decision makers. American interests in the Middle East have historically been to maintain secure access to oil, contain the spread of Soviet influence in the region, maintain a favorable climate for American investment in the Middle East, and promote regional stability. This last point has historically been defined as checking leftist nationalist or other ideological movements that would imperil the fulfillment of the above. In the 1950s and 1960s this meant actively seeking to weaken Arab nationalism such as that articulated by Nasser of Egypt, while at the same time supporting conservative Arab states such as Saudi Arabia. In the 1980s and 1990s the emphasis has been to check what has been labeled Islamic fundamentalism as exemplified by the Islamic Republic of Iran. Finally, there was massive political, economic, and military support for Israel.

The U.S. alliances with Iran and Saudi Arabia protected American oil interests and promoted a pro-Western economic business climate in the region as a whole. These alliances also integrated these nations into the American security network, allowing these states, and particularly Iran, to build up their military capabilities to defend oil facilities, as well as the sea-lanes of the Persian Gulf.

In examining this issue it is also difficult to determine whether these alliances could have been implemented any differently. These pacts reflected the interests of politically and economically important groups within American society, such as business interests, in particular oil and defense corporations, sectors of the American bureaucracy, and conservative political groups. In the case of Israel there was also support based on ethnicity. In examining these case studies historically, it can be illustrated that interest groups have provided support for the respective ally and gained benefits from the way these relationships were implemented.

The growth of Iranian military capabilities along with American political and strategic support enabled the United States to maintain control over the Persian Gulf region and have a buffer against the spread of Soviet influence. In addition, this military buildup permitted resources to be channeled into strategic sectors, such as the aerospace industry, of the American economy. This allowed important defense contractors to maintain their production lines as well as acquire funding for research and development. This at a time when the winding down of the war in Southeast Asia and public protest made large expenditure outlays for defense not politically or economically feasible. A specific example of this was the sale of F-14 aircraft to Iran, which saved the Grumman Corporation from bankruptcy and allowed the U.S. Navy to continue the procurement of this system. In addition, the oil shocks of the 1970s allowed Iran to greatly expand economic development projects that benefitted many sectors of the American economy.

Saudi Arabia served much the same function as Iran. The relationship with Saudi Arabia has provided numerous benefits for the United States that were in the interests of the dominant political and economic groups in American society. By the late 1970s the Saudis had emerged as the seventh largest trading partner with the United States, supplied 25 percent of America's oil, and were one of the largest purchasers of American military equipment. Geopolitically, Riyadh was emerging as the leader of the Arab states in the Gulf and American military aid to Saudi Arabia was indirectly protecting these states as well. They were also working aggressively to support pro-Western states in the Middle East and the Third world as a whole such as Oman, North Yemen, Zaire, and Somalia among others. At the same time the Saudis were trying to weaken and destabilize pro-Soviet regimes such as Ethiopia and the People's Democratic Republic of Yemen. In addition, both the Shah of Iran and the Saudi monarchy were able to gain political prestige from their association with the United States. This political and military support allowed them to pursue their own foreign policy goals, which for the most part complemented the U.S. goal of containing political movements and regimes supported by the Soviet Union. These included, among others, supporting the Iraqi Kurds in their conflicts with Baghdad, attempting to destabilize the governments of both North and South Yemen in an effort to weaken the socialist government in Aden while keeping Sanaa on a pro-Western course, as well as assisting various conservative states in Africa. This also contributed to enhancing a generally pro-American attitude within the elites of these states to purchase American products and have U.S. corporations establish facilities within the respective countries.

Support for Israel also reflected many of these same concerns. By building up ties with Israel politically and militarily, Tel Aviv served most of the same functions as the Iranians and Saudis. Israel was able to become a regional military power and to use its forces to check anti-American states and movements. Examples of these include Syria and the Hezbollah of Lebanon among others. The Israelis were also able to furnish aid to pro-Western countries throughout the third world, specifically in Africa and Latin America, which would have cost the United States politically to do so itself. In addition, there was the not-so-secret alliance between Israel and Iran that featured close political, economic, and military contacts between the two countries. Israel also provided technical and research and development support for American military systems as well as served as a potential deterrent to the Soviet Union should a major conflict occur in the region. The most significant reason for the Israeli-American alliance was the implications it had for U.S. domestic politics.

While there were inconsistencies in these alliances, such as the relationship with Israel that could have weakened American ties with Saudi Arabia, both nations, as well as Iran, had similar foreign policy orientations. Essentially these were to maintain the status quo and keep radical nationalistic forces in check. Those who argue that these alliances were detrimental to the United States also must consider that either because, or in spite of these alliances, Washington has achieved all of the above foreign policy goals it has established since World War II. These objectives were met despite the loss of a major ally in the region, Iran. The United States was able to compensate for this by intensifying its buildup of Saudi Arabia as well as getting more militarily involved itself in the region. It can be argued that despite the criticisms of the alliance with Iran, it established and maintained a strongly pro-American regime for 25 years. In retrospect, the alliance with Iran allowed, at least on paper, a strong, indigenous, pro-American force to be established in the region. This occurred during the 1970s when it was politically, economically, and militarily not feasible for the United States to garrison its own forces in the region. Proponents of this policy would also argue that this system of alliances paid off handsomely during the Gulf War, as the American forces sent to Saudi Arabia already had infrastructure and supplies available to them to carry out their operations.

The Weaknesses of American Alliance Policy

The question of international alliances historically has had negative connotations in American political thought. For most of its history the United States has stayed away from permanent alliances and long-term foreign entanglements. In debating foreign policy, the words of Washington and Jefferson often have been quoted. George Washington in his farewell address stated, "It is our true policy to steer clear of permanent alliance with any portion of the foreign world." This sentiment was echoed by Thomas Jefferson in his inaugural address when he said, "Peace, commerce, and honest friendship with all nations—entangling alliances with none."[25]

It is difficult to measure the success of American containment policy as one cannot know for sure what the international system and American diplomatic history would look like if these were not initiated. Arguments can be presented that while these policies were in place they were effective strategically, politically, and economically. Certainly one can look at some "success stories," at least from the perspective of American decision makers, as opposed to the citizens of these countries who had to live under authoritarian governments. Korea and Taiwan, it can be argued, were successful, as the commitment of American forces and the extension of U.S. economic and military aid allowed these nations to develop economically. They were also able to develop credible military forces that are less draining to the United States than at the inception of these alliance relationships. However, one can also cite the Philippines and Korea as examples of where American alliances contributed to the political stagnation of the country. Many commentators have also credited the American alliance and official presence in Iran as contributing to the overthrow of the Shah.[26]

The United States has been very active in formulating coups against unfriendly third world leaders and governments. Examples of these include Iran in 1953, Guatemala in 1954, Chile in 1971, as well as the various coups in Vietnam during the 1960s. Historically, coups were a way for American decision makers to gain short-term benefits, such as the elimination of a troublesome leader and changes in policy to make the country more amenable to America politically and economically. In the case of Iran the nation became a significant component in American containment strategy. Overall, however, they have worked to hinder American interests by stagnating political and economic development in the cases mentioned above. As a result the United States became identified with corrupt authoritarian regimes that cost the United States political support in world opinion, and in many cases caused long-term liabilities.[27]

On balance, the American postwar alliance system, rather than supporting American interests, has involved the United States in entangling relationships with few real allies, many clients that have to be supported, and some states that are an obvious drain on American resources. It is argued this has evolved as a result of overcommitment, miscommitment, and mismanagement of American alliances. Overcommitment is identified as formulating alliances with no real conception of where they fit American interests and with little thought to developing a comprehensive strategy. Miscommitment is the American relationship with authoritarian regimes whose only connection with U.S. interests were that they espoused an anti-communist political ideology. In these relationships, however, the United States was unable to extend massive support should it be needed because of the cost involved. In addition, it would not be willing to incur the cost of a possible loss of influence should it attempt to coerce its ally into initiating political reforms. Mismanagement in an alliance occurred when the smaller states were unable to contribute significantly to American global strategy while at the same time used the American political system to exercise a great deal of leverage within the relationship.[28]

A problem of American alliances is that very often American administrations, because of other interests such as domestic politics, electoral pressures, or questions of credibility, have been too cavalier in articulating that a particular situation was of a "vital interest." The worst example of this was the escalation of the Vietnam conflict during the Johnson administration. In attempting to gather domestic support for this effort, President Johnson argued that "there are great stakes in the balance." He even declared that the principles of the conflict were equal to those of the American revolution.[29]

These factors were illustrated in the case studies discussed in this work. In looking at the formulation and much of the implementation of the American-Israeli alliance one can observe the importance of American domestic politics. This was the case in the Truman administration's decision to support the Zionist position on the U.N. partition vote in 1947. This was also the case with the decision by the Johnson administration to sell F-4 Phantoms to Israel in 1968. This improved Israel's offensive capabilities greatly and reinforced earlier decisions taken by the Johnson administration that had already made the United States Israel's major arms supplier. Johnson at first was reluctant to go ahead with the sale, however, he was pressured by a combination of factors. First, the Israeli lobby was gaining support from members of Congress to agree to the sale. Second, there were electoral pressures, as 1968 was a presidential election year and the Republican Party's candidate, Richard Nixon, had on several occasions expressed support for the sale. Third were domestic economic and political pressures. Senator Stuart Symington of Missouri, whose state the F-4 was built in, threatened to derail the entire Military Sales Bill if this sale did not go through. Finally, there were foreign policy pressures. The conflict in southeast Asia was causing foreign policy as well as political problems due to international and domestic opinion turning against the war. As a result, the administration did not want to get into a major political battle with supporters of Israel.

Similar dynamics were at work in the Iranian and Saudi cases as well. The intensification of the American alliance with Iran, reinforced by large-scale arms transfers, were justified as being significant for both domestic and foreign policy interests. Similar justifications were also made for selling arms to Saudi Arabia during this period as well as throughout the 1980s when Saudi Arabia, to a certain extent, replaced Iran as the major American ally in the region. Domestically, sales such as the F-14, F-16, and AWACS to Iran, as well as AWACS and the F-15 to Saudi Arabia, were defended as being important to subsidize research and development costs, maintain key production lines in operation, maintain a favorable balance of trade, as well as assist in paving the way for American exports in general to these nations.

The foreign policy pressures to expand this alliance through arms transfers concerned not only issues pertaining to the region, such as maintaining American access to oil and maintaining the status quo in the region, but also had importance in the international system as a whole. In the Iranian case, a major American goal was to illustrate to the Soviet Union that despite detente, the United States would still pursue its interests in the third world. American policy makers also recognized that Iran was important in insuring Soviet compliance with future strategic arms limitations agreements as a result of the American intelligence facilities located on the Iranian-Soviet border. In the Saudi case the foreign policy considerations included the United States seeking to bolster Saudi Arabia's position in the Arab world, as well as the recognition of the Saudi role in OPEC and in international finance in general.

American Allies and the Manipulation of United States Policy

One argument against American alliances is that U.S. allies can and have manipulated the foreign policy of the United States. Robert Keohane argues that America's allies have frequently been able to gain leverage over the United States as a result of manipulating the internal dynamics of the American political system.[30] Part of the reason for this, Keohane states, is that America's anticommunist ideology has traditionally been used against it. Therefore, since the United States must interact with its allies, this enables them to have bargaining leverage as threats to their interests are translated against threats to the United States. This is a factor of alliances in general that promotes an "internationalization" of American politics as coalitions of interest groups, public officials, and elements of the U.S. government, along with representatives of foreign government, interact to influence policy.[31]

Keohane maintains that small powers can influence the United States on three levels. First, there is formal bargaining in which the smaller state negotiates through diplomatic channels. A second method that the smaller power can use is to develop working relationships with components of the American government. This is usually done with the military, CIA, or the Agency for International Development (AID). Common interests are developed around such factors as military bases, aid programs, and shared intelligence. This can be effective, as a component of the American bureaucracy could become dependent on the ally and is particularly true regarding military bases. The respective service involved tends to be more favorable towards the country than the State Department as they have more at stake.[32]

A third pattern of influence occurs when the smaller power can count on the support of groups within the United States. This could include political, religious, and economic groups. The focus of politics switches to Congress and the presidency as opposed to the bureaucracy. This strategy filters the ally's demands through domestic groups so it is couched in references to American interests.[33] For the ally, successful leverage over the United States depends on four factors. First, the small ally must not be viewed as hostile. Second, it needs to establish itself as anticommunist and play this up to be attractive to American decision makers. Third, it must develop strong working relationships with sectors of the American government that encourage mutual dependence. Finally, whenever possible it should build the support of organized groups within the United States. This can include ethnic and religious groups in the case of Israel or smaller, politically oriented groups such as anticommunist organizations that have traditionally supported Taiwan.[34]

In sum, an alliance with the United States gives the small country the prestige and ability to consult with the United States on matters of mutual security and gives these nations opportunities to sway the United States. Therefore the power that these smaller allies derive from the United States is due to the American policy of accumulating global alliances.[35]

This process of penetration for influence in alliances is also recognized by Stephen Walt, who argues that penetration can take three forms. First, public officials may by choice attempt to move their nations closer to another in an alliance framework. An example of this was Franklin D. Roosevelt's gradual erosion of American neutrality in favor of Great Britain at the beginning of World War II. Second, interest groups may attempt to use their ability to influence public opinion and decision makers in order to get policies adopted that are favorable to the ally. Third, foreign propaganda can be used to manipulate decision makers and the public in general in an effort to implement policy.[36] Walt argues that this can be especially effective against large powers. Smaller powers can manipulate larger states, who have to take into account their global interests, particularly if they have knowledge of the political system.[37]

The dynamic of a foreign power gaining influence within the American political system was evident in the three case studies discussed in this work. The Iranian and Saudi cases are similar, as American decision makers perceived that these states were important to maintaining U.S. interests in the region as well as in the international system as a whole. Therefore, these alliances were initiated out of at least perceived strategic interests on the part of American decision makers. During the 1970s the military component of these alliances became predominant. This was reflected by the huge quantity and quality of American arms that were sold to these nations. The arms sales reinforced these alliances, as they created constituency groups in the United States to maintain and expand these relationships. These groups included sectors of the American government, notably the military services and the Commerce and Treasury Departments. For the military, their research and development costs were subsidized as a result of the greater quantities of arms that were produced, costs per item of various weapons systems were also lowered. The Commerce and Treasury Departments were supportive, as these arms transfers helped U.S. balance of payments as well as encouraged future exports of both military and civilian goods. This was a major factor for the generally enthusiastic role played by the American business community, which hoped to be able to take advantage of the overall climate of relations to gain additional market share in these nations. This was significant, as American policy makers and corporate leaders frequently pointed out the potential ramifications should a particular weapons sale to either Iran or Saudi Arabia be rejected by Congress. An example of this in both the Iranian and Saudi cases was the sale of AWACS highlighted in earlier chapters.

The integration of these states into the U.S. alliance framework created a generally favorable climate in the American press and public that these governments were "modernizing states" who shared similar values and goals with the United States. Conservative political groups in the United

States valued these alliances as important components in the Cold War with the Soviet Union.

The Israeli case differs from Iran and Saudi Arabia because domestic constituencies within the United States served to bring about the establishment of the alliance. Once the alliance was established it was justified for strategic reasons. Over time, the base of support for the alliance within the American political system expanded as well. In addition to getting support from many American Jewish groups as well as Congress, components of the U.S. Defense Department came to view Israel as being important for a variety of factors. First, the growth of Israeli military power served as a check on states that were hostile or potentially hostile to American interests in the region, as well as serving as a possible deterrent to direct Soviet military involvement in the Middle East. Second, Israel served as a testing ground for American weaponry in combat conditions against comparable Soviet weapons systems. This benefited the companies that produced them as well as sectors of the U.S. military that used them. As was discussed in other parts of this work, with regard to the cases of the Maverick and Sparrow missiles during the 1973 war, the measures of military success were questionable. In the case of the Maverick air-to-ground missile, the system was used against targets identified as enemy command facilities that were in actuality a group of tents spread over a wide area of desert. The missile was counted as scoring a hit if it landed within the perimeter of these group of tents even though in most cases the damage caused was minimal. The case of the Sparrow is even more dubious. The problem with the Sparrow system was that it could not identify friend from foe and during aerial combat the chances were good that friendly aircraft could be shot down. The Israelis grounded their entire air force for a period of time, sending up only one plane armed with Sparrow missiles. As a result, any aircraft encountered would be certain to be hostile. The favorable reports the Israelis generated from these "successes" pleased elements of the U.S. Air Force. Third, Israel served as an important source of research and development given the improvements that they were able to make to adapt American equipment to warfare conditions in the Middle East. In addition, Israel entered into partnerships with American firms to produce weapons systems, notably the partnership of the Israeli Aircraft Industry and the Grumman Corporation to produce the Lavi fighter. Fourth, Israel became valuable to sectors of the American military because of the intelligence it was able to furnish regarding the strengths and weaknesses of Soviet equipment. This included allowing the American military to inspect and take possession of captured Soviet equipment. This began relatively early on in the relationship in the aftermath of the 1956 Suez War. In addition to sectors of the Defense Department, the U.S. intelligence community also by and large became supportive of the alliance with Israel. The Israelis, as discussed in other parts of this work, supported conservative pro-Western states and movements in many parts of the world, some of whom the United States would have found difficult to ally with openly. Specific examples of this include Israel's military and economic cooperation with South Africa, and cooperation with Iran in assisting the Iraqi Kurds in their attempt to gain autonomy from Baghdad in the early 1970s as well as the military training missions that the Israeli military performed in parts of Africa and Latin America. The Israelis were also used in covert operations in various parts of the Third World that were funded by the CIA. This was known within the American intelligence community as project KK Mountain.

The Implications of the Gulf War

On the surface it appeared that the Gulf War was a vindication of Washington's Middle East policy, especially the development of military infrastructure in Saudi Arabia. The prepositioning of military equipment and the establishment of an American-Saudi political/military alliance facilitated the rapid U.S. military buildup in the Middle East. The Gulf War and the ending of the Cold War seemed to promise a new era for the international system. In the aftermath of the Gulf War there was some movement in the Israeli-Palestinian peace process. The PLO's initial support of Iraq caused a loss of credibility in general, and more importantly within most Arab governments. Israel was pushed to agree to negotiations by their fears that Washington no longer considered them a strategic asset in the region. This development resulted from the end of American-Soviet competition in the region, as well as the political liability of Israeli retaliation against Iraqi SCUD missile attacks which threatened to unravel the coalition against Baghdad. As a result Israel was more vulnerable to American economic pressure. A similar dynamic was working in Syria as Damascus lost the backing of its superpower patron.[38]

The conflict was a limited success for the United States as it did not realize all of the war aims identified by George Bush at the outset: the unconditional withdrawal of all Iraqi forces from Kuwait; the restoration of Kuwait's legitimate government; the protection of the security and stability of the region; and the protection of American lives abroad. Certainly the first two, and for the most part, the last aim were satisfied.[39]

However, Saddam Hussein was not removed from power when the ground war stopped after 100 hours. This was time enough to evict the Iraqi military from Kuwait but not to dislodge Saddam Hussein from his control over Iraq. Legitimate military and political factors account for this. The Bush administration did not want to defeat Iraq absolutely and risk the fragmentation of the state which might have politically benefitted Iran and/ or Syria. Conversely President Bush's fragile political coalition might have fractured had the western powers taken the war deeper into Iraq. Finally, the administration did not want to risk greater American casualties by pursuing Republican Guard Divisions into Iraq, shifting fighting from the open deserts to the narrow confines of cities and towns and limiting

American advantages in firepower.[40]

The Bush administration encouraged the Iraqi people to rise up and overthrow Saddam Hussein. Washington hoped that disaffected elements of the Iraqi military would stage a coup and overthrow the regime. Due to Saddam Hussein's control of the military this was, and remains, an unlikely scenario. Washington's encouragement, however, did help to stimulate the revolt of the Kurds in the north and the Shia in the south. The United States did not provide concrete support to these movements other than supplying humanitarian aid to the Kurds and establishing no fly zones in the north and south because it did not want to see the fragmentation of Iraq. While these no fly zones did, and still do, limit Baghdad's ability to freely control and move military forces about the country, they could not prevent the regime from defeating its domestic opponents. The defeat of the Kurds and Shia has given the regime a new lease on life in the aftermath of its defeat in the Gulf War by allowing Saddam Hussein to reconsolidate his power over his core base of support among the Sunni Arab component of the population.[41] It also demonstrated to opponents the futility of opposing the regime, as despite its glaring military defeat, the central government still had enough military forces to put down internal insurrection. Furthermore, the lack of support from the coalition illustrated that it was divided and would not provide significant support to any internal rebellion.

The failure to remove Saddam Hussein from power has caused the United States to expend greater resources to maintain the security and stability of the region. Initially there was support for sanctions against Baghdad and the inspection regime. However, Washington has become increasingly isolated on the issue of sanctions and has been forced to expend a great deal of economic, political, and military resources to contain Iraq and limit its ability to develop weapons of mass destruction. It can be argued that the fact that the commitment of a substantial amount of military forces to roll back Iraq's aggression illustrated the weakness of Washington's policy of arming regional allies in an effort to safeguard its interests in the region. The close political relationship and the arming of Iran could not forestall the Iranian revolution, and critics argue contributed to the weakening of the regime. Likewise the political and military support extended to Israel and Saudi Arabia did not deter Iraq from invading Kuwait.[42]

Conclusions

There are four conclusions of this study that contribute to the alliance literature on international relations. First, these cases illustrate that alliances can evolve through stages. Second, the orientation of an alliance can change when the larger power fosters the expansion of its ally's military and political influence. As a result, the alliance takes on a life of its own and the relationship becomes important for its own sake. This occurs at the systemic level where the emphasis becomes one of credibility. At the domestic level the constituency groups around the alliance act as a reinforcement as well as contribute to alliance reformulation. Third, the emphasis on military relations in these alliances, which increased over time, prevented them from evolving into more broad-based relationships. Finally, because of strategic reasons, these alliances came to have great importance with American decision makers. In the case of Iran and Saudi Arabia it was access to oil and issues of containment. The Israeli case is different, as there was a strong domestic constituency for initiating the relationship and strategic rationales were developed later. Thus, these states to a large degree were able to manipulate the United States in gaining support for their own foreign policy goals despite the contradictions these could have with American interests.

Both Iran and Saudi Arabia saw alignment with the United States as being in the interests of the regime. In the Iranian case it was the United States that facilitated the royalist coup in 1953 that established the Shah as the absolute monarch of the country. A dual dependency emerged as the Shah was dependent on American military and political support. The United States in turn was dependent on Iran for maintaining its strategic interests in the region. These strategic interests included: providing secure access to oil to the industrialized world; becoming a pro-American regional surrogate in the region by building up Iranian military capabilities to basically keep in check other anti-Western states such as Iraq; providing its territory for American intelligence-gathering facilities so the United States could monitor and gather information on the Soviet Union; and providing a market for American goods.

The American relationship with Saudi Arabia was driven by similar factors. However, the Saudi monarchy differed from Iran as, until recently, it was more subtle in maintaining its links with America. As a result of these strategic interests, the United States became interlocked with the fate of the respective regimes, thus limiting the options of American decision makers. The Israeli case is different as the evidence indicates that the alliance was formulated to a large degree out of domestic political considerations. Strategic considerations became important after the establishment of the relationship as a United States justification, specifically during the Reagan administration. Although it should be noted that some analysts, as well as sectors of the American military, viewed Israel as a strategic liability to American geostrategic interests in the region.

The United States continues to adopt a static policy with regard to international relations as a whole. I would agree with those scholars who argue that America has consistently overcommitted to its allies. In many cases the policies of the ally become American policies, and the U.S. ties itself to a narrow elite in these nations and is dependent on its survival. This is especially true with regard to Iran and Saudi Arabia, while Israel is a more complex case. This reinforces the notion that these alliances are not made with nations so much as with a narrow segment of the elite. As a result overcommitment militarily and politically to these states has locked the United States into the fate of these regimes. It would seem therefore that American foreign policy has come full circle. From the early postwar era to the late 1960s American allies were dependent on the United States. Currently, however, it seems that the United States has lost its dominant position with respect to many of its allies. In some cases the United States has subordinated certain of its regional interests in the Middle East to its allies as a result of both systemic and domestic conditions. Therefore, in conclusion, it is necessary for the United States to reevaluate its military commitments in the Middle East, and more generally in the international system. Many of these alliances are no longer useful and some are detrimental, as they foster the concept that these states, many of whom are undemocratic, are essential to the security of the United States. As a result, too much emphasis has been placed by the United States in both the formation and implementation of these alliances on strategic aspects, and not enough attention has been placed on political and economic cooperation. This would create longer-lasting bonds with a greater number of states rather than having the primary focus of the relationship based on military interaction.

From a policy perspective it would be more beneficial politically, economically, and military for the United States to adopt a less interventionist military policy, while placing a much greater emphasis on political and economic cooperation. As Paul Kennedy points out, economic and military power is relative. Great powers decline as they become overextended militarily. This occurs as a result of changes in the international system. Great powers are confronted by economic and military rivals so they spend more on defense, which contributes to their economic erosion.[43]

This has been the situation the United States has found itself in during the postwar period. From 1945 until the late 1960s the United States was the major power in the international system. It sought to rebuild this system after World War II so as to make it receptive to the expansion of Liberal Capitalism. This served to enhance American economic, political, and strategic interests. However, with its role as the hegemon of the international system came responsibilities, which became evident with the development of the Cold War in the late 1940s. In the name of defense the United States allowed its alliance partners, specifically West Germany and Japan, to violate the rules of the Liberal Economic Order by engaging in protectionism. This was justified, because it was argued, in order for these states to become stronger allies they needed to reindustrialize rapidly. Therefore the United States, with the goal of defense, fostered the development of economic rivals. More significantly, in seeking to maintain its position in the international system the United States got involved in conflicts in Korea and Vietnam that weakened itself economically, militarily, and politically. Thus by the early 1970s the United States, while a superpower militarily, was becoming one of several major powers economically. However, its alliance policies toward its major allies,

Western Europe and Japan, did not reflect this. The United States still contributed a disproportionate amount of resources toward the defense of these areas.

American alliance policy did shift, however, in the third world, particularly in the Middle East, as the United States sought to build up regional surrogates as a way of divesting itself of costly military burdens. However, this posed a more serious problem as the United States, to a large degree, allowed these countries to exercise a great deal of control over the alliance. Therefore the goals and interests of these states became those of the United States as well. These nations were able to gain leverage over America as the United States had invested its political credibility in these alliances, as well as building up economic and strategic incentives for the maintenance of these relationships. This was illustrated by the support domestic groups and sectors of the U.S. government gave to these alliances. It was perceived that a failure to support these allies would result in a loss of credibility for the United States in the international system and call into question the strength of American commitments elsewhere.[44]

In initiating and maintaining alliance commitments, it is imperative for American leaders to be clear on the concrete purposes of the alliance. The idea of maintaining an alliance simply for its own sake ultimately costs the United States economically, politically, and strategically. It is imperative for the United States to develop clear priorities in foreign policy.[45] In formulating and evaluating American alliances, decision makers and scholars should remember the words of Frederick the Great. In a conversation with his generals he stated, "he who seeks to defend everything ultimately defends nothing."[46]

Notes

1. Franklin B. Weinstein, "The Concept of a Commitment in International Relations," *Journal of Conflict Resolution* 13, no. 1 (March 1969): 52-53. Also see Hans Morgenthau, "Alliances in Theory and Practice," *American Political Science Review* 56, no. 2 (June 1962): 210-11; Norman A. Graebner, "Alliances and Free World Security," *Current History* 38 (1960): 214-19, 227.

2. Alexander L. George and Robert O. Keohane, "The Concept of National Interests: Uses and Limitations," in *Presidential Decisionmaking in Foreign Policy*, Alexander George ed. (Boulder, Colo: Westview Press, 1980), 232-33.

3. Alan Tonelson, "The Real National Interest," *Foreign Policy*, no. 61 (Winter 1985-1986), 65. He points out that credibility theory emphasizes that officials cannot attempt to classify parts of the world as more important than others. He cites the example of Dean Acheson excluding Korea from American security interest in Asia, which critics have argued helped to precipitate the North invading the South six months later.

4. Tonelson, "The Real National Interest," 49-50.

5. Jack L. Snyder, *Myths of Empire: Domestic Politics and International Ambition* (Ithaca, N.Y.: Cornell University Press, 1991), 256-57. Also see Robert A. Pollard, *Economic Security and the Origins of the Cold War, 1945-1950* (New York: Columbia University Press, 1985), 194-95. It would seem that the repercussions of this policy was seen twenty years later with the American intervention in Vietnam, as Snyder identifies this as an example of American overextension, (262). Domestic factors also become apparent when one considers the major escalation of this conflict in 1965 under Lyndon Johnson. He felt he had to continue Kennedy's policy, as a failure to do so on his part could jeopardize his domestic legislative agenda.

6. Snyder, *Myths of Empire*, 264-65. For example, Acheson argued that areas of Southeast Asia and Korea were important for Japan to reindustralize. Kennan stated that Greece and Turkey were important to prevent communism from spreading into the core area of Western Europe. For a discussion of George Kennan's views see Terry L. Deibel "Alliances for Containment," in *Containing the Soviet Union: A Critique of U.S. Policy*, Terry L. Deibel and John Lewis Gaddis eds. (New York: Pergamon-Brassey, 1987), 104. He states that Kennan opposed the establishment of a huge network of alliances because it focused just on the military means of containment. Kennan's strategy of containment was to build up those areas that were considered important for the United States, such as Western Europe and Japan, economically, socially, and politically. Eventually, he argued, these states would be able to resist Soviet influence on their own. Kennan was against the model of containment that the United States eventually established of attempting to ring the Soviet Union with pro-American allies. He felt that this strategy would preputate military confrontation and impede negotiations.

7. Terry L. Deibel, "Changing Patterns of Collective Defense: U.S. Security Commitments in the Third World," in *Alliances in U.S. Foreign Policy: Issues in the Quest for Collective Defense*, Alan Ned Sabrosky ed. (Boulder, Colo.: Westview Press, 1988), 108-9. Deibel characterizes these alliances as significant because they aligned the United States with, for the most part, similar socioeconomic and political societies. As a result, the interests of the Western coalition were complementary, sharing, among other factors, historic immigration patterns, common language, and wartime cooperation. In addition, they were reinforced by personal and cultural ties (109).

8. Stalin's suspicious view of American motives after World War II is illustrated by Adam Ulam, *The Rivals: America and Russia since World War II* (New York: Viking Press, 1971), 3-11, and 95-151. Cited in Melvyn P. Leffler, "From the Truman Doctrine to the Carter Doctrine: Lessons and Dilemmas of the Cold War," *Diplomatic History* 7, no. 4 (Fall 1983): 250-51.

9. Deibel, "Changing Patterns of Collective Defense," 109. Deibel argues that since Dulles' strategy was based on massive nuclear retaliation in confronting Soviet expansion, these alliances were stopgap measures designed to deal with more immediate contingencies (110).

10. Jack L. Snyder, *Myths of Empire*, 265. Acheson stated that this directive was used to get the American government to line up behind this view of containment. It was further used as a means of gaining public support. See Dean Acheson, *Present at the Creation* (New York: Norton, 1969), 374-75. Cited in Snyder.

11. "Review of Basic National Security Policy," NSC 162/1, October 30 1953. Reprinted in *The Pentagon Papers: The Defense Department History of United States Decision making on Vietnam*, The Senator Gravel ed. (Boston: Beacon Press, 1971), 1: 424; Cited in Walt, 3.

12. Weinstein, "The Concept of A Commitment," 52.

13. Weinstein, "The Concept of A Commitment," 113-15.

14. Text of speech published in *The Washington Post*, 23 February 1983, 12(A). Quoted in Deibel, "Changing Patterns of Collective Defense," 115. Deibel states that the view of the Reagan administration was that third world states would be better able to resist Soviet pressures if it were aligned with the Western alliance system.

15. George Schultz, Address before the Southern Center for International Studies, Atlanta, Georgia, February 24,1983, quoted in *USAF Selected Statements* 83-1, (January-March 1983), 76. Cited in Deibel, "Changing Patterns of Collective Defense," 115-16.

16. George Liska, *The New Statecraft: Foreign Aid in American Foreign Policy* (Chicago: University of Chicago Press, 1960), 226-27. He cites the example of NATO.

17. Steven R. David, *Third World Coups d'Etat and International Security* (Baltimore, Md.: Johns Hopkins University Press, 1987), 21. He argues that the third world is significant to the United States as it desires an international system that reflects its dominant values. This would help promote its security aims as well as serve a domestic political function of popular confidence in the government's ability to conduct foreign policy (24).

The significance of American military bases in the third world was also articulated by William R. Van Cleave, "The Military Sinews of a Global Strategy," in *Security Commitments and Capabilities: Elements of an American Global Strategy*, Uri Raanan and Robert L Pfaltzgraff eds. (Hamden, Conn.: Archon Books, 1985), 172. He argues that the United States and its allies needed to do more to cope with Soviet threats.

18. Charles William Maynes, "America's Third World Hang-ups," *Foreign Policy*, no. 71 (Summer 1988): 132. Among the restrictions that third world countries have placed on American use of military facilities are: Turkey will not let American forces use its bases in an out-of-area conflict; the Philippines required prior consultation before the United States could use its bases in that country in a conflict. Examples of host country restrictions that affected American military operations were: most European states refusing to allow their bases to be used to launch an attack on Libya in 1986, and the refusal of most NATO countries, except Portugal, to allow the United States to use bases in Europe to resupply Israel during the 1973 war.

The establishment of overseas bases was an important advantage that the United States had vis-à-vis the Soviet Union throughout most of the Cold War period. This factor gave the United States overwhelming strategic superiority; while America had an array of bases from which to attack the Soviet Union directly the USSR had none to reciprocate against the United States. It was only with the development of ballistic missile technology by the late 1960s that the need for bases from which to launch a nuclear attack became obsolete. Throughout the Cold War the Soviet Union was only able to really establish extensive base facilities outside of the Warsaw Pact in a few places, notably Cuba, Ethiopia, the PDRY, and Vietnam.

19. Norman Myers, *Not Far Afield: U.S. Interests and the Global Environment* (Washington, D.C.: World Resources Institute, June 1987), 8-9. Cited in Maynes, "America's Third World Hang-ups," 134. Maynes also indicates the significance of American investment in the third world as well as the importance of the commodity trade with the third world. The United States has been dependent on the importation of strategic minerals such as tin, columbium, aluminum, and manganese. In addition, the United States imports much of its agricultural output to the third world.

20. Andrew Pierre, "The Future of America's Commitments and Alliances," *Orbis* 16, no. 3 (Fall 1972): 701-2. See also Tonelson, "The Real National Interest," 53.

The Nixon Doctrine was also important in allowing American policy makers to withdraw from Vietnam. See Joo-Hong Nam, *America's Commitment to South Korea* (Cambridge: Cambridge University Press, 1986), 64.

It can be argued that the Nixon Doctrine sought to substitute American weaponry for a United States physical presence. See Ilan Peleg, "Models of Arms Transfer in American Foreign Policy: Carter's Restraint and Reagan's Promotion, 1977-1987," in *Arms, Politics and the Economy,* Robert Higgs ed. (New York: Holmes and Meier, 1990), 142-43. It is significant to note that the Nixon Doctrine stressed the selective intervention of American forces. See Stephen P. Gilbert, "The Nixon Doctrine and Military Aid," *Orbis* 16, no. 3 (Fall 1972): 667.

21. For a discussion of the Carter and Reagan Administrations' policies towards arms sales see Peleg, "Models of Arms Transfers," 149. He argues that Carter's arms sales policy failed for two reasons. First, there was inconsistency in its application that led to opposition from elements of Congress. Second, many nations viewed Carter's emphasis on human rights as another form of American intervention. It is significant to note also that to a certain extent Reagan campaigned against Carter's security assistance policy by indicating his administration would not abandon American allies. This was a reference to the Shah of Iran and Somoza of Nicaragua.

Also see William D. Hartung, *And Weapons for All* (New York: HarperCollins Publishers, 1994), 63-83. Discusses especially the bureaucratic attempts to circumvent limitations on arms transfers under Carter.

For a discussion of the history of American arms transfers and military assistance in general see Robert Jefferson Wood, "Military Assistance and the Nixon Doctrine," *Orbis* 15, no. 1 (Spring 1971); and Chester J. Pach Jr., *Arming the Free World: The Origins of the United States Military Assistance Program, 1945-1950.* (Chapel Hill, N.C.: The University of North Carolina Press, 1991).

22. Philip C. Rusciolelli, "Security Assistance: An Applicable Strategy for the 1990s?" in *Can American Remain Committed? U.S. Security Horizons in the 1990s* (Boulder, Colo.: Westview Press, 1992), 237. Another important factor that Rusciolelli cites is that America must develop a policy on security assistance that takes into account national security interests, as opposed to parochial domestic economic incentives.

23. Hartung, *And Weapons For All,* 274-75, 283. See also Lee Feinstein, "Administration to Sell Advanced F-16 fighters to Taiwan," *Arms Control Today,* September 1992; Don Oberdorfer, *Washington Post,* 4 September 1992. It is significant to note that during the Reagan administration it was then Vice-President Bush that negotiated the pledge with Beijing that the United States was not to exceed American arms transfers to Taiwan.

Governor Clinton supported the sale of the F-15 so long as it was not the most modern ground attack version of the system that could affect Israeli security. More importantly, Clinton made the promise two-and-half weeks prior to the Bush administration's agreeing to sell the planes. Hartung argues that this was a reason for Bush to go ahead with the sale. See "Governor Clinton Supports F-15 Sale to Saudi Arabia," Clinton/Gore Campaign Press Release, 26 August 1992. Cited in Hartung. Press release issued one day after Clinton's appearance.

24. William D. Hartung, "Breaking the Arms Sales Addiction: New Directions for U.S. Policy," *World Policy Journal* 8, no. 1 (Winter 1990-1991): 4.

25. Cited in David Fromkin, "Entangling Alliances," *Foreign Affairs* 48, no. 4 (July 1970): 688.

26. Deibel, "Alliances for Containment," 112-13.

27. David, *Third World Coups d'Etat*, 68.

28. Alan Ned Sabrosky, "Alliances in U.S. Foreign Policy," *Alliances in U.S. Foreign Policy: Issues in the Quest for Collective Defense* (Boulder, Colo.: Westview Press, 1988), 8. These views were also articulated by Terry Deibel writing in the same work. He stated, "Alliances should always be seen as means to an end—the end being U.S. national security—never as ends in themselves." Deibel, "Changing Patterns of Collective Defense," 123.

Ted Galen Carpenter discusses the problems of seeking to maintain the vestiges of imperial dominance. While it may have some value for prestige, it ultimately drains resources in keeping up useless alliance commitments. He articulates these views in examining the United States-South Korean alliance which Carpenter argues is not and never was a vital American interest (13).

29. Comments made by President Johnson in an address at Johns Hopkins University, "Peace without Conquest," April 7, 1965, *Public Papers of the Presidents: Lyndon B. Johnson, Volume I, 1965*. (Washington, D.C.: U.S. Government Printing Office, 1966), 394-99. Cited in Ted Galen Carpenter, "South Korea: A Vital or Peripheral U.S. Security Interest," *The U.S.-South Korean Alliance: Time for a Change*, Doug Bandow and Ted Galen Carpenter eds. (New Brunswick, N.J.: Transaction Publishers, 1992), 1-2.

30. Robert Keohane, "The Big Influence of Small Allies," *Foreign Policy* 1, no. 2 (Spring 1971).

31. Robert Keohane, "The Big Influence of Small Allies," 163-64.

32. Robert Keohane, "The Big Influence of Small Allies," 164-66. He cites congressional testimony discussing this issue. Keohane cites as examples of this the U.S. Navy and Portugal and Greece, as well as the U.S. Air Force with Spain.

33. Robert Keohane, "The Big Influence of Small Allies," 166.

34. Keohane, "The Big Influence of Small Allies," 167.

35. Keohane, "The Big Influence of Small Allies," 180-82, cites as an example Australia's right to consult the United States through its membership in the Australian, New Zealand, United States (ANZUS) pact. See also Thomas B. Millar, "Australia and the American Alliance," *Pacific Affairs* 37 (Summer 1964), 150. Cited by Keohane.

36. Walt, *The Origins of Alliances*, 46.

37. Walt, *The Origins of Alliances*, 48-49. See also Yaacov Bar-Siman-Tov, "Alliance Strategy: U.S.-Small Allies Relationships," *Journal of Strategic Studies* 3, no. 2 (September 1980): 202-16.

38. John Pimlott, "The International Ramifications" in *The Gulf War Assessed*, John Pimlott and Stephen Badsey eds., (New York: Sterling, 1992) 207, 265. Provides a good discussion of the early negotiations and the U.S. role. As was mentioned in Chapter 5 Israel was actually a burden during the Gulf War, as Washington was forced to divert political and military resources to keep Israel out of the conflict to preserve the coalition. The military resources expended included diverting coalition air power to seek and destroy mobile SCUD missiles in western Iraq as opposed to bombing targets in Iraq and Kuwait thought necessary to facilitate the ground offensive. See chapter 5 (174). The American economic pressure included withholding loan guarantees in an effort to get Israel to cease building new West Bank settlements. This was also discussed in chapter 5. See (147).

39. Steve A. Yetiv, *The Persian Gulf Crisis* (Westport, Conn: Greenwood Press,

1997), 104.

40. For a discussion of the threats coming from Iraq as well as other regional states see Jim Hoagland, "A Year After Desert Storm: What the War Didn't Resolve," *Washington Post*, 12 January 1992, C1. He cites a statement from Assistant Secretary of State Edward P. Djerejian who stated in congressional testimony that Iraq still posed a threat to Saudi Arabia. Hoagland also cited an official who discussed the potential military threat from Iran.

41. Jeffrey Record, *Hollow Victory: A Contrary View of the Gulf War.*(New York: Brassey's, 1993), 157.

For a brief discussion of the significance of the Kurdish and Shia rebellions see Yetiv, *The Persian Gulf Crisis,*108-10.

It has been stated that Saddam Hussein has been able to reconstitute his armed forces in both size and equipment. One year after the Gulf War, Iraq had retained an estimated 2,400 tanks, 4,400 armored personnel carriers and infantry fighting vehicles, 1,000-2,000 artillery pieces, and 250 multiple rocket launchers as well as about 200 SCUD missiles. Charles Lane, "The Stalking of Saddam," *Newsweek,* January 20, 1992, 27. Cited in Record, 156.

42. Shahram Chubin has made the argument that, "some twenty years of major defense expenditures($150-$200 billion), Saudi Arabia still needs to call upon Western allies for most security problems." Shahram Chubin, "Post-War Gulf Security," *Survival* 23, no. 2 (March-April 1991): 146. Jeffrey Record also makes the argument that the continued American military presence threatens to delegitimize the Saudi government and conveys the image that the monarchy is a surrogate for American interests in the region. This was what happened to the Shah by the late 1970s and contributed to the downfall of the Iranian monarchy. See Record, 158. For a good brief discussion of the threats emerging from Iraq in the immediate aftermath of the Gulf War see Elaine Sciolino, "Iraqis Could Pose A threat Soon, CIA Chief Says," *New York Times*, 16 January 1992, A9. She cites CIA chief Robert Gates as stating in Congressional testimony that Iraq retained the ability to develop weapons of mass destruction as Baghdad still retained a cadre of skilled engineers and scientists. See also Barton Gellman, "One Year Later: War's Faded Triumph," *Washington Post*, 16 January 1992, A1.

43. For a discussion of this argument see Paul Kennedy, *The Rise and Fall of the Great Powers* (New York: Vintage Books, 1987).

44. See Yacov Bar-Siman-Tov, "Alliance Strategy American-Small Allies Relationships." He argues that small allies were able to gain leverage over the United States due to their perceived value by American decision makers during the Cold War (204).

45. Tonelson, "The Real National Interest," 72.

46. Tonelson, "The Real National Interest," 72.

Bibliography

Books

International Relations Theory, American Foreign Policy

Anderson, Terry H. *The United States, Great Britain, and the Cold War: 1944-1947.* Columbia: University of Missouri Press, 1981.

Badar, William. *The United States and the Spread of Nuclear Weapons.* New York: Pegasus, 1968.

Baldwin, David. *Economic Statecraft.* Princeton, N.J.: Princeton University Press, 1985.

Ball, Nicole. *Security and Economy in the Third World.* Princeton, N.J.: Princeton University Press, 1988.

Bandow, Doug, and Ted Galen Carpenter, eds. *The U.S.-South Korean Alliance.* New Brunswick, N.J.: Transaction Publishers, 1992.

Benoit, Emile. *Defense and Economic Growth in the Developing Countries.* Lexington, Mass.: D.C. Heath, 1974.

Bently, Arthur. *The Process of Government.* San Antonio, Tex.: Principia Press, 1949.

Beer, Francis A. *The Political Economy of Alliances: Benefits, Costs, and Institutions in NATO.* Beverly Hills, Calif.: Sage Publications, 1972.

Beer, Francis A., ed. *Alliances: Latent War Communities in the Contemporary World.* New York: Holt, Rinehart, and Winston, 1970.

Braum, Aurel, ed. *The Middle East in Global Strategy.* Boulder, Colo.: Westview Press, 1987.

Brzezinski, Zbigniew. *Power and Principle.* New York: Farrar, Strauss, Giroux, 1983.

Campbell, John. *Defense of the Middle East.* New York: Praeger, 1960.

Carpenter, Ted Galen. *A Search for Enemies: America's Alliances after the Cold War.* Washington, D.C.: CATO Institute, 1992.

Cervenka, Zdenek, and Barbara Rogers. *The Nuclear Axis: Secret Collaboration between West Germany and South Africa.* New York: Times Books, 1978.

Cingranelli, David Louis. *Ethics, American Foreign Policy and the Third World.* New York: St. Martin's Press, 1993.

Claude, Inis. *Power and International Relations.* New York: Random House, 1962.

Dahl, Robert. *A Preface to Democratic Theory.* Chicago: University of Chicago Press, 1956.

David, Steven R. *Choosing Sides: Alignment and Realignment in the Third World.*

Baltimore, Md.: Johns Hopkins University Press, 1991.

David, Steven R. *Third World Coups d'Etat and International Security*. Baltimore, Md.: Johns Hopkins University Press, 1987.

Deibel, Terry L., and John Lewis Gaddis. *Containing the Soviet Union: A Critique of U.S. Policy*. Washington, D.C.: Pergamon-Brassey's, 1987.

Dougherty, James E., and Robert L. Pfaltzgraff Jr. *Contending Theories of International Relations*. New York: Harper and Row Publishers, 1990.

Farley, Philip, Stephen S. Kaplan, and William H. Lewis. *Arms across the Sea*. Washington, D.C.: The Brookings Institution, 1978.

Fedder, Edwin. *NATO: The Dynamics of Alliance in the Postwar World*. New York: Dodd, Mead & Company, 1973.

Feinberg, Richard. *The Intemperate Zone*. New York: W.W. Norton, 1983.

Fox, Annette Baker. *The Power of Small States*. Chicago: University of Chicago Press, 1959.

Friedman, Julian et al., ed. *Alliance in International Politics*. Boston: Allyn and Bacon, Inc., 1970.

Gaddis, John Lewis. *The United States and the Origins of the Cold War: 1941-1947*. New York: Columbia University Press, 1972.

George, Alexander. *Managing the U.S.-Soviet Rivalry: Problems of Crisis Prevention*. Boulder, Colo.: Westview Press, 1983.

George, Alexander, ed. *Presidential Decision making in Foreign Policy*. Boulder, Colo.: Westview Press, 1980.

George, Alexander, and Richard Smoke. *Deterrence in American Foreign Policy*. New York: Columbia University Press, 1974.

Gilpin, Robert. *War and Change in World Politics*. Cambridge: Cambridge University Press, 1981.

Granfelt, Helge. *Alliances and Ententes As Political Weapons: From Bismarck's Alliance System to Present Time*. Lund, Sweden: Fahlbeck Foundation, 1970.

Gulick, E. *Europe's Classical Balance of Power*. New York: W.W. Norton and Company, 1955.

Haas, Ernst. *Tangle of Hopes: American Commitments and World Order*. Englewood Cliffs, N.J.: Prentice-Hall, 1969.

Hadar, Leon. *Quagmire: America in the Middle East*. Washington, D.C.: Cato Institute, 1992.

Haglund, David G. *Can America Remain Committed?* Boulder, Colo.: Westview Press, 1992.

Hammond, Paul Y., David J., Louscher, Michael D. Salomone, and Norman A. Graham. *The Reluctant Supplier: U.S. Decisionmaking For Arms Sales*. Cambridge, Mass.: Oelgeschlager, Gunn & Hain, Publishers, 1983.

Harkavy, Robert E. *The Arms Trade and International Systems*. Cambridge, Mass.: Ballinger Publishing Company, 1975.

Hartung, William D. *And Weapons for All*. New York: HarperCollins Publishers, 1994.

Hermann, Charles F., Charles W. Kegley Jr., and James Rosenau, eds. *New Directions in the Study of Foreign Policy*. Boston: Allen & Unwin, 1987.

Herz, John H. *International Politics in the Atomic Age*. New York: Columbia University Press, 1959

Higgs, Robert. *Arms, Politics, and the Economy*. New York: Holmes and Meier, 1990.

Hoffmann, Stanley. *Gulliver's Troubles, or the Setting of American Foreign Policy*. New York: McGraw-Hill, 1968.

Holsti, K. J. *Why Nations Realign*. London: George Allen & Unwin, 1982.

Holsti, Ole R., Terrence P. Hopmann, and John D. Sullivan. *Unity and Disintegration in International Alliances: Comparative Studies.* New York: John Wiley and Sons, 1973.

Hopmann, P. Terrence, Dina A. Zinnes, and J. Singer, eds. *Cumulation in International Relations Research.* Denver, Colo.: Monograph Series in World Affairs, 1981.

Jervis, Robert, and Jack Snyder. *Dominoes and Bandwagons.* Oxford: Oxford University Press, 1991.

Joffe, Josef. *The Limited Partnership: Europe, the United States, and the Burdens of Alliance.* Cambridge, Mass.: Ballinger, 1987.

Joseph, Paul. *Cracks in the Empire: State Politics and the Vietnam War.* Boston: South End Press, 1981.

Kaldor, Mary, and Richard Falf, eds. *Dealignment: A New Foreign Policy Perspective.* Oxford: Basil Blackwell Ltd., 1987.

Kaldor, Mary, and Asborn Eide eds. *The World Military Order.* New York: Praeger, 1979.

Kaplan, Morton. *Systems and Processes in International Politics.* New York: John Wiley and Sons, 1957.

Kegley, Charles W. Jr., and Gregory A. Raymond. *When Trust Breaks Down.* Columbia, S.C.: University of South Carolina Press, 1990.

Kennan, George. *The Fateful Alliance: France, Russia, and the Coming of the First World War.* New York: Pantheon Books, 1984.

Kennedy, Paul. *The Rise and Fall of the Great Powers.* New York: Vintage Books, 1987.

Keohane, Robert O., ed. *Neorealism and its Critics.* New York: Columbia University Press, 1986.

Kissinger, Henry. *A World Restored.* Boston: Houghton Mifflin Company, 1973.

Klare, Michael. *American Arms Supermarket.* Austin, Tex.: University of Texas Press, 1984.

Klare, Michael, and Cynthia Arnson. *Supplying Repression.* Washington, D.C.: Institute for Policy Studies, 1981.

Knorr, Klaus, ed. *Historical Dimensions of National Security Problems.* Lawrence, Kans.: University Press of Kansas, 1976.

Kolko, Gabriel. *The Roots of American Foreign Policy.* Boston: Beacon Press, 1969.

Kolko, Gabriel. *The Politics of War.* New York: Random House, 1968.

Krasner, Stephen D. *Defending the National Interest.* Princeton, N.J.: Princeton University Press, 1978.

Krause, Keith. *Arms and the State: Patterns of Military Production and Trade.* Cambridge: Cambridge University Press, 1992.

Kuniholm, Bruce. *The Persian Gulf and U.S. Policy.* Claremont, Calif.: Regina Books, 1984.

Kuniholm, Bruce. *The Origins of the Cold War in the Near East.* Princeton, N.J.: Princeton University Press, 1980.

Labrie, Roger P., John G. Hutchins, and Edwin W. A. Peura. *U.S. Arms Sales Policy: Background and Issues.* Washington, D.C.: American Enterprise Institute, 1982.

Lauren, Paul Gordon. *Diplomacy: New Approaches in History, Theory, and Policy.* New York: The Free Press, 1979.

Lee, Manwoo, Ronald D. McLaurin, and Chung-in Moon. *Alliance under Tension: The Evolution of South Korean-U.S. Relations.* Boulder, Colo.: Westview Press, 1988.

Lenczowski, George. *American Presidents and the Middle East.* Durham, N.C.: Duke University Press, 1990.

Levy, Jack S. *War in the Modern Great Power System 1495-1975.* Lexington, Ky.: The University Press of Kentucky, 1983.

Liska, George. *Quest for Equilibrium: America and the Balance of Power on Land and Sea.* Baltimore, Md.: Johns Hopkins University Press, 1977.

Liska, George. *Alliances and the Third World.* Baltimore, Md.: Johns Hopkins University Press, 1968.

Liska, George. *Nations in Alliance: The Limits of Interdependence.* Baltimore, Md.: Johns Hopkins University Press, 1962.

Liska, George. *The New Statecraft: Foreign Aid in American Foreign Policy.* Chicago: The University of Chicago Press, 1960.

Litwak, Robert. *Detente and the Nixon Doctrine: American Foreign Policy and the Pursuit of Stability, 1969-1976.* New York: Cambridge University Press, 1984.

Lowi, Theodore. *The End of Liberalism.* New York: W. W. Norton, 1969.

Louscher, David J., and Michael D. Salomone, eds. *Marketing Security Assistance.* Lexington, Mass.: Lexington Books, 1987.

McKinley, R. D., and A. Mughan. *Aid and Arms to the Third World.* New York: St. Martin's Press, 1984.

Machiavelli, Niccolo. *The Prince.* Translated by George Bull. New York: Penguin Books, 1961.

Magdoff, Harry. *The Age of Imperialism.* New York: Monthly Review Press, 1969.

Michon, Georges. *The Franco-Russian Alliance: 1891-1917.* New York: Howard Fertig, 1969.

Mills, C. Wright. "The Power Elite," in *The American Polity Reader.* 2nd ed. Edited by Ann S. Serow, W. Wayne Shannon, and Everett C. Ladd. New York: W.W. Norton, 1993.

Morgenthau, Hans J. *Politics among Nations.* New York: Alfred A. Knopf, 1978.

Nachmias, Nitza. *Transfer of Arms, Leverage, and Peace in the Middle East.* New York: Greenwood Press, 1988.

Nagai, Yonosuke, and Akira Iriye, eds. *The Origins of the Cold War in Asia.* New York: Columbia University Press,

Nam, Joo-Hong. *America's Commitment to South Korea.* Cambridge: Cambridge University Press, 1986.

Neumann, Stephanie E. *Military Assistance in Recent Years.* New York: Praeger, 1986.

Neumann, Stephanie E., and Robert E. Harkavy, eds. *Arms Transfers in the Modern World.* New York: Praeger, 1979.

Niou, Emerson M. S., Pewter C. Ordeshook, and Gregory F. Rose. *The Balance of Power: Stability in International Systems.* Cambridge: Cambridge University Press, 1989.

Nuechterlein, Donald R. *America Recommitted: United States National Interests in a Restructured World.* Lexington, Ky.: University Press of Kentucky, 1991.

Olson, Mancur Jr. *The Logic of Collective Action: Public Goods and the Theory of Groups.* New York: Schocken Books, 1965.

Onkar, Marwah, and Ann Schulz, eds. *Nuclear Proliferation and the Near Nuclear Countries.* Cambridge, Mass.: Ballinger Publishing Company, 1975.

Osgood, Robert E. *Limited War Revisited.* Boulder, Colo.: Westview Press, 1979.

Osgood, Robert E. *Alliances and American Foreign Policy.* Baltimore, Md.: Johns Hopkins University Press, 1968.

Osgood, Robert E., and R. W. Tucker. *Force, Order, and Justice.* Baltimore, Md.: Johns Hopkins University Press, 1967.

Osgood, Robert E. *NATO: The Entangling Alliance*. Chicago: University of Chicago Press, 1962.

Osgood, Robert E. *Limited War: The Challenge to American Strategy*. Chicago: University of Chicago Press, 1957.

Paarlberg, Robert L. *Diplomatic Disputes*. Cambridge, Mass.: Center for International Affairs, Harvard University, 1978.

Pach, Chester Jr. *Arming the Free World*. Chapel Hill, N.C.: University of North Carolina Press, 1991.

Pierre, Andrew J., ed. *Arms Transfers and American Foreign Policy*. New York: New York University Press, 1979.

Pierre, Andrew J. *The Global Politics of Arms Sales*. Princeton, N.J.: Princeton University Press, 1982.

Pimlott, John, and Stephen Badsey eds. *The Gulf War Revisited*. New York, Sterling, 1992.

Plischke, Elmer. *Foreign Relations: Analysis of Its Anatomy*. New York: Greenwood Press, 1988.

Polk, William R. *The Arab World*. Cambridge, Mass.: Harvard University Press, 1982.

Pollard, Robert A. *Economic Security and the Origins of the Cold War, 1945-1950*. New York: Columbia University Press, 1985.

Ra'anan, Uri, and Robert L. Pfaltzgraff Jr. *Security Commitments and Capabilities*. Hamden, Conn.: Archon Books, 1985.

Rais, Rasul B. *The Indian Ocean and the Superpowers*. Totowa, N.J.: Barnes and Noble Books, 1987.

Record, Jeffrey. *Hollow Victory: A Contrary View of the Gulf War*. New York: Brassey's 1993.

Rosenau, James N., ed. *Domestic Sources of Foreign Policy*. New York: The Free Press, 1967.

Rosenau, James N., ed. *International Politics and Foreign Policy*. New York: The Free Press of Glencoe, Inc., 1961.

Rothstein, Robert L. *The Evolution of Theory in International Relations*. Columbia, S.C.: University of South Carolina Press, 1991.

Rothstein, Robert L. *The Weak in the World of the Strong*. New York: Columbia University Press, 1977.

Rothstein, Robert L. *Alliances and Small Powers*. New York: Columbia University Press, 1968.

Rusciolelli, Philip C. *Can America Remain Committed? U.S. Security Horizons in the 1990s*. Boulder, Colo.: Westview Press, 1992.

Russett, Bruce M. ed. *Peace, War, and Numbers*. Beverly Hills, Calif.:Sage, 1972.

Rustow, Dankwart A. *Oil and Turmoil: America Faces OPEC in the Middle East*. New York: W.W. Norton, 1982.

Sabrosky, Alan Ned, ed. *Alliances in U.S. Foreign Policy: Issues in the Quest for Collective Defense*. Boulder, Colo.: Westview Press, 1988.

Sabrosky, Alan Ned. *Polarity and War: The Changing Structure of International Conflict*. Boulder, Colo.: Westview Press, 1985.

Sampson, Anthony. *The Arms Bazaar: From Lebanon to Lockheed*. New York: Viking Press, 1977.

Schattschneider, E. E. *The Semi-Sovereign People*. New York: Holt, Rinehart, and Winston, 1960.

Schell, Jonathan. *The Time of Illusion*. New York: Vintage Books, 1975.

Schelling, Thomas C. *The Strategy of Conflict*. Cambridge, Mass.: Harvard University Press, 1976.

Schelling, Thomas C. *Arms and Influence.* New Haven, Conn.: Yale University Press, 1966.
Schlesinger, Arthur M. Jr. *A Thousand Days.* Boston: Houghton Mifflin Company, 1965.
Schlesinger, Stephen, and Stephen Kinzer. *Bitter Fruit.* New York: Doubleday Press, 1982.
Shoemaker, Chistopher C., and John Spanier. *Patron-Client State Relationships.* New York: Praeger Publishers, 1984.
Simowitz, Roslyn. *The Logical Consistency and Soundness of the Balance of Power Theory.* Denver, Colo.: Monograph Series in World Affairs, 1982.
Singer, J. David, and M. Small. *The Wages of War 1816-1965.* New York: John Wiley and Sons, 1972.
Singer, J. David, ed. *Quantitative International Politics: Insights and Evidence.* New York: The Free Press, 1968.
Snyder, Jack. *Myths of Empire: Domestic Politics and International Ambition.* Ithaca, N.Y.: Cornell University Press, 1991.
Snyder, Glenn H. *Deterrence and Defense: Toward a Theory of National Security.* Princeton, N.J.: Princeton University Press, 1961.
Stahl, Shelly A., and Geoffrey Kemp. *Arms Control and Weapons Proliferation in the Middle East and South Asia.* New York: St. Martin's Press, 1992.
Stanley, John, and Maurice Pearton. *The International Trade in Arms.* New York: Praeger, 1972.
Stockholm International Peace Research Institute. *The Arms Trade with the Third World.* New York: Holmes and Meier, 1975.
Tillman, Seth. *The U.S. and the Middle East.* Bloomington, Ind.: Indiana University Press, 1982.
Truman, David. *The Governmental Process.* New York: Alfred A. Knopf, 1951.
Walt, Stephen M. *The Origins of Alliances.* Ithaca, N.Y.: Cornell University Press, 1987.
Waltz, Kenneth. *Theory of International Relations.* Reading, Mass.: Addison-Wesley Publishing Company, 1979.
Ward, Michael Don. *Research Gaps in Alliance Dynamics.* Denver, Colo.: Monograph Series in World Affairs, 1982.
Wolfers, Arnold. *Alliance Policy in the Cold War.* Baltimore, Md.: Johns Hopkins University Press, 1959.
Wright, Martin. *International Theory: The Three Traditions.* New York: Holmes & Meier, 1992.
Yager, Joseph A., ed. *Nonproliferation and U.S. Foreign Policy.* Washington, D.C.: The Brookings Institution, 1980.
Yetiv, Steve A., *The Persian Gulf Crisis.* Westport, Conn.: Greenwood Press, 1997.

Iran

Abrahamian, Ervand. *Iran between Two Revolutions.* Princeton, N.J.: Princeton University Press, 1982.
Alexander, Yonah, and Allan Nanes, eds. *The United States and Iran: A Documentary History.* Frederick, Md.: University Publications of America, 1980.
Amirsadeghi, Hossein, ed. *The United States and the Middle East.* Albany: State

University of New York Press, 1993.

Amirsadeghi, Hossein, ed. *The Security of the Persian Gulf.* London: Croom Helm, 1981.

Amirsadeghi, Hossein. *Twentieth-Century Iran.* London: Heinemann, 1977.

Azimi, Fakhreddin. *Iran: The Crisis of Democracy, 1941-1953.* New York: St. Martin's Press, 1989.

Banani, Amin. *The Modernization of Iran: 1921-1941.* Stanford, Calif.: Stanford University Press, 1961.

Bill, James A. *The Eagle and the Lion: The Tragedy of American-Iranian Relations.* New Haven, Conn.: Yale University Press, 1988.

Bill, James A., and William Roger Louis, eds. *Musaddiq, Iranian Nationalism, and Oil.* Austin, Tex.: University of Texas Press, 1988.

Bill, James A., and Robert W. Stookey. *Politics and Petroleum: The Middle East and the United States.* Brunswick, Ohio: King's Court Communications, 1975.

Cottam, Richard W. *Iran and the United States.* Pittsburgh: University of Pittsburgh Press, 1988.

Cottrell, Alvin J., and James E. Dougherty. *Iran's Quest for Security.* Cambridge, Mass.: Institute for Foreign Policy Analysis, 1977.

Cottrell, Alvin J., and R. M. Burrell, eds. *The Indian Ocean: Its Political, Economic, and Military Importance.* New York: Praeger, 1972.

Council on Foreign Relations. *Great Power Interests in the Persian Gulf.* New York: Council on Foreign Relations, 1989.

Dorman, William, and Mansour Farhang. *The U.S. Press and Iran.* Berkeley, Calif.: University of California Press, 1987.

Elm, Mustafa. *Oil, Power, and Principle.* Syracuse, N.Y.: Syracuse University Press, 1992.

Fatemi, Nasrollah Saifpour. *Oil Diplomacy.* New York: Whittier Books, Inc., 1954.

Gasiorowski, Mark J. *U.S. Foreign Policy and the Shah: Building a Client State in Iran.* Ithaca, N.Y.: Cornell University Press, 1991.

Ghareeb, Edmund. *The Kurdish Question in Iraq.* Syracuse, N.Y.: Syracuse University Press, 1981.

Goode, James F. *The United States and Iran, 1946-1951.* New York: St. Martin's Press, 1989.

Graham, Robert. *Iran: The Illusion of Power.* New York: St. Martin's Press, 1980.

Grayson, Benson Lee. *United States-Iranian Relations.* Washington, D.C.: University Press of America, 1981.

Halliday, Fred. *Iran: Dictatorship and Development.* New York: Penguin Books, 1979.

Heiss, Mary Ann. *Empire and Nationhood: The United States, Great Britain, and Iranian Oil, 1950-1954.* New York: Columbia University Press, 1997.

Hulbert, Mark. *Interlock: The Untold Story of American Banks, Interests, the Shah's Money, Debts, and the Astounding Connections between Them.* New York: Richardson and Snyder, 1982.

Huyser, Robert E. *Mission to Tehran.* New York: Harper and Row, 1986.

Ismael, Tareq Y. *Iraq and Iran: Roots of Conflict.* Syracuse, N.Y.: Syracuse University Press, 1982.

Katouzian, Homa. *The Political Economy of Modern Iran: 1926-1979.* New York: New York University Press, 1981.

Keddie, Nikki, and Mark J. Gasiorowski, eds. *Neither East nor West.* New Haven, Conn.: Yale University Press, 1990.

Keddie, Nikki. *Roots of Revolution: An Interpretive History of Modern Iran.* New Haven, Conn.: Yale University Press, 1981.

Kedourie, Elie, and Sylvia G. Haim, eds. *Towards a Modern Iran.* London: Frank
    Cass and Company, Ltd., 1980.
Ledeen, Michael, and William Lewis. *Debacle: The American Failure in Iran.* New
    York: Random House, 1981.
Lenczowski, George, ed. *Iran under the Pahlavis.* Stanford, Calif.: Hoover
    Institution Press, 1978.
Lenczowski, George. *Russia and the West in Iran, 1918-1948: A Study in Big-
    Power Rivalry.* Ithaca, N.Y.: Cornell University Press, 1949.
Looney, Robert E. *Economic Origins of the Iranian Revolution.* New York:
    Pergamon, 1982.
Lytle, Mark Hamilton. *The Origins of the Iranian-American Alliance: 1941-1953.*
    New York: Holmes and Meier Publishers, 1987.
Marlowe, John. *Iran.* New York: Praeger, 1963.
Marr, Phebe, and William Lewis. *Riding the Tiger: The Middle East After the Cold
    War.* Boulder, Colo.: Westview Press, 1993.
Nirumand, Bahman. *Iran: The New Imperialism in Action.* New York: Monthly
    Review Press, 1969.
Nissman, David B. *The Soviet Union and Iranian Azerbaijan.* Boulder, Colo.:
    Westview Press, 1987.
Noyes, James. *The Clouded Lens.* Stanford, Calif.: Hoover Institution Press, 1979.
Parsons, Anthony. *The Pride and the Fall: Iran 1974-1979.* London: Jonathan
    Cape, 1984.
Ramazani, R. K. *The United States and Iran: The Patterns of Influence.* New York:
    Praeger, 1982.
Ramazani, R. K. *The Persian Gulf and the Strait of Hormuz.* Netherlands: Sijthoff
    and Noordhoff, 1979.
Ramazani, R. K. *Iran's Foreign Policy 1941-1973: A Study of Foreign Policy in
    Modernizing Nations.* Charlottesville, Va.: University Press of Virginia, 1975.
Ramazani, R. K. *The Persian Gulf: Iran's Role.* Charlottesville, Va.: University
    Press of Virginia, 1972.
Ramazani, R. K. *The Foreign Policy of Iran, 1500-1941: A Developing Nation in
    World Affairs.* Charlottesville, Va.: University Press of Virginia, 1966.
Razavi, Hossein. *The Political Environment of Economic Planning in Iran, 1971-
    1983: From Monarchy to Islamic Republic.* Boulder, Colo.: Westview Press,
    1984.
Rubin, Barry. *Paved with Good Intentions.* New York: Penguin Books, 1980.
Rubinstein, Alvin Z. *Soviet Policy toward Turkey, Iran, and Afghanistan: The
    Dynamics of Influence.* New York: Praeger, 1982.
Rubinstein, Alvin Z. *The Great Game.* New York: Praeger, 1983.
Saikal, Amin. *The Rise and Fall of the Shah.* Princeton, N.J.: Princeton University
    Press, 1980.
Schulz, Ann Tibbitts. *Buying Security: Iran under the Monarchy.* Boulder, Colo.:
    Westview Press, 1989.
Sick, Gary. *All Fall Down.* New York: Random House, 1985.
Sicker, Martin. *The Bear and the Lion: Soviet Imperialism and Iran.* New York:
    Praeger, 1988.
Singh, K. R. *Iran: Quest for Security.* New York: Advent Books, Inc., 1980.
Sirriyeh, Hussein. *U.S. Policy in the Gulf, 1968-1977: Aftermath of British
    Withdrawal.* Ithaca, N.Y.: Ithaca Press, 1984.
Stempel, John D. *Inside the Iranian Revolution.* Bloomington, Ind.: Indiana
    University Press, 1981.
Taylor, Alan R. *The Arab Balance of Power.* Syracuse, N.Y.: Syracuse University

Press, 1982.
Yodfat, A., and Abir, M. *In The Direction of the Gulf.* London: Frank Cass and Company, 1977.

Israel

Alteras, Isaac. *Eisenhower and Israel: U.S.-Israeli Relations, 1953-1960.* Gainesville, Fla.: University Press of Florida, 1993.
Aronson, Sholomo. *The Politics and Strategy of Nuclear Weapons in the Middle East: Opacity, Theory, and Reality, 1960-1991 An Israeli Perspective.* Albany: State University of New York Press, 1992.
Bahbah, Bishara, and Linda Butler. *Israel and Latin America: The Military Connection.* New York: St. Martin's Press, 1986.
Ball, George W., and Douglas B. Ball. *The Passionate Attachment: America's Involvement with Israel 1947 to the Present.* New York: W.W. Norton, 1992.
Bard, Mitchell Geoffrey. *The Water's Edge and Beyond.* New Brunswick, N.J.: Transaction Publishers, 1991.
Beit-Hallahmi, Benjamin. *The Israeli Connection: Who Israel Arms and Why.* New York: Pantheon Books, 1987.
Beling, Willard A. *The Middle East: Quest for an American Policy.* Albany: State University of New York Press, 1973.
Ben-Zvi, Abraham. *The United States and Israel: The Limits of the Special Relationship.* New York: Columbia University Press, 1993.
Ben-Zvi, Abraham. *Alliance Politics and the Limits of Influence: The Case of the U.S. and Israel, 1975-1983.* Jerusalem: The Jerusalem Post, 1984.
Black, Ian, and Benny Morris. *Israel's Secret Wars: A History of Israel's Intelligence Services.* New York: Grove Weidenfeld, 1991.
Blitzer, Wolf. *Between Washington and Jerusalem.* New York: Oxford University Press, 1985.
Brecher, Michael. *Decisions in Israel's Foreign Policy.* London: Oxford University Press, 1974.
Cobban, Helena. *The Superpowers and the Syrian-Israeli Conflict.* New York: Praeger Publishers, 1991.
Cockburn, Andrew, and Leslie Cockburn. *Dangerous Liaison: The Inside Story of the U.S.-Israeli Covert Relationship.* New York: HarperCollins Publishers, 1991.
Cohen, Michael J. *Truman and Israel.* Berkeley: University of California Press, 1990.
Crosbie, Sylvania. *A Tacit Alliance: France and Israel from Suez to the Six Day War.* Princeton, N.J.: Princeton University Press, 1974.
Curtis, Michael, and Susan Aurelia Gitelson, eds. *Israel in the Third World.* New Brunswick, N.J.: Transaction Books, 1976.
Curtiss, Richard. *Stealth PACS: How Israel's American Lobby Seeks to Control U.S. Middle East Policy.* Washington, D.C.: The American Educational Trust, 1990.
El-Khawas, Mohamed, and Samir Abed-Rabbo. *American Aid to Israel: Nature and Impact.* Brattleboro, Vt.: Amana Books, 1984.
Evensen, Bruce J. *Truman, Palestine, and the Press.* New York: Greenwood Press, 1992.

Feldman, Lily Gardner. *The Special Relationship between West Germany and Israel.* Boston: George Allen & Unwin, 1984.

Feldman, Shai *Israeli Nuclear Deterrence.* New York: Columbia University Press, 1982.

Findley, Paul. *Deliberate Deceptions: Facing the Facts About the U.S.-Israeli Relationship.* Brooklyn, New York: Lawrence Hill Books, 1993.

Findley, Paul. *They Dare to Speak Out.* Westport, Conn.: Lawrence Hill & Company, 1985.

Freedman, Robert O. *Soviet Policy Toward Israel Under Gorbachev.* New York: Praeger, 1991.

Friedman, Thomas L. *From Beirut to Jerusalem.* New York: Anchor Books, 1989.

Fuller, Graham E. *Central Asia: The New Geopolitics.* Santa Monica, Cal.: The Rand Corporation.

Gaffney, Mark. *Dimona: The Third Temple? The Story Behind the Vanunu Revelation.* Brattleboro, Vt.: Amana Books, 1989.

Gazit, Mordechai. *President Kennedy's Policy toward the Arab States and Israel.* Tel Aviv: Shiloah Center for Middle Eastern and African Studies, Tel Aviv University, 1983.

Glick, Edward Bernard. *The Triangular Connection: America, Israel, and American Jews.* London: Allen and Unwin, 1982.

Gold, Dore. *Israel As an American Non-NATO Ally: Parameters of Defense Industrial Cooperation in a Post-Cold War Relationship.* Boulder, Colo.: Westview Press, 1992.

Green, Stephen. *Living by the Sword.* Brattleboro, Vt.: Amana Books, 1988.

Green, Stephen. *Taking Sides: America's Secret Relations with a Militant Israel.* New York: William Morrow and Company Inc., 1984.

Grose, Peter. *Israel in the Mind of America.* New York: Alfred A. Knopf, 1983.

Halsell, Grace. *Prophecy and Politics: The Secret Alliance between Israel and the U.S. Christian Right.* Chicago: Lawrence Hill Books, 1986.

Hersh, Seymour M. *The Samson Option: Israel's Nuclear Arsenal and American Foreign Policy.* New York: Random House, 1991.

Herzog, Chaim. *The Arab-Israeli Wars.* New York: Vintage Books, 1984.

Issacs, Stephen D. Jews and American Politics. New York: Doubleday, 1974.

Indyk, Martin, Charles Kupchan, and Steven J. Rosen. *Israel and the U.S. Air Force.* AIPAC Papers on U.S.-Israeli Relations, Washington, D.C.: American Israel Public Affairs Committee, 1983.

Joseph, Benjamin M. *Besieged Bedfellows: Israel and the Land of Apartheid.* New York: Greenwood Press, 1988.

Kenen, I. L. *Israel's Defense Line.* Buffalo, N.Y.: Prometheus Books, 1981.

Klieman, Aaron. *Israel and the World After 40 Years.* New York: Pergamon-Brassey's 1990.

Klieman, Aaron. *Israel's Global Reach: Arms Sales As Diplomacy.* Washington, D.C.: Pergamon-Brassey's, 1985.

Klieman, Aharon, and Reuven Pedatzur. *Rearming Israel.* Boulder, Colo.: Westview Press, 1991.

Lambeth, Benjamin S. *Moscow's Lessons from the 1982 Lebanon Air War.* Santa Monica, Calif.: The Rand Corporation, 1984.

Mansour, Camille. *Beyond Alliance: Israel in U.S. Foreign Policy.* New York: Columbia University Press, 1994.

Melmann, Yossi, and Dan Raviv. *Friends in Deed: Inside the U.S.-Israel Alliance.* New York: Hyperion, 1994.

Mills, Walter, ed. *The Forrestal Diaries.* New York: The Viking Press, 1951.

Novik, Nimrod. *The United States and Israel: Domestic Determinants of a Changing U.S. Commitment.* Boulder, Colo.: Westview Press, 1986.

Ojo, Olusola. *Africa and Israel: Relations in Perspective.* Boulder, Colo.: Westview Press, 1988.

Organski, A. F. K. *The $36 Billion Bargain: Strategy and Politics in U.S. Assistance to Israel.* New York: Columbia University Press, 1990.

Penniman, Howard R., and Daniel J. Elazar, eds. *Israel At the Polls, 1981.* Bloomington, Ind.: Indiana University Press, 1986.

Peters, Joel. *Israel and Africa: The Problematic Friendship.* New York: St. Martin's Press, 1992.

Pollock, David. *The Politics of Pressure.* Westport, Conn.: Greenwood Press, 1982.

Pry, Peter. *Israel's Nuclear Arsenal.* Boulder, Colo.: Westview Press, 1984.

Puschel, Karen L. *U.S.-Israeli Strategic Cooperation in the Post-Cold War Era: An American Perspective.* Jerusalem: The Jerusalem Post Press, 1992.

Rabie, Mohamed. *The Politics of Foreign Aid: U.S. Foreign Assistance and Aid to Israel.* New York: Praeger Publishers, 1988.

Rabin, Yitzhak. *The Rabin Memoirs.* Boston: Little Brown, 1979.

Ray, James Lee. *The Future of American-Israeli Relations.* Lexington, Ky.: University Press of Kentucky, 1985.

Reich, Bernard. *The United States and Israel: Influence in the Special Relationship.* New York: Praeger, 1984.

Reiser, Stewart. *The Israeli Arms Industry.* New York: Holmes and Meier, 1989.

Reppa, Robert B. Sr. *Israel and Iran: Bilateral Relationships and Effect on the Indian Ocean Basin.* New York: Praeger Publishers, 1974.

Rubenberg, Cheryl A. *Israel and the American National Interest.* Urbana, Ill.: University of Illinois Press, 1986.

Safran, Nadav. *Israel the Embattled Ally.* Cambridge, Mass.: Harvard University Press, 1981.

Safran, Nadav. *The United States and Israel.* Cambridge, Mass.: Harvard University Press, 1963.

Sanders, Ralph. *Arms Industries: New Suppliers and Regional Security.* Washington, D.C.: National Defense University, 1990.

Schaar, Stuart. *Patterns of Israeli Aid and Trade in East Asia: Part I* AUFS. East Africa Series. Vol. 7, No. 1. New York: American Universities Field Staff, 1968.

Schoenbaum, David. *The United States and the State of Israel.* Oxford: Oxford University Press, 1993.

Segev, Samuel. *The Iranian Triangle: The Untold Story of Israel's Role in the Iran-Contra Affair.* New York: The Free Press, 1988.

Sheffer, Gabriel, ed. *Dynamics of Dependence: U.S.-Israeli Relations.* Boulder, Colo.: Westview Press, 1987.

Sicker, Martin. *Israel's Quest for Security.* New York: Praeger, 1989.

Snetsinger, John. *Truman, the Jewish Vote and the Creation of Israel.* Stanford, Calif.: Hoover Institution Press, 1974.

Sobhani, Sohrab. *The Pragmatic Entente: Israeli-Iranian Relations, 1948-1988.* New York: Praeger, 1989.

Souresrafil, Behrouz. *Khomeini and Israel.* England: I Researchers, 1988.

Spiegel, Steven L. *The Other Arab-Israeli Conflict: Making America's Middle East Policy, from Truman to Reagan.* Chicago: University of Chicago Press, 1985.

Steven, Stewart. *The Spymasters of Israel.* New York: Macmillan, 1980.

Stevens, Richard P. *American Zionism and U.S. Foreign Policy, 1942-1947.* New York: Pageant Press, 1962.

Tivnan, Edward. *The Lobby.* New York: Simon and Schuster, 1987.

Toscano, Louis. *Triple Cross.* New York: Birch Lane Press, 1990.
Weinstein, Allen, and Moshe Ma'oz. *Truman and the American Commitment to Israel.* Jerusalem: The Magnes Press, 1981.
Yaniv, Avner. *Deterrence without the Bomb: The Politics of Israeli Strategy.* Lexington, Mass.: Lexington Books, 1987.

Saudi Arabia

Abir, Mordechai. *Saudi Arabia in the Oil Era: Regime and Elites; Conflict and Collaboration.* Boulder, Colo.: Westview Press, 1988.
Acharya, Amitav. *U.S. Military Strategy in the Gulf.* London: Routledge, 1989.
Ali, Sheikh Rustum. *Saudi Arabia and Oil Diplomacy.* New York: Praeger, 1976.
Anderson, Irvine H. *ARAMCO, the United States and Saudi Arabia.* Princeton, N.J.: Princeton University Press, 1981.
Axergard, Frederick W., ed. *Iraq in Transition: A Political, Economic, and Strategic Perspective.* Boulder, Colo.: Westview Press, 1986.
Badeeb, Saeed M. *The Saudi-Egyptian Conflict over North Yemen, 1962-1970.* Boulder, Colo.: Westview Press, 1986.
Beling, Willard A. *King Faisal and the Modernisation of Saudi Arabia.* Boulder, Colo.: Westview Press, 1980.
Bidwell, Robin. *The Two Yemens.* Boulder, Colo.: Westview Press, 1983.
Bligh, Alexander. *From Prince to King.* New York: New York University Press, 1984.
Braun, Aurel, ed. *The Middle East in Global Strategy.* Boulder, Colo.: Westview Press, 1987.
Brown, L. Carl. *International Politics and the Middle East.* Princeton, N.J.: Princeton University Press, 1984.
Bryson, Thomas A. *United States-Middle East Diplomatic Relations 1784-1978.* Metchen, N.J.: Scarecrow Press, Inc., 1979.
Casillas, Rex J. *Oil and Diplomacy: The Evolution of American Foreign Policy in Saudi Arabia 1933-1945.* New York: Garland, 1987.
Chubin, Shahram, and Charles Tripp. *Iran and Iraq at War.* Boulder, Colo.: Westview Press, 1988.
Chubin, Shahram. *Security in the Persian Gulf: The Role of Outside Powers.* London: Allanheld and Osmun, 1982.
Cole, Juan R. I., and Nikki R. Keddie. *Shi'ism and Social Protest.* New Haven, Conn.: Yale University Press, 1986.
Conant, Melvin A. *The Oil Factor in U.S. Foreign Policy, 1980- 1990.* Lexington, Mass.: Lexington Books, 1982.
Cordesman, Anthony H. *The Gulf and the West: Strategic Relations and Military Realities.* Boulder, Colo.: Westview Press, 1988.
Cordesman, Anthony H. *Western Strategic Interests in Saudi Arabia.* London: Croom Helm, 1987.
Cordesman, Anthony H. *The Gulf and the Search for Strategic Stability.* Boulder, Colo.: Westview Press, 1984.
Cottrell, Alvin J., and Frank Bray. *Military Forces in the Persian Gulf.* Beverly Hills, Calif.: Sage, 1978.
Darius, Robert C., John W. Amos II, and Ralph H. Magnus, eds. *Gulf Security into the 1980s.* Stanford, Calif.: Hoover Institution Press, 1984.

Dawisha, Adeed, and Karen Dawisha, eds. *The Soviet Union in the Middle East.* London: Holmes and Meier, 1982.

Dekmejian, Hrair. *Islam in Revolution.* Syracuse, N.Y.: Syracuse University Press, 1985.

Draper, Theodore. *A Very Thin Line: The Iran-Contra Affairs.* New York: Hill and Wang, 1991.

Emerson, Steven. *The American House of Saud: The Secret PetroDollar Connection.* New York: Franklin Watts, 1985.

Freedman, Robert O. *Moscow and the Middle East.* New York: Cambridge University Press, 1991.

Gause, F. Gregory. *Saudi-Yemeni Relations: Domestic Structures and Foreign Influence.* New York: Columbia University Press, 1990.

Goldberg, Jacob. *The Foreign Policy of Saudi Arabia.* Cambridge, Mass.: Harvard University Press, 1986.

Goldman, Marshall I. *Soviet Foreign Aid.* New York: Frederick A. Praeger, 1967.

Golub, David B. *When Oil and Politics Mix: Saudi Oil Policy, 1973-1985.* Cambridge, Mass.: Harvard University, Center For Middle Eastern Studies, 1985.

Grayson, Benson Lee. *Saudi-American Relations.* Washington, D.C.: University Press of America, 1982.

Halliday, Fred. *Soviet Policy in the Arc of Crisis.* Washington, D.C.: The Institute for Policy Studies, 1981.

Halliday, Fred. *Arabia without Sultans.* New York: Vintage Books, 1975.

Hameed, Mazher A. *Saudi Arabia, the West and the Security of the Gulf.* London: Croom Helm, 1986.

Hanks, Robert J. *The U.S. Military Presence in the Middle East: Problems and Prospects.* Washington, D.C.: Institute for Foreign Policy Analysis, Inc., 1982.

Hiro, Dilip. *The Longest War: The Iran-Iraq Military Conflict.* London: Grafton Books, 1989.

Holden, David, and Richard Johns. *The House of Saud.* New York: Holt, Rinehart and Winston, 1981.

Hurewitz, J. C. *Middle East Politics: The Military Dimension.* Boulder, Colo.: Westview Press, 1982.

Ismael, Tareq Y. *The Middle East in World Politics: A Study in Contemporary International Relations.* Syracuse, N.Y.: Syracuse University Press, 1974.

Katz, Mark. *Russia and Arabia: Soviet Foreign Policy toward the Arabian Peninsula.* Baltimore, Md.: Johns Hopkins University Press, 1986.

Korany, Bahgat, and Ali E. Hillal Dessouki. *The Foreign Policies of Arab States.* Boulder, Colo.: Westview Press, 1991.

Kupchan, Charles A. *The Persian Gulf and the West: The Dilemmas of Security.* Boston: Allen & Unwin, 1987.

Lackner, Helen. *A House Built on Sand: A Political Economy of Saudi Arabia.* Ithaca, N.Y.: Ithaca Press, 1978.

Lefebvre, Jeffrey A. *Arms for the Horn: U.S. Security Policy in Ethiopia and Somalia 1953-1991.* Pittsburgh: University of Pittsburgh Press, 1991.

Long, David E. *The United States and Saudi Arabia: Ambivalent Allies.* Boulder, Colo.: Westview Press, 1985.

Longrigg, Stephen Hemsley. *Oil in the Middle East.* London: Oxford University Press, 1968.

Louis, William Roger. *The British Empire in the Middle East: 1945-1951.* Oxford: Clarendon Press, 1984.

Makinda, Samuel M. *Superpower Diplomacy in the Horn of Africa.* New York: St.

Martin's Press, 1987.

Miller, Aaron David. *Search for Security: Saudi Arabian Oil and American Foreign Policy, 1939-1949.* Chapel Hill, N.C.: University of North Carolina Press, 1980.

Nash, Gerald D. *United States Oil Policy 1890-1964.* Westport, Conn.: Greenwood Press Publishers, 1968.

Niblock, Timothy. *State, Society, and Economy in Saudi Arabia.* New York: St. Martin's Press, 1982.

Nonnemann, Gerd *Iraq, the Gulf States and the War.* London: Ithaca Press, 1986.

Nyrop, Richard F. et al. *Area Handbook for Saudi Arabia.* Washington, D.C.: U.S. Government Printing Office, 1977.

O'Ballance, Edgar. *The War in the Yemen.* Hamden, Conn.: Archon Books, 1971.

Olson, William J., *U.S. Strategic Interests in The Gulf Region.* Boulder, Colo.: Westview Press, 1987.

Painter, David S. *Oil and the American Century.* Baltimore, Md.: Johns Hopkins University Press, 1986.

Peterson, J. E. *Defending Arabia.* New York: St. Martin's Press, 1986.

Piscatori, James, ed. *Islam in the Political Process.* New York: Cambridge University Press, 1983.

Polk, William R. *The Arab World.* Cambridge, Mass.: Harvard University Press, 1980.

Quandt, William B. *Saudi Arabia in the 1980s: Foreign Policy, Security, and Oil.* Washington, D.C.: The Brookings Institution, 1981.

Quandt, William B. *Decade of Decisions.* Berkeley, Calif.: University of California Press, 1977.

Rabinovich, Itamar, and Jehuda Reinharz, eds. *Israel in the Middle East.* Oxford: Oxford University Press, 1984.

Randall, Stephen J. *United States Foreign Oil Policy 1919-1948.* Montreal: McGill-Queen's University Press, 1985.

Rubin, Barry. *The Great Powers in the Middle East: 1941-1947.* London: Frank Cass, 1980.

Rustow, Dankwart A. *Oil and Turmoil.* New York: W.W. Norton, 1982.

Safran, Nadav. *Saudi Arabia: The Ceaseless Quest for Security.* Ithaca, N.Y.: Cornell University Press, 1988.

Saivetz, Carol R. *The Soviet Union and the Gulf in the 1980s.* Boulder, Colo.: Westview Press, 1989.

Schmnidt, Dana Adams. *Yemen: The Unknown War.* New York: Holt, Rinehart, and Winston, 1968.

Shadran, Benjamin. *The Middle East, Oil and the Great Powers.* New York: John Wiley and Sons, 1973.

Smolansky, Oles M., and Bettie M. Smolansky. *The USSR and Iraq.* Durham, N.C.: Duke University Press, 1991.

Spiegel, Steven, Mark Heller, and Jacob Goldberg. *The Soviet-American Competition in the Middle East.* Lexington, Ky.: Lexington Books, 1988.

Spiegel, Steven, ed. *The Middle East and the Western Alliance.* London: George Allen & Unwin, 1982.

Stoff, Michael B. *Oil, War, and American Security.* New Haven, Conn.: Yale University Press, 1980.

Stookey, Robert W. *South Yemen: A Marxist Republic in Arabia.* Boulder, Colo.: Westview Press, 1982.

Stookey, Robert W. *Yemen: The Politics of the Yemen Arab Republic.* Boulder, Colo.: Westview Press, 1978.

Szyliowicz, Joseph S., and Bard E. O'Neill. *The Energy Crisis and U.S. Foreign Policy.* New York: Praeger, 1975.

Tahtinen, Dale R. *National Security Challenges to Saudi Arabia.* Washington D.C.: American Enterprise Institute for Public Policy Research, 1979.

Tillman, Seth P. *The United States in the Middle East.* Bloomington, Ind.: Indiana University Press, 1982.

Tripp, Charles, ed. *Regional Security in the Middle East.* New York: St. Martin's Press, 1984.

Troeller, Gary. *The Birth of Saudi Arabia.* London: Frank Cass, 1976.

Winder, R. Bayly. *Saudi Arabia in the Nineteenth Century.* New York: St. Martin's Press, 1965.

Yodfat, Aryeh Y. *The Soviet Union and the Arabian Peninsula.* New York: St. Martin's Press, 1983.

Articles

Alliances, American Foreign Policy, Arms Sales

Albrecht, Ulrich, Dieter Ernst, Peter Lock, and Herbert Wulf. "Arming the Developing Countries." *International Social Science Journal* 28, no. 2 (1976): 326-40.

Ball, George. "What is an Ally?" *American-Arab Affairs* 6, no. 6 (Fall 1983): 5-14.

Barnett, Michael, and Jack Levy. "Domestic Sources of Alliances and Alignments: The Case of Egypt, 1962- 1973." *International Organization* 45, no. 1 (Summer 1991): 369-95.

Bar-Siman-Tov, Yaacov. "Alliance Strategy: U.S.-Small Allies Relationships." *Journal of Strategic Studies* 3, no. 2 (September 1980): 202-16.

Becker, Avi. "The Arms-Oil Connection." *Armed Forces and Society* 8, no. 3 (Spring 1982): 419-42.

Beres, Louis Rene. "Bipolarity, Multipolarity, and the Reliability of Alliance Commitments." *The Western Political Science Quarterly* 25, no. 4 (December 1972): 702-10.

Betts, Richard. "The Tragicomedy of Arms Trade Control." *International Security* 5, no. 1 (Fall 1980): 80-110.

Blechman, Barry M. et al. "Pushing Arms." *Foreign Policy* 46 (Spring 1982): 138-54.

Bueno de Mesquita, Bruce. "Measuring System Polarity." *Journal of Conflict Resolution* 19, no. 2 (June 1975): 187-216.

Bueno de Mesquita, Bruce. "Systemic Polarization and the Occurrence and Duration of War." *Journal of Conflict Resolution* 22, no. 2 (June 1978): 241-67.

Campbell, John C. "The Middle East: A House of Containment Built on Shifting Sands," *Foreign Affairs* 60, no. 3 (1981-1982): 593-628.

Christensen, Thomas J., and Snyder, Jack. "Chain Gangs and Passed Bucks: Predicting Alliance Patterns in Multipolarity." *International Organization* 44, no. 2 (Spring 1990): 137-168.

Chubin, Shahram. "Post-War Gulf Security," *Survival* 23, no. 2 (March-April 1991): 140-57.

Deutsch K. W., and Singer, J. D. "Multipolar Power Systems and International Stability." *World Politics* 16, no. 3 (April 1964), 390-406.

Fedder, Edwin. "The Concept of Alliance." *International Studies Quarterly* 12, no. 1 (March 1968): 65-85.

Feinstein, Lee. "Administration to Sell Advanced F-16 fighters to Taiwan." *Arms Control Today* 22, no. 7 (September 1992): 25.

Fromkin, David. "Entangling Alliances." *Foreign Affairs* 48, no. 4 (July 1970): 688-700.

Gilbert, Stephen P. "The Nixon Doctrine and Military Aid," *Orbis* 16, no. 3 (Fall 1972): 643-81.

Goldgeier, James M., and Michael McFaul. "A Tale of Two Worlds: Core and Periphery in the Post-Cold War Era." *International Organization* 46, no. 2 (Spring 1992): 467-91.

Graebner, Norman A. "Alliances and Free World Security." *Current History* 38, no. 223 (1960): 214-27.

Haas, Ernst. "The Balance of Power As a Guide to Policy Making." *The Journal of Politics* 15, no. 3 (August 1953): 370-98.

Hartung, William D. "Breaking the Arms Sales Addiction: New Directions for U.S. Policy." *World Policy Journal* 8, no. 1 (Winter 1990-1991): 1-26.

Healy, Brian, and Arthur Stein. "The Balance of Power in International History." *Journal of Conflict Resolution* 17, no. 1 (March 1973): 33-61.

Jentleson, Bruce W. "American Commitments in the Third World: Theory vs. Practice." *International Organizations* 41, no. 4 (Autumn 1987): 667-704.

Johnson, Robert H. "Exaggerating America's Stakes in Third World Conflicts." *International Security* 10, no. 3 (Winter 1985-1986): 32-68.

Kann, Robert A. "Alliances Versus Ententes." *World Politics* 28, no. 4 (July 1976): 611-21.

Kennedy, Paul. "The First World War and the International Power System." *International Security* 9, no. 1 (Summer 1984): 7-40.

Keohane, Robert. "Alliances, Threats, and the Uses of Neorealism." *International Security* 13, no. 1 (Summer 1988): 169-76.

Keohane, Robert. "The Big Influence of Small Allies." *Foreign Policy* 1 (Spring 1971): 161-82.

Keohane, Robert. "Lilliputians Dilemmas: Small States in International Politics." *International Organization* 23, no. 2 (Spring 1969): 291-310.

Kirkpatrick, Jeanne. "Dictatorship and Double Standards." *Commentary* 68, no. 5 (November 1979): 34-45.

Klingsberg, Frank L. "The Historical Alternation of Moods in American Foreign Policy." *World Politics* 4, no. 2 (January 1952): 239-73.

Leffler, Melvyn P. "From the Truman Doctrine to the Carter Doctrine: Lessons and Dilemmas of the Cold War." *Diplomatic History* 7, no. 4 (Fall 1983): 245-66.

Levy, Jack. "Alliance Formation and War Behavior." *Journal of Conflict Resolution* 25, no. 4 (December 1981): 581-613.

McDonald, H. Brooke, and Richard Rosecrance. "Alliance and Structural Balance in the International System." *Journal of Conflict Resolution* 29, no. 1 (March 1985): 57-82.

McGowan, Patrick, and Robert M. Rood. "Alliance Behavior in Balance of Power Systems: Applying a Poisson Model to Nineteenth-Century Europe." *The American Political Science Review* 69, no. 3 (1975): 859-70.

Maynes, Charles William. "America's Third World Hang-ups." *Foreign Policy,* no. 71 (Summer 1988): 117-40.

Modelski, George. "The Study of Alliances: A Review." *Journal of Conflict Resolution* 7, no. 4 (December 1963): 769-76.

Morgenthau, Hans. "A Political Theory of Foreign Aid." *American Political*

Science Review 56, no. 2 (June 1962): 301-9.
Morrow, James D. "Arms Versus Allies: Trade-offs in the Search for Security." *International Organization* 47, no. 2 (Spring 1993): 207-21.
Neumann, Stephanie G. "Coproduction, Barter, and Countertrade: Offsets in the International Arms Market." *Orbis* 29, no. 1 (Spring 1985): 183-213.
Neumann, Stephanie G. "Security, Military Expenditures and Socioeconomic Development: Reflections on Iran." *Orbis* 22, no. 3 (Fall 1978): 569-94.
Nuechterein, Donald E. "The Concept of National Interest: A Time for New Approaches." *Orbis* 23, no. 1 (Spring 1979): 73-92
Oberg Jan. "Arms Trade with the Third World As an Aspect of Imperialism." *Journal of Peace Research* 12, no. 3 (1975): 213-34.
Olson, Mancur Jr. and Richard Zeckhauser. "An Economic Theory of Alliances." *The Review of Economics and Statistics* 48, no. 3 (1966): 266-79.
Oppenheimer, Joe. "Collective Goods and Alliances." *Journal of Conflict Resolution* 23, no. 3 (September 1979): 387-407.
Park, Chang Jin. "The Influence of Small States upon the Superpowers: United States-South Korean Relations As a Case Study, 1950-1953." *World Politics* 28, no. 1 (October 1975): 97-117.
Pierre, Andrew J. "Arms Sales: The New Diplomacy." *Foreign Affairs* 60, no. 2 (Winter 1981-1982): 266-86.
Pierre, Andrew J. "The Future of America's Commitments and Alliances." *Orbis* 16, no. 3 (Fall 1972): 696-719.
Singer, J. D., and M. Small. "Formal Alliances, 1815-1939: A Quantitative Description," *Journal of Peace Research* 3 (January 1966): 1-31.
Slater, Jerome. "Dominos in Central America: Will They Fall? Does It Matter?" *International Security* 12, no. 2 (Fall 1987): 105-34.
Snyder, Glenn H. "Alliances, Balance, and Stability." *International Organization* 45, no. 1 (Winter 1991): 121-42.
Snyder, Glenn H. "Alliance Theory: A Neorealist First Cut." *Journal of International Affairs* 44, no. 1 (Spring 1990): 103-23.
Synder, Glenn H. "The Security Dilemma in Alliance Politics." *World Politics* 36, no. 4 (July 1984): 461-95.
Teune, Henry, and Sig Synnestvedt. "Measuring International Alignment." *Orbis* 9, no. 1 (Spring 1965): 171-89.
Tonelson, Alan. "The Real National Interest." *Foreign Policy,* no. 61 (Winter 1985-1986): 49-72.
Van Evera, Stephen. "The Cult of the Offensive and the Origins of the First World War." *International Security* 9, no. 1 (Summer 1984): 58-107.
Wallace, Michael. "Alliance Polarization, Cross-Cutting, and International War, 1815-1964." *Journal of Conflict Resolution* 17, no. 4 (December 1973): 575-604.
Walt, Stephen M. "Testing Theories of Alliance Formation: The Case of Southwest Asia." *International Organization* 42, no. 2 (Spring 1988): 275-316.
Weinstein, Franklin B. "The Concept of a Commitment in International Relations." *Journal of Conflict Resolution* 13, no. 1 (March 1969): 39-55.
Wood, Robert Jefferson. "Military Assistance and the Nixon Doctrine." *Orbis* 15, no. 1 (Spring 1971): 247-74.

Iran

Ball, Nicole, and Milton Leitenberg. "The Iranian Domestic Crisis: Foreign Policy Making and Foreign Policy Goals of the U.S." *Journal of South Asian and Middle East Studies* 2, no. 3 (Spring 1979): 36-56.

Clark, Jane Perry, and Andrew G. Carey. "Industrial Growth and Development Planning in Iran." *Middle East Journal* 29, no. 1 (Winter 1975): 1-15.

Cottam, Richard W. "American Policy and the Iranian Crisis." *Journal of Iranian Studies* 13, no. 1-4 (1980): 279-305.

Cottam, Richard W. "The United States, Iran and the Cold War." *Iranian Studies* 2, no. 1 (Winter 1970): 2-22.

Cottrell, Alvin. "Iran, the Arabs and the Persian Gulf." *Orbis* 27, no. 3 (Fall 1973): 978-88.

Doenecke, Justus D. "Revisionists, Oil, and Cold War Diplomacy." *Iranian Studies* 3, no. 1 (Winter 1970): 23-33.

Englehardt, Major Joseph P. "American Military Advisors in Iran: A Critical Review." *Joint Perspectives* (Summer 1981): 28-37.

Fatemi, Khosrow. "The Iranian Revolution: Its Impact on Economic Relations with the United States." *International Journal of Middle East Studies* 12, no. 3 (November 1980): 303-17.

Gasiorowski, Mark J. "The 1953 Coup D'Etat in Iran." *International Journal of Middle East Studies* 19, no. 3 (August 1987): 261-86.

Klare, Michael. "America's White-Collar Mercenaries." *Inquiry* (October 16, 1978): 14-19.

Looney, Robert E. "The Role of Military Expenditure in Pre-revolutionary Iran's Economic Decline." *Iranian Studies* 21, no. 3-4 (1988): 52-83.

McFarlane, Stephen L. "A Peripheral View of the Origins of the Cold War: The Crises in Iran, 1941-1947." *Diplomatic History* 4, no. 4 (Fall 1980): 333-51.

Mahdavy, Hossein. "The Coming Crisis in Iran." *Foreign Affairs* 44, no. 1, (October 1965): 134-46.

Moran, Theodore H. "Iranian Defense Expenditures and the Social Crisis." *International Security* 3, no. 3 (1978-1979): 178-92.

Neumann, Stephanie G. "Security, Military Expenditures, and Socioeconomic Development: Reflections on Iran." *Orbis* 22, no. 3 (Fall 1978): 569-94.

Pajak, Roger F. "Soviet Military Aid to Iraq and Syria." *Strategic Review* 4, no. 1 (Winter 1976): 51-59.

Pryor, Leslie M. "Arms and the Shah." *Foreign Policy*, no. 31 (Summer 1978): 56-71.

Quester, George. "The Shah and the Bomb." *Policy Sciences* 8, no. 1 (March 1977): 21-32.

Ramazani, R. K. "Emerging Patterns of Regional Relations in Iranian Foreign Policy." *Orbis* 28, no. 4 (Winter 1975): 1043-69.

Ricks, Thomas M. "U.S. Military Missions to Iran, 1943-1978: The Political Economy of Military Assistance." *Iranian Studies* 12, no. 3-4 (Fall 1979): 163-93.

Rubinstein, Alvin. "The Evolution of Soviet Strategy in the Middle East." *Orbis* 24, no. 2 (Summer 1980): 323-37.

Weinbaum, M. G. "Iran and Israel: The Discreet Entente." *Orbis* 28, no. 4 (Winter, 1975): 1070-87.

Young, T. Cuyler. "Iran in Continuing Crisis." *Foreign Affairs* 40, no. 2 (January

1962): 275-92.

Israel

Aronson, Geoffrey. "Hidden Agenda: U.S.-Israeli Relations and the Nuclear Question." *The Middle East Journal* 46, no. 4 (Autumn 1992): 617-30.

Aruri, Nasser. "The U.S.-Israeli Special Relationship after Shamir and the Cold War." *Middle East International* no. 433 (September 11, 1992): 21-22.

Ball, George. "The Coming Crisis in Israeli-American Relations." *Foreign Affairs* 58, no. 2 (Winter, 1979-1980): 231-56.

Bialer, Uri. "The Iranian Connection in Israeli's Foreign Policy 1948-1951." *Middle East Journal* 39, no. 2 (1985): 292-315.

"Bomblets Away." *Time Magazine* 124, no. 9 (August 27, 1984): 34.

Clarke, Duncan L., and Alan S. Cohen. "The United States, Israeli, and the Lavi Fighter." *Middle East Journal* 40, no. 1 (Winter 1986): 16-32.

Cobban, Helen. "Israel's Nuclear Game: The U.S. Stake." *World Policy Journal* 5, no. 3 (Fall 1988): 415-33.

Jalal, Ayesha. "Toward the Baghdad Pact: South Asia and Middle East Defense in the Cold War, 1947-1955." *International History Review* 11, no. 3 (August 1989): 409-33.

Mintz, Alex. "The Military-Industrial Complex: The Israeli Case." *Journal of Strategic Studies* 6, no. 3 (September 1983): 103-27.

Nadelmann, Ethan A. "Israel and Black Africa: A Rapproachement?" *The Journal of Modern African Studies* 19, no. 2 (June 1981): 183-219.

Neff, Donald. "America's Unconditional Hand-outs to Israel." *Middle East International* no. 435 (October 9, 1992): 3-4.

Ojo, Olusaola. "Israeli-South African Connections and Afro- Israeli Relations." *International Studies* 21, no. 1 (January-March 1982): 37-51.

Roosevelt, Kermit. "The Partition of Palestine: A Lesson in Pressure Politics." *Middle East Journal* 2, no. 1, (January 1948): 1-16.

Shaw, Harry J. "Strategic Dissensus." *Foreign Policy,* no. 61 (Winter 1985-1986): 125-41.

Speigel, Steven. "US Relations with Israel: The Military Benefits." *Orbis* 30, no. 3 (Fall 1986): 475- 97.

Wheelock, Thomas R. "Arms for Israel: The Limit of Leverage." *International Security* 3, no. 2 (Fall 1978): 123-37.

Saudi Arabia

Aburdene, Odeh. "U.S. Economic and Financial Relations with Saudi Arabia, Kuwait, and the United Arab Emirates." *American-Arab Affairs* no. 7 (Winter 1983-1984): 76-84.

Anderson, Irvine H. "Lend-Lease for Saudi Arabia: A Comment on Alternative Conceptualizations." *Diplomatic History* 3, no. 4 (Fall 1979): 413-23.

Bligh, Alexander, and Steven E. Plaut. "Saudi Moderation in Oil and Foreign Policies in the Post-AWACS-Sale Period." *Middle East Review* 14, no. 3-4 (Spring- Summer 1982): 24-32.

Carapico, Sheila. "From Ballot Box to Battlefield: The War of the Two 'Alis'."
    Middle East Research and Information Project 24, no. 5 (September-October
    1994): 24-27.
Dawisha, Adeed I. "Internal Values and External Threats: The Making of Saudi
    Foreign Policy." *Orbis* 23, no. 1 (Spring 1979): 129-43.
Dunn, Michael Collins. "Soviet Interests in the Arabian Peninsula: The Aden Pact
    and Other Paper Tigers." *American-Arab Affairs* no. 8 (Spring 1984): 92-98.
Gerner, Deborah J. "Petro-Dollar Recycling Imports, Arms, Investment, and Aid."
    Arab Studies Quarterly 7, no. 1 (Winter 1985): 1-26.
Hoagland, Jim, and J. P. Smith. "Saudi Arabia and the United States: Security and
    Interdependence." *Survival* 20, no. 2 (March-April 1978): 80-82.
Klare, Michael T. "The Political Economy of Arms Sales." *Society* 2, no. 6
    (September-October 1974): 41-49.
Kurth, James R. "Why We Buy the Weapons We Do." *Foreign Policy*, no. 11
    (Summer 1973): 33-56.
McNaugher, Thomas L. "Arms and Allies on the Arabian Peninsula." *Orbis* 28, no.
    3 (Fall 1984): 489-526.
Middle East Journal. "Chronology." *The Middle East Journal* 38, no. 3 (Summer
    1979): 305-7.
Pounds, Bonnie, "The U.S.-Saudi Arabian Joint Commission: A Model for Bilateral
    Economic Cooperation." *American-Arab Affairs* no. 7 (Winter 1983-1984): 60-
    68.
Quandt, William. "Riyadh between the Superpowers." *Foreign Policy* no. 44 (Fall
    1981): 37-56.
Stork, Joe. "The CIA in Afghanistan: 'The Good War.'" *Middle East Research and
    Information Project* 16, no. 4 (July-August 1986): 12-13.
Valenta, Jiri. "The Soviet Invasion of Afghanistan: The Difficulty of Knowing
    Where to Stop." *Orbis* 24, no. 2 (Summer 1980): 201-18.
Van Hollen, Christopher. "North Yemen: A Dangerous Pentagonal Game."
    Washington Quarterly 5, no. 3 (Summer 1982): 137-42.
Volman, Daniel. "Commanding the Center." MERIP Reports 14, no. 6-7 (July-
    September 1984): 49-50.
Weintraub, Sidney. "Saudi Arabia's Role in International Financial System."
    Middle East Review 10, no. 4 (Summer 1978): 16-47.
Wright, Claudia. "Implications of the Iraq-Iran War." *Foreign Affairs* 59, no. 2
    (Winter 1980-1981): 275-303.

Unpublished Sources:

Gerner, Deborah J. "Consistencies and Contradictions: U.S. Foreign Policy toward
    Saudi Arabia and the Arab States of the Gulf, 1945-1973." Paper presented at
    the annual meeting of the American Political Science Association, Washington
    D.C. September 1-4, 1988.
Lytle, Mark Hamilton. "American-Iranian Relations 1941-1947 and the Redefini-
    tion of National Security." Unpublished Ph.D. Dissertation, Yale University,
    1973.
Peck, Malcolm C. "Saudi Arabia in United States Foreign Policy to 1958: A Study
    in the Sources and Determinants of American Policy." Unpublished Ph.D.

Dissertation, Fletcher School of Law and Diplomacy, Tufts University, April, 1970.
Pfau, Richard. "The United States and Iran." Unpublished Ph.D. Dissertation, University of Virginia, 1975.
Shah, Safqat A. "The Political and Strategic Foundations of International Arms Transfers: A Case Study of American Arms Supplies to and Purchases by Iran and Saudi Arabia, 1968-1976." Unpublished Ph.D. Dissertation, University of Virginia, August 1977.
Trice, Robert H., Jr. "Domestic Political Interests and American Policy in the Middle East: Pro-Israel, Pro- Arab and Corporate Non-governmental Actors and the Making of American Foreign Policy, 1966-1971." Unpublished Ph.D. Dissertation, University of Wisconsin-Madison, 1974.

U.S. Government Sources

Arms Control and Disarmament Agency

U.S. Arms Control and Disarmament Agency, *World Military Expenditures and Arms Transfers.* Washington, D.C.: U.S. Government Printing Office, Years 1988, 1982, 1978.

Agency for International Development

U.S. Agency for International Development, Office of Planning and Budgeting, Bureau for Program and Policy Coordination, *U.S. Overseas Loans and Grants and Assistance from International Organizations Obligations and Loan Authorizations.* Washington, D.C.: U.S. Government Printing Office, 1989, 1988, 1979.

Congressional Hearings and Reports: U.S. House of Representatives

U.S. House of Representatives Foreign Affairs Committee. *Documents.* 96th Cong., 1st sess., 1979.
U.S. House of Representatives Subcommittee on Commerce, Consumer, and Monetary Affairs. *Federal Response to OPEC Country Investments in the United States.* 97th Cong., 2nd sess., 1982.
U.S. House of Representatives Select Committee on Intelligence. *Iran: Evaluation of U.S. Intelligence Performance Prior to November 1978.* Staff Report. 96th Cong., 1st sess., 1979.
U.S. House of Representatives International Relations Committee, *Letter from President Carter to Speaker O'Neill.* 95th Cong., 1st sess., 1977.
U.S. House of Representatives Foreign Affairs Committee. *New Perspectives on the Persian Gulf.* 93rd Cong., 1st sess., 1973.
U.S. House of Representatives International Relations Committee. *The Persian Gulf, 1975: The Continuing Debate on Arms Sales. Hearings* before the Special Subcommittee on Investigations, 94th Cong., 1st sess., 1976.

U.S. House of Representatives Foreign Affairs Committee. *The Persian Gulf 1974: Money, Politics, Arms and Power.* Report to the U.S. House of Representatives, Foreign Affairs Committee, Subcommittee on the Near East and South Asia, 1974, by Richard P. Berman, *The Shah's Iranian Empire: Old Games, New Stakes.* 93rd Cong., 2nd sess., 1974.

U.S. House of Representatives International Relations Committee. *Perspective Sale of Airborne Warning and Control System to Iran.* 95th Cong., 1st sess., 1977.

U.S. House of Representatives International Relations Committee. *Proposed Aircraft Sales to Israel, Egypt, and Saudi Arabia,* 95th Cong., 2nd sess., 1978.

U.S. House of Representatives. *Proposed Sale of AWACS and F-15 Enhancement to Saudi Arabia.* 97th Cong., 1st sess., 1981.

U.S. House of Representatives International Affairs Committee. *Saudi Arabia and the United States: The New Context in an Evolving Special Relationship.* Staff Report by Richard M. Preece for the Subcommittee on Europe and the Middle East, House of Representatives, 97th Cong., 1st sess., 1981.

U.S. House of Representatives Foreign Affairs Committee, *Supplemental 1979 Middle East Aid Package for Israel and Egypt.* 96th Cong., 1st sess., 1979.

U.S. House of Representatives Foreign Affairs Committee. *United States Arms Sales to the Persian Gulf, Report of a Study Mission to Iran, Kuwait, and Saudi Arabia.* 94th Cong., 1st sess., 1975.

U.S. House of Representatives International Relations Committee. *U.S. Arms Policies in the Persian Gulf and Red Sea Areas: Past, Present, and Future.* Report of a Staff Survey Mission to Ethiopia, Iran, and the Arabian Peninsula, 95th Cong., 1st sess., 1977.

U.S. House of Representatives, Foreign Affairs Committee. *United States Arms Sales to the Persian Gulf.* 94th Cong., 1st sess., 1975.

U.S. House of Representatives International Relations Committee. *U.S. Arms Policy and Recent Sales to Europe and the Middle East.* 95th Cong., 2nd sess., 1978.

Congressional Hearings and Reports: U.S. Senate

U.S. Senate Committee on Energy and Natural Resources. *Access to Oil-The U.S. Relationship with Saudi Arabia and Iran.* Staff Report by Fern Racine and Melvin Conant. 95th Cong., 1st sess., 1977.

U.S. Senate Committee on Foreign Relations. *The AWACS.* 90th Cong., 1st sess., 1981.

U.S. Senate Committee on Foreign Relations. *Disapproval of the Proposed Sales to Saudi Arabia of E-3A Airborne Warning and Control Systems.* Hearings before the Foreign Relations Committee, U.S. Senate. 97th Cong., 1st. sess., 1981.

U.S. Senate Committee on Armed Services. *Military and Technical Implications of the Proposed Sale of Air Defense Enhancements to Saudi Arabia.* 97th Cong., 1st sess., 1981.

U.S. Senate Committee on Foreign Relations. Subcommittee on Multinational Corporations, *Multinationals and U.S. Foreign Policy, Part 17.* Committee on Foreign Relations and the Committee on Armed Services. *The President's Proposal on the Middle East (Eisenhower Doctrine). Hearings* on S.J. Res. and H.J. Res. 117, pt. 2. 84th Cong., 1st sess., 1957.

U.S. Senate Committee on Foreign Relations. *Enhancement Sale to Saudi Arabia.* Staff Report. *The Proposed AWACS/F-15 Sale.* 97th Cong., 1st sess., 1981.
U.S. Senate Committee on Foreign Relations. *Proposed U.S. Sales of Fighter Aircraft to Saudi Arabia, Egypt, and Israel.* 95th Cong., 2nd sess., 1978.
U.S. Senate Committee on Foreign Relations. *Sale of AWACS to Iran.* 95th Cong., 1st sess., 1977.
U.S. Senate Committee on Foreign Relations. *U.S. Arms Sales Policy.* 94th Cong., 2nd sess., 1976.

Articles in Congressional Quarterly

Maxfield, Daivd. "Senate Panel Deadlocks on Mideast Plane Sales; Fight Moves to Floor." *Congressional Quarterly* 36, no. 19 (May 13, 1978): 1159-61.
"Reagan Sends Aid, Troop to Lebanon." *Congressional Quarterly Almanac* 38 (1982): 167-71.
Whittle, Richard. "Instability and Soviet Pressure Seen as Persian Gulf Threats." *Congressional Quarterly* 39, no. 42 (October 17, 1981): 2009-16.
Whittle, Richard. "Reagan Loses AWACS Votes, but Picks Up Some Support among Senate Republicans." *Congressional Quarterly* 39, no. 42 (October 17, 1981): 2006-8.

U.S. General Accounting Office

U.S. General Accounting Office. *Critical Factors Affecting Saudi Arabia Oil Decisions.* Washington, D.C.: U.S. Government Printing Office, 1978.
U.S. General Accounting Office. *Perspectives on Military Sales to Saudi Arabia.* Washington, D.C.: U.S. Government Printing Office, 1977.
U.S. General Accounting Office, National Security and International Affairs Division. *U.S. Assistance to the State of Israel.* Washington, D.C.: U.S. Government Printing Office, 1983.

U.S. Department of Defense

U.S. Department of Defense. *Foreign Military Sales, Foreign Military Construction Sales, and Military Assistance Facts.* Washington, D.C.: U.S. Government Printing Office, 1992, 1982, 1978, 1975.
U.S. Defense Department. Special Regional Studies. *The Growing U.S. Involvement in Iran.* January 22, 1975. Washington, D.C.: National Security Archive, 1989.
U.S. Department of Defense, Office of the Assistant Secretary of Defense International Security Affairs. *U.S.-Iranian Arms Transfers Relationship: A Historical Analysis* by David Ranfeldt, The Rand Corporation, October 1976. Washington, D.C.: National Security Archive, 1989.

U.S. Department of State

U.S. Department of State. *American Foreign Policy, Basic Documents, 1977-1980.* Washington, D.C.: U.S. Government Printing Office, 1983.

U.S. State Department, *Briefing Memorandum.* January-February, 1957, from *Declassified Documents*, no. 00894. Washington, D.C.: Carrolton Press, 1988.

U.S. Department of State. *Department of State Bulletin* 82, no. 2058 (January 1982). Washington, D.C.: U.S. Government Printing Office.

U.S. Department of State. *Congressional Presentation: Security Assistance Programs, FY 1984.* Washington, D.C.: U.S. Government Printing Office, 1985.

U.S. Department of State, Bureau of Intelligence and Research. *Iran: The External Threat to Iran.* June 9, 1970. Washington, D.C.: National Security Archive, 1989.

U.S. Department of State. *Foreign Relations of the United States.* Washington, D.C.: U.S. Government Printing Office, 5, 1944; 8, 1945; 7, 1950; 9, 1952-1954; 17, 1954- 1957.

U.S. Department of State. Letter, Walter B. Smith undersecretary to Harold E. Stassen, Director for Mutual Security. *Declassified Documents.* Washington, D.C.: Carrolton Press, 1990.

U.S. Department of State. *Iran.* February 28, 1978. Washington, D.C.: National Security Archive, 1989.

U.S. Department of State. *Iran Study.* February 28, 1978. Washington, D.C.: National Security Archive, 1989.

U.S. Department of State. *Secret telegram 86 from Secretary of State to U.S. Embassy, Port-au-Prince, August 4, 1964. Declassified Documents*, 433D. Washington, D.C.: Carrolton Press, 1979.

U.S. Department of State. *Security Assistance Programs, FY 1980.* Washington, D.C.: U.S. Government Printing Office, 1978.

Lyndon B. Johnson Presidential Documents

Department of State. Memorandum of Conversation, *U.S.-Israeli Talks.* NSF Country File: Middle East/Israel, Box no. 141, Document 153A. January 7, 1968.

Department of State. Memorandum for the President, Military and Economic Assistance to Israel: The Arab-Israel Arms Race and Status of U.S. Arms Control Efforts.: NSF Country File: Middle East/Israel, Box no. 145, Document no. 1F. May 1, 1967.

W. W. Rostow. *Memorandum for the President.* NSF Country File: Middle East/India, Box no. 136, no. 266B. May 21, 1966.

Harold Wiggins. *Memorandum for Mr. Rostow, Call to Secretary McNamara, re: F-4s to Shah.* NSF Country File: Middle East/India Box no. 136, Document no. 265.

Directorate of Intelligence. *Intelligence Memorandum: The Arab Threat to Iran.* NSF Country File: Middle East/India, Box no. 136, Document no. 270. May 21, 1966.

Directorate of Intelligence. National Intelligence Estimates, Iran NSF Country File: Middle East/India, Box no. 6, Document no. 6. March 24, 1966.

R. W. Komer. Memorandum for the President, *Prime Minister Eshkol's Visit.*
NSF Country File: Middle East/Israel, Box no. 143, Document no. 17A. May 28,
1964.
National Security Action Memorandum. *Meeting Israeli Arms Requests.* April 28,
1964. NSAM no. 290, Box no. 3, Document no. 2. April 28, 1964.

Miscellaneous Government Sources

Nyrop, Richard F. et al. *Area Handbook for Saudi Arabia.* Washington, D.C.: U.S.
Government Printing Office, 1977.
National Security Archive, "Survey of U.S.-Iranian Relations 1941-1979: The
Evolution of the U.S.-Iranian Relationship," in *The Making of U.S. Policy, Iran:
1977-1980.* January 29, 1980, document no. 03556. Washington, D.C.: National
Security Archive, 1989.
U.S. National Technical Information Service. *An Analysis of the Impact of
American Arms Transfers on Political State in Iran,* by Gregory Francis Gates.
AD-AO93255, September 1980. Springfield, Va.: National Technical Informa-
tion Service, 1980.

Newspapers

New York Times

June 9, 1992
February 6, 1992
January 16, 1992
March 5, 1991
November 5, 1989
September 29, 1989
February 3, 1989
December 17, 1987
September 16, 1985
July 21, 1983
February 3, 1983
December 14, 1981
October 18, 26, 29, 1981
February 22, 1981
March 23, 1978
February 15, 1978
December 23, 1977
August 31, 1977
July 12, 16, 20, 1977
May 29, 1977
April 27, 1977
August 8, 1976
January 25, 1976
November 2, 1975
March 5, 15, 1975

June 9, 1974
July 29, 1973
December 28, 1968
October 23, 1953
February 13, 1948
May 15, 1947
October 7, 1946

Washington Post

September 14, 1992
January 16, 1992
January 12, 1992
February 22, 1987
January 24, 1985
August 17, 1983
February 23, 1983
December 7, 1982
November 1, 8, 1981
October 9, 28, 30, 1981
September 19-20, 29, 1981
May 9, 1981
April 24, 1981
October 25, 1979
August 15, 1979
May 6, 1979
January 12, 1979
May 2, 4-5, 7, 1978
March 15, 1978
January 6, 26, 1978
July 18, 22, 27, 1977

Wall Street Journal

June 24, 1987
February 26, 1985
October 2, 14, 21, 28, 29, 1981
September 21, 29, 1981
April 20, 1981
February 12, 1979
May 4, 17, 1978

Christian Science Monitor

December 27, 1985
September 17, 1985
October 27, 29, 1981
July 5, 1979

April 10, 1978
March 6, 1978
February 23, 1978
July 6, 1973

Index

About the Author

John Miglietta received his B.A. degree in political science from Fordham University, and his M.A. and Ph.D. degrees from New York University, focusing on international relations and Middle East politics. He has taught at Lock Haven State University of Pennsylvania, Caldwell College in New Jersey, and is currently an Assistant Professor of Political Science at Tennessee State University in Nashville. Dr. Miglietta has taught, and continues to teach, a variety of courses in political science primarily focusing on international relations, Middle East politics, and American politics. His research interests are international organizations, security issues, and foreign policy processes, particularly as they apply to American foreign policy formulation in the Middle East. He is an active member of many academic associations including the American Political Science Association, International Studies Association, Middle East Studies Association, the Southern Political Science Association, and the Tennessee Political Science Association. He has participated in numerous national and regional academic conferences as a paper presenter, panel chair, and discussant. Dr. Miglietta is also active in Model United Nations, serving as the faculty advisor for Model UN at Tennessee State University. Outside the classroom John enjoys playing chess, racquetball, and softball. He also enjoys listening to country music and walking his dog Flash. He and his wife Beth live in Nashville, Tennessee.